Miners and the State in the Ottoman Empire

International Studies in Social History
General Editor: Marcel van der Linden
International Institute of Social History, Amsterdam

Volume 1
Trade Unions, Immigration, and Immigrants in Europe 1960–1993
Edited by Rinus Penninx and Judith Roosblad

Volume 2
Class and Other Identities
Edited by Lex Heerma van Voss and Marcel van der Linden

Volume 3
Rebellious Families
Edited by Jan Kok

Volume 4
Experiencing Wages
Edited by Peter Scholliers and Leonard Schwarz

Volume 5
The Imaginary Revolution
Michael Seidman

Volume 6
Revolution and Counterrevolution
Kevin Murphy

MINERS AND THE STATE IN THE OTTOMAN EMPIRE
The Zonguldak Coalfield, 1822–1920

Donald Quataert

Berghahn Books
NEW YORK • OXFORD

Published in 2006 by
Berghahn Books

www.berghahnbooks.com

© 2006 Donald Quataert

All rights reserved.
Except for the quotation of short passages
for the purposes of criticism and review, no part of this book
may be reproduced in any form or by any means, electronic or
mechanical, including photocopying, recording, or any information
storage and retrieval system now known or to be invented,
without written permission of the publisher.

Library of Congress Cataloging-in-Publication Data

Quataert, Donald, 1941–
  Miners and the state in the Ottoman Empire : the Zonguldak coalfield, 1822–1920 / Donald Quataert
   p. cm. — (International studies in social history; v. 7)
  Includes bibliographical references and index.
  ISBN 1-84545-133-3 (alk. paper) — ISBN 1-84545-134-1 (pbk.)
    1. Coal miners—Turkey—Zonguldak—History. 2. Coal mines and mining—Turkey—Zonguldak—History. 3. Coal mine accidents—Turkey—Zonguldak—History. 4. Turkey—History—Ottoman Empire, 1288–1918. I. Title. II. Series.

HD8039.M62T96 2005

331.7'62233409563—dc22

2005048299

British Library Cataloguing in Publication Data

A catalogue record for this book is available from
the British Library.

Printed in the United States on acid-free paper

To Jean Helen,
for everything

Contents

List of Illustrations — viii

Acknowledgments — xi

1. Introduction and Historiographical Essay — 1
2. The Ottoman Coal Coast — 20
3. Coal Miners at Work: Jobs, Recruitment, and Wages — 52
4. "Like Slaves in Colonial Countries": Working Conditions in the Coalfield — 80
5. Ties That Bind: Village-Mine Relations — 95
6. Military Duty and Mine Work: The Blurred Vocations of Ottoman Soldier-Workers — 129
7. Methane, Rockfalls, and Other Disasters: Accidents at the Mines — 150
8. Victims and Agents: Confronting Death and Safety in the Mines — 184
9. Wartime in the Coalfield — 206
10. Conclusion — 227

Appendix on the Reporting of Accidents — 235

An Ottoman Miner's Glossary — 242

List of Abbreviations — 243

Notes on Calendar System — 244

Bibliography — 245

Index — 250

Illustrations

Maps

2.1	The Ereğli Coalfield	23
3.1	Sources of Mine Labor outside of the Coalfield, 1840s–1914	72

Figures

4.1	Room-and-Pillar Method of Mining	83
7.1	Aboveground Rail Accident, October 1913	157
7.2	Accident at Air Door, Ikinci Makas Mine, June 1913	165
7.3	Accident on Winch Cable, Tünel Mine, October 1917	166
7.4	Rockfall in Giurgiu Mine, July 1913, I	172
7.5	Rockfall in Giurgiu Mine, July 1913, II	173
7.6	Rockfall in the Boyacıoğlu Mine, June 1913	175
8.1	Air Ventilation Proposals, at Alacaağzı #364 Mine, June 1913	199
8.2	Fire in the Çamlı #188 Mine, 1913	200

Tables

2.1	Types of Trees in Selected Mine Districts, 1915 (in %)	26
2.2	Coal Production in the Coalfield, 1848–1940 (1,000 tons)	28
2.3	Number of Villages in the Coalfield, ca. 1895	32
2.4	Population of Coalfield Districts, 1898 and 1914	32
2.5	Population of Ereğli District, 1870–1915	37
2.6	Population of Ereğli Town, 1840–1910	37
2.7	Directors and Superintendents of Mines, 1865–1921	40
2.8	State Mining Engineers, 1910	45
2.9	Monthly Work Schedule of a Mine Engineer, March 1914	46
3.1	Monthly Wage Payments (in krs), Kozlu Locale, 1906–1907	68
3.2	Median Monthly Wages for Various Aboveground Occupations, 1905–1907	70

3.3	Median Monthly Wages for Aboveground Workers (1910 and 1911 fiscal years)	71
3.4	Raises by Occupational Group (1911 fiscal year)	73
5.1	Mine Operators' Debts Incurred for Labor, 1894–1895 (in krs)	105
5.2	Labor Payments of Kozlu #5 Mine, 1895	111
5.3	Relative Rate of Donations (in krs)	115
5.4	Payments to Workers, 1894 and 1895 (in krs)	118
5.5	Population of Ereğli and Devrek Districts, ca. 1898	118
5.6	Villages Supplying Labor to Mines, 1894–1895	119
5.7	Villages and Town Quarters Providing Labor to Mines, mid 1890s	120
5.8	Villages Sending Compulsory Labor to Multiple Mines	121
6.1	Terms of Military Service, 1843–1914 (in years)	131
6.2	Origins of Soldiers Working in the Kozlu Locale, October 1907	139
6.3	Wages of Workers and Soldier-Workers, 1907 (in krs)	139
6.4	Wages of Soldier-Workers and Workers in the Kozlu Locale, October 1907	140
6.5	Potential and Actual Conscripts, 1912	143
6.6	Ages of Accident Victims and Witnesses, 1893–1919 (in %)	146
7.1	Mining Accidents of All Kinds, 1893–1907, 1912–1919	154
7.2	Frequency of Accidents, 1893–1907, 1912, 1913	156
8.1	Distribution of Accidents by Occupation, 1893–1907	186
8.2	Occupational Distribution of Accident Participants, 1912–1914	187
8.3	Ages of Accident Victims, 1912–1914	187
8.4	Age and Occupation Distribution of Accident Victims, 1913–1914	188
8.5	Ages of Accident Victims and Witnesses, 1912–1914, 1917	188
8.6	Size of Families of Accident Victims, 1912–1914, 1917	190
8.7	Hospitalization of Accident Victims, 1893–1907, 1912, 1913	192
9.1	Labor Shortages in the Asma Mine, April 1918	221
9.2	Per Capita Productivity Levels at Various Mines, 1914–1919	223

Photographs

Following page 128

2.1 Kozlu Kılıç Mine, Workers, and Supports
2.2 Armutçuk Mine of the Merchant Ahmed Efendi, Inclined Plane
2.3 Gelik Mines Inclined Plane, Ereğli Company
2.4 Domuz Mine, Kozlu
2.5 Aerial Cable, Main Station toward Gelik, Ereğli Company, 1917
2.6 Zonguldak Port View, Ereğli Company
2.7 Zonguldak Port
2.8 Zonguldak Port and Breakwater

2.9 Second Ereğli Company Coal Scrubber, Zonguldak, Cornerstone Ceremony
2.10 Kozlu, Giurgiu Company Mine, Machine Room
2.11 Kozlu, Çatal Dere, Ahmed Efendi Mine Tunnel
2.12 Kozlu, Giurgiu Company Mine, Machinery
2.13 Çatalağzı Railroad, Opening Ceremony
2.14 Zonguldak, Coke Production
2.15 Zonguldak Street, Entrance to Market
2.16 Zonguldak Plateau Quarter, 1917
2.17 Ereğli Town, View from Sea
2.18 Kozlu Town
3.1 Muleteer at Mine Entrance, ca. 1926
3.2 Muleteer at SA Mine Entrance (doctored photo)
3.3 Kozlu, Workers at the Petri Mine
3.4 Boy Basket Carrier
3.5 Worker before SH (Ereğli Company?) Mine
3.6 Worker with Lamp (photo perhaps reversed)
3.7 Zonguldak, Boat-Launching Area
3.8 Kozlu Coal-Loading Pier
3.9 Armutçuk Mine of Ahmed Efendi, Workers, and Equipment
3.10 Armutçuk Mine of Ahmed Efendi, Workers, Machinery, and Machine Shop

Acknowledgments

A clear view of the everyday lives of Ottoman subjects has been an important and elusive goal for me. Over several decades, frustrations far outnumbered successes in ferreting out the few materials about Ottoman workers in the Istanbul-based Prime Ministry Archives, an otherwise marvelous repository of millions of documents. By the early 1990s, after publishing a book and several articles that touched on workers' lives, it seemed to me that I had run out of documents relating to workers, and so I began to consider abandoning labor history. At that juncture, in early 1996, I received a letter from Erol Kahveci, then a graduate student in sociology at Bristol University, who had just returned from substantial fieldwork on the coal miners of Zonguldak during the 1990s. He asked for my help in locating some sources because, in a chapter of a 1983 book, I had written all that I knew about the miners during the late Ottoman period. After some further correspondence, he mentioned that he had seen Ottoman- and French-language materials about Ottoman-era mining while carrying out his own research in Zonguldak. One thing led to another, and I made three research trips to Zonguldak in 1997, 1998, and 2004. This book is the result.

I am profoundly grateful to Erol Kahveci for his extraordinary courtesy and help, without which I literally could have neither begun nor completed this book. He not only told me about the existence of the research materials but also introduced me to a host of mining engineers, workers, and officials in the Zonguldak coalfield who opened the doors that made the research possible. Some have become dear friends; among these I count Nevzat Ünlü, Aydın Kasapoğlu, and Avni Özerkan. Hüseyin Toraman and Kemal Kutlu provided invaluable aid, as did Fevzi Engin and Emine Uzun. I offer my respects to Erol Çatma, a retired mine foreman who has learned Ottoman Turkish on his own initiative and is now writing on the history of the Ottoman Zonguldak miners.

Nearly all of the materials that I consulted are housed in two locations around or in the city of Zonguldak. Most are in a reading room at Karaelmas

University, under the watchful eye of Professor Mustafa Yüce; his vigilance in protecting these documents deserves our profound thanks and gratitude. I am indebted to Erol Şeref at the Education Bureau of the Mining Ministry in Baştarla, who offered essential cooperation and support for my research. Nadir Özbek, once my graduate student and now on the faculty at Boğaziçi University, accompanied me on all three visits, acting as my eyes, voice, and coordinator. On these trips we formed a lasting friendship for which I am grateful. I wish to single out the generosity of M. Arsen Yarman and Orlando Carlo Calumeno in providing me with scanned images of their incredible collections of Zonguldak postcards.

Thanks to Kevin Heard of the Binghamton University GIS Core Facility for the wonderful maps.

Nancy Micklewright, Mary Guillochon, Margarita Poutouridou, Christoph Neumann, Yavuz Karakışla, and Nalan Turna helped me in locating other important materials, and Mert Sunar, Selim Deringil, and Mike Hanagan provided additional invaluable assistance. Mel Dubofsky and Tom Dublin, experts in U.S. mining, provided helpful comparative contexts. Jean Quataert, as always, offered invaluable criticisms at every stage of the research and writing.

This project was a long time in the making and would not have been possible without sustained financial support from various sources. The Social Science Research Council funded my second research visit in 1998. In 1999–2000, I spent my entire tenure as a Senior Fellow of the National Endowment for the Humanities organizing and translating the vast body of materials that I had assembled. In 2003 and then in 2004–2005, a sabbatical leave from Binghamton University and a Guggenheim Fellowship allowed me the time to write, reorganize, and complete the manuscript.

There is a Web site, prepared with the assistance of Thomas M. Sliva, that contains a host of photographs, illustrations, maps, and documents relevant to this volume. Please visit the following site: http://bingweb.binghamton.edu/~coal/index.htm.

I am very pleased to have this book appear in a series under the editorial supervision of Marcel van der Linden. And finally, I wish to thank the two readers for Berghahn Books, who saved me from many errors, Jaime Taber, for the very careful copyediting, and Shawn Kendrick, for outstanding typesetting and proofreading. The remaining mistakes are my own.

1

Introduction and Historiographical Essay

The narrative setting for this account centers on the coalfield of Zonguldak, a few hours' drive eastward along the Black Sea coast from modern Istanbul. Exploitation of the Zonguldak mines began in the early nineteenth century, as Ottoman leaders confronted the implications of the steam revolution and sought coal to power the war fleet and state factories. Steam and coal, after all, were accelerating the ongoing shift in the balance of wealth and power toward Western Europeans, a process underway since their conquest of the New World and domination of the human, mineral and other natural resources of the newly discovered continents. As the Ottoman economy increasingly entered the steam age, state planners looked for indigenous mines to maintain uninterrupted supplies, even in wartime. After several false starts that may date back to the 1820s, coal began to flow from the Zonguldak mines around 1850, promising a richly abundant supply independent of foreign control. Mine workers were recruited in large numbers to dig the coal; and on the eve of World War I, they totaled more than 10,000 persons, the largest concentrated labor force in the 600-year history of the Ottoman Empire. These workers are the focus of the present study.

For labor historians of the Americas, Europe, Africa and Asia, coal miners are a familiar sight, the subject of a rich literature. From the perspective of the history of the world's workers, the appearance of a book on Ottoman coal miners requires no justification. As I will explain shortly, this history of Ottoman coal workers both draws upon and enriches the efforts of labor historians in general. But from the viewpoint of my colleagues in Ottoman history, some discussion of these miners and their place in our historiography is a good beginning point, before moving on to situate the subject in labor history writing. Coal miners at first appear to be an odd vehicle for exploring some of the major themes in Ottoman social, economic, and political history. After all,

---

Notes for this chapter begin on page 18.

aren't miners an exception in the Ottoman world? Aren't mine labor experiences idiosyncratic, with little general explanatory power? As the following pages make clear, the story of the miners of Zonguldak presents a particularly graphic local lens through which to examine questions that have been of major concern to historians—both within and outside of Ottoman history writing-most prominently, the nature of labor, the development of the state, the nature of capitalism, and the role of the working classes in these large processes.

The development of the state remains a predominant preoccupation among Ottoman historians who have generated a comparatively rich literature on this subject. Although many still disagree, it now seems clear that the formation of the modern Ottoman state can best be understood as part of a long, ongoing, and continuous evolutionary process from the sixteenth through the nineteenth centuries. In this view, events such as the Tanzimat reforms of the 1830s and 1850s are regarded as part of a domestically inspired continuum of change, rather than radical westernizing breaks with the past imposed from outside. Nineteenth-century reforms derived from ongoing internal dynamics, not from programs suddenly imposed or inspired by the West.[1]

Yet many of the revisionists arguing for domestically driven continuity seem to agree with their opponents supporting westernization from without that the hegemonic power of the central Ottoman state is the force before which pale all other agents at work in Ottoman history. I certainly will not disagree with the notion of the Ottoman state as an important actor equipped with a host of tools to maintain control. For example, during the 1830s, in the general area of the coalfield, it sought to keep track of the daily movements of its subjects, recording their goings and comings in registers.[2] Similarly, at about the same time, it planted spies in Istanbul coffeehouses who wrote down conversations, passing these on to spymasters in the state apparatus.[3] Later in the century, the sultan subtly dispensed charity not merely as a humanitarian gesture but also to enhance his own power and bind to him the objects of his generosity.[4]

The study of the state and its elites certainly is appropriate since its decisions and actions powerfully affected the nature and evolution of not only the Ottoman body politic but society as well. It is, however, not appropriate for a field as rich and developed as Ottoman history to continue to neglect the history of workers and other non-elite groups. Ottoman historians' unwillingness or reluctance to move beyond elite groups and examine those populating the rest of the Ottoman past has had many causes. First, there are the long-established patterns of historical writing, dating back to the Ottoman era, which heavily emphasize the deeds of sultans and other state policy makers. The authors usually were members of the elite literati, often on royal appointment. When the empire vanished, these traditions continued into the era of the Ottoman successor states, of which the Turkish republic was one among many. The historical writing that had served the empire now propped up the nation-state. History writing in the successor states became distorted by nation-building projects in the post-Ottoman world. In their quests to form new identities and make new states, writers vilified their own Ottoman pasts and sought to make them irrelevant. Thus, whatever the experiences of workers were in, for example, Syria or Iraq, they were seen as part of the history of the Syrian or Iraqi nation rather than Ottoman history as a whole.[5] More generally, history writing emphasized nation-state building. Non-elites' success depended on following the paths set down for them by the elites (as the Uzun Mehmed story later in this chapter illustrates). Thus, the histories of workers (or other non-elites) either were related within the nation-state master narrative or went untold.

The geopolitical position of the republic of Turkey has played a particular role in discouraging history from below. This aspect of Turkey's story is especially important considering that the main Ottoman archives are located in Istanbul and that, thanks to linguistic similarities between Ottoman and modern Turkish (among other reasons), most Ottomanists from the successor states are Turkish nationals.[6] During the first decades of the new republic, Turkish historians, like their nation-building colleagues in many other post-Ottoman states, emphasized state elites and ignored the non-elites. But within Turkish historical writing there was a twist, one tied to the later emergence of the Cold War. Turkey's role in its front lines meant that workers' histories often were linked to Communism and the Soviet Union, reinforcing already-negative attitudes concerning the field. Even after the fall of the Berlin Wall, the writing of workers' history continues to be seen as a subversive activity.

In addition, the nature of the historical records left by the Ottoman state stressed elites at the expense of the non-elites. Until quite recently, almost all of Ottoman history writing relied upon documents found in the central archival repository, the Prime Ministry Archives in Istanbul. For all their wonderful revelations, these millions of documents suffer from several deficiencies. First, because they are by definition materials that replicate official interests and concerns, workers appear only when they become interesting to the state—often at times of labor unrest in the form of guild petitions or strikes. Second, these archives usually record activities at a high societal level. Documents might record the outcome of a guild or village petition for tax relief, but omit the details that permit discussion of the guild members or villagers involved.[7]

This study devotes considerable attention to the state and, by demonstrating its powerful effect on coalfield residents, in many respects reinforces the prevailing sense of extensive state control. Thanks to a registration system they maintained from the 1860s, state officials knew precisely the street and house addresses and physical descriptions of individuals in remote villages of the Black Sea littoral, from whom the state demanded mine work (see chapter 2). This information enabled it to dragoon villagers into the mines against their will, sometimes using naked military force. State officials employed less direct methods as well. An extraordinary series of mine inspectors' reports describe, in increasing detail, the accidents that killed or wounded many hundreds of workers (chapters 7 and 8). Indeed, Zonguldak miners were hurt and killed in relative numbers far greater than their contemporaries in Western Europe and the United States. These reports illustrate the growing intrusiveness of the state into the everyday lives of its subject/citizens. They also offer irreplaceable insights into laboring conditions. The details they present on the site and nature of the accidents as well as on the personal lives of accident victims and witnesses offer an otherwise unobtainable profile of the labor force. Relevant to the point at hand is the notion that the safety regulations and reports did not spring merely from government concern for workers. Rather, they were part of an effort to discipline the work force into a malleable body, one more amenable to state control. Like the sultan's spies and charity, safety rules formed part of the drive to create a disciplined and responsible citizenry.

If my study thus depicts the state as increasingly intruding into the lives of its citizens, it also helps to demystify the central Ottoman state that too often has been oversimplified as all-powerful. Indeed, this volume demonstrates the total and complete failure of the state to achieve its most basic goal in coal mining—the assurance of adequate coal supplies in wartime. Despite all efforts of the government and the policing infrastructure that it had created, the mines produced no more coal during World War I than they had four decades before in the 1870s.

The reasons are detailed in the following chapters: simply put, the state could not overcome the forces in Ottoman society that worked against official objectives. Workers refused to work, or they fled after being dragged to the mines. And the villages that were to send allotments of workers sometimes refused to cooperate with the central state in forcing residents into the mines. Indeed, an important finding concerns the central state's use of village authorities—the headmen and councils of elders—to discipline workers. On the one hand, this shows the power of the state's enforcement apparatus. But the persistent shortages of mine workers meant that the headmen, elected by the villagers and appointed by the state, were not fulfilling the tasks assigned to them by their superiors. So on the other hand, the headmen were part of the historic compromise the central state made with local elites over the course of the nineteenth century. Across the empire, and in the coalfield, local notables *were* part of the central state apparatus, serving it even as they guarded local interests from centralist encroachments. In this way, they resembled local elites elsewhere in the empire, for example, the council of elders in faraway Nablus during the 1830s. When Istanbul imposed new instruments of centralizing control on Nablus, the notables gained entrance to the council and there continued to defend local interests against central state encroachment.[8] In Zonguldak, village headmen served as central state functionaries, directing the recruitment of villagers for mine labor (and financially profiting from the task) but also mediating and guarding the village against levies that would damage its fabric—hence, the chronically inadequate supplies of mine labor. In the end, the villagers never constituted the reliable work force envisaged by state planners.

Thus, the story of the coal miners helps to present an alternative to the paradigm of an all-powerful nineteenth-century Ottoman state effortlessly imposing its will. The central Ottoman state was an uneasy union between imperial and local interests in a relationship filled with tension, conflict, and compromise. And, to repeat, it utterly failed to achieve its fundamental objective in opening the coalfield in the first place—to gain assured coal supplies in wartime.

The story of the miners also reveals much about the nature of capital in this corner of the world. Indeed, in the coalfield, the workings of capital were constrained on the one side by the Ottoman state and on the other by the labor force. Worldwide, most coal mines came into being through the efforts of private entrepreneurs using their own and investors' capital to open and operate mines. For example, coal mining in three of the world's most prolific producers—Britain, France, and the United States—depended on private capital. Somewhat by contrast, the Zonguldak mines owed their opening and initial exploitation to state efforts, to the Ottoman regime's determination to have steam power for its fleet and industries. Early efforts at state management of the mines quickly failed, however, and by the late 1860s they had yielded to a hybrid system of exploitation. The coal belonged to the state, or more accurately to the sultan, who leased exploitation rights to private operators. Production stagnated at first because the state, reluctant to surrender control, imposed prohibitively onerous terms on would-be entrepreneurs. But over the period studied here it steadily surrendered control to private interests. In 1882, when it partially yielded to operators' demands for better terms, production began to climb.

The entrepreneurs who came to play an increasing role included both Ottoman subjects, some with connections to the court, and foreigners. Chief among the latter, as of the 1890s, was the French-financed Ereğli Company, which came to control three-quarters of total coal production. In this regard, the Ottoman coal-mining experience did not follow the British, French, or U.S. pattern, but rather resembled that of contemporary Czarist Russia. In both Russia and the Ottoman Empire, state sponsorship and a dependence on French capital combined to exploit coal resources. In the Ottoman case, the state continuously battled with the Ereğli Company. Fearful that French money would corrode its sovereignty, the Istanbul government often impeded the company's natural quest for profits, seeing this as a French plot for domination. More generally, however, local and international capital alike obtained poor rates of return from the Zonguldak mines. The Ereğli Company was a special case and could place the blame for its mediocre performance on tense relations with the state. But in fact, all operators (including those with royal connections) suffered from the nature of the mine labor force. In the end, increasingly capitalist relations did emerge, but their structure proved too fragile to withstand the pressures of war.

As I hope the above makes clear, this study of coal workers adds to our understanding of the state and of capital during the last Ottoman century. Yet this story of miners is most of all a history of workers, an effort to present

Ottoman "lives of labor." For Ottoman specialists, therefore, the book offers a rare focus on the popular classes. It portrays their worlds of work and of home life. It hopes to encourage and point the way to other studies of Ottoman workers. For labor historians reading this book, it will become clear that while the fate of Zonguldak workers was much like that of miners elsewhere, there also is much that is unique in their story. Because of the inherent nature of mine work, the lives of coal miners everywhere have been brutish, nasty and brief. It is true that today, the life expectancy of miners in some countries is close to the national averages. But the high incidence of catastrophic accidents in China reminds us that coal mining remains among the most dangerous of all occupations. Now, as in the past, the specific conditions of recruitment and work imposed by states and entrepreneurs make a considerable difference, for better or worse. There is no doubt that because of the diversity of these imposed conditions, the fate of miners in different regions of the world at particular times has varied enormously.

During the period under study here, states and entrepreneurs worldwide employed a host of stratagems to recruit and retain mine labor. There were nearly as many methods of mine work recruitment and treatment of labor as there were mining work forces. Whether or not laborers were abundant or scarce was not necessarily the determining variable in how workers were treated. In some cases, labor scarcities provoked what appears to be relatively generous treatment. But, contrariwise, shortages of workers also prompted coercive and cruel measures. Sometimes states and employers have relied on cash bonuses, decent housing, and medical care to attract and retain their work force. In some areas they provided food, free of charge. At the other end of the spectrum, brutal coercion, whippings, and forced labor were frequent tactics under conditions amounting to slavery. In the nineteenth-century United States, many operators used cash wages to attract some of the then vast and continuing inflows of cheap immigrant labor into mine work. In the Donbass region of Russia during the later nineteenth century, mine operators found seasonal village labor unsuitable and sought to recruit full-time workers, offering them better wages and conditions attractive to their families.[9] Across the Atlantic, in Peru, mine labor slowly evolved, between 1906 and 1945, from temporary migrant labor into a permanent, stable, work force.[10] Here too, employers aimed to create a labor force that was married, believing it to be more stable and reliable. Somewhat similarly, the white colonial state in Rhodesia at first, during the late nineteenth century, tried to rely on a mix of permanent, married workers living at the mine sites and temporarily employed migrant workers. But when this hybrid failed, it implemented a truly brutal forced labor system on African workers in order to obtain a sufficient supply of low-cost labor. This mine force became proletarianized, in the sense that it was fully dependent on wage labor without access to other forms of subsistence.[11]

In this global variety of labor systems, the Ottoman miners share characteristics with workers in many regions, but—to my eyes, at least—they still seem somewhat special. This Zonguldak mining work force derived from an extraordinary and changing mix of unfree and free labor that, toward the end of the period under study, drew upon at least six distinct sources of workers. There were three groups of unfree workers: villagers from the coalfield region who were forced to perform rotational labor (the majority of all workers); townsmen from the coalfield; and lastly, active-duty soldiers. Free laborers also fall into three groups: aboveground workers from various extra-coalfield Ottoman regions, recruited to fill technologically more difficult jobs; underground miners from Ottoman provinces in eastern Anatolia, who were recruited once the rotational work force proved problematic for the state and the mine operators; and very small numbers of foreigners, including foremen.

The complexion of the aggregate work force evolved over time. In the following chapters, the narrative traces the formation and hybrid nature of the labor force, especially the unfree local villagers. The Ottoman state's search for mine labor was mired in its own practices of compulsory labor recruitment, which dated back centuries. Thus, dating from 1867, it required all males in the coalfield to be available for mine work on a rotational basis—which divided the miner's month equally between the time of work in the mines and the "rest" time back in the village. In exchange, the workers received cash wages and exemption from active-duty military service. In this way the Ottoman state adopted an allegedly pre-capitalist form of labor to exploit coal, that most capitalist of commodities.

Four decades after initiating this rotational labor system, the state yielded to private mine operators' complaints about the quality and quantity of the rotational labor, allowing them to recruit free labor from metal mining regions in the Ottoman east. This experiment, however, failed. Labor agitation mounted and accident rates skyrocketed with the arrival of the new workers, who in the end did not provide the hoped-for reliable work force. The narrative also reveals how, from the outset, the state violated its own regulations—which divided local residents into those who mined and those who soldiered—to keep the mines working. Throughout the period, the mine superintendent's office employed active-duty soldiers, conscripted from the coalfield region, in a variety of mine tasks to supplement the rotational work force, paying them a tiny fraction of the already-low rotational worker wage. The final major component of the work force consisted of the free workers, recruited from outside the coalfield, who labored in aboveground jobs different from the tasks carried out by the rotational workers. Altogether it was predominantly a male work force, although women regularly were present in both above- and belowground work.

More than three hundred villages sent rotational workers, who labored in more than 100 different mines. Every twelve days, thousands of workers put down their tools and walked home to their villages to be replaced by the second shift of village workers. From a global perspective, this rotational system seems rather unusual in its formality and regularity. These village-mine connections, moreover, reveal the power that village headmen and councils of elders wielded over fellow villagers. Indeed, the state's rotational system gave these authorities a chilling tool of control: they determined which young men's names were placed on the mine-worker rosters and which were inscribed in the registers of those eligible for military service. Thus, mine work transferred the existing system of power relations within the village to the new setting of the worksite (the mine), enhancing the position of the community authorities back in the village. Numerous additional illustrations of unbalanced power relations are provided later in this volume. Workers often were paid in promissory notes, not in specie. Unable to cash these, the workers sold them at a fraction of face value to village leaders and town merchants, who bought them as investment opportunities and then used their leverage to seek full payment. So for many workers, mine work did not inject cash into their homes but furthered subordination to local authorities and notables.

These relations between mines and villages forged the long-term identity of the rotational mine labor force as villager-worker, a concept fraught with powerful consequences for worker, mine operator, and state. This Ottoman example demonstrates how, in a modern state during the age of high capitalism, mine labor could be the province not of a landless, uprooted class but of workers with enduring ties to the land. Again, the Zonguldak case seems rather special in that its work force, despite five decades of involvement with mine work, had not been proletarianized. This is quite unlike many studies of French and English miners, whose ultimate proletarianization historians have dissected into stages. It also is unlike the cases of the Rhodesian and Peruvian miners noted above, for in the Ottoman instance, workers remained deeply connected to the village and indeed, to this day, identify as villager-miners rather than merely miners. Their adherence to village life while mining allowed villager-miners to remain uncommitted to mine labor. They stayed away from the mines because they feared accidents, because of religious holidays, because the crops needed tending, even at times because they didn't need or want the cash incomes provided by mine work.

Such behavior was a double-edged sword. On the one hand, since they did not identify with the workplace, the villager-miners remained more vulnerable to exploitation than contemporaries who formed militant working-class identities. For example, their wages remained fixed for decades while those of the free mine workers rose. The villager-miner syndrome badly hurt the state and capital as well. When the state fell short of coal in wartime because of these labor problems, it sustained grave injury. These same labor issues also caused mine operators to fail financially, over and over again. And to boot, exploitation of the coalfield did not trigger the accumulation of capital for investment elsewhere in the Ottoman economy, retarding the entire empire's further development.

The Historiography of the Zonguldak Mines

Uzun Mehmed's Discovery of Coal

The story of how Uzun Mehmed, a villager from the Ereğli area, first discovered coal in 1829 is a familiar one to citizens of today's Turkish republic. His name and story are embedded in Turkish national memory, long a part of the education of schoolchildren growing up in the republic. The construction and propagation of this Uzun Mehmed narrative helped to shape the Turkish nation-state; the structure of the story and its wide dissemination tell a great deal about the formation of republican ideals and of the state itself. This famous tale, however, derived from an Ottoman narrative that was selectively built upon during the Turkish republican era.

Intellectuals and officials in the coal basin prepared the most widely circulated account of the Uzun Mehmed story, which appeared in two somewhat different versions published in 1933 and 1934, as part of the tenth anniversary celebration of the Turkish republic. The first appeared as part of an extensive monograph published by the Zonguldak People's House (*halkevi*), established just months before on 24 June 1932. Ultimately, the ruling Republican People's Party founded some 500 of these People's Houses in Turkey; they were intended, in the words of one author, "to spread nationalist, positivist and secularist ideas."[12] Their main goal, according to another writer, "was to educate people in the Kemalist ideals and to create ideological unity between the educated elite running the party and the [Grand National] Assembly, and the masses."[13] The large monograph, entitled *Zonguldak and the Coalfield on the 10th Anniversary of the Republic*, traced the history of the coal region and its development and was perhaps the first fruit of the new local institution.

The Zonguldak People's House had charged a research team of three persons with the duty of determining the history and chronology of the coalfield's discovery.[14] These included the head editor of the *Zonguldak* newspaper, Tahir Kara Uğuz Bey, as well as Hüseyin Fehmi, a former superintendent of the mines (1910–1921) who, no longer a pasha of the empire but a bey of the Republic, was serving as president of the Zonguldak Chamber of Commerce. The third was Ahmet Naim, representative of the People's House publication committee.

In the subsequent year, 1934, Naim (1904–1967) published his own account of the Uzun Mehmed story, a condensed version of the collectively authored account that had just been published, as part of his book entitled *The Zonguldak Coalfield: From Uzun Mehmed to Today*. We must see the 1933 collective account as the more official story since it had the imprimatur of the state-organized People's House. The plot lines of the two versions are essentially identical, but there are some important differences in the details.

In brief, both the People's House and Naim's accounts relate how Uzun Mehmed returned from military service in the Istanbul naval yards, remembering how he and other discharged soldiers were shown coal samples and promised rewards should they find coal in their home districts. Constantly searching for the stones that burned, he found them one day in the autumn of 1829, as he was killing time waiting near a mill to grind his grain. Keeping his discovery a secret, he went to Istanbul in the spring of 1830, and there received both a cash award and a lifetime salary. Richly rewarded and honored, the hero incurred the jealous wrath of a local notable, whose lackeys poisoned Uzun Mehmed on his return visit to the capital.

Both versions dismiss rival stories that attributed the discovery of coal to a wandering shepherd or local notable. Instead, they focused on the person of Uzun Mehmed, "a quick-witted man"; the discovery of coal "in Turkey" was no accident but derived from his actions, his taking advantage of an opportunity. Thus, the authors offered a vision of great deeds springing from individual peasant initiative and an eye to opportunity. Both versions drive home the message that the common man could score important achievements and gain wealth and fame, regardless of rural, peasant origins. Pointedly, in both versions the initiative for Uzun Mehmed's actions comes from above, from the state that offers the common man the necessary direction and opportunity for success. The lesson seems clear enough: in republican Turkey the key to success was a resourceful peasantry following the lead of an informed state elite, pursuing opportunity. "Uzun Mehmed is a national hero."

Their Uzun Mehmed story, which was disseminated nationally, also illustrated for its republican audience the callous disregard of the Ottoman state for the common man. After Uzun Mehmed was murdered, the state punished the killers[15] but took no action of any kind to help his widow and children. The "sultanate remained indifferent to the family of Uzun Mehmed which had lost its head." Under the Ottomans they remained in poverty, uncared for and neglected. "But the sunshine of the Republic shed light on this event which no longer remained in darkness." Thanks to the investigations of the People's House committee, a holiday was established in the name of Uzun Mehmed, a monument was built, and his name was given to streets, avenues, and gardens. "The republican administration [also] ... took the family of Uzun Mehmed under its protection ... [and] "assistance was given to individuals of the poor family of Uzun Mehmed which exists today."[16] Thus, the republic succeeded in caring for the deserving, while the empire had utterly failed in this duty.

Turning now to the differences between these two versions, we see that Naim's later 1934 story is a bit more dramatic and heroic, for example, in its description of Uzun Mehmed climbing by his fingernails up a mountain road to keep his secret. Meanwhile, the more official 1933 version credits anonymous officials of the (Ottoman) state for ordering the search for coal and for rewarding our hero, without any mention of the monarchy. After describing the murder, it strongly condemns the sultanate for ignoring the victim's family. But in Naim's story, it is the person of the sultan who plays the central role in the chain of events leading to the discovery: to avoid spending vast sums on imported coal, Sultan Mahmud II himself ordered explorations for coal in every corner of the empire. Too, the sultan personally rewards, pensions, and honors Uzun Mehmed. Naim's story, after narrating Uzun Mehmed's murder, refrains from criticizing the sultan for failing to help the widow and children.

In a number of other differences, Naim deviates from the official version in ways that suggest he was bothered by inconsistencies in the People's House story and was trying to paper over the cracks. The People's House committee relates without comment how Uzun Mehmed was near a mill when he found the coal. But Naim notes that the mill was distant from Uzun Mehmed's village and spends some energy explaining, rather lamely, why he chose this particular mill and not the one next to his village. Also, the 1933 version simply states that Uzun Mehmed waited until spring before traveling to Istanbul. Naim, for his part, sounds puzzled when he comments that the information available to him indicates a spring departure and therefore a delay that is difficult to understand, considering the importance of the discovery. As an explanation for the delay, his speculations again seem contrived.

There are other differences between the account of Naim and that published by the full People's House committee. For example, Naim relates that the local notable, on ordering the killing, said to his two henchmen: "As soon as you find him, cut the throat of that Turk pig"[17]—a curious remark since almost surely the notable also was an ethnic Turk and certainly a Muslim. Here, I believe, Naim was arguing to his readers that the Ottoman Empire had a non- or even anti-Turkish nature and that its provincial elite, in this telling, was at liberty to murder Turks who were performing great deeds for the common good.

In 1932, just one year before the appearance of the People's House version, an alternate story of Uzun Mehmed had appeared in Turkish, written by Ahmed Cemal as part of a booklet on the provinces of Kastamonu and Zonguldak. He previously had published at least nine other provincial studies.[18] Given the timing of its appearance, the Zonguldak People's House committee and Naim likely completed and published their separate Uzun Mehmed tales with the text of this alternate version before them. They both chose to prepare versions that differ in important details from the 1932 study—which turns out to be based, sometimes verbatim, on a 1903 Ottoman account.

And so here I present the available Ottoman version, Cemal's digressions from it, and their differences from the People's House and Naim accounts. The Ottoman story appeared in a December 1903 issue of the *Sabah* newspaper, published in Istanbul. During those years, writers were giving considerable attention to the entrepreneurial ethos; it was a time, for example, when many self-help manuals appeared in print.[19] Noted for its efforts to curb European investors' domination of the Ottoman economy, the *Sabah* newspaper published an extensive account of the geology and production of the Zonguldak coalfield.[20] It impressively reproduced the best geological information on the deposits then available and gave a succinct summary of the major production locales. At the end of this long article, the author dates and describes the initial discovery of coal, in 1829. In both the structure and the sequence of the factual presentation, this is the same story that appeared in 1933 and 1934. These versions contain many details that are tellingly different from the Ottoman newspaper account, but those that they share make clear that the republican authors had access to either the *Sabah* version or a report on which it was based (and not merely the 1932 Cemal account).

In the 1903 tale, Ottoman subscribers and listeners learn of the imperial factories' dependence on foreign sources and Sultan Mahmud's orders to look for coal in every corner of the empire. The promises of imperial rewards reach Ereğli, and it is only there and then that Uzun Mehmed is introduced, not as a returned veteran who once had served in Istanbul but as a "Kestanelik" village resident near Ereğli learning of the reward. Seeking to take advantage of "the things promised," he becomes very active in searching the area of his village. "The more he searched about, the more this person's peace of mind became spoiled." Wishing to mill flour, he goes to the Köşeağzı mill, which the newspaper story inaccurately locates near his village. Here the *Sabah* account offers a detail not present in the 1933–1934 accounts. Wandering the stream shores and becoming cold, he tries to warm himself at a village called Limancık. Inadvertently, he starts the fire on an exposed coal vein, which begins to burn.[21] As the black stones burn, Uzun Mehmed understands that he has discovered the coal sought by the sultan, exclaiming "I found it." He puts out the fire, retrieves his flour from the mill, goes home, and secretively returns the next day to fill a sack with coal.

At this juncture, the 1903 account again relates a detail that does not reappear in the People's House or Naim versions: that is, he leaves immediately for Istanbul, without waiting for spring. He presents his sack to officials at the imperial mint (*Darphane*) who examine the sample and pronounce it to be coal. The sultan then issues a decree, awarding Uzun Mehmed a decoration, a 5,000 kuruş (hereafter krs) reward, and a lifetime monthly salary of 600 krs. Here the story abruptly stops, without any mention of the Ereğli notable or the untimely death of Uzun Mehmed.[22]

This 1903 account is remarkable for the individuation of the discoverer.[23] The sultan certainly is credited, and the state in his person is the ultimate author of the discovery. But in the *Sabah* newspaper story, more agency than in the People's House or Naim version is given to the person of Uzun Mehmed, a "curious person" who acts tirelessly and decisively to take advantage of an available opportunity to enrich himself. In its recounting, *Sabah* implies that he left immediately for Istanbul. Moreover, he summons his determination to find coal not for the sake of the empire, nor even for the sultan but rather for his own profit. The *Sabah* story, in my view, is presenting Uzun Mehmed as a role model, an Ottoman entrepreneur diligently striving for gain who becomes wildly successful. Thus, the story ends as he gains his recognition, reward and pension.

The 1932 Cemal version follows the 1903 Ottoman account in a nearly verbatim fashion, also stopping at a successful, un-murdered Uzun Mehmed. Most but not all of the few variations from the 1903 story are populist or Turkish embellishments. In the 1932 account the sultan's order is to find coal in

Anatolia, not in every corner of the empire. To this end, the sultan is encouraging the masses (*halk*) to look for coal. Uzun Mehmed is described as "a very poor villager." He does not cry out "I found it" (as he does in the *Sabah*, People's House, and Naim versions). But otherwise, the structure and the details of the 1932 story are identical to those in the 1903 newspaper—including the burning earth, the Limancık locale, the immediate Istanbul departure via the same road, and the audience with the grateful sultan. The hero in 1932 is nearly the same as in 1903—an enterprising peasant who makes his fortune—but with a slight Turkish nationalist twist. It is quite likely that Cemal had direct access to the newspaper story.

With varying degrees of emphasis, all four versions—1903, 1932, 1933, and 1934—feature an energetic and creative Uzun Mehmed. Cemal, in his 1932 study, uncritically takes the 1903 Ottoman story, translates it into modern Turkish, and disseminates it to his Turkish audience essentially without modification. As stated, the only differences, beyond the missing "I found it" quote, concern his mild introduction of Turkish nationalist themes. Beginning just one year later, however, the intellectuals and officials in the coalfield would produce a radically different version with a considerably beefed-up Turkish nationalist component that went well beyond Cemal's presentation. As part of this endeavor, they insert and bring into high relief a tale of Ottoman corruption and decadence. In the 1933 and 1934 accounts, agents of the corrupt and ungrateful Ottoman state strike down the hero at the very moment of his success. Thus, three decades after Uzun Mehmed appeared in the 1903 story as an entrepreneurial model for individual action in a capitalist world, that story is revised: now, cast in a republican aura, he has evolved into a model of a different sort, a patriotic common man being accorded his just recognition by a grateful nation.

Moreover, to repeat, the differences between the 1932 version by Cemal and those by the People's House and Naim are truly striking, given that only a single year separates the appearance of the first and the latter two. Surely we are witnessing the impact of the emergence of the People's House on the writing of the past. The publication of the story, in both its People's House and Naim versions, aimed to disseminate a tale of an energetic national hero brutally murdered by local notables who sought only their own interests, unrestrained by a cold and indifferent Ottoman state. By contrast, the republic thanks, recognizes, honors, and rewards the obedient and productive sons of the fatherland. The Uzun Mehmed memorials, holidays, and parades similarly intended to promote a unified vision of this newly reconstructed past, shared by Kemalist elites and the masses alike. The Uzun Mehmed story thus illustrates the process of value formation and nation-building by the Turkish republican elite through the vehicle of the People's Houses.[24]

Since 1934, nearly all of the studies (approximately a dozen in number) that discuss the Ottoman-era coalfield at any length follow the Uzun Mehmed story as related by the Zonguldak People's House and Ahmet Naim. The vast majority of their authors had a direct personal connection with the coalfield: prominent among them are Sina Çıladır, Zonguldak newspaper editor and son of Ahmet Naim, and several professional engineers, many of whom wrote after they had moved away from the coalfield. They include just one former miner, Erol Çatma, and two academics, Özeken and Kıray.[25] None of the authors focuses exclusively on the Ottoman era, which normally is presented as a cautionary preamble, a reminder of the bad old days before the Turkish Republic.

In a 1944 article, the former mine superintendent, Hüseyin Fehmi, repeats the finding of the People's House commission in which he participated (but does not offer Naim's later justification for Uzun Mehmed's traveling to a distant flour mill).[26] In his 1970 study, Sina Çıladır acknowledges the existence of a rival 1822 dating of coal's discovery (see below) but accepts as definitive the 1933–1934 findings of the People's House committee and of Naim.[27] In the substantial 1977 revision of his earlier book, Çıladır reiterates his position and introduces new material to explain the murder of Uzun Mehmed, basing his explanation on a 1964 study by M. Kıray. In her field research, Kıray found that the village near Uzun Mehmed's discovery had "belonged to" a notable family, the Karamahmudzadeler. Having based its fortunes on coal, this family emerged later in the nineteenth century as one of the most powerful in the region but, during the 1820s, it was rivaled by the Hacı Ismailoğluları. The head of this family, Hacı Ismailoğlu, was angered by the discovery that enhanced the wealth of his opponents, so he ordered Uzun Mehmed's murder.[28] Similarly, a chief mining engineer, Savaşkan, in a concise and useful 1990s history of the coalfield, summarizes the transmission of the Uzun Mehmed story and its rival discovery alternatives.[29] After evaluating the various stories, he comes down on the side of the 1829 Uzun Mehmed version.

A number of alternate accounts to the Uzun Mehmed story have remained in circulation since 1933–1934, but so far to little effect. Özeken offered the most complete presentation of the main rival version in 1944. He presents the discoverer of the coal as Hacı Ismail, a discharged marine from Kestaneci village near Ereğli who in 1822 responds to the appeals, finds coal, and is awarded 5,000 krs by the sultan. Yet the deposit lay undeveloped for years when Uzun Mehmed appears and enters the service of the Safranbolu head administrator, then in charge of Ereğli. He is none other than Ismail Agha, the son of the original discoverer. Following several years of searching, Uzun Mehmed discovers the coal, receives his reward in Istanbul and is then murdered by the jealous Ismail Agha.[30] A brief 1976 account supports the 1822 date.[31] Most recently, in 1998, the former miner Çatma accepts 1822 as the initial discovery date but says that the importance of coal did not become clear until later. Hence, the first real exploitation occurred only in 1848.[32]

The triumph of Uzun Mehmed over Hacı Ismail as the discoverer of coal surely is linked generally to the populist impulses of the Kemalist state and in particular to the labors of the People's House to forge links between the state and the peasants. Given the goals of the People's House and its efforts to create a common vision between state elites and the people, the victory of the version crediting the poor peasant Uzun Mehmed over the story supporting Hacı Ismail, scion of an aristocratic family, seems inevitable. Uzun Mehmed served as a vehicle to disguise the real differences between republican peasants and elites, and all could enjoy his enshrinement as national hero. A victorious Hacı Ismail, for its part, symbolically would have meant the triumph of notable over peasant, an impossibility given the populist logic of early 1930s Turkey.[33]

Uzun Mehmed in Global Perspective and the Historiography of the Coalfield

There is a false ring to the entire Uzun Mehmed (and Hacı Ismail) story, in both its Ottoman and Turkish versions. Namely, the premise that the local population was unaware of the existence of the coal until 1829 (or 1822) is implausible, given both the exposed nature of the rich seams, on the very surface, and the history of other coal discoveries across the globe. For many centuries elsewhere in the world, such as in England and China, populations of coal-bearing regions knew about and used the "stones that burned" for heating and cooking well before the industrial revolution. Similarly, Native Americans were very familiar with the coal seams of Pennsylvania and helped European settlers locate the deposits.[34] Discoveries of coal, other minerals, or valued commodities commonly were serendipitous, if not apocryphal. For example, I remember reading about the accidental discovery of coffee, by a shepherd in the Yemeni hills who noticed the strange behavior of goats feeding on certain bushes. Similarly, Sutter's great discovery of California gold was purely by accident.

In most coal discovery tales though, its presence is well known and the crucial factor becomes the economic motive for its exploitation. In our story, we are supposed to believe, local villagers were unaware of these abundant, visible deposits until the state intervened to set in motion the chain of events leading to the coal's discovery by a local. That is, the Ottoman-era and the 1932, 1933 and 1934 versions generally share a vision of the state as the *primum mobile*, the agent responsible for the subsequent chain of events. In the *Sabah* account, this quality is filtered through the economic liberalism of the editors. The statist version is most starkly evident in the People's House account which, after all, was an officially sponsored writing project. In sum, the Uzun Mehmed (or Hacı Ismail) story illustrates the centrality of the state in the historiographical tradition of both the empire and its Turkish successor republic.

The shadow of the state is similarly present in the periodization of the mines' history. This completely state-centered chronological ordering is organized to narrate the succession of government ministries' supervision of the mines. The early studies by the Zonguldak People's House and Naim not only established the Uzun Mehmed orthodoxy but also set the periodization of coal-mining history. This chronology emerges more clearly in Naim, who plainly organizes the history according to the government body administering the coalfield.

1848–1865	Privy Purse
1865–1909	Ministry of Marine
1909–1920	Ministry of Commerce
post-1920	Ministry of the Economy[35]

With minor adjustments to some of the dates, this periodization prevails up to the present, adopted by virtually all of those writing on the mines. Even authors who quarrel with the Uzun Mehmed story follow this ministerial timetable.[36] This chronology implies that state actions drove the tempo, timing, and course of events and were the crucial variable that explains the history of the Zonguldak mines.

But such a periodization is not terribly useful if we seek to explain unfolding developments in the coalfield, except for its 1848 starting date, when real exploitation apparently began. Whether it was the Ministry of Marine or the Ministry of Commerce that was in charge is irrelevant to the story, and the shift from one ministry to another was not a decisive turning point. Rather, we should look to new demands for coal that emerged thanks to vast increases in the number of steamships plying Black Sea and other Ottoman ports, in urban utilities, and in Ottoman steam-powered factories. There were turning points: for example, a decision taken in 1882 to permit free sales of coal. It was, to be sure, a result of state action, but one taken only after enormous pressure from entrepreneurs. Similarly, other key events in the history of the mines—such as ending the restrictions on labor recruitment in 1906 and the civilianization of the mining administration in 1910—resulted from private initiatives and lobbying. The claim that such state decisions were decisive interventions is true only in the very narrowest meaning of the phrase—if the state had not acted then labor supplies would have been worse and the administration would have remained a military one. Yet these state decisions were the effects of ongoing changes, not their cause. Therefore, the continuing primacy of a state-based chronology in coal-mining history is not actually a function of governmental importance; rather, it mainly derives from the ongoing dominance of a state-centered historiographical tradition in both Ottoman and republican Turkish historical writing.

Since nearly all the authors focus on the state and its actions or inactions, they view workers through state-ground lenses. These authors often are respectful of workers and their rights. Özeken, for his part, expresses great frustration over their lack of full-time proletarian status, which to his mind would assure a more regular labor supply. With an eye on the state, most of these histories are mainly concerned with coalfield operations, production, state policies, imperialism, and issues of non-Muslim mine ownership. In these areas of concern, they offer a great deal of valuable information. But rarely do the authors discuss working conditions or wages, even though elsewhere in the world, the miners usually are the center of attention in coal-mining narratives. Some writers, such as Naim and Çıladır, are deeply sympathetic to workers and accord them much space in their narratives. But in my view, theirs is always sympathy from a distance or, more precisely, from above. These two discuss workers mainly as victims of Ottoman state neglect and beneficiaries of enlightened republican state policies. Indeed, this is the generally shared view of workers among our authors, when they discuss workers at all. Only Çatma, himself a former miner, maintains a focus on workers and their living conditions, making them the central subject of his narrative.

This state-focused approach distorts both the chronology and our understanding of the engines of change in the coalfield. In addition, it promotes a view of legislation as an actual description of conditions rather than a normative set of rules. Thus, there is nearly unanimous uncritical praise for the 1867 regulations, named for the first mine superintendent, Dilaver Pasha, who created the compulsory rotational labor system. Without much discussion, nearly all writers on the topic equate these regulations with actual working conditions after 1867 (which, as I will demonstrate, was clearly not the case). Yet, they go on to discuss the appalling working conditions of the later Ottoman era, not seeing the contradiction between their acceptance of the 1867 rules as reality and their critique of working conditions supposedly governed by those rules. They then discuss the new mine labor laws of the early republic that, they argue, ameliorated these deplorable conditions. Consistent with their statist bias, they do not consider such legislation from the workers' perspective or ask if, indeed, the legislation enacted actually ever was implemented. Their goal is to assert the beneficent intentions of state elites and the consequent identity of interests between state and worker.

The present study is a break, but only a partial one, with prevailing trends in Ottoman history writing. It diverges from the statist perspective of most Ottoman historians' narratives to present a history from below—so called not because of the underground worksites but because workers and villagers stand at the very center of the narrative. This study contributes to the modest but important body of scholarship narrating the lives of workers, peasants, and other non-elite groups in Ottoman society,[37] who together with their families constituted 90 percent of the total Ottoman population and generated most of the wealth that financed the ambitions of the elites.

It also differs from most Ottoman historical writing in the nature of the sources utilized. The majority of Ottoman historical narratives have their source in the massive archives of the central Ottoman state, located in Istanbul, with the disadvantages that I mentioned above. More recently, a second set of sources has emerged. The records of the Ottoman courts have offered a valuable local rather imperial perspective and present a better view of non-elite Ottoman life.[38] A different source base is used here and suggests the value of a third kind of data set for labor and other historians. Within the empire were thousands of large and small concentrations of labor, ranging from home manufacturing and small workshops to factories (as well as mining enterprises). There can be no doubt that the records of some of these concentrations, whether generated by the state or privately, have survived in scattered provincial locations. Nearly all of the documents used in this study were generated on the spot, in the coalfield; that is, they originated in the provinces and not within the Istanbul-based bureaucracy. They thus offer a perspective that is much closer to the actors: as records written very close to the action, they perhaps represent the closest view that Ottoman historians will be able to have of the non-elite subjects of their study.

It remains nonetheless true that state officials, not workers, wrote these documents. Given the illiteracy rates of 85 to 90 percent, the dearth of workers' written testimony is not surprising. So, the testimony of the documents used in this project remains at a distance, even when we read inspectors' reports offering us workers' words wrapped in "quotation marks." Again unsurprisingly, such quotations are remarkable and quite rare in Ottoman documents. But in the final analysis, the historical record tells us only what a state official, in this case an expert mine engineer, chose to write down.

In sum, this study's break with the existing scholarship is incomplete because of the continuing need to depend on state sources in the absence of a rich set of alternative records.[39] And the writing of workers' history remains a particularly difficult task in the Ottoman context in that biases dating back to the empire continue to favor elites and are compounded by the discipline's own biases toward the multiple issues surrounding nation-state building. For many scholars in this field, writing the history of workers is seen as a polemic whereas that of the elites is considered normal, non-polemical history.

Notes

1. For an early formulation of this position, see Abou El-Haj (1991).
2. Abdulkadiroğlu et al. (1998).
3. Kırlı (2000).
4. Özbek (2001).
5. Longueness (1978) and Batatu (1978).
6. See Quataert (2000).
7. See Quataert (2000).
8. Doumani (1995).
9. Izmestieva (2000).
10. DeWind (1987).
11. Van Onselen (1976), esp. 91–114.
12. Zürcher (1993), 188.
13. Shaw and Shaw (1976), II, 383.
14. İmer (1973), 6, who likely was chair of the committee, says that it was formed in 1930. Either this is a typographical error or the group had begun the project under the *Türk Ocakları*, institutions abolished in 1932, that had functions similar to those of the People's Houses.
15. It is unclear if this reference is to the notable or to merely his henchmen.
16. People's House (1933), 113–115.

17. Naim (1934), 16–17.
18. Cemal (1932). See back cover for listing of published and projected provincial studies in this series.
19. I am indebted for this point to my colleague, Çağlar Keyder.
20. Published on 26 Aralık 1903. Certainly, this account rests on a story then currently known and in circulation.
21. This kind of burning earth story is consistent with discovery tales elsewhere in the world.
22. Significantly, the official yearbooks of Kastamonu province for the years 1892–1899 make no mention of the coal discovery event. *Kastamonu vs 1310,1311, 1312, 1314, 1317* (1892–1899). The 1915 yearbook for Bolu province, *Bolu vs 1334*, 139, briefly presents a rival version, that coal first was found in 1822, in the area of Tiran village. And this was repeated nearly verbatim in Cemal (1922), 9. The central Ottoman state, in a 1909 statistical survey of the empire, summarily gives a version that could refer to either the 1822 or the 1829 discovery (more likely it is the latter). Turkey (1327), *Ihsaiyati maliye 1325*, 262, asserts that during the reign of Mahmud II, "Ereğli ahalisinden biri" (one of the people of Ereğli) discovered coal for the first time, took a sackful to Istanbul, and presented it to the sultan, thus leading to scientific studies early in the era of Sultan Abdulmecid. Among European writers, Spratt (1877), 528, reporting in 1854, says that the "existence of these coal beds was first brought into notice about the year 1838 or 1840." Cuinet (1895) makes no comment. These are all the discovery references made during the Ottoman period that I have uncovered.
23. Surely there are earlier versions on which the *Sabah* article is drawing, but they have not yet come to my attention.
24. During the 1930s, recall, regimes in Russia, Germany, and Italy were all extolling the omnipotence of the state and its unique ability to realize the potential of the individual. Again, thanks to Çağlar Keyder for this point.
25. I am unaware of any personal link between either Özeken or Kıray and the coalfield.
26. İmer (1944), 36–37. He does not mention Uzun Mehmed in his 1973 memoir.
27. (1970), 5, n. 1.
28. Çıladır (1977), 26, n. * and 64, n. *, citing Kıray (1964). The murderer, identified only as "H.I.," is doubtless Hacı Ismailoğlu. See also Çıladır (1977), 14–15.
29. Savaşkan (1993).
30. I consulted three similar versions: Özeken (1944a), 33, n. 1; (1944b), 14 and 14, n. 1; and (1955), 4–5.
31. Etingü (1976), 23–24. This work offers a Turkish translation of the important 1867 regulations, which set up the rotational labor system.
32. Çatma (1998), 68–69.
33. The extent to which the local politics of the early 1930s influenced the decision in favor of Uzun Mehmed is uncertain. The Karamahmudzadeler had been very prominent in mining over the past century, and was perhaps the leading local family. The Hacı Ismailoğlu family, for its part, fell into the second rank, having derived its wealth from the business of providing mine supports. How their influence affected the People's House deliberations is uncertain. See Kıray (1964), 64–65.
34. Freese (2003).
35. Naim (1934), 20.
36. For example, all three of the Özeken studies. Gürol (1997) is a partial exception and characterizes 1884–1908 as the "companies" period.
37. For example, see Burke (1993), Goldberg (1996), Quataert (2001), and Beinin (2001).
38. Jennings (1975) was a pathfinder in the use of these court records; for a more recent effort, see Peirce (2003).
39. A striking exception is the recorded memoir of the miner Ethem Çavuş, who for decades worked in the coal mines of the Ottoman Empire and the Turkish Republic. See Quataert and Duman (2001).

2

The Ottoman Coal Coast

General Introduction

Located in a geologically complex region along the southern Black Sea coast, the Zonguldak coalfield is among the richest mineral deposits in the eastern Mediterranean. Its beautiful geography disguises twisted strata that helped to restrict mechanization and production levels throughout the Ottoman period. The surface soils are not rich, supporting only marginal agriculture; residents in this comparatively densely populated area combined farming and animal husbandry with activities such as nut gathering, forestry, and shipbuilding.

Commercial coal mining entered the inhabitants' lives quite late in the Ottoman era, when the state, seeking coal for strategic purposes, began mining operations during the decades before 1850. In 1867, unable to find sufficient labor otherwise, the central government inaugurated a compulsory mine work system that would indelibly mark the region. Villagers (and some townsmen) in a newly formed coalfield administrative district (*havza*) thereafter labored in the mines for wages and release from active military service. Rotating work gangs rotationally left the villages to work in the mines, returning home after a half-month's labor.

Stifling state control took the form of a military administration between 1867 and 1910 but failed to gain the needed coal. As the late Ottoman period unwound, free market forces played an increasing role and the mine administration finally was civilianized. Simultaneously, an ever larger and more specialized cadre of state engineers and officials emerged to organize and control coal output.

Physical Setting and Human Setting

Introduction

The Zonguldak coalfield, around 1914, contained the largest industrial work force in the Ottoman world. More than 10,000 rotational and permanent workers, nearly all of them Ottoman subjects, labored above- and belowground in

---

Notes for this chapter begin on page 46.

the richest coal beds—indeed, the richest mineral deposits except for oil—in the Middle East. The coalfield of the Ereğli-Zonguldak district lies some 135 nautical miles east of the Ottoman imperial capital—an overnight nineteenth-century steamship voyage—along the southern shore of the Black Sea, part of an area nicknamed the "sea of trees" because of its heavily forested mountain slopes.[1] In the official history, a veteran discovered coal there in the 1820s, remembering the sultan's admonition to the troops to search for coal upon returning home. The area of production expanded fitfully but steadily over the nineteenth century: between the 1850s and the 1890s, working mines hugged a stretch of coastline about 80 km wide. In 1854, the known deposits began 5–6 km of Ereğli on the west and extended eastward to within 1.6 km of the town of Amasra. At that time, some mines were 5 to 19 km from the coast. In the 1890s, most operations were between two and ninety minutes distance from the sea. Thereafter, production rapidly mounted, and the area of known deposits expanded considerably inland, now 3.5 hours into the mountains, and an additional 10 km eastward past Amasra along the coast.[2] Today, the field is 180–200 km in width. In 1915, the coalfield area equaled 1,335 sq km.[3] During the entire Ottoman period, one 1920s report estimated, only around 15 million tons of coal had been extracted, less than 1 percent of the then-known coal deposits of 1.5–2.0 billion tons.[4]

Geology

The nineteenth-century miners of Zonguldak cut coal that a complex geology had created over an extraordinarily long period of time. During the Carboniferous era over 250 million years in the past, vast accumulations of plant matter trapped between great folds of the earth began to transform into coal. Many millions of years later, in the Cretaceous period some 65 million years ago, enormous swamps began to sink and yet more coal materials began to form. The land within the district of Zonguldak consisted of layers of pisolite, limestone, and sandstone. Coal lies between sandstone layers and schist layers, and the coal-bearing strata often run roughly parallel to the coast. Tectonic forces before, during, and after these formative processes have created the twisted and tortured strata that make up the diverse coalfield of the Black Sea littoral. Carboniferous and Cretaceous coals often lay near the surface and, at some locations, are virtually adjacent to one another. Thus, miners within walking distance of each other could be working coal millions of years apart in age. At their deepest, coal layers reached depths up to 1–2,000 meters.[5] The heavy fracturing resulted in coal seams that often were and are "discontinuous, and difficult to mine."[6] Problems in extracting the coal already had been noted by an 1854 expedition that provided the first scientific analysis. "These [coal] drifts extended from about 100 to nearly 400 yards only into the hill; for the district was so disturbed by faults and displacements, which occurred at every 200 or 300 yards, that ... few extended a greater distance before a fault was met with."[7]

The first band of coal appears just east of Ereğli—quite near where coal officially was discovered. Farther along, some 25 km away, is the wide valley of Kozlu, the early center of exploitation. At this point begins a series of parallel stream valleys—Zonguldak, Kilimli, and Çatalağzı—that became the site of some of the most intensive Ottoman operations. Millions of years after its creation, coal (and its workers) was transported between these valleys and from the valleys to the coast by a combination of railways and aerial cables.

The principal areas of known coal deposits in the Ottoman era were (moving from west to east): Ereğli, Çamlı, Kandilli, Alacaağzı, Tefenli, Kozlu, Zonguldak, Inağzı, Kilimli, Çatalağzı, and, finally, Tarlaağzı at Amasra to the east.[8] These were organized into six distinct coal locales (*mevki*): Alacaağzı, Kozlu, Zonguldak, Kilimli, Çatalağzı, and Amasra (see map 2.1). Historically and today, the coalfield was quite compact, and most mines along the coast were within several hours' sea journey (by steam) of one another. Alacaağzı, an area of rich veins, lay three hours by land or one hour by sea from Ereğli, to its northeast. Farther west, the small town of Kozlu lay in the very heart of the coal district and was 0.75 hours by sea and 1.5 hours by land from Zonguldak. Karadon, inland on the southeast side of Zonguldak and 300 meters in elevation was, by land transport, two hours from Çatalağzı, three hours from Kilimli, and three hours from Zonguldak.

By the late nineteenth century, geologists had determined the presence of three distinctive coal strata in the planet's crust—lower, middle and upper. For example, coal mines in America often were of the lower strata type, some 4,000 meters down, while France's upper strata mines were 800 meters deep. In 1894, a Greek-French engineer named Ralli, who then served as head engineer for the important Giurgiu Company, went into every mine in the Zonguldak coalfield and collected fossils to date the strata in which they were found. He organized his finds and sent them for analysis to the Paris Mining School,[9] and the coal-bearing strata of Zonguldak coalfield were categorized according to Ralli's finds.

The lowest stratum locally, named the Alacaağzı type, was the richest in volatile materials (40–44 percent), a positive measure of coal quality. Around 1913 there were some fifteen differently named seams averaging 0.75 meters in thickness in this stratum, mainly located in the western part of the coalfield, and about 17 meters (54 feet) thick. The middle, Kozlu, stratum (30–40 percent volatile materials) overall about 49 meters (158 feet) thick, appeared most commonly in the valleys of Zonguldak, Kilimli and Çatalağzı. There were at least twenty-five known seams of this coal, averaging 1.5 meters in thickness. The uppermost, Karadon, stratum held eight seams in the east-central area of the field, near Karadon and Çatalağzı, and another five seams lay still farther east, near Amasra.[10]

Before the first scientific examination of the fields in 1854, it mistakenly had been assumed that the Zonguldak fields were entirely of the low-quality lignite found in the Sea of Marmara.[11] Since then, specialists have described Zonguldak coals variously, depending on the specific location, as both poor

Map 2.1 The Ereğli Coalfield

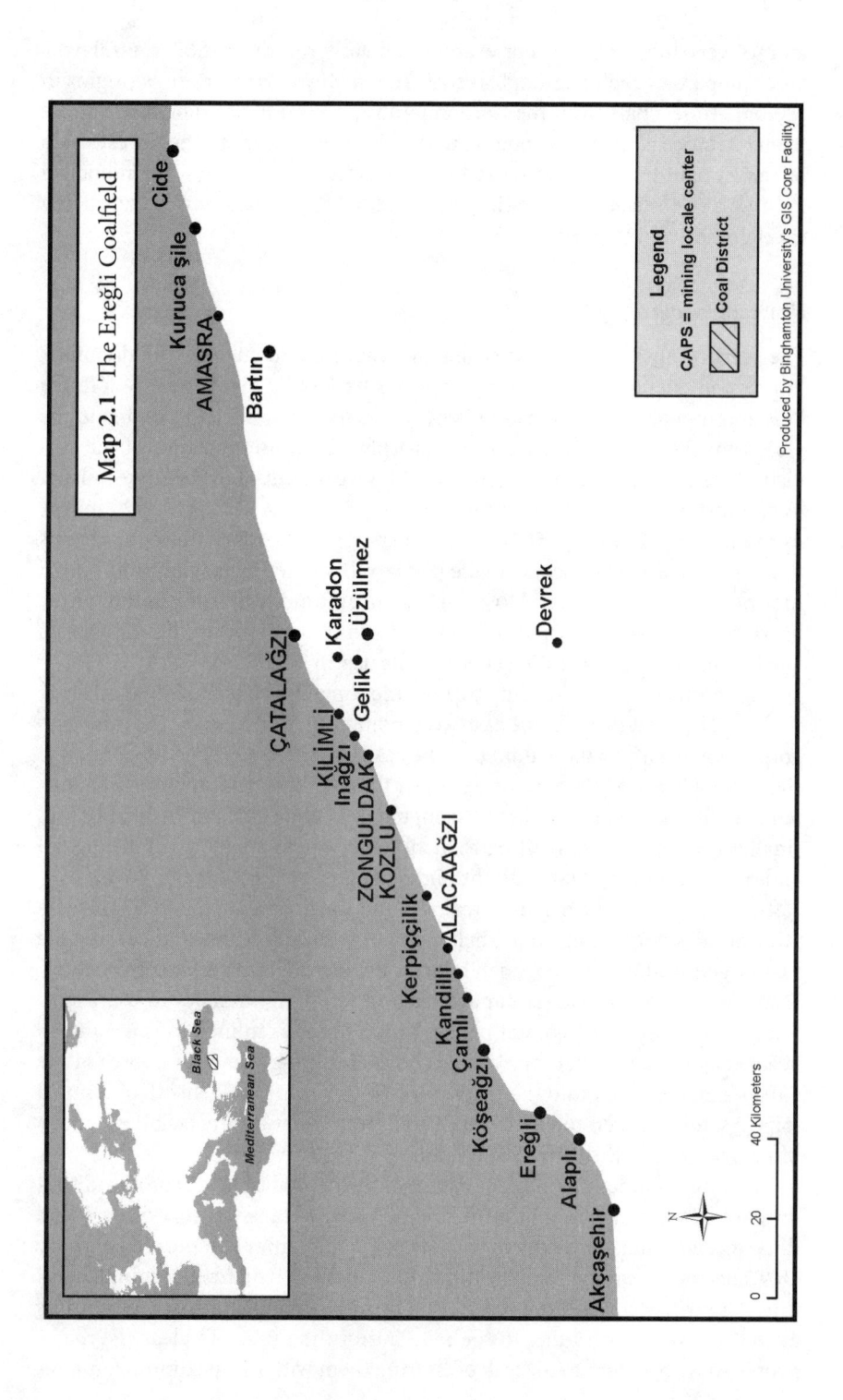

and "of very high grade."[12] For example, an early report in 1867 not unfavorably compared Ereğli and English coal. The quality derives from its origins in geologic time: coals from the Carboniferous era overall are superior to those from Cretaceous time.[13] Belonging to the bituminous variety, the lowest strata of the Zonguldak coals were used chiefly to manufacture gas for municipal lighting and for steam generation. The middle, Kozlu variety was considered excellent for coking purposes.[14]

Physical Geography

The scenery of the coalfield is strikingly beautiful and rugged. The dominant impression is one of narrow sandy beaches backed by green, heavily forested hills and mountains of increasing height, intersected by streams flowing to the sea. From the beaches, the land rises sharply. The coastal uplands of the coal district are quite steep and rocky and quickly give way, in 4 km (1.5 miles) inland, to 550-meter (1,800 foot) elevations and then in just 26–32 km (15–20 miles), to mountain heights of 1,500–2,200 meters (5–7,000 feet). These mountains trap the moisture of the sea, so the region is well watered, averaging around 1.25 meters (50 inches) per year. Most rains fall in autumn with some in the spring; in winter, snow falls to depths of 10 to 100 cm (4 to 40 inches) but disappears quickly thanks to the warming effects of the nearby Black Sea.[15]

Numerous small rivers and streams, the longest being the Filyos River at some 200 km, cut through the east-west mountains, and most cascade through gorges northward as they tumble to the sea.[16] The streams generally are quite short: the Catalağzı stream, for example, flows 15 km from the Gelik Mountains to the sea while another at Zonguldak is about 10 km in length. Still smaller is a 5 km stream at Kozlu. In all these waters are plentiful during fall and spring, but from May until the end of August very little water flows.[17]

In geologic time the narrow streams found weaknesses in the rock and wore away at the surrounding strata, helping to expose coal seams that became the first targets of the emerging coal industry during the mid nineteenth century: "Narrow valleys and ridges parallel each other at right-angles to the shoreline."[18] There are a few coastal plains. In the times examined in this volume, beaches gradually turned black from the coal mining along the shores of the streams that emptied into the sea; from coal transport accidents that dumped tons in shallow waters along the coast; and from coal washing facilities built by mine operators at the turn of the century.

The mountainous and broken nature of the coastal uplands and the abrupt drop into the sea, however beautiful, rendered land transport very difficult and thus worked against the exploitation of coal. A government report in February 1878 succinctly summarized the difficulties posed to land transport in this setting: "Snow has covered the roads used by the workers and coal transporters as well as the paths leading to the railroads of the mines. To clear the roads, people were thrown into the task of clearing them with the maximum [amount of effort]. There has been snow and rain and no coal is being delivered. The workers and coal transporters are without barley and hay and it is insufferably cold. The *poyraz* and *yıldız* and *karayel* winds are raging back and forth; it's a huge storm and it's continuing."[19]

The coal extracted in those days left the region only by sea. Even today, only a few roads and railroads connect the mining area to the wider region. Thus, about two dozen tiny estuaries formed by the streams served as loading spots for the coal. These transfer points were exposed to every vagary of the weather and the sea, which became particularly dangerous as terrible storms lashed the coasts, especially in the winter season. In all of the coal-bearing region there is only one decent natural port, at Ereğli, located on the far west of the district. A storm on 19–20 March 1878 (just a month after the one described in the quote above), for example, drove a ship carrying a cargo of wood up onto the rocks in front of the mine administration building, drowning two of eight crew members.[20] By the end of the century, Zonguldak—located in the geographic center of the coalfield—had become the chief exit point for the coal, although the man-made port there was tiny and dangerous.

Agriculture

In summer, the agricultural setting could appear idyllic: lush green hills surrounding homesteads with small plots growing cereals, legumes, and occasionally, fruits for family consumption. But steep slopes, the scarcity of level ground, and thin soils afforded a meager agricultural base for the region. Characteristically, these small farmers grew cereals, especially wheat, barley, and maize as well as legumes, particularly chickpeas.[21] A government assessment in 1915 painted a far-from-rosy picture of agriculture in the Zonguldak district, where mining was the most intense. Analysts noted that cultivators were not producing enough for the needs of the district and generally were using antiquated methods. The most common crops in the district at the time were wheat, corn, rye, barley, oats, lentils, and beans. For personal use, many families maintained small orchards in front of their homes that produced some apples, pears, plums, and figs. Generally, however, fruits were being brought from the outside.[22]

Forests

Abundant nearby forests[23] were crucial to the development of the mining industry. The western Black Sea littoral of the coalfield was heavily wooded overall, and unusually for the Ottoman world, forestry was a mainstay of the regional economy. The forests of the coal-mining areas were remarkable for their extent and for the presence of trees of soaring heights and vast girth. These mainly consisted of oak, elm, chestnut, and "all kinds of conifers," especially firs and black and yellow pines. Forests in the interior region behind the mines, administered by the Devrek district, which sent both timber and men to the mines, covered two-thirds of the area and consisted of "magnificent, chiefly old, oaks, enormous beeches and gigantic conifers." In around 1890, forty-two named forests covered some 4,544 sq km of the administrative unit[24] in which the coalfield was situated, or 22 percent of the total land area of the unit (21,000 sq km).[25] At the time, a European observer reported that exploitation was very limited and that there were "no forest roads."[26] Surely this is an underestimation since mining had been going on in the region for nearly four decades.

Mines, to mix metaphors, were voracious consumers of trees. Take the year 1895, for example, when coal production totaled 151,000 tons, one-sixth of its peak during the Ottoman era. At that time, some 89 mines were operating at least nominally and annually advanced a total of about 15,000 meters into the earth. For every new meter dug, eight mine supports were needed. An additional six supports per meter maintained the already existing mine surfaces, shoring up the walls and ceilings and buttressing the entrances to the stone tunnels that led into the work areas. Altogether, in this year of relatively slight coal production, the mines consumed 330,000 mine supports, or to put it another way, as many as 330,000 trees (photograph 2.1).[27] The impact was clear. As a leading Istanbul newspaper put it in 1898: "[F]rom the forests near the mines, operators have been taking out all the wood that they needed. Thus, over time, the forests near the mines were destroyed."[28]

By 1915, the mines annually were requiring 1.5 million supports.[29] Nonetheless, forest-covered mountains remained a characteristic feature of the region in Ottoman times. Take, for example, the enumeration of 1915, when the administrative region holding the coalfield measured some 35,000 sq km. (The administrative boundaries in the meantime had been redrawn repeatedly, so there can be no direct comparison with the 1890 evaluation.) Forests at this later period accounted for 27 percent, some 5,400 sq km of the total land mass of the administrative region.[30] These figures suggest that, despite the many millions of trees cut down to provide mine supports between the 1890s and 1915, forest reserves remained immense. In 1915, in the Zonguldak district where the most important mines were located, specialists measured 26,900 hectares of forest land in seventeen named forests (table 2.1).[31]

Table 2.1 Types of Trees in Selected Mine Districts, 1915 (in %)

	Ereğli	Devrek	Zonguldak
Fir	5	30	—
Pine	5	20	20
Beech/alder	45	20	45
Oak	25	20	25
Other	20	10	10

Source: *Bolu vs 1334*, 185, 246, and 288, respectively for the three districts.

These forests provided a variety of livelihoods, for example, from the sale of millions of kilograms of acorns, gall nuts, chestnuts and other forest products.[32] Within the coalfield, the primary forestry occupations were cutting trees for construction lumber and shaping them into mine supports. An indirect measure of forests' importance was that during the early 1890s, taxes on forestry accounted for 60 percent of all government revenues from the province of Kastamonu, the general region in which the coalfield was located.[33] Lumber milled in many districts of the province primarily went to local villages or down narrow trails to nearby towns.[34] In districts outside of the coalfield, such as Safranbolu, Tatai, Inebolu, and Cide, foresters brought the harvested timber to various small docks for export to Istanbul. The mines drew on forest resources both within and outside the coalfield. By the 1890s, several districts outside of the coalfield, including İskilip and Taşköprü on its east and south borders, were already sending their logs for use in the coal mines.[35]

Coal Production and the Mining Infrastructure: An Overview

During the decades between the opening of the first mines and the end of World War I, production mounted thanks to a partial resolution of problems concerning the supply of labor, animals and materials (see chapter 3). This in turn led to an expansion in the geographic scale of mining, increases in the number of operational mines, and major technological improvements in the physical infrastructure, both above- and belowground. Overall, annual production levels which had averaged perhaps 20,000 tons in the 1840s, had surpassed 900,000 tons by 1911 (see table 2.2). More specifically: annual levels of about 30,000 tons until the 1860s doubled and redoubled during the next decade and then leveled off, more or less, until the 1890s. By that date, some ninety mines had been opened, a number that would not change significantly in later years. But owing to a subsequent host of technical and administrative changes, production jumped from around 200,000 to over 500,000 tons in the decade around the turn of the century. Still later, during its peak years of 1906–1914, production annually averaged 750,000 tons.

The first mines were in Tiran village, quite near the town of Ereğli on the western edge of the coalfield. By the 1850s, mines had opened farther east, mostly around Kozlu and around the future site of Zonguldak. As they spread out geographically from the sites of the first exploitation, at first the mines were barely holes in the ground, worked under very primitive conditions. Numerous small operators worked mines as close to the coast as possible so that in many cases, e.g., Yeni Harman at Kozlu, the coal was loaded directly from the mine onto the boat, a practice persisting for decades.

Initial infrastructural support was sparse: transport largely consisted of mules, horses, and buffalo wagons. In the 1850s during the Crimean War, the first recorded railroads appear, built by the English engineers, the Barkley brothers, who also were constructing coal chutes at a number of coastal locations. In

Table 2.2 Coal Production in the Coalfield, 1848–1940 (1,000 tons)

1848–1865	20–30*	1895	151*	1911	904
1860	35*	1896	176*	1912	810
1861–1865	35–40*	1897	123	1913	827
1865	61*#	1898	212	1914	651
1870	64*#	1899	258	1915	420*#
1875	142*#	1900	388 (420*#)	1916	208*#
1880	56*#	1901	341	1917	158*#
1882	65	1902	388	1918	186*#
1883	71	1903	454	1919	381*#
1884	79	1904	519	1920	569*#
1885	55 (79#)	1905	590 (622*)	1921	342*#
1886	101	1906	611	1922	411*#
1887	109	1907	736	1923	596*#
1888	147	1908	698	1930	1.6*#
1889	—	1909	794	1935	2.3*#
1890	149*#	1910	764*#	1940	3.0*#

Sources: Unless otherwise noted, figures are drawn from Özeken (1944a), 26.
As noted, the following offer the same figures as Özeken.
* Savaşkan (1993), 12, 38, 55–56.
# Naim (1934), 88–89.
Ihsaiyati 1325, 263, gives the same figures as Özeken for 1900–1909.
Maden 1323, 80–81, gives the same figures as Özeken for 1902–1907.
Estimates that differ from Özeken are in parentheses.

the late 1860s, state officials of the newly formed coalfield district rebuilt the existing railroad and narrow-gauge lines and coal chutes along the coast. It was perhaps these railroads that an 1871 visitor recorded: in the valleys at Kozlu, Kilimli, and Zonguldak, he said, rails had been laid that were 2.5, 1.2, and 5 km in length respectively (with 1.4-meter gauge), along which animals pulled 1,600-kg wagons. In addition, a number of inclined planes were constructed to bring coal down the steep slopes.[36] Photographs 2.2 and 2.3, likely from the 1890s or later, show a two-track inclined plane moving full cars down and empty cars up for reloading. In earlier years, the plane likely contained just one set of tracks.

During the early 1890s, transport at Zonguldak reportedly consisted of "a small railroad," that is, wagons on rails pulled by mules to the coast.[37] There was a small loading dock but, "thanks to the sultan," construction had begun, around 1895, on a jetty.[38] Until just before the turn of the century, transport facilities throughout the coalfield remained remarkably primitive. Coal came by rail, sometimes pulled by animals to the coast where at a number of spots it slid down chutes into small boats. Photograph 2.4, which is quite remarkable in other respects, shows the Domuz mine at Kozlu (1888–1914), one of the more important mine operations. Notice the narrow and frail pier of boards leading from the mine to the sea. Coal was moved along these boards and then, via a chute, dropped down into the waiting small boats. The boatmen then rowed away and pulled broadside along ships out in the open anchorage, to shovel the coal into wicker baskets and then dump it from the baskets into the holds.[39]

Over the decades, the mines progressively went farther and deeper into the earth and, finally, under the sea. In the 1870s, the deepest mine in perpendicular distance reached 70 meters and ran 1,000 meters in length. Just four mines of the eighty in operation went vertically into the earth at that time, relying on steam to move the men and the coal.[40] In these early decades there were few investment incentives for private entrepreneurs. Until 1882, the state demanded the right to purchase all the coal, at prices it determined. Once the state took the modest step of allowing 40 percent of production to be sold on the open market, the investment climate improved immediately. The first significant private entrepreneur, the foreign shipping magnate Giurgiu Pano, was soon followed by others. Within a decade after free market sales were thus permitted, radical improvements in the technological infrastructure became apparent.

A significant set of changes accompanied the formation of the Ottoman Ereğli Company (Société anonyme ottomane d'Héraclée/Ereğli Şirketi Osmaniyesi). Thinly disguised as an Ottoman enterprise and guided by a number of well-placed Ottoman investors of high official position, the company largely was financed with French capital via the Ottoman Bank, which actually was French-capitalized. There were a number of false starts following the original concession in 1891.[41] The port originally was planned for Kozlu. But two local coal operators, Eseyan and Karamanyan, had rich holdings away from Kozlu and closer to Zonguldak.[42] They appealed to the Ottoman Bank, arguing that a port located at Zonguldak would be more profitable for investors and for their own operations. The final concession (with the port at Zonguldak) was let in 1896, and the Ereğli Company began operations in earnest, quickly coming to occupy the dominant position in the coalfield around the turn of the century. By 1902, the company accounted for 79 percent of total output; in 1915 the company was operating twenty-two mines.[43]

The company set out to improve transport facilities, the key to successful exploitation of the mines. Renovating and extending government-built lines in the spring of 1899, the company opened 25 km of track (1-meter gauge), running between the mines at Çatalağzı and Zonguldak to the new port under construction. Lacking the finances to build a more complete network of rail lines, the company constructed cheaper aerial tramways. The two went into service in 1899 and descended to existing rail lines in two different valleys. And in 1902 it opened a 5.2-km aerial cable between the important Gelik mines and Üzülmez, with its rail connections to the coast (photograph 2.5). Some of the coal thus flowed to the coast at Çatalağzı. But most of the transport links brought coal to the port of Zonguldak, then under construction.

A modern port facility lay at the heart of company plans to exploit the coalfield. The company ignored the superior natural port at Ereğli, abandoned an earlier plan to develop a port at Kozlu, and finally pressed ahead in favor of a man-made port at Zonguldak, close to the best coal mines in the region.

Construction was begun in 1897, but the Ottoman-Greek War and then a storm delayed completion. Finally, in the fall 1902 the port opened behind the shelter of a 320-meter breakwater. Colliers and ships taking on fuel were now loaded directly in the sheltered port, with the use of powerful cranes. At last, the labor-intensive and slow loading (and weighing) by small boat and basket could be bypassed (photographs 2.6, 2.7, and 2.8).[44] Still many other operators continued to use these older technologies.

The company also built several coal scrubbers. Previously, the combustibility and therefore the sales of coal had been retarded by the presence of impurities, such as schist, which accounted for 20–25 percent of the total matter extracted from the mines. To wash away such foreign matter, the company built two scrubbers, respectively in about 1897 and 1903, each with an hourly capacity of 200 tons (photograph 2.9).[45] Among other facilities, it opened a casting factory; separate repair shops for locomotives, wagons, and machinery; and a small factory to make coke and briquettes.[46] These improvements were considerable and help explain the leap in company production in just a few years. Moreover, other operators, for a fee, could use the port, railroads, narrow-gauge lines, scrubbers, and repair facilities of the Ereğli Company. They also could purchase supplies from the extensive stockpiles of materials that the company maintained.[47]

Other entrepreneurs made important if less extensive improvements (photographs 2.10, 2.11, and 2.12). During the 1880s, the Karamanyan Company had led the way, briefly monopolizing the coal trade. In 1884 it built the first privately owned inclined plane in the district and played an important role in extending the existing rail system.[48] The Giurgiu Company, for its part, established the first air cable car in the region, using cables strung between towers, not unlike today's chair ski lifts.[49] Near the turn of the century, an Austrian engineer working for the Karamanyan Company doubled the vertical depths being exploited when he opened a 150-meter deep shaft in the Kozlu area, "using the latest mechanical means with real success."[50] The Ereğli notable Halil Pasha Karamahmudzadeler, a member of one of the most powerful local families in the coalfield, introduced electric power to the Çamlı mine.[51]

Raghip Pasha, a court chamberlain turned entrepreneur, was perhaps the most important technological leader after the Ereğli Company. His seventeen operations, collectively called the Sarıcazadeler mines after his family name, crossed what were reportedly the best veins in the basin,[52] perhaps because of his political connections. At the time he entered operations at Kozlu, no Ottoman subject had dug under the Black Sea because of the capital such an underwater operation required. Mining beneath the seabed necessitated steam and electric power for the pumps and for the elevators that brought up the coal. Until then only two operators—Giurgiu Pano and Petro Gregoviç—had had the wherewithal to operate below the floor of the Black Sea.[53] Raghip Pasha went twenty meters deeper to go after this underwater coal.[54] He made a number of other investments, including the construction of air cable cars.

And, aiming to break the monopoly of the Ereğli Company, he built a scrubber at Kozlu to wash the coal from the seventeen mines he operated under the Sarıcazadeler name plus others that his sons were operating.[55]

Until the entry of private entrepreneurs such as the Ereğli Company and Raghip Pasha, the mine administration, as seen, had been nearly the sole source of infrastructural improvements. In the mid 1890s, for example, a mining official who had grown up near Zonguldak established a coke oven as well as a briquette and firebrick factory.[56] Early on, the state had built the railroads from the mines down to the coast at Kozlu and Kilimli, and it remained responsible for these lines throughout the period.[57] By 1912, it had renovated and reopened repair facilities at the two locations to service the locomotives and wagons.[58] Thus, ownership of the few railroads in the region was divided between the state and the Ereğli Company. Early in his tenure as mine superintendent (1910–1921), Hüseyin Fehmi Pasha took steps to modernize the state-supported infrastructure. He compared the railroads of the Ereğli Company and the government. The former, he noted, owned new locomotives and eight-ton wagons, while the state still operated engines and wooden wagons dating from the Crimean War. Therefore, he bought modern engines from Germany and rebuilt the rail bed in the Kozlu and Kilimli valleys; in his estimation, rail facilities were now on a par with those of the Ereğli Company. Just before the war, Hüseyin Fehmi Pasha also renovated and lengthened the dock at Kozlu, repaired docks at several other locations, and installed facilities for weighing entire carloads of coal and not just baskets, as had been the case (photographs 2.13 and 2.14).[59]

In sum, a modest modern infrastructure had emerged to extract coal, bring it to central storage locations, wash it for sale, and load it onto ships. There can be no doubt of the improvements. By 1915, the railroads together could carry 5,000 tons daily. The handling capacity of the port of Zonguldak alone equaled 3,000 tons a day while the improved docks at Kozlu, Kilimli, and the smaller facilities at Alacaağzı, Kandilli and Çamlı together could handle an additional 4,500 tons daily.[60] And yet, the primitive methods and wearying means that had characterized mine work in the 1860s persisted in some locales, notably the less well-financed operations. Basket carriers remained commonplace, as did animal transport, wooden wagons, and a heavy reliance on small boatmen. The relatively very high accident rates in the Zonguldak coalfield underscore the transitional character of the infrastructure at the end of the Ottoman era.

Human Setting

Throughout the Ottoman era, the area immediately surrounding the mines provided the bulk of the labor force (see chapter 3). In 1867 this region was bureaucratically constituted as a separate entity—a coalfield district, consisting of fourteen administrative units that made up the manpower pool for the mines.[61] As soon will be made clear, manpower shortages plagued the mines. Thus, it seems striking to note that the province of Kastamonu, which contained the mine district, was a densely populated one, containing twenty-eight persons per sq km and ranking fifth among the sixteen administrative units in Ottoman Anatolia. A mid-1890s enumeration, likely including nearly all of the mine district area, offers a total population of approximately 325,000 inhabitants, males being in the slight majority.[62] There were at this time more than 1,100 villages in the coalfield (see table 2.3). Only some villages sent workers to the mines. During the 1890s, for example, some 230 villages and five town quarters furnished mine labor (see chapter 5).[63]

While the mines drew on the entire mine district, most workers came from two of the administrative units, the districts of Ereğli and especially that of Devrek, also named Hamidiye. In 1898, the villages of these two districts held about 41,000 persons and the towns, some 7,100 individuals (table 2.4).[64] By 1914, two districts bearing the same name but (almost certainly) different geographic parameters, contained 96,000 rural and urban dwellers. At both dates, Muslims constituted nearly the entire rural population of the general coalfield. Non-Muslims, for their part, lived almost exclusively in the few urban centers of the region. By 1914, rising urbanization (see below) had increased the number of non-Muslims, who formed about 2 percent of the total coalfield population.[65]

Table 2.3 Number of Villages in the Coalfield, ca. 1895

Bolu district	187
Ereğli district	63
Bartın district	58
Göynük district	119
Gerede district	56
Düzce district	133
Mudurnu district	175
Devrek district	340
Total	1,131

Source: Cuinet (1895), 493.

Table 2.4 Population of Coalfield Districts, 1898 and 1914

District	Quarters	Villages	Quarter population	Village population	Total 1898	1914
Ereğli	7	137	5,298	22,336	27,634	
Devrek	2	169	1,776	18,476	20,252	
Zonguldak						30,008
Bartın						65,903

Sources: *Kastamonu vs 1314*, 320–358; Karpat (1985), 184–185.

The Town of Zonguldak

The town of Zonguldak owes its very existence to the opening of the coal mines. In the 1860s, the uninhabited site of the future mining town was a swampy morass of malarial infection. Indeed, the terrain unsuitability for human habitation is evident in two of the favorite explanations of how the town obtained its name. In one account, the name stems from the Turkish *Zongalik*, 'a place of reeds and rushes'. An equally unreliable account notes its derivation from *Zonklamak*, 'a place of pain'.[66] Situated at the confluence of two small rivers (10 km in length, the Acılık and Üzülmez) whose deposited sediments would demand constant dredging when the port was built, the location held no particular promise. One former resident remembered: "In the area around Zonguldak there was neither agriculture nor farmlands, no rural shrines or holy springs."[67] Moreover, the indentation that later became a small port was fully exposed to the sea and to violent winds sweeping off the heights on both sides.[68] During the mining activity of the Crimean War days, the coastal indentation at Zonguldak was not singled out for any particular attention.[69]

But over time, ease of access to the rich coal deposits of the immediate hinterland came to outweigh the obvious disadvantages of the spot. Between the emptiness of the 1860s and the construction of the port three decades later, a small community slowly emerged to service the mining activities that fitfully were developing. At one stage, between the 1860s and the early 1890s, the area of Zonguldak—not yet a town and perhaps not even a village—administratively was subordinate to Çaycuma, an inland community that held a market, two mosques, a church, and a public bath.[70] Around this time, by one account, Zonguldak held between five and ten houses[71] as well as a market and an office of the coal-mining administration.[72] Another report noted the presence of about fifteen houses, all belonging to "Serbs from Montenegro" who had come to work the coal, settled down, and married Ereğli women. These Greek Orthodox, who spoke Serbian but knew Greek as well, the first to settle at Zonguldak, were followed by four-five Greek-speaking families from Ereğli.[73] As the Ereğli Company centered its activities at Zonguldak in the 1890s, the number of families from Ereğli who moved there rose to 150.

In the early 1890s, the "only decent place in town" was the lodging of the mine authorities. The encyclopedic observer Cuinet found the population of Zonguldak more animated and numerous than at Kozlu but added that life was about the same in the two places. Those who weren't miners, he said, either smuggled or fished, subsisting on goat meat, mutton, fish, and game. They avoided beef, he added, "because of the bad health in the area." Wheat was hard to come by and locals ate mainly maize flour.[74] Until 1896, when it was constituted as a district in its own right, Zonguldak officially was a sub-district of the village of Elvan, part of Ereğli district.[75]

As more mines and the port opened, businessmen and workers filtered in from across the empire and beyond. Two expatriates later remembered Zonguldak as a magnet for immigration, a new town in the making.

> You could find people of all nationalities there: Greeks, Armenians, French, Turks, Italians, Kurds.[76]

> In the past Zonguldak was insignificant.... Everybody, Turks as well as Greeks came from somewhere else. There was no native population. There were no indigenous Zonguldaklis [native inhabitants]. Whoever settled there was a foreigner.[77]

In 1895, the town still lay on only the right bank of the Acılık stream.[78] But, apace with coal mining, the town continued to grow. In 1896, either immediately or within a few months after creation of the separate administrative district of Zonguldak, the former hamlet became the administrative center of the coalfield region.[79] As the French company came in during the later 1890s, building the jetty and behind it a sheltered space for a handful of ships, the town began to boom.[80] Houses arranged themselves like seats in an amphitheatre, from the narrow flatland at the seaside spreading steeply uphill. The marketplace was on the flats, not far from the shore (photograph 2.15). Starting from the market area, residential quarters climbed upwards. Although the streets were unpaved, mud was not a problem because of the coal dust that drained well. Some quarters up the hill were high; by around 1900, the houses farthest from the flats were ten minutes' walk from the beach.[81] Notice (in photograph 2.16) the villa-like quality of the houses, certainly those of the European personnel and, perhaps, the merchants and mine operators.

Expatriate memories and official Ottoman records offer different points of emphasis concerning the populace of this new town. In the 1960s, many former Ottoman Greeks who now were living in Greece gave interviews about their lives in the Ottoman Empire.[82] In their recorded statements, they remembered the coal districts as communities in which Muslims provided the bulk of the mining labor force while Christians dominated the merchant class of the various towns. Regarding Zonguldak, one refugee recalled two or three grocery shops and smithies in Muslim hands.[83] Virtually all of the remaining commerce, he said, had rested in the hands of Greeks and Armenians. Another former resident remembered some 300 "Christian houses" and fewer Muslim ones. The French colony, he recalled, contained some fifty families. Among these was M. Paul Fauzon, who took credit for founding the "first European store" for the provisioning of miners, in 1897.[84] The Armenians numbered thirty families; there also were one or two Jewish families and a handful of Italians and Maltese. Most of the Ottoman Greek speakers, several of the interviewees stated, had migrated from Ereğli, but there were many other Anatolian Greek speakers from nearby Safranbolu in the interior and from more distant Kayseri. Most islanders came from Mytilene and from the Dodecanese. And finally, there were some settlers from mainland Greece.[85]

There are no available population statistics for the town itself but Ottoman records from 1915 flatly state that most residents were Muslim and Turkish-speaking, thus contradicting the impression given by the testimonies of the expatriates. The numbers of places of Muslim and Christian worship and education lend favor to the official view. The town supported three mosques, two of them in the market district, as well as a number of schools for religious education (*medrese*). It also possessed fourteen state-run primary schools (*iptidai*), attended mostly by Ottoman Muslim subjects. The Greek Orthodox community, by contrast, maintained two primary schools, one each for boys and girls, as well as one Greek Orthodox Church.[86] In addition, there was a school for both boys and girls offering instruction in French.[87] At the turn of the twentieth century, the district of Zonguldak held 28,607 Muslims and 1,856 non-Muslims.[88]

The town of Zonguldak owed its existence to and profited from the economic stimulus of the nearby coal mines, from its status as a port shipping coal from these mines as well as those scattered along the Black Sea coast, especially to the east, and from its capacity as a government administrative center, at the level of both the district and the coalfield. It must have been a rough-and-tumble place. Coal dust filled the air, whipped about by sometimes-fierce winds, and covered the streets. The fine sandy beaches slowly were turning black thanks to the coal scrubbers and the many tons of coals inadvertently dumped in the sea. Many hundreds of miners, away from their families for weeks and, in the case of the permanent workers, for months and perhaps years, found shelter and recreation in the town. Many shops and coffeehouses sprang up to serve their needs. Also, as prostitutes migrated to the area, syphilis became rampant.[89]

Unlike most Ottoman communities, there was no set market day in Zonguldak. Markets existed to supply the workers and the ships calling at the port. Thus, the town erupted into activity as the work shifts changed (see chapters 3 and 4) or ships arrived. "Every fifteen days on payday, the Turkish peasants [mine workers] would come down to Zonguldak. They would buy whatever they needed at the bazaar and then go back to their villages. Turkish workers who had gotten their wages would be much the same—they would do their shopping and leave for their villages."[90] As another former resident reminisced, "every day" there were five or six ships loading coal for their own consumption or for transport. Besides coal, they took on supplies from merchants in the ship provisioning business. Knowing the schedule of the arriving ships, these merchants placed orders with surrounding villagers, who would bring in eggs, chickens, meat, and vegetables. Additional supplies of vegetables, fruit, and fish came from Ereğli, while Safranbolu over the mountains supplied butter and cheese. A ship from Istanbul, he remembered, called twice weekly, bringing butter, cheese, and "all kinds of grocery supplies," some of them for reshipment, one hour by boat, to Kozlu.[91] You could buy "everything" in the town market, even champagne from Marseilles and Metaxa cognac from Athens.[92]

Ereğli

Farther to the west, Ereğli, by contrast, was not quite so dependent on coal for its existence and growth, although mining clearly was crucial to the local economy (photograph 2.17). Ereğli offered the best natural port in the region of the coalfield—the only good one between Istanbul and Sinop. Just east of Ereğli, the coastline makes an abrupt ninety-degree turn northward from its east-west axis, a geography that afforded the port considerable protection under most conditions. Ereğli could hold dozens of ships while the artificial port constructed at Zonguldak managed only a fraction as many.[93] All ships seeking to load coal (except at Zonguldak) first called at Ereğli to obtain the services of lighter boats and workers.[94]

As storms approached, ships from the entire coal coast would flee (towing the lighter boats behind them) and take refuge at Ereğli, which under steam power was not more than one hour's distance from any loading point. But when powerful storms blew directly from the west, the harbor was fully vulnerable to assault. Official sources reported one such storm that, in 1903, destroyed five steamships and more than seventy sailing vessels.[95] It may have been this storm that one former resident remembered many decades later. Thirteen years old at the time, he recalled a storm that wrecked nearly 100 ships in the harbor (most seeking refuge, others loading coal).

> What a huge catastrophe that day! All along the shore and even up to fifty meters into the sea you could see all kinds of merchandise, fruits and timber floating on the water. All the ships were pushed ashore by the storm. For days after, barefooted, we would collect fruit.... [E]verything was wrecked, nothing was spared. So many people were drowned. At night you could hear the wild whistling of the ships while they were hit by the waves so that the ropes holding their anchors broke. Their sirens cried out for us to go help them. The ships crashed on the beach. There were so many drowned, so many frozen people.... Whoever was able to lend a helping hand would run to assist, there were no exceptions—Greeks and Turks—everybody was on the run, everybody was doing their best.[96]

The presence of the natural port sustained a certain amount of activity in the town of Ereğli, independent of the coal mines. In 1840, before any real coal exploitation had occurred, the town numbered some 2,000 persons. It certainly received an impetus when, in 1865, Ereğli district became the administrative center of the coalfield and the town became the seat of the mine administration (table 2.5). In 1877, Ereğli was said to contain 370 houses, 300 of them "Turkish," i.e., Muslim.[97] Between 1840 and 1899, as trade increased and the coalfield exploitation developed in earnest, the town tripled in size (table 2.6). In response to growing opportunities, not only in coal but also in the lumber trade, Ottoman Greek and Armenian merchants from Konya and Kayseri moved into the area in significant numbers between 1860 and 1890.[98]

In the early 1890s, on the eve of the coal boom, the town held a certain modest infrastructure including a "beautiful" government building, a granary,

Table 2.5 Population of Ereğli District, 1870–1915

Date	Muslim	Non-Muslim	Male (all)	Female (all)
1870	14,696	275	14,971	not counted
1878	23,242	543	23,885	not counted
1890	41,186	1,242	22,319	20,109
1892	38,668	854	20,590	18,932
1895	38,668	854	20,590	18,932
1896	40,020	858		
1901	40,650	980		
1915	40,467	227	21,251	20,643

Note: Boundaries may have changed over the years.
Sources: *Kastamonu vs 1310, 1311,* and *1317,* 203; *Yurt Ansik* 10, 7727; *Bolu vs 1334,* 164.

Table 2.6 Population of Ereğli Town, 1840–1910

ca. 1840	2,000
1880s	4,000
1890	6,274
1899	6,274
1910	6,000+

Sources: Kıray in Çıladır (1977), 62–63; Cuinet (1895), 513; Winkler (1961), 93.

and a garrison for the local troops. Two state primary schools for boys and one for girls, as well as one secondary school for boys (ages 10–15) educated the children of Ereğli. For the Muslims the town contained seven larger and four smaller mosques; in 1896, a public subscription funded a six-room school for religious education that initially trained twenty-five students. In the district surrounding the town, some 100 state primary schools were operating before the turn of the century, serving a population of around 40,000 (table 2.5). In addition, the countryside held eleven larger mosques and twenty-three smaller ones that provided for the spiritual needs of the 5,395 households in the district.[99]

A Turkish anthropologist in the 1960s interviewed the town elders, who agreed that in Ottoman times, Greeks had monopolized the town's trade while Armenians dominated transport and peddling.[100] There also were a few prominent and wealthy Greek merchants from Gelveri in the Kayseri region, who had settled in Ereğli after 1880.[101]

Kozlu

Even though Kozlu served as an early site of coal exploitation and became the administrative center of the coalfield after 1910, it seems to have changed relatively little over the decades. During the Crimean War era, the town of

Kozlu "was recognized by the few houses forming the settlement that stood near the shore of the little bay, as well as by the heap of coal."[102] In the 1890s the locale was still considered unhealthy, a "small village" of little importance that received free medicines from the state, presumably to fight malaria. At the time, it contained a military hospital and an arms depot and was noted for its fields of wild rhododendrons.[103] Even in 1903, well into the era of expanding coal production, Kozlu remained "a very small town"[104] (photograph 2.18). When Hüseyin Fehmi Pasha arrived as mine superintendent in 1910, the administrative center had just been moved from Ereğli to Kozlu. He remarked on the ready availability of beautiful homes for bureaucrats in Kozlu for just 20 krs a month; but at Zonguldak, he said, these were scarce and cost 200 krs and more.[105]

Devrek

Unlike Zonguldak, which was born in the steam age, the town of Devrek already was millennia-old when the mines opened. Located to the south and slightly east of Zonguldak, eight hours' journey from the sea, it was as far from the coal center as Zonguldak was from Ereğli. The Filyos River flowed through the town on its way to the sea, and before the mines were opened its course, choked up with swamps near the coast, was un-navigable. But Devrek timber was to shore up the walls and ceilings of mines, so the river was cleared to provide ready transport for the felled trees along their 200 km journey to the sea. During the immediate pre–World War I years, when coal production was booming (table 2.2), the town population grew considerably, at an estimated 3 percent per year. Devrek's children attended six primary state schools, three each for boys and girls, while village children in the surrounding area had access to another fifty primary state schools. Devrek town, in 1915, numbered some 5,000 inhabitants.[106]

State Administration of the Coalfield

State, not private, initiative played the crucial role in the early development and exploitation of the coalfield. Sustained government efforts to develop the mines, however, started only in 1865, as the Marine Ministry began its thirty-three-year supervision of the coalfield. Until then, administrative responsibility for the mines had drifted uncertainly within the state apparatus, and apparently there were very few state regulations overseeing mine operations in the area.[107] The mines remained under the competence of the Marine Ministry until 1908, when they passed briefly to the Public Works Ministry and then, in 1909, to the Ministry of Commerce, Agriculture and Mines, remaining there through the end of the Ottoman era and beyond, until 1939.[108]

The few mines operating prior to 1848 had a nebulous administrative and legal existence, probably under the haphazard authority of local officials in the area. At that time, the administration of the Privy Purse of the central government established a separate mine district, with the apparent intent to coordinate coal-mining activities and assure the flow of both revenues to the state and coal to Ottoman warships and state factories. The Ereğli coalfield (*Ereğli kömür havzası*) functioned as a separate and special administrative category, beyond the normal Ottoman practice of classifying areas as province and sub-province, district and sub-district. The boundaries at first were coterminus with those of the Ereğli district; later on, additional districts, such as Zonguldak district, were formed as coal production mounted. The ranking official, initially appointed and stationed at Ereğli in 1849, had dual functions, serving simultaneously as both director of the coalfield and district official of Ereğli district.[109] In theory, as both mine director and administrative district chief, he held considerable power over the workers and mine operators. But this potential went completely unrealized for a time: the initial appointees to the position possessed no apparent knowledge of or connection to the coal industry, and there was considerable turnover. Along with the director/chief administrator, clerks arrived to record the quantities of coal shipped from each of the various docks already in existence, as did watchmen to look over activities at the few mines in operation.[110] Several years later, around 1852, Sultan Abdulmecid sent two officials charged with the task of preparing a registry of the coal seams, their locations, and the borders of the newly founded coalfield.[111]

Government administration of the coalfield became established in these early years, and a number of precedents that were followed in later decades fell into place. Thus, entrepreneurs extracting coal could be operators of mines but never their owners. Legally, the land on which the first coal deposits officially had been discovered[112] was imperial property (*emlâki humayun*) and at the disposal of the monarch, the sultan having decreed these lands to be his property in 1848. Entrepreneurs purchased a license for the right to exploit the mine, but the mine remained the property of the ruler. From the outset, the sultan set aside a modest fixed sum of the coal-derived revenues for specific religious and pious purposes, in an endowment instrument called a pious foundation (*vakıf*). And indeed, these sums flowed regularly until the first years of the World War I period.[113]

For most of the years between 1848 and 1865, the coalfield legally fell under the competence of the Privy Purse (*hazine-i hassa*), but by all accounts the mines were administered rather badly during these years. Sometimes the Privy Purse subcontracted out the actual administration. During the Crimean War years of 1854–1856, the legal status of the mines remained the same but an English company administered them to supply coal to French and English warships in the Black Sea. After the war, the mines reverted to the direct administration of the Privy Purse. But, during the later 1850s and early 1860s, when neither the Arsenal nor the Navy obtained enough coal, the state in desperation turned unsuccessfully to private Ottoman subjects and then back to the English company to run the coalfield.[114]

In early 1865, the central government transferred administration of the coalfield from the Privy Purse to the Marine Ministry. During the subsequent decades, the state's regulatory powers mounted considerably. Under the new administration, the executive's dual position was modified somewhat: the mine directorship component was upgraded to a superintendency, but the district official post remained the same. Subsequently, not later than 1892, the superintendency was spun off into an independent position and a different person held the chief administrator position. Up to the end of the empire, no fewer than six individuals served as mine superintendent, not one of them an expert in mining (table 2.7).

The first occupant of the new office (*Ereğli livası kaymakamı ve madeni hümayunu nazırı*) was one Dilaver Pasha, "an influential high-ranking Marine Ministry official"[115] who was to achieve fame in local coal-mining circles for his regulatory work. He arrived at the head of a special mining commission in 1865 and set about trying to bring order to the coalfield. The commission based its activities at Kozlu, close to the center of mining activities.[116] It fixed the boundaries of the Ereğli coalfield: on the west from the Taşsuyu stream between Alaplı and Akçaşehir, and on the east the Kapısuyu stream, between Kuruca şile and Cide (see map 2.1). And under its auspices, an actual map of the coalfield was prepared, apparently for the first time.[117] After two years of work, the special commission led by Dilaver Pasha issued a regulatory document that sought to assure both manpower and material supplies for the mines and the conditions of their exploitation (see chapters 3 and 4). Officially entitled the Ereğli Imperial Mines Regulations (*Nizamname-i Madeni Hümayunu Ereğli*), it later acquired the nickname Dilaver Pasha Regulations, in recognition of the superintendent/chief administrator.[118]

These regulations owed their existence to local villagers' refusal to either enter the mines or furnish sufficient supplies of the wooden mine supports (see chapter 3). The new rules both accompanied and initiated a process of change in the conditions of work, exploitation, and administration that gradually took hold in the coalfield, if only imperfectly, during the subsequent decades. The 100-article document regulated a multitude of issues ranging from the granting and retention of mine concessions, to the opening of shops

Table 2.7 Directors and Superintendents of Mines, 1865–1921

Name	Dates of Tenure
Dilaver Pasha	1865–
Grammar Hasan Pasha	
Arif Pasha	
Sami Bey	
Eşref Bey	January 1908–February 1909
Hüseyin Fehmi Pasha	May 1910–May 1921

Sources: Hasan Pasha is listed in *Kastamonu vs of 1310, 1311*, and *1312*, but in *1317*, the name of the superintendent is left blank on the page. Also see İmer (1973).

and stores, to the rights of way for coal transport across cultivators' fields. The regulations delineated the responsibilities of mine operators in some detail and admonished that they "must, must, must" follow these dictates.[119] Treatment of the animals to be used for coal transport and the duties of those operating the scales to weigh the coal were carefully elaborated. And one section regulated the supply of the timber used to provide supports within the mines: knowledgeable observers later on would credit this as a major accomplishment.[120]

Other articles (comprising about 15 percent of the total body of regulations) focused on the recruitment and conditions of labor, including daily periods of work and rest. They defined various categories of mine labor; villagers as well as the townspeople of Ereğli who lived within the coalfield were compelled to serve. Moreover, the compulsory labor was established as rotational, twelve days at mine work and twelve days at home, with three days transport time in each direction.

The 1867 Dilaver Pasha regulations, for all of their 100 articles and the attention allotted them in the historiography, cannot be studied as a depiction of actual conditions in the mines. As will be made abundantly clear elsewhere in this study, many of its provisions remained unenforced and ultimately served only as a blueprint for proposed change. In many respects, it was a Potemkin village on paper, an officially projected image of conditions only dimly reflecting the reality of mine life.[121]

Yet, the crucial nature of these regulations and their importance for understanding the history of the coal miners must be acknowledged. Life in the coalfield was definitively altered by this state intervention. These procedures began to mold life, work, and leisure in patterns that persist to the present day, though compulsory labor ended with the death of the empire and, still later, the period of rotational labor changed, to shifts of thirty days. Thanks to these 1867 regulations, local workers during the 1990s continued to refer to themselves with pride as villager-workers, attesting to the continued prevalence of patterns set in another age and political space.

The 1867 regulations articulated the state's determination to play the central role in coal exploitation. Needing the coal for its factories and fleet, the state attempted to monopolize production and sales. To that end, it assumed responsibility for the development of production and placed the coalfield under military administration. Because the coal fueled naval vessels and because the coalfield was a maritime region, it was the Marine and not the War Ministry that assumed control.

Beginning in 1867, an administrative and military cadre from the Marine Ministry took up stations in "every corner of the coalfield."[122] The newly created policies of compulsory labor and compulsory delivery of mine supports and transport animals were enforced by maritime soldiers. For four decades, administrative officials working locally in mine operations usually held a military rank.[123] Some were clerks keeping records of the quantities of coal extracted and shipped, or of wages and salaries paid; other officials weighed coal at a number of state-run seaside facilities, many too small to be called a port. Yet others supervised railroad construction and operations and staffed maintenance workshops, while yet other higher-ranking administrators carrying military rank supervised the port, the various mine locales and the supporting workshops. Soldiers, the soldier-bureaucrats of the Marine Ministry and the personnel it hired from the outside were involved at every stage of the industry—from the recruitment of the labor to the loading of the coal onto ships. Just over fifty officials of military rank were working in all tasks by the early-mid 1890s (exclusive of maritime soldiers loading coal), when annual coal production averaged about 150,000 tons.[124]

While the state sought to provide the infrastructure for handling and moving coal from the mine head to the ships, the extraction tasks were left to private corporations and individuals within the mine. There, they were to use the human labor and transport animals provided through state coercion. Thus, the state intended the coal industry of Zonguldak to be a hybrid of public and private initiative. It inserted itself into every stage of production and demanded monopolistic purchase of the coal to boot. In this new post-1867 system, private capital theoretically would profit from state intervention and extract the coal more effectively than in the preceding decades.

State efforts to the contrary notwithstanding, a distinctive pattern subsequently emerged in which state control of the mines gradually and incompletely gave way to private capital. On the one hand, the provisions for compulsory labor and sales decisively affected life in the coalfield. On the other, the Ottoman government ultimately could not extract the coal without increasingly surrendering control to private enterprise, in a word, to capitalism. And yet, as we will see, despite the concessions to capitalism, the results were not very successful.

After 1867, state policies simultaneously proceeded down two paths. On the first path, the Istanbul regime gave way to market forces and became less decisive in shaping events. The state itself continued to evolve, developing different and less direct methods of control (see chapters 7 and 8). Yet it remained powerful enough to retard the fuller private exploitation that might have occurred in the absence of government controls. Whether or not workers benefited from this mix of capitalism and a dirigist state is explored later. Here, I offer three examples of diminishing state control and the increasing importance of the market.

First, take the conversion from state monopoly purchases of coal to free market sales. Until 1882, the Marine Ministry had the exclusive right to buy the coal extracted by private companies, which obtained their licenses from the mining administration. Mine operators were obligated to sell all of their production to the state, at officially set prices. This system, however, repressed production and discouraged the entry of mine entrepreneurs. Disastrous shortfalls in coal supplies during the recent Ottoman-Russian War of 1877–1878 (chapter 9), along with great pressure exerted by larger mine operators, led the state to reluctantly abandon its stranglehold on sales. As of 1882, operators could legally sell 40 percent of their output on the open market.[125] This modest step had an immediate and positive impact on production. But, in 1882, to compensate itself for the loss of cheap coal purchases, the state began taxing the coal sold in the marketplace.[126] Over time, however, the nominal amount of this tax fell steadily: it declined 86 percent between 1882 and 1920, from 18 to 2.5 krs per ton.[127] As the introduction of free-market sales and declining taxes on production indicate, the entrepreneurs (who included top-ranking state officials) repeatedly won their battles with bureaucrats who sought to run the mines for the benefit of the state alone.[128]

A second major example of diminishing state control involves the decision to open up the labor supply to all Ottoman subjects and end the restriction of some jobs to local residents. Free market sales of the 40 percent share had prompted a rise in the number of companies, accelerating production to new levels. A labor crisis began to erupt and both companies and entrepreneurs began pressuring the government to eliminate the restriction to local workers. Events took a decisive turn when Raghip Pasha, who at the time held the high-ranking post of chamberlain, aggressively entered coal operations.[129] Beginning in 1900, he and his sons bought up about two dozen mines from at least four separate companies. Unable to obtain sufficient labor supplies for his new acquisitions, he used his political influence with the governor of Kastamonu province who ordered a subordinate in Zonguldak to study the matter. In 1906, the governor abolished the forty-year practice embedded in the 1867 provisions, and permitted all Ottoman subjects to work in the coalfield.[130] Thus, it was an entrepreneur-capitalist within the state apparatus who promoted further changes that reduced government control in the coalfield.

The third example of diminishing state control involves the outcome, in early 1911, of negotiations between the state and the Ereğli Company. In this agreement, the two parties revisited the terms of their original agreement, which had unleashed the most important entrepreneurial force in the history of the coalfield. In this 1911 renegotiation, the government yielded to company demands on a number of crucial points. The state relinquished claims to a host of controls and revenues that it had demanded in the 1896 concession and to its right, embraced in the 1867 regulation, to buy back mines at its pleasure.[131]

These three examples together illustrate the first path followed by state policies: a decline of state control over coal sales, the labor market, and generally, exploitation of the coalfield. The agents of these changes driving out the state were capitalists from every quarter. They included, to be sure, the French corporate interests that came to play a dominant role, but there were many others as well. Ottoman entrepreneurs sometimes played a vital role, as seen in the intervention by the palace chamberlain who crucially affected the labor supply, hardly a unique example of the influence of indigenous capital. As we also will see, a host of smaller operators joined together in pressing the state to replace its military administration with a civilian one.

We now turn to the second path that state policies followed after 1867 as the state gradually gave way to capital in the shaping of exploitation. Namely, an ever-larger state bureaucracy utilized increasingly scientific and rational procedures, both to govern exploitation and, of particular interest here, to supervise, discipline, and control the labor force (chapters 7–8). For example, it acted to end the chaos resulting from unregulated mining, when operators willy-nilly cut drift mines that often ran into each other. The superintendent's office responded by defining mine boundaries to eliminate conflicts among operators. The concession area, the exact length and width of which varied according to circumstances, originally had a total radius of 250 sq m; later this was expanded to 450 sq m and finally to 1,200 sq m.[132] Also, mine officials assigned a number to each mine when they issued the exploitation permit, a procedure that began in 1878. Initially, sequenced numbers were assigned to the various locales; thus numbers 1 through 33 went to mines in the Kozlu locale. But thereafter, rather haphazardly, officials assigned the next number in the sequence to whatever mine opened in whichever locale, be it Kozlu, Zonguldak, or Amasra. Thus, when a new mine opened, it obtained the next available number, which, confusingly, could be out of sequence with mines in that same locale.[133] In another process formalized in 1896, the administration adopted the practice of naming coal veins, usually after the entrepreneur who first exploited them.[134]

In 1892, as stated above, two individuals came to occupy the once-unified post of district chief and mine superintendent. At this time, a superintendent headed the Ereğli Imperial Mine Administration (*Ereğli madeni hümayunu nezareti*) while another person was chief administrator of the Ereğli district.[135] This administrator also served both as head of the scientific commission and assistant superintendent (*nazır muavini*) of the coalfield.[136] This division reflected a more general trend in the nineteenth-century Ottoman bureaucracy: the mining bureaucracy was becoming larger and more specialized in function. Too, it was acquiring a more civilian character.[137] Much of this development came quite late, between 1907 and 1910.

Until around 1899, for example, only a single, state-salaried engineer watched over the safety of all workers in the entire coalfield, when production had increased to 250,000 tons. In 1892 he was a foreign civilian named "Mister William," while in 1896 Osman Cevdet Efendi, who held military rank, occupied the post. Each was based in Kozlu and from there traveled about to the different mine locales.[138] Except for the foreigner, virtually all other mining officials who were serving in the region, including Mr. William's assistant engineer, were Ottoman subjects and held military ranks such as captain and lieutenant. By 1899, Osman Nuri, also with a military rank, had joined Osman Cevdet on the engineering staff at Kozlu.[139] Somewhat later, an expansion of the state engineering staff began. When the current engineer, one Istiolyanos Istabolos Efendi, lost his job in July 1907, plans were afoot for the hiring of a "head" engineer (who presumably came with a staff of engineers reporting to him).[140] Two years later, as part of this ongoing professionalization, the Ministry of Forests, Mines, and Agriculture temporarily assigned Behçet Bey, an Istanbul-based engineer, to the coalfield. Following a methane gas explosion that killed six workers, he filed a report that included a recommendation for a permanently assigned mine engineer (a post he himself later assumed).[141]

The Young Turk Revolution in 1908 prompted a series of changes in the administration of the coalfield.[142] The Marine Ministry lost its jurisdiction over the coalfield, first to the Public Works Ministry and a year later to the Ministry of Commerce, Agriculture, and Mines. In addition, after decades of military rule, a civilian superintendent of mines took charge (table 2.7). According to the mine superintendent—who benefited from this change in policy—disgruntled mine operators residing in Zonguldak, Kozlu, and Istanbul played the key role in the shift from a military to a civilian administration. On Easter Sunday, 1910, he said, some of them gathered in a "lokal" in Istanbul and complained about the pending appointment of yet another superintendent of military rank and about their own suffering under "50 years of military discipline. In the Constitutional era we expect a civilian director and some respite. The Constitution and justice are not compatible with [the appointment of] another soldier and former member of the Marine Ministry."[143] Immediately thereafter, the memoir's author, Hüseyin Fehmi Pasha, who had worked for many years in the civilian forestry service bureaucracy, became mine superintendent.

Shortly after his arrival in the coalfield, he hired a cohort of professional mining engineers, mostly trained in Germany, to work at the various mine centers (table 2.8)[144] With the recruitment of these engineers, government supervision of coal operations reached a new intensity. Safety inspections became more commonplace and accident reports more frequent and thorough (see chapters 7 and 8). These inspectors certainly were busy. The following report by one of them, in March 1914 (table 2.9), summarizes the course of his duties during a presumably typical month, as he moved constantly among the various mine sites. Many days were taken up inspecting sites where accidents had already occurred (1, 6, 7, 17, 18, 21, 24 March). But the number of visits he made to promote safe operational procedures in the absence of a specific accident is noteworthy (see entries for 14, 15, 16, 18 March). His activities underscore the mounting professionalization of this engineer cohort, itself a measure of the state's steadily increasing commitment to safe and healthy worksites (see chapter 8).

Table 2.8 State Mining Engineers, 1910

Chief engineer	Wilhelm Hühner
Chief assistant engineer	"Ştronuz"
Mining engineer for Ereğli, Çamlı, Kandilli	Emin Bey
Mining engineer for Kozlu	Said Bey
Mining engineer for Kilimli	Kenan Bey
Mining engineer for Zonguldak	Setrak

Source: İmer (1944), 49–50. The chief engineer's tenure spanned from May 1910 until April 1921. He left office just weeks before the superintendent who had hired him.

Table 2.9 Monthly Work Schedule of a Mine Engineer, March 1914

Date	Activity
1	I investigated an accident in the Tünel mine of Ereğli Company.
2	I organized the maps of the Ereğli coal district.
3	" " "
4, 5	[blurred in original].
6	I visited an accident site at Kandilli and returned to Ereğli
7	I [again] inspected the accident at Kandilli.
8	I filed a report concerning the Zonguldak railroad.
9	[blurred in original].
10	I worked at the ??? at Çamlı.
11	" " "
12	I delivered ??? the maps of the Ereğli basin.
13	M. Istavro ???
14	I inspected the Rombaki mine.
15	I visited the Pavli mine with Çakır Efendi.
16	I inspected Çay Damarı mine and reduced the methane levels there.
17	I organized a report on the accident in the Pavli mine.
18	I prepared a report on the accident in the Rombaki mine and I presented a report on the inspection which I made at the Cay Damarı mine of the Ereğli Company.
19	I was at the central mine administration, busy with geometry instruments.
20	I went to Ereğli.
21	I inspected the accident at the Kandilli mine.
22	I was at Ereğli.
23	I returned from Ereğli.
24	I organized and presented the report on the accident at Kandilli mine.
25, 26, and 27	I calculated the expenses for the geometry instruments and for the translation of the report prepared by M. Istavro, Reçet Bey, and head engineer M. Hühner.
28	I had the day off.

Source: ED 16, 249–250, from Zonguldak mine engineer (Behçet?), 4 Mart 1330/17 March 1914.

Notes

1. *Yurt Ansik* 10, 7712. Turkey in the 1960s and 1970s produced far less than 1 percent of the world's coal and had even less of the world's known coal reserves.
2. Spratt (1877), 528, for the 1850s. For later dates, compare *Kastamonu vs 1314*, 431; Turkey (1327) *Ihsaiyati maliye 1325*, 262, states the breadth at 56 miles and 4–5 hours. Dominian (1913) says 60 miles.
3. *Bolu vs 1334*, 133–134. Also, Kahveci (1997), 68, citing a 1926 U.S. Department of Commerce report, states the coalfield stretched 90 miles across, encompassing the newly formed province of Zonguldak.
4. Kahveci (1997), 69–70, citing a 1926 U.S. Dept. of Commerce report. See ibid., 148–150, for estimates of the coal reserves in the later twentieth century. At that time, some one-sixth of the coal operations were undersea.
5. *Yurt Ansik* 10, 7712.

6. Dates from *Yurt Ansik* 10, 7712, and quote from Fisher (1966), 344. This assessment appears in the earliest scientific study of the coalfield. Spratt (1877), 525-528.
7. Spratt (1877), 525-526.
8. After Solakian (1923), 101. The importance of the stream mouths is underscored by these place names—*ağız* in Turkish means 'stream' or 'river mouth'.
9. Ralli (1933) and Ralli (1895).
10. *Sabah*, 26 Aralık 1903; Dominian (1913), 4-5; Solakian (1923), 100-106 and Kahveci (1997), 68, citing a 1926 U.S. Department of Commerce report.
11. Spratt (1877), 524, report on a March 1854 investigation of the coalfield.
12. Fisher (1966), 344, offers the optimistic view. But http://www.zonguldak.gov.tr states that the hard coal generally burned poorly and was considered to be of low quality.
13. See Cuinet (1895), 422-423 and 498.
14. After Dominian (1913), 5. Fisher (1966), 344-345, is confusing and misleading.
15. Fisher puts the total precipitation amount at 1-2 m/year; *Yurt Ansik* says 1,243 mm at Zonguldak, 7708. *Bolu vs 1334*, 277.
16. After Fisher (1966) and Dominian (1913).
17. *Bolu vs 1334*, 277.
18. Dominian (1913), 3.
19. ED 4, 25 ks 1293/6 February 1878.
20. ED 4, 138, 7 Mart 1294/19 March 1878. For major storms in December 1878, see ibid., 269, 25 ts 1294/7 December 1878 and 272, 5 kl 1294/17 December 1878.
21. Referring to the sub-province of Bolu and the district of Devrek; see Cuinet (1895), 497-498, who usually presents a rosy picture. They also harvested millions of kilograms of acorns, gall nuts, chestnuts, and other forest products.
22. *Bolu vs 1334*, 287.
23. *Kastamonu vs 1310*, 394; ibid. for *1312 vs*, 198, 205; ibid. *1311*, 166, 283.
24. Bolu sub-province, part of Kastamonu province.
25. Cuinet (1895), 537.
26. Cuinet (1895), 499-500.
27. ED 3, 15 Mayıs 1312/27 May 1896, 149-150. In the later 1870s, Alaplı sub-district alone annually provided 45-60,000 supports. ED 4, 137, 7 Haziran 1293/19 March 1878.
28. *Sabah*, 19 Ağustos 1898.
29. *Bolu vs 1334*, 139.
30. *Bolu vs 1334*, 133-134. In yet another enumeration, from 1933, forests were 52 percent of the total land surface of the then-province of Zonguldak. While some of the relative increase in the forested proportion may have been due to republican reforestation policies, it could also simply be a matter of the boundaries drawn.
31. *Bolu vs 1334*, 288.
32. *Kastamonu vs 1308* and *1309*, 49. Also, Cuinet (1895), 499-500.
33. This does not include the trees cut for use in the mines since these were exempt from forest duties.
34. For example, the İskilip district in the southeast; see *Kastamonu vs 1311*, 283. In the early 1890s, the coal areas held virtually no roads according to Cuinet (1895), 436-437ff.
35. *Kastamonu vs 1311*, 283 and *vs 1312*, 198. A possible indicator of growing demand for forest resources is the transformation of the legal status of the forests of Devrek district. In 1890 these were not under state control; by 1915, the situation had reversed itself so that all forests belonged to the state and there was *baltalık* in Devrek district—*baltalık* being the right of inhabitants to cut the forests. Compare Cuinet (1895), 537 with *Bolu vs 1334*, 246.
36. Winkler (1961), quoting an 1871 source, de Johannes.
37. Cuinet (1895), 421-422.
38. Likely this is a reference to the breakwater being built by the Ereğli Company. *Kastamonu vs 1314*, 240.

39. *Sabah*, 1 Nisan 1899.
40. ED 4, 253–255, 25 tl 1294/6 November 1878.
41. Savaşkan (1993), 22–23. The first concession, including the port at Kozlu, is dated May 1891. See *Sabah*, 27 Temmuz 1308/8 August 1892, for a lengthy report on the concession.
42. Later the Ereğli Company bought some rich mines from these two companies. Savaşkan (1993), 24.
43. For details, see Thobie (1977), 406–410, and Quataert (1983), 47–50. Also, Etingü (1976), 63. The final concession, dated May 1896, was capitalized in Paris at 10 million francs. Notably present among Ottoman investors was Minister of Forests, Mines, and Agriculture Selim Melhame Pasha. *Bolu vs 1334*, 150.
44. Naim (1934), 61 says a storm in 1316/1900 destroyed the port but other sources say January 1898.
45. Özeken (1944a), 22. I have preferred to use his dates and capacities. Tesal (1957), 87 gives dates of 1899 and 1907 and says they each had an hourly capacity of 1,680 tons. Savaşkan (1993), 25 says 1,200 tons daily.
46. *Bolu vs 1334*, 145–146; also Etingü (1976), 63–64.
47. Özeken (1944a), 22–23.
48. Özeken (1944a), 20 and 38, n. 19.
49. Özeken (1944a), 20.
50. *Bolu vs 1334*, 146; Etingü (1976), 63.
51. Etingü (1976), 63.
52. Savaşkan (1993), 35. Raghip later sold his interests to a Belgian company.
53. İmer (1944), 49, and Savaşkan (1993), 26, who adds that Raghip Pasha didn't compete for long and sold his interests to a "*Rum*" named Abacıoğlu.
54. Özeken (1944a), 25–28; Naim (1934), 65–66; Savaşkan (1993), 26; İmer (1944), 49.
55. People's House (1933), 167 notes the presence of four scrubbers, two of them run by the Ereğli Company, a third operated by the mining works (*maden kömürü işleri*) at Üzülmez in 1907, and the last built at Kozlu in 1911. See also Özeken (1944a), 25. By 1915, however, the Sarıcazadeler family had sold off many of its interests.
56. *Bolu vs 1334*, 138–139; Naim (1934), 35. Özeken (1944a), 29–30, notes that imported firebricks proved to be cheaper and the factory was closed later on.
57. See KU KD 23 5 Mart 1328 and 76, 14 Mart 1328, for measures to rebuild the Kilimli railroad.
58. People's House (1933), 196.
59. İmer (1944), 52–53.
60. *Bolu vs 1334*, 148.
61. I have not been able to find a map that illustrates the boundaries of the coalfield (*havza*), which complicates precise tallies of its population. Nor have I found, in Ottoman or later documents, a list of the fourteen districts. The Ottoman names and republican Turkish equivalents generously were given to me by the former miner Erol Çatma on the occasion of my first visit to Zonguldak. Here are the Ottoman names: Panıklıbolu, Bartın/Divan, Devrek/Hamidiye, Zerzene, Akçaşehir, Ereğli, Aktaş, Karasu, Eflani, Ulus, Viranşehir, Yenice, Tefen, and Amasra.
62. Cuinet (1895), 411–412.
63. KU 64.
64. *Kastamonu vs 1314*, 320–358, and Karpat (1985), 183–184. As an example of the rapid and radical shifting of administrative boundaries, compare the 340 villages in Devrek district in around 1895 with the 169 villages in about 1898. Thus, the district population figures are low, and safely could be doubled.
65. Karpat (1985), 184–185.
66. Savaşkan (1993), 66. Also, less convincingly, see http://www.zonguldak.gov.tr.
67. CAMS file Pf4, Zonguldak, informant Michalis Christoforidis, 5/5/1963.

68. *Bolu vs 1334*, 277.
69. Spratt (1877); Özeken (1944a), 17ff.
70. *Kastamonu vs 1314*, 440.
71. Etingü (1976), 62.
72. *Kastamonu vs 1314*, 440.
73. CAMS file Pf4, Zonguldak, informant Evangelos Paslidis, 6/5/1963.
74. Cuinet (1895), 421.
75. Kahveci (1997), 202.
76. CAMS file Pf4, Zonguldak, informant, Yiannis Kaptanidis; interviewer, Christos Samouilidis, 19/2/1963.
77. CAMS file Pf4, Zonguldak, informant Michalis Christoforidis, 5/5/1963.
78. Winkler (1961), 88, quoting Ralli. Winkler's study is exhaustive in the languages he uses; he states that no population figures for Zonguldak town before World War I could be found. In 1927, for what it is worth, the town had 11,947 inhabitants, 8,500 male and 3,447 female.
79. *Bolu vs 1334*, 278 is the reference for the center of coalfield statement. *Yurt Ansik* 10, 7729, states that Zonguldak, in 1899, became the district center (*kaza merkezi*). A decade later, in 1909, it became the administrative center of the coalfield region, replacing Kozlu, the "very small" town to its immediate east. People's House (1933), 38, states that in Eylül 1896, Zonguldak became the district center.
80. *Kastamonu vs 1314*, 428.
81. CAMS file Pf4, Zonguldak, informant Michalis Christoforidis, 5/5/1963; CAMS file Pf4, Zonguldak, informant, Yiannis Kaptanidis; interviewer, Christos Samouilidis, 19/2/1963.
82. CAMS. By the 1920s, most of the Ottoman Christians once resident in the coalfield (and in the rest of the new Turkey for that matter) had vanished. Their fate is the subject of a growing literature that points to massacre, population exchanges between the new republic of Turkey and the state of Greece, and voluntary self-exile.
83. CAMS file Pf4, Zonguldak, informant Michalis Christoforidis, 5/5/1963.
84. Postcard, "Souvenir de Zongouldak," No. 9, courtesy of Orlando Carlo Calumeno.
85. CAMS file Pf4, Zonguldak, informant Michalis Christoforidis, 5/5/1963. CAMS file Pf2, Ereğli, several families from Gelveri, east of Kayseri and south of Nevşehir.
86. *Bolu vs 1334*, 286. CAMS file Pf4, Zonguldak, informant, Yiannis Kaptanidis; interviewer, Christos Samouilidis, 19/2/1963.
87. *Bolu vs 1334*, 286. In 1915, however, that school was closed.
88. *Yurt Ansik* 10, 7726 attributes this population to the town, but *Bolu vs 1334*, 278, on which this account is based, makes clear that the reference is to the district not to the town.
89. *Bolu vs 1334*, 287–290.
90. CAMS file Pf4, Zonguldak, informant, Yiannis Kaptanidis; interviewer, Christos Samouilidis, 19/2/1963.
91. CAMS file Pf4, Zonguldak, informant Evangelos Paslidis, 6/5/1963.
92. CAMS file Pf4, Zonguldak, informant Michalis Christoforidis, 5/5/1963.
93. *Kastamonu vs 1310*, 509–510.
94. CAMS file Pf2, Ereğli, informant Ioakeim Yailaoglou, 18/3/1963.
95. *Bolu vs 1334*, 162. The date is stated as 1321, presumably in the hicri calendar and therefore 1903.
96. CAMS file Pf2, Ereğli, informant Ioakeim Yailaoglou, 18/3/1963.
97. Murray's Handbook (1877–1878), 356. In the late 1860s, the central sub-district of Ereğli district held some 69 villages. People's House (1933), 42.
98. Çıladır (1977), 62–63, quoting Kıray (1964), 185ff.
99. *Kastamonu vs 1310*, 206, 508–509; *Kastamonu vs 1314*, 427–428. The *1310 vs* says 70 boys' schools (*sibyan mektebi*), including those in town, while the *1314 vs* gives the figure as 127, including those in town.

100. Kıray (1964), 44.
101. CAMS Pf2, Ereğli, informant Despoina Makroskoudfidou, May 1951.
102. Spratt (1877), 525.
103. Cuinet (1895).
104. *Sabah*, 26 Aralık 1903.
105. İmer (1944), 46.
106. *Bolu vs 1334*, 235–244. In 1887, the central sub-district held 77 villages. People's House (1933), 45.
107. Özeken (1944a), 8–9, who points to some general provisions of the Land Law of 1858 and the mining laws of 9 Muharrem 1278/1861 and 23 Zilhicce 1283/1867 as the only governing legislation.
108. Özeken (1944a), 7. More accurately, the mines passed briefly to the Public Works Ministry in 1908–1909.
109. Savaşkan (1993), 11; Özeken (1955), 6, n. 3.
110. Savaşkan (1993), 11.
111. Naim (1934), 19, in the sultan's 13th regnal year.
112. See chapter 1 for a discussion of the discovery of the coalfield.
113. Naim (1934), 19–20, and Çıladır (1977), 19. Also see Özeken (1944a), 4. For a list of the intended recipients, see Naim (1934), 20. I do not know if these sums increased with production. The annual bequest was a modest 30,000 krs.
114. Savaşkan (1993), 11–17; Özeken (1944a), 3–5; Naim (1934), 20–29.
115. Özeken (1955), 7, n. 5.
116. Naim (1934), 4–6 and 33, n. 4.
117. Naim (1934), 33–34.
118. For the original, see OA, DUIT, Dosye: 21, Gömlek: 2–3, Madeni humayun nizam defteri, 1283 senesi. Turkish transliteration of Ottoman original, dated 4 Muharrem 1284, 26 Nisan 1283 in *TTBD* 23 (1998): 123–146, which mistakenly gives the citation as Dos: 21, Göm: 2–1. For a complete Turkish translation, see Etingü (1976), 28–52. At a key juncture, in Article 21, Etingü mistakenly writes "support maker" (*direkçi*) rather than "transporter" (*kiracı*).
119. Articles 43–100; see Article 86 in particular.
120. Naim (1934), 32.
121. Özeken (1944a), 8–9, states that the regulations were never given formal imperial approval (*irade*) and so technically did not have the proper legal force of a "regulation." In 1882, he says, new regulations referred to it as "the 1867 document of practices in the Imperial Ereğli mines."
122. Savaşkan (1993), 151.
123. *Kastamonu vs 1310*, 504–507, and *Kastamonu vs 1314*, 186.
124. *Kastamonu vs 1310*, 504–507, and *Kastamonu vs 1314*, 186.
125. Özeken (1944a), 4–6; Naim (1934), 33–35, 38, 40. Shortly thereafter, in 1896, operators were permitted to sell 90 percent of the coal dust on the open market.
126. Until 1911, the ministry in charge of the mines collected the tax; the separate treasury of the mine administration then was abolished and collection fell to the district treasury (*kaza mal müdürlüğü*).
127. Özeken (1944a), 37, n. 14 and Naim (1934), 41 offer the same figures. But Özeken (1944a), 11 says the tax was abolished in 1920 while Naim claims it was set at 5 percent.
128. İmer (1973), 58–59, who was superintendent between 1910 and 1921, successfully urged the new state to raise the tax. He discusses how this tax was too low and deprived the state of needed revenues. Mine operators, he said, were profiting excessively and some of the profits needed to go to the state.
129. Çıladır (1977), 61. See 61, n.* for his excellent detective work on the dating of the decision to end the restrictions on labor recruitment.
130. Naim (1934), 65–66, 111; Özeken (1944a), 23–24. Savaşkan (1993), 26 after Özeken. The governor in question was Nazım Pasha, later murdered in the Babıali assassination affair.

131. The original concession to a front man was signed in 1891 whereas that acknowledging the actual presence of the Ereğli Company was signed in 1896. See Thobie (1977), 406–407, for details. See Savaşkan (1993), 34, for the 1911 agreement, in exchange for which the state obtained an important international loan. While this example is about state-international capital relations, I prefer here to focus on the state-capital issue.
132. Savaşkan (1993), 18–19.
133. Through the 1990s, there were 399 mines open and operating, at least nominally. Savaşkan (1993), 19–20.
134. Savaşkan (1993), 19.
135. Namely, Mirliva Hasan Pasha (presumably Grammar), while the chief administrator was Veledin Bey.
136. *Kastamonu vs 1310*, 504 and ibid. *1311*, 202.
137. For the general growth of the Ottoman bureaucracy in the nineteenth century, see Quataert (2000), chapter 4.
138. *Kastamonu vs 1310*, 504, and ibid. *1314*, 185.
139. *Kastamonu vs 1317*, 207.
140. Presumably, the hiring of a "head engineer" meant also hiring a staff of subordinate engineers under his authority. In 1907, we read of the dismissal of engineer Istiolyanos Istabolos Efendi; his last report is dated 23 Haziran 1323/6 July 1907. The first report in ED 3 is dated Şubat 1309/February 1893, but the reports in the intervening years could have been written by various individuals. Head engineer Rasım Bey prepared the report dated 6 Temmuz 1323/19 July 1907. ED 3. İmer (1944), 44, takes the credit for making the appointments in 1910.
141. OA DH.MUI.C.II (22/f-2); Sıra 552; Dosye 17-2, 18 Ramadan 1327/3 October 1909.
142. The administration of the mines shared in the general shakeup of the Ottoman bureaucracy after the July 1908 Young Turk Revolution.
143. İmer (1944), 44.
144. At this time, a large number of students were sent abroad, especially to Germany, to train as future government mine inspectors, agronomists, and forestry specialists. See Quataert (2000). By 1913, the engineer Behçet Bey, who had filed the 1909 report recommending a permanent appointment, had joined the staff.

3

Coal Miners at Work
Jobs, Recruitment, and Wages

Introduction

The work force of the coalfield took shape in the 1840s in the form of free labor that was ethnically homogenous and displayed little task differentiation. Over the decades, its character changed in nearly every possible way. Its numbers increased from perhaps several hundred during the 1840s to 6,000 unskilled workers and hewers who annually were employed in the mid 1890s. By World War I, at least 8–10,000 unskilled workers annually labored, plus several thousand uncounted, skilled above- and belowground workers. When the original reliance on free labor failed to provide sufficient workers, the Ottoman state erected a corvée-style labor system to supply the mines, building on centuries-old imperial practices of dragooning labor whenever necessary to fill its needs. Thus, after 1867, unfree labor from surrounding communities became commonplace, indeed predominant, in the mine labor force, working on a semi-monthly rotation with equal amounts of time in village and mine. But a free labor force persisted alongside these compulsory workers, especially in the aboveground jobs.

In another development, as the mines went farther and deeper into the earth, mine work demanded ever greater skill. Cutting tunnels to the coal surfaces, pumping air in and water and gases out, guarding against coal dust, gas, and methane accumulations, and providing transport within the mines— all were tasks gaining in complexity. Similarly, outside jobs increased both in numbers and the skills they required. The widening use of technology within the mines meant a growing need for support and maintenance workers aboveground: these included trainmen, switchmen, pumpers, machinists, iron workers, carpenters, and boatmen, to name just a few occupations. As labor needs grew, free-market labor for aboveground jobs migrated from near and distant Ottoman provinces as well as the Balkan lands and the wider Eastern Mediterranean region. As production mounted later in the century, the compulsory

---

Notes for this chapter begin on page 76.

labor supply for underground work increasingly came to be seen as inadequate. By the early twentieth century, a supplementary free labor force flowed in, almost exclusively from Ottoman provinces farther east in Anatolia. But it too failed to solve the labor problem.

Thus, an always-inadequate but ever larger and increasingly task-differentiated and ethnically diverse labor force emerged in the coalfield, growing in spurts after the opening of free market coal sales, an event that also prompted the beginnings of Ereğli Company operations in the late 1890s. Visible labor unrest, which became increasingly frequent among under- and aboveground workers alike, accompanied the subsequent fifteen years of rapid growth in the size and diversity of the work force. Between 1908 and 1913, strikes repeatedly wracked the coalfield. Sources concerning strikes during World War I are silent, but since such protests again are visible after that war and the Turkish War of Independence, their continuation through the war years (or at least a continuation of the grievances) is likely.

The sources consulted do not permit rigorous analysis of the surely profound differences between the working conditions of the compulsory and free labor forces. Compulsory workers quite frequently did not receive the wages they had earned (see chapter 5). Many hundreds of workers' wages simply were noted as "in arrears" and went unpaid for years at a time. Also, the wages earned often were channeled away to pay the workers' taxes or for the bread they ate while on the job. Basket carriers, the truly unskilled and numerically most important, clearly fared the worst. Meanwhile, the wages of compulsory workers barely moved over the decades. But the free labor force won significant increases that are most manifest in the post-1908 era, which was rife with strikes and other labor actions. Most of the benefits from health and housing improvements, moreover, fell to these free workers.

On the one hand, the compulsory workers' stubborn adherence to the village frustrated the Istanbul government and mine operators and perhaps was the major factor in the disappointing performance of the Zonguldak coalfield. The mines needed full-time workers who, fully dependent on their wages, would keep hard at work. Instead, they relied on workers who notoriously were uncommitted to mine work, leaving willy-nilly to mark holidays, gather harvests, or because they feared mine accidents.

On the other hand, their lack of class consciousness left them very vulnerable to exploitation. Their primary ties to their villages left them at the mercy of the headmen, from whom they had little escape either at work or at home. Similarly, they were vulnerable to the demands of the labor bosses (many of whom probably were headmen), who profited by sending compulsory workers to the mines. Compulsory workers labored in appallingly bad conditions, even after improvements during the later period. Again, the engine for improvements may well have been the free-market workers who were recruited from outside the coalfield. They likely forced the reforms and played the key role in worker activism—actions that remain largely invisible to us.

Workers During the Early Years, 1848–1867

The earliest reports indicate that, during the 1840s and perhaps sooner, "Croat squatters worked some of the best-developed and most easily worked seams near the coast."[1] The government had contracted an English company to work the coal in the late 1840s, but the venture met with little success. Faced with the lack of experienced miners in the region and the locals' refusal to work underground, the company brought in experienced Montenegrin and Croatian quarry workers. During the Crimean War era, most of the hewers were Croats and Montenegrins, assisted by local villagers who were hauling out the coal on their backs. The government also required soldiers in the local army barracks around Zonguldak to work as coal miners during their period of service. However, once the Crimean War began, these soldier-miners had to return to military activities.[2] There also were a small and, by 1854, declining number of English miners.[3] Brought in by John Barkley, many "had suffered greatly from the malignant fever that prevailed in the autumn months."[4]

Many years later, in 1915, the (Bolu) provincial government offered an analysis of mine work in the early years that, unlike the above findings, specifically indicates the presence of compulsory labor. In the pre-1867 period, it reported, the mines had been exploited by two quite different groups of workers. Marines (naval soldiers) and local villagers serving as compulsory labor worked in some of the mines, while Montenegrins and workers previously employed by the English company worked under contract to mine operators.[5]

Compulsory Labor

The Ottoman state's persistent failure to obtain sufficient coal finally led to a two-year commission from Istanbul that toured the coalfield and made a sweeping series of recommendations. In consequence, the state promulgated the 1867 Dilaver Pasha regulations, established a coalfield with defined boundaries, and installed a military regime to govern the inhabitants and material of its fourteen administrative divisions. The integrity of these coalfield boundaries was maintained over the decades, marking off its inhabitants as distinct.[6] The compulsory labor system defined by these regulations endured, without interruption, until 1921. In so many ways, as already indicated, the 1867 regulations remained on paper only, the fictive vision of bureaucrats with scarce little connection to reality. These cannot provide insight into the actual conditions of labor during the later nineteenth and early twentieth centuries. And yet, as seen in chapter 2 above, they decisively affected the structure of the labor force, up to the present day.

The new regulations sought to organize and assure adequate flows of supplies and labor to the mines. All males between the ages of 13 and 50 years who lived in the fourteen administrative districts of the designated coalfield (*havza*) were set aside in a special category as persons "necessary for work" in the mines, and their names and places of origins were inscribed in ledgers. All except the sick or crippled were eligible for mine labor, in one form of work or another. If selected for mine work, they had to serve, on a rotational basis, for a certain number of days each year. The nature of the rotation and the degree of compulsion varied depending on the kind of labor provided—but, overall it is clear, massive coercion was the norm. A host of authorities—ranging from the mine superintendent to military troops to the village headmen—worked together to discipline the labor force. The "Dilaver Pasha" system was a variation, not markedly different, on other versions of Ottoman corvée labor. By early modern times, Ottoman corvée labor regulations in general required males to build roads, cut wood, mine, or build fortifications. In exchange, these workers (usually but not always villagers) often received tax exemptions or wages. Such practices generally continued well into the nineteenth century. The provisions enacted to regulate coalfield workers are not unusual in form, but they appear to be harsher than normal corvée practices in that they demanded more of a laborer's time. Thus, for example, regulations in the late 1860s required villagers elsewhere to provide four days of labor per year for road construction. Also, corvée labor prepared the right of way for at least some railroads in the later nineteenth century.[7]

In the case of the coal mines, the remuneration for labor apparently did not include tax exemptions. Instead, workers were to receive two different forms of compensation. First, depending on the labor performed, they obtained wages on either a piecework or a daily basis. And second, in exchange for their mine work, they were not required to serve on active duty in the Ottoman military. Moreover, the mine work technically counted as fulfillment of non-active reserve obligations (see chapter 6).

In essence, the regulations divided the male population of the coalfield into those who were subject to mine labor and those who were not. Hence, some in a particular village went off to work the mines while others entered military service. Within the same family, some young men became soldiers whereas their fathers or brothers took up mining. As we will see, the choice was not theirs but rather that of the community authorities, the village headmen and council of elders.

A key provision of the 1867 regulations stipulated that, from the lists of able-bodied males "necessary for work," boys and men from the fourteen administrative districts that made up the coalfield could be called upon to perform labor in one of three distinct categories—either as transporters (*kiracı*), basket carriers or unskilled workers (*amele*), or hewers (*kazmacı*).[8] With these designations, the state sought to assure adequate numbers of workers in the core occupations, where the need for workers was the greatest. No mention is made of the many other above- and underground personnel required to maintain mining operations. Significantly, the tasks in the three categories of work exclusively were reserved for the residents of the fourteen administrative units that made up the coalfield.

In a study that I did more than twenty years ago, I sought to explain these provisions as the state's effort to obtain a mining labor force while at the same time maintaining the stability of the agrarian work force. A rotational labor force, I argued, kept the boys down on the farm, helping to assure political stability by maintaining the agrarian population that was the basis of the Ottoman state. At the same time, it also assured the continued flow of agrarian taxes, the fiscal foundation of the regime. The provision restricting the work to these local villagers marked their special status as exempt from active military service, which may have been meant as an enticement, a way of assuring them access to mining jobs and the cash income they provided. The restriction also limited erosion of the manpower base of the military by flatly asserting that males in these fourteen districts, and nowhere else, had the exemption privilege.[9]

The transporters were to provide, supervise and feed their own mules, oxen, and other animals, and sometimes furnish wagons as well (photographs 3.1, 3.2, and 3.3). They worked inside the mines hauling coal both on animal back and sometimes in wagons on tracks. They also hauled coal from the mines to weighing stations, railroads, other transport centers, and to the seashore. The animals used by the transporters were divided into two groups, each serving semi-monthly shifts.

Under the compulsory labor system, most laborers inside the mines were the unskilled workers whose tasks included bringing coal out of the mines, on their backs, in baskets weighing 40–50 kg.[10] Also called basket carriers (*küfeci*), these unskilled workers were numerically the most important single group in the coalfield (photographs 3.4, 3.5 and, perhaps, 3.6). Indeed, they simply were called "workers" (*amele* in the Ottoman), whereas all the other categories had specific names that designated the particular job being done.[11] Like the animals, the basket carriers were divided into two shifts, in this case of twelve days each. The former miner, Ethem Çavuş, whose memoir forms an invaluable source that I frequently cite on the everyday life of miners in the late Ottoman era, reports on the recruitment and rotation of basket carriers during the 1890s: "As I said previously, the village boys who were able carry thirty *okka* black stones on their backs [that is, qualified to be basket carriers] would be separated into two groups. While the first rotation of workers came back to the village after performing their compulsory labor for twelve days, the second rotation of workers would leave the village to replace the first."[12]

Those who worked at the coal face cutting or hewing coal (*kazmacı*) formed the third category of compulsory labor in the coalfield. Some mining historians assert that hewers should not be considered highly skilled workers, saying that cutting coal is a task quickly and easily learned. Such arguments miss the point that cutting coal also means intimate knowledge of the coal face and the surrounding strata. Anyone, it is true, can hack at a coal face. But to cut it in a consistently safe manner is quite another task. Experienced hewers listen to the mine and from the sounds seek to know whether a rock fall or explosion is imminent. Consider the words of a Zonguldak hewer in the 1990s: "You can't start digging just anywhere, you have to know where to start. You have to find the soft point. When you find that point the coal rises itself up. We can understand when the coal is about to explode or the ground is about to fall, it tells you before it comes. You have to listen to the coal, the hanging wall and the wooden pit props."[13]

It is these kinds of knowledge that make the job a highly skilled one and, in Zonguldak, a highly prized one as well. The elite status of these workers in the Zonguldak fields is attested by the special treatment they were accorded in the 1867 regulations and by the higher wages they received throughout the subsequent decades.[14] Sina Çıladır, an eminent mine labor activist and newspaper editor in twentieth-century Ereğli, remarks that the 1867 compulsory labor regulations were not enforced on the hewers. Rather, he said, these hewers could choose their place of work and change jobs at will.[15] Indeed, as he points out, one article of the regulations specifically states that "hewers are not under the compulsory labor requirements for mine work" and that they could negotiate individually with mine operators for an appropriate salary. Their names were inscribed in the ledgers, but they were not obliged to remain at a particular mine and in principle could move to wherever wages were the highest.[16] The actual ability of the hewers to move about, of course, was another matter. In August 1878, the right of some hewers to choose their jobs was protected by the mine superintendent.[17] And yet on other occasions, he acted in quite the opposite manner. In a case from October 1877, he noted that the hewers from one hamlet who for a long time had been allotted to a certain mine had not been arriving as scheduled. His response was to order soldiers (*zabıta*) to go to the hamlet and take the hewers to their assigned mine by force.[18] The particular status of hewers is also marked by another provision that, oddly enough, permitted foreigners to take on such work.[19]

In addition to the transporters, basket carriers, and hewers, there were two other groups of workers incorporated into the compulsory labor schema. The first is discussed in the 1867 provisions; but the second is not. It is certain, however, that both bore the burden of compulsory labor.[20]

Let me turn to the first of these. In the 1867 regulations, the state created a somewhat indirect compulsory labor requirement for workers who would provide the wooden supports needed to prop up the walls, ceilings, and coal faces of the mines. In this heavily forested region, the supply of mine supports was given priority over firewood. Indeed, many local forests, such as those in the Alaplı Mountains, were set aside for mine use. The 1867 regulations dictated that, first of all, mine operators formally present their mine support needs for the coming year—including the numbers and dimensions. Next, the local authorities sent on these requirements for the various villages to satisfy. Village headmen dispatched the workers, called *sütunkeş*, who ventured into the forests of the region, felled the trees, and cut them into mine supports of two different standard lengths (three and four *arşın* each). These workers obtained piecework wages, depending on the length of the support. In addition, for most of the period between

1865 and 1909, they were exempted from the forestry tax (*orman resmi*).[21] On the average, during the 1870s, one worker cut and trimmed three supports in two days. After preparation, the villages were required to transport the supports before the beginning of the winter season. At this time, the shorter pieces came from three to six hours distance. Sometimes, villagers brought the supports to the mine itself using oxen, the average being one support per ox per day. Otherwise, they hauled them to the landing place for boat transport to a landing area and then farther overland to the mine.[22] Mine support workers were not subject to rotational labor. Their labor obligations for the year were met once they had furnished the requisite number of supports.

The second group of workers is not mentioned in the 1867 provisions, but their presence was noted by the 1870s and they regularly appear in the wage ledgers of later decades. These were the boat launchers (*felenkeci*), who helped to move boats on and off the beaches through the use of rollers. These vessels moved coal, supplies, and personnel and filled a yawning gap left by the general absence of railroads and good harbor facilities along the coal coast. The even, unprotected coastline that made the boat launchers existence possible also spelled danger for the small vessels, which for safety, were pulled up onto the beaches. Rollers, made of round tree trunks laid parallel to each other on the sand, made it easier to pull the boats onto and off of the beaches (photograph 3.7). The hard work of hauling the boats on and off the rollers was the special task of various neighborhoods (*mahalle*) in the town of Ereğli. With this exception, townspeople generally did not work in the mines. [23] All of the other compulsory labor classifications mentioned above drew on villages as their source of supply. The workers who helped roll boats in and out of the water were paid in cash, in some cases with revenues generated by the animal tax.[24]

The Free Labor Force: Underground Workers

Workers who did not fall under the jurisdiction of the 1867 regulations also played a vital role in the development of the coalfield where two quite different groups of workers generally were present. On the one hand, the local compulsory labor villagers (and townsmen) grew up, worked in the mines, and died, all within a radius of a few miles. Locals labored under provisions stating that only they had the right to such labor. On the other hand, the mines assembled workers from a host of locations across the Ottoman, wider Mediterranean, Balkan, and Western European worlds. Croatian and Montenegrin miners attended the birth of Zonguldak coal mining and played a crucial, if scarcely visible, role in transferring the necessary mining technologies and skills to a completely inexperienced local population. And surely a similar role was played by the English workers who, in the 1850s, found the region so unhealthy. These were the vanguard of a steady influx of outsiders who continued to flow in and play a vibrant part in Zonguldak mining life.

During the 1870s, mine operators recruited both foreigners and Ottoman subjects from the Balkans. Croats and Montenegrins continued to arrive, even after the home areas became independent, and some workers arrived from Ottoman Bulgaria. There were a number of Italian, Montenegrin and other foreign hewers at work in the early 1890s, thanks to a loophole that allowed such work to foreigners.[25] The Italians were perhaps ethnic Croats of Italian nationality or natives of Piedmont and other areas of the peninsula, part of the vast wave of Italian immigrant labor then sweeping the Mediterranean and global economies.[26] And from an early date, metal miners from the eastern Black Sea regions worked in the mines.

Many outsiders—here meaning both Ottomans from beyond the fourteen districts and non-Ottomans—routinely were engaged in hewing as well as other tasks that allegedly were the prerogative of the local work force. After all, the provision (Article 53) that permitted the hiring of foreign hewers required only that they adhere to Ottoman law. The reason for inclusion of such a measure in the 1867 regulations is unclear but its presence constantly worried the state, which feared the dangers that foreign workers might pose to Ottoman sovereignty and to the control of these strategic coal resources. Thus, it generally insisted on Ottoman workers and repeatedly blocked the entry of foreigners. Recognizing the technological need for their services, it did allow foreign engineers and supervisory personnel, as well as hewers (although the total number of foreigners seems very low). But it drew the line at workers, insisting on an Ottomans-only policy. There can be no doubt that these policies frustrated foreign entrepreneurs, including the Ereğli Company, and harmed their profitability.[27] Nonetheless, despite its genuine reluctance to do so, in subsequent decades the state permitted the hire of persons whom existing legislation barred. Take the example, dated 1912, of an Iranian worker who stated his intention to come and work in the Zonguldak mines. The official with competency in the matter reviewed the standard practices and quoted the relevant mining regulations that should have specifically blocked the Iranian worker—but then went on to open the door for his hiring.[28] In fact, Iranian workers seldom were present in the coalfield. More generally, foreign workers migrated from the Eastern Mediterranean and Balkan lands, such as Greece and the Aegean Islands, and Bulgaria. There were a few Western Europeans, mostly engineers.

When, in 1882, the state succumbed to pressures from mine entrepreneurs and allowed the free-market sale of 40 percent of the mined coal, production mounted and so did the demand for more miners. Labor shortages were curtailing the mine operations of Raghip Pasha, the sultan's chamberlain, when in 1906 he quite self-interestedly began to lobby to end the restriction of mine work to residents of the fourteen administrative districts. His cajoling won the day for a wider labor market. As a result of his actions, the forty-year old restrictions on jobs in the three categories of compulsory mine labor—hewer, transporter and unskilled worker—were abolished and these positions became open to all Ottoman subjects. Local villagers, however, remained subject to compulsory labor until its abolition by the Ankara government in 1921, and even after this the rotational labor system was continued.[29]

The results of this labor market decision were immediate: mine operators hastened to recruit experienced Ottoman miners from areas outside of the coal district, notably metal miners from the Trabzon and Sivas regions of eastern Anatolia. In its 1907 annual report to stockholders, the Ereğli Company announced (somewhat prematurely, as it turned out) its "solution to the worker question," referring to the recruitment of these miners. The report also noted sharp increases in the company payroll and a record surge in output.[30] The new workers' presence also is attested by the accident statistics for the years 1912–1914 (also see chapter 8). While it is true that 80 percent of the recorded accident victims were residents of the fourteen administrative districts, one in five victims were Ottoman subjects who came from outside the coalfield. The presence of these outsiders indicates that Raghip Pasha's recruitment efforts had borne fruit. And given that fewer than a handful of the 200 persons recorded in the accident reports had names of Western European origin, the statistics also reveal that the state's policies against the employment of foreigners had held fast. In sum, Ottoman subjects from outside the coalfield came to participate in relatively meaningful numbers, but Western European workers remained a rare sight inside the mines. The state's profound distrust of foreigners is evident in its response, during the war year of 1912, to petitions from a number of companies to hire foreigners as a special exception to the general rule. The mine superintendent reluctantly agreed and, to limit the damage, demanded preparation of a ledger showing the names and nationalities of each and every engineer, official, master craftsman and worker who was to be employed.[31]

The Free Labor Force: Aboveground Workers

During the post-1882 era, the need for aboveground workers increased along with mounting coal production and the demand for underground labor. The number of aboveground workers in the late 1890s is unknown though records do show that at that time 6,000 hewers and unskilled workers annually were being employed.[32] Later statistics provide some guidance in discerning the population of aboveground workers. In 1917, at one mine, there were two aboveground for every three underground workers, while at another mine, one-eighth of the labor force worked aboveground. Extrapolating from these figures, it seems possible to estimate a force of between 1,500 and 4,000 aboveground workers in the late 1890s. Yet these are minimal figures. Both examples only consider aboveground workers in a single mine operation and do not include workers who provided support between and among mines—for example, workers in animal and train transport, workshops, scrubbers, and repair facilities. In the case of these Ottoman mines, boatmen also must be counted;

in fact, their presence is so unusual in a coal-mining story that I begin my account of aboveground workers with them.

As has been mentioned elsewhere, lighter boatmen played a vital role in the life of the coal mines because of the difficult terrain in which the mines were situated. Even in the twenty-first century, land transport in the region is difficult because of the rugged mountains set parallel to the coast and intersected by sharp valleys plunging to the sea. In the nineteenth century, it was far easier to bring coal down to the sea for water transport than to haul it across the uneven landscape. Thus, the animal drivers and railroads brought the coal to numerous locations along the shore, often at stream mouths (see photographs 3.7, 3.8, and 2.18).

The opening of the Zonguldak port and its mechanized loading facilities around the turn of the century must have jeopardized the operation of some of these small loading locations. But as late as 1913, these lighter boat loadings were continuing at six different locations—Kandilli, Kirelik, Kozlu, Zonguldak-Inağzı, Kilimli, and Çatalağzı—there workers sent coal down chutes into these small transport boats and the boatmen then rowed the coal either out to ships anchored in safety or on to the port at Ereğli or perhaps Zonguldak. A former Ereğli resident, relying on his living memory, testifies to the laborious, time-consuming and tedious lighter boat business in the early twentieth century.

> All the ships seeking to load coal ... had to make port in Ereğli first to get lighters and workers.... These lighters were smaller ships, their capacity varying between five and ten tons. They were oared ships. On its way to load coal each freighter would stop at Ereğli, where we would provide them with five to ten lighters and about twenty workers. They would tie the lighters to the ship and tow them along. The ship then went to the *stomio* where it was supposed to load; but the sea there was open, there was no port. If the weather was good, then they could load. Each lighter would approach the company's storage place, which was right on the beach, on the rocks. Then the *olouki* [chute]would open and thus they would fill the ship. When this was over the lighter went to the ship. The sailors on the ship would throw rope ladders over the side, and the porters would lift the coal by hand in wicker baskets. It was such a primitive routine! It could take five and even ten days for a ship to load.[33]

When there was no work or when the weather was bad, the boats were pulled onto the land for safety. During such times neither the boatmen nor the coal loaders received any wages.[34] Wages were piecework, by weight, and varied between summer and winter seasons. The warden (*kethuda*) of the boatmen kept accounts of the wages received and from these deducted common expenses, including the shares due to the boatmen, the warden, and the head of the guild.

In a fascinating turn of events in 1912, the warden of the Ereğli boatmen petitioned the mine superintendent to change the formal status of these workers from free to compulsory laborers, a ploy to avoid mobilization. The names of the boatmen, he argued, were inscribed in rosters and they were continuously working in the transport of coal to ships. Therefore, he argued, boatmen had the same status as compulsory workers, who also worked regularly and were listed in register books. To bolster his request, he correctly recalled events thirty-five years in the past, during the Ottoman-Russian War of 1877–1878, when, he said, so many boatmen were taken into active duty that there were not enough of them to load coal onto the ships. To prevent such shortages from recurring, he successfully petitioned the mine superintendent that the boatmen were not to be mobilized and were to serve only their active and inactive reserve obligations.[35]

The expansion of production both hurt and bolstered the livelihoods of these boatmen and coal loaders at the turn of the century. The construction of the Zonguldak port and mechanical facilities for directly loading coal onto ships meant that much, likely most, of the Ereğli Company–inspired production could now exit the region without being handled by the boatmen (see photographs 2.6, 2.7, and 2.8). And since these facilities were available to other mine operators, at least some of their production also flowed through these mechanized facilities. A strike that erupted among the boatmen and coal loaders in January 1913 indicates the impact of the new port on their livelihoods. The strikers demanded wage increases averaging more than 70 percent, pitting them against twelve mine operators who banded together and petitioned the state to reject the workers' demands. Among them were some of the more important companies in the coalfield, such as the Sarıcazadeler, the company of the chamberlain Raghip Pasha. Significantly, the Ereğli Company was not included; its absence suggests that boatmen were no longer loading any of its coal.[36]

The boatmen's skills were ancient ones, heavily dependent on a profound knowledge of their vessels and the sea. In contrast, most aboveground workers were needed in skilled occupations that were generated by the increasing mechanization of facilities. In the earlier years, the compulsory work force of transporters must have handled much, likely most, of the coal as it emerged from the mine, hauling it with their animals either to storage areas or to coastal spots. But as steam-powered railroads and aerial cables were installed, specialized workers were required for the loading and unloading of the coal. In addition, the machine shops and other facilities for their repair and maintenance required a skilled labor force (photographs 2.10 and 2.14 and 3.9 and 3.10). When the coal scrubbers finally were built, these too required both operational and repair personnel, as did the cranes, conveyer loaders, and other motorized equipment at the new Zonguldak port.

Workers flowed in to fill these new needs from a variety of departure points, mainly within the empire. The heavy reliance on Ottoman subjects indicates the extent to which technological expertise had become available domestically. Immediately after the 1882 shift to free market coal sales, aboveground, year-round workers from the Eastern Anatolian districts such as Trabzon, Rize, and Artvin began migrating to the region, remaining to work for periods as long as several years.[37] Many were from Gümüşhane, an ancient silver mining region in the Anatolian Black Sea area. Interestingly, most of them were not hewers as might be expected, but rather wagoners or unskilled workers, suggesting that imported workers were filling shortages not just in the skilled categories but across the board.[38] These workers became a regular part of the work force, establishing chain migrations patterns that echo through to the present and shape Zonguldak work life into the twenty-first century.[39] In 1882, the state also acknowledged its dependence on outsiders when it signed a mining concession expressly permitting the hire of foreign foremen and workers in the aboveground repair facilities that were being planned.[40]

A half century later, a former resident of the region remembered the coming of the Ereğli Company and its efforts to recruit workers:

> So, from 1890 on the company started looking for personnel. They had representatives everywhere recruiting people and sending them to Zonguldak. The company would pay those representatives 5 kuruş for each person they would send back: skilled workers, laborers, tunnel-diggers—mostly Greeks, but Turks as well. They had representatives all over the area between Thrace and Trabzon who were hiring people. If a representative sent fifty people, for example, he would get two hundred and fifty kuruş—five kuruş a head![41]

Workers' Wages: The Compulsory Labor Force

In many coal-mining regions of the world, workers were simultaneously compensated via both the daily wage and piecework/tonnage forms of payments.[42] One or the other method prevailed partly as a function of the kind of labor being performed. Thus, work involving the actual extraction and sometimes the transport of coal involved tonnage rates or a mix of piecework and daily wages. Support workers, such as machinists and repair shop or railroad workers, often received fixed wages.

In the Zonguldak coalfield, similarly, both compensatory forms were present from an early date. We can surmise but not know the methods of payment for workers before 1867. During the 1870s, transporters received daily wages of three krs from which they had to supply barley and straw for their animals. Two decades later, their method of payment had shifted and they were receiving piecework wages—between 15 and 90 *paras* (per 100 *atik kantar* of coal), depending on the distance.[43] Thus, in 1900, transporters at one mine were receiving 68 *paras* per (100 *kiyye*s) for a 2,200-meter distance (and were demanding an increase). At another mine, also in 1900, the transporters' fee for the 940-meter trip from the Abdi Bey mine in Kozlu to the depot in Zonguldak increased from 32 to 40 *paras* (per 100 *kiyye*s).[44]

The villagers who cut and transported mine supports received piecework rates from the outset. In the 1870s, they were paid 3.5 krs for the shorter (3 *arşın*) supports and 4.5 krs for the longer (4 *arşın*) supports. In the 1890s, we learn only that mine operators were paying them 2 and 4 krs for each piece.[45]

The basket carriers received fixed daily wages that seem to have remained frozen at six krs during the four decades leading up to World War I.[46] Given the especially brutal treatment meted out to these workers, this impression of wage stagnation may indeed be correct. It is unlikely that hewers, when they themselves were receiving higher wages, offered extra compensation to the basket carriers on whom they relied. Unlike their equivalents in the United States, workers carrying coal away from the face were not, in any sense, employees of the hewers.[47]

Hewers: Daily Wages or Piecework?

If my reading is correct, the 1867 regulations perhaps recognized both the daily wage and the piecework forms of payment for hewers. The provision allowing hewers freedom to negotiate a wage with a mine operator (Art. 22) may simply be referring to daily wages. But it also seems possible to understand the article as countenancing negotiations over piece rates as well. Between the 1870s and World War I, hewers' wages, stated to be daily wages, fluctuated within a wide range, between 8 and 20 krs. In the mid 1870s, hewers' wages equaled between 15 and 18 krs a day while, in 1900, they fluctuated between 8 and 20 krs. In 1907, the rate was 12 krs a day; in 1911, it ranged between 10 and 20 krs.[48] These figures may represent different daily wages at different mines, designed to recruit and hold scarce workers. Or, they may represent piece rates averaged out on a daily basis, or a combination of wages and piece rates.

Scattered evidence suggests that piecework became increasingly prevalent for hewers late in the period, a trend perhaps accelerated by the increasing dominance of the Ereğli Company. Indeed, soon after it began operations the company reported that, in 1899 "for the individual recruitment of workers and daily wage payments we gradually are substituting piece work contracts arranged with the small entrepreneurs of the countryside who are responsible for their workers."[49] An engineer's report prepared in 1902 on Ali Efendi's #226 mine in Kilimli offers further evidence of piecework. It is an extremely detailed accounting of monies owed to "a person named Petro who is doing piecework [*kesenecilik*] and receiving so many krs for each meter of work that he does." The text of this document spells out in exquisite detail the amount and location of the coal he has cut, the expenses he has incurred, and the sums owed to him by the mine operator. Its detail and subject matter make it unique among the thousands of documents consulted for this study and seem to suggest that piecework was not a process commonly encountered by the engineer who filed the report.[50]

Nearly simultaneously, another engineer reported a fatal accident 650 meters inside mine #216 in the Alacaağzı locale. He explicitly mentions that the headman of Tiran village had hired a group of workers on a piecework basis. (Three of them, one from Tiran village, died when a 100-kg rock fell from the ceiling.)[51] In a third case from 1902, in the Kozlu locale, the engineer notes a Montenegrin working in mine #232 of the Giurgiu Company and, again explicitly, mentions that his labor was on a piecework basis. The Montenegrin was supervising two hewers and two basket carriers when a methane explosion injured two of them.[52] In these two accident reports, piecework is specified as something noteworthy. In contrast, hundreds of other accident reports simply discuss the presence of hewers and other workers, without elaboration. This singling out of piecework seems to suggest that it was an unusual form of compensation at the turn of the century.

Another documented instance of piecework, dated March 1919, appears in the context of a labor dispute in the Ereğli Company's Ikinci Makas mine, reportedly the most productive of all the mines on a per capita basis. From this incident, we learn interesting details of workers' lives otherwise not often visible in the documents. It took place after World War I, during the French occupation of the coalfield, when production was well below pre-war levels. In the mine, the engineer reports, "anarchy" prevailed and supervisory personnel were refraining from introducing "scientific procedures" because of workers' resistance and hostility. Workers and children were stealing coal from the storage areas, the coal wagons, and within the mine itself. One worker, a repairman (*tamirci*) from the Trabzon area on the eastern Black Sea coast, had been filling sacks with coal, smuggling them back to his dormitory, and from there hauling them to the coal market for sale during the late winter season. He was arrested inside the mine. But then, the engineer reports: "I heard threats like, 'we are going to bash your head,' and, 'bad things are going to happen,' addressed to the guard and the accountant. Subsequently, the aforementioned Mustafa Ibrahim said, 'I'm leaving the mine. Come to the mouth of the mine and look, there are lots of people [ready to attack the officials].' Subsequently, the workers left work and went to their dormitory."[53]

At this point, the incident takes on meaning for our inquiry into piecework. There were fifteen workers involved in the walkout, about half the work force at that spot. Three were locals, one hailed from Monastir province in the Balkans, and the remaining eleven were from Trabzon province. A number of them, including three foremen, two of them from Trabzon and the third from a local village, had been receiving piecework wages. The foremen, the engineer wrote, began to fear for the loss of wages that would follow if the work stoppage continued. Acting together, the three foremen ordered their crews back to work. When the mine manager visited the coal face an hour later, he reported that work had resumed.[54] In the report, piecework is offered as the reason behind the foremen's intervention, though not in a manner suggesting that it was an unusual form of compensation.

A final example of documented piecework dates from 1923, just after the end of the empire, when a widespread strike erupted among the miners. Originating in the Asma mine of the Ereğli Company, it was triggered by hostility to the company's piecework policies (*araba kesenesi*). Here is Ethem Çavuş's explanation of the piecework system and why workers were opposed to it.[55]

The company, after a time, began a practice called piecework (*kesenecilik veya götürücülük*). The company liked this practice and said to the workers: finish the job I give you and earn your daily wage. This system was a way of reckoning on the very high side the work that could be done in a day. For example, three workers are sent to work in a coal vein. They are told "today you will yield 20 wagons." But it's impossible for three workers to get 20 wagons from this vein. Forced to work at a horrible pace, most become sick and leave the mine half-crazy. They were asked for too much and would quit the company which then would hire new workers. Also, the workers learned to cheat. But how to cheat! They worked longer than they should have and began taking coal from dangerous places. The company was thinking of nothing but profit; and the workers began secretly taking coal from places without permission, working to receive the designated amount of wage. Gradually, the company shut its eyes to this. And much of the time the workers, who paid with their blood, began to extract coal from dangerous places under orders of the company.[56]

The above accounts indicate that piecework for hewers was likely a factor in the work life of the region from the early years of mining. The various reports and accounts make clear that it was being practiced in a number of widely separated mines, with different owners, at the beginning of the twentieth century. By the end of World War I it had become commonplace, especially, it seems, in the mines of the Ereğli Company, which then furnished three-quarters of all production. Moreover, it had become accepted practice, requiring neither definition nor defense. Finally, the 1923 strike indicates that the Ereğli Company was applying piecework quotas that workers considered unreasonable.

Aboveground Workers, 1905–1912: A Critical Look at Wage Ledgers

A series of wage ledgers for several years between 1905 and 1912 variously lists names, occupations, and monthly sums paid to individuals and groups engaged in aboveground mine work. Yet despite the hundreds of pages, thousands of entries, and many hundreds of workers' names recorded, the ledgers are a very disappointing source of information for the labor historian.[57] The causes for the disappointment are many. The records usually note total wages paid to the individual worker during a month but not the number of days or hours worked. Wages that different persons received for the identical occupations during a given month sometimes vary dramatically (see the median wage analysis below as a corrective). The fluctuating sums recorded usually do not correspond to fractions of any presumed monthly wage or to the wages paid to other persons in the same occupation. Surely these differences reflect not only variations in skill level but also the amount of time worked. They might even reflect a wage paid for work carried out over a period of several months. In the end, the work period being compensated remains uncertain, and therefore so too does the base wage.

Also, the monthly patterns of work as recorded in the ledgers do not reflect reality. For example, according to one ledger covering the period between

March 1905 and March 1906, only during that final March were more than two-thirds of the workers on the roster. Meanwhile, all except two of the remaining workers received wages for just two months' labor.[58] Thus, all but a handful of workers worked only one or two months. Only one worker, and the best paid at that, is noted as receiving wages for most months of the year: a master iron worker named Bartınlı Mustafa Usta who is recorded to have received the same rate of pay for ten months.[59] Here, the reader has two choices: either to accept the notion that two-thirds of the labor force were working one month and the rest two months, or to posit that the records are misleading. I prefer the latter course. A more realistic picture of work patterns appears in a ledger for the period 1915–1920.[60] Therein workers are recorded as present, month in and month out and, with some fluctuations, throughout the year. These workers are in the same occupations as those named in the above ledger from 1905–1906, where they were recorded as being present during just one month. The later ledger has a different format—a separate page for each individual for each year. By contrast, all workers and occupations being paid were listed in a monthly section of the earlier ledger. The varying formats of the two ledgers offer completely different pictures of the work force present. Yet since coal production was about the same during the two periods, I can assume the working hours and the monthly patterns of work would have been more or less the same.

Several other major weaknesses make use of these data problematic. Wages often were paid to workers who are listed by name only, without any suggestion of their occupation. And workers with unspecified occupations form a large share, sometimes over half, of the entries. For example, wages paid to named workers whose occupations are not identified make up one-third of all recorded wage payments during the period between April 1906 and March 1907. In several months, workers with unspecified occupations account for 73 to 90 percent of all the wages reported (table 3.1). Such large proportions limit the significance of the remaining information.

Moreover, the very large sums of wages recorded during the months of February and March 1907 (table 3.1), when aboveground work usually was at a standstill (as coal production and accident statistics make clear), raise suspicions.[61] Can it be true, as the ledger payments indicate, that one-third of all aboveground labor occurred during these two winter months? Since most of these winter wages were paid for unspecified occupations, the suspicion of misleading accounting procedures seems doubly justified. The sums recorded likely do not reflect any burst of actual work activity in February and March but rather derive from bookkeeping practices—when debits previously not recorded were swept up at the turn of the Ottoman fiscal year. The workers listed for February and March almost certainly had labored during the high season—June through September. That is, remuneration for unspecified labor that the ledgers record as paid to workers during February and March could have compensated any task done in any month.

Table 3.1 Monthly Wage Payments (in krs), Kozlu Locale, 1906–1907

	1906						1907		
	Apr.	July	Aug.	Sept.	Oct.	Nov.	Feb.	Mar.	Total
Ironworker						550	550	550	
Boat launcher		548					9		
Bathhouse construction				2,444			57		
Quarry worker				133			326		
Kılıç bridge repair							665		
Machinist				122	410		410		
Carpentry house			870	85	1,176				
Railroad	1,700		1,904	735	705		509		
Railroad repair			1,214	874	730				
Brick factory				660	1,508	275	285		
Aerial car worker	249		776	2,341	5,690			1,383	
Unspecified		5,124					7,498	2,741	15,663
Grand totals	1,949	5,672	4,764	7,394	10,219	825	10,309	4,674	45,806

Source: KU 207, Kozlu locale only. There were no itemizations offered during May, June, December, and January.

Yet another major shortcoming of these data is the inconsistent method of recording individuals' names. To give but one example: in August 1906, Mustafoğlu Ali b. Osman received payment for services rendered. Later in the ledger, on the pages presenting wages paid in September and October, a person named only Osman is paid.[62] Is this the same person? More detailed information is given about more highly skilled and paid workers such as machinists and ironworkers, so we are better able to trace their employment month by month, throughout the year. But apart from these kinds of exceptions, tracing the presence of a worker over the course of time would pose great difficulties yet still would involve making an ongoing series of assumptions, even guesses.[63]

In addition, there are problems of terminology. In most of the registers and documents consulted, the term *amele* refers exclusively to the basket carriers, the unskilled underground workers. But here, in presenting the aboveground labor force, the register employs the term *amele* to denote all workers, including machinists who earned monthly 550 krs, master craftsmen who earned slightly less, and unskilled workers who were paid as little as 15 krs a month. Sometimes a named person is designated as an *amele* without further elaboration when in another month he is specifically noted to be a carpenter in the carpentry shop. Lists of the wages of unnamed individual *amele* often are presented without reference to occupation, obscuring the livelihoods of those listed. Therefore, despite the records listing many hundreds of workers' names, issues relating to wage levels, job continuity, and turnover cannot be explored adequately. The ledgers available for the years 1905–1912 are misleading and incomplete.[64]

These caveats notwithstanding, the wage ledgers do tell a great deal about aboveground labor. First of all, they indicate that all of these workers were paid on a monthly basis, not semi-monthly or weekly. If true, this is an important finding. Such long intervals between pay periods generally operate against the workers' interests, encouraging indebtedness and leaving them vulnerable to debt servitude.[65]

Next, the ledgers help to identify workers. Persons with names that are clearly identifiable as Muslim, such as Ismail, routinely held highly technical and skilled positions including that of machinist or boiler fireman on the railroad. Although Armenian or Greek names occasionally are recorded, Muslims account for well over 95 percent of all aboveground workers. This pattern hammers yet another nail into the already-studded coffin of the ethnic division of labor, a concept whose advocates held that non-Muslims inherently were more skilled and able than Muslims.[66] At this date, in this coalfield, Muslims were an integral, indeed dominant, part of the skilled aboveground labor force.

The wage ledgers yield glimpses into everyday work life that are especially valuable since direct testimonies generally are absent except in times of labor strife. Expenditures such as those on construction of a bathhouse in September 1906 point to the developing infrastructure of facilities in the coalfield, in this case, amenities for some elements of the work force. But the ledgers do not reveal who the intended users of the bathhouse were—workers, employees, or officials—or whether it was intended for females (it most likely was built for the use of male Muslim workers). Wages paid for repairs at boat launch sites attest again to the character of small boat transport and the crucial role it played in the life of the coalfield. From these ramps, recall, small boats traveled all along the coast to bring coal to the harbor facilities at Ereğli or Zonguldak, or from shore to ships waiting on the open sea. And small boats using these launches routinely transported personnel between worksites, taking mine inspectors up and down the coal coast, shuttling between headquarters and the mines.[67]

When the ledgers record the presence of carpenters, machinists, and brick makers, they testify to the presence of the support facilities needed to maintain coal production. For example, a carpentry shop at Kozlu employed four to seven workers in 1905–1906.[68] At least as many worked in the brick factory. Transport, of course, was a key occupation; a large proportion of the aboveground work force was employed either in maintaining the transport facilities or doing the actual transportation work.[69] Thus it is documented that workers repaired a particular bridge, but whether this was routine maintenance or an emergency remains unknown; wages for railroad repairs appear regularly in the ledger. Part of the aboveground transportation work, which involved animals carrying mine supports or coal, fell to the compulsory labor workers, so it is invisible in these ledgers. But free-market wage labor worked in relatively large numbers on the aerial tramways and the railroads. The heads of the aerial tramways, where workers loaded or unloaded the coal, were dangerous places where many accidents occurred. Between August and September 1906, the wages paid to workers on these cable systems tripled, and in October 1906, they more than doubled again, fluctuations that are either merely statistical or suggestive of the volume of coal being shipped.[70] By contrast, wage payments for railroad (perhaps construction) work fell by three-quarters between August and September and then halted altogether in October, possibly reflecting the onset of the bad weather season. Many of the workers receiving pay for unspecified labor (as in, for example, table 3.1) surely worked loading and unloading coal on the aerial tramways or the railroads.[71]

Vast disparities in earning power separated the occupations (tables 3.2. and 3.3). Between 1905 and 1907, workers in all categories earned a median wage of 190 krs; by 1910, the median wage equaled 300 krs.[72] Given the labor unrest following the Young Turk Revolution of 1908, it seems reasonable to accept such a sharp increase. Highly skilled workers such as machinists and ironworkers stood near the top of the wage hierarchy. During the earlier period, they earned about four times more than workers on the railroad and five times more than stone quarry workers. Carpenters, too, were relatively well-paid, as were boiler firemen.[73] Aerial tramway workers earned more than railroad workers and a bit less than brick makers. The low wages recorded for railroad repair workers likely reflects the casual, day-labor nature of roadbed repair work.

The ledgers shed meager light on the origins of aboveground workers but it is enough to underscore the presence of a geographically diversified work force.[74] Local workers, both townsmen and villagers, were well represented. But most aboveground workers came from Ottoman regions outside the coalfield, mainly from locations to the east, especially Kurds from the area of Van in Eastern Anatolia. A few migrated from Izmir and Eskişehir in the west (see map 3.1).

A different kind of ledger, dated 1910 and 1911 (table 3.3), shows a wage hierarchy among aboveground workers that is not dissimilar from that of 1905–1907

Table 3.2 Median Monthly Wages for Various Aboveground Occupations, 1905–1907

Occupation	Krs	No. of Positions
Ironworker	445	7
Machinist	410	1
Bathhouse construction	379	6
Carpenter (*dülger*)	260	4
Carpenter (*marangoz*)	256	23
Boiler fireman	228	9
Unskilled worker	209	110
Brick factory	209	14
Aerial car worker	160	45
Railroad worker	109	90
Quarry worker	3	7
Railroad repair	49	19
Qur'an reciter	34	1
Total		336

Sources: KU 76, KU 207.

Table 3.3 Median Monthly Wages for Aboveground Workers (1910 and 1911 fiscal years)

Occupation, 1910	Krs	No. of Positions	Occupation, 1911	Krs	No. of Positions
Foreman	500	2	Foreman	550	2
Machinist	425	5	Machinist	400	5
Carpenter	350	5	Carpenter	530	7
Iron foundry	350	11	Iron foundry	700	7
Oiler	300	1	Unskilled worker	330	2
Boiler waterman	300	3	Boiler fireman	250	9
Switchman	300	8	Conveyer worker	300	4
Conveyer worker	275	6	Oiler	300	1
Boiler fireman	240	6	Boiler waterman	300	2
			Switchman	300	2
			Railroad boiler waterman	285	1
			Locomotive guard	270	1
			Railroad worker	270	3
Kozlu mosque	150	2	Kozlu mosque	150	2

Note: The 1911 wages include raises. A direct comparison between the 1910–1911 and the 1905–1907 wages cannot be made because of fundamental differences in reporting. In the case of 1910, monthly payments of wages to 36 workers were recorded; these received 96 percent of their nominal, full-time salary over the course of the fiscal year. In 1911, the nominal wage was presented and the arrival and departure of workers noted, but without monthly notations of wages paid. See the above discussion for the reporting in 1905–1907. These discrepancies permit comparisons only within the given year and not, alas, between years.
Source: KU 158, 47–139.

(table 3.2). This later ledger reported almost exclusively on skilled workers. Machinists, ironworkers, and carpenters were among the best-paid. The relative differences in wages among other technical workers—such as switchman, boiler waterman, oiler and conveyer worker—were small. Moreover, the movement of workers from one to the other of these occupations was common. Foremen received salaries much higher than most rank-and-file workers.

Only rarely (on just three occasions among more than 100 records) do the ledgers record supervisors as granting permission for aboveground workers to take leave for personal business. Two instances involved the head machinist at Kozlu, one of the highest-paid of all aboveground workers. Just before the onset of Ramadan, he sought and received permission to return to his family's village for four days. He spent a week at home celebrating the most important holiday of the Muslim calendar, at the end of the fast month of Ramadan. In the only other instance recorded, the Kozlu fireman Tahir obtained official permission to return home the same holiday week.[75]

The frequency of wage raises and high turnover rates indicate considerable job instability in the coalfield. During the fiscal year of 1910, a period of international peace, nearly 20 percent of aboveground workers received raises. In the very next 1911 fiscal year, when the Tripolitanian War with Italy broke

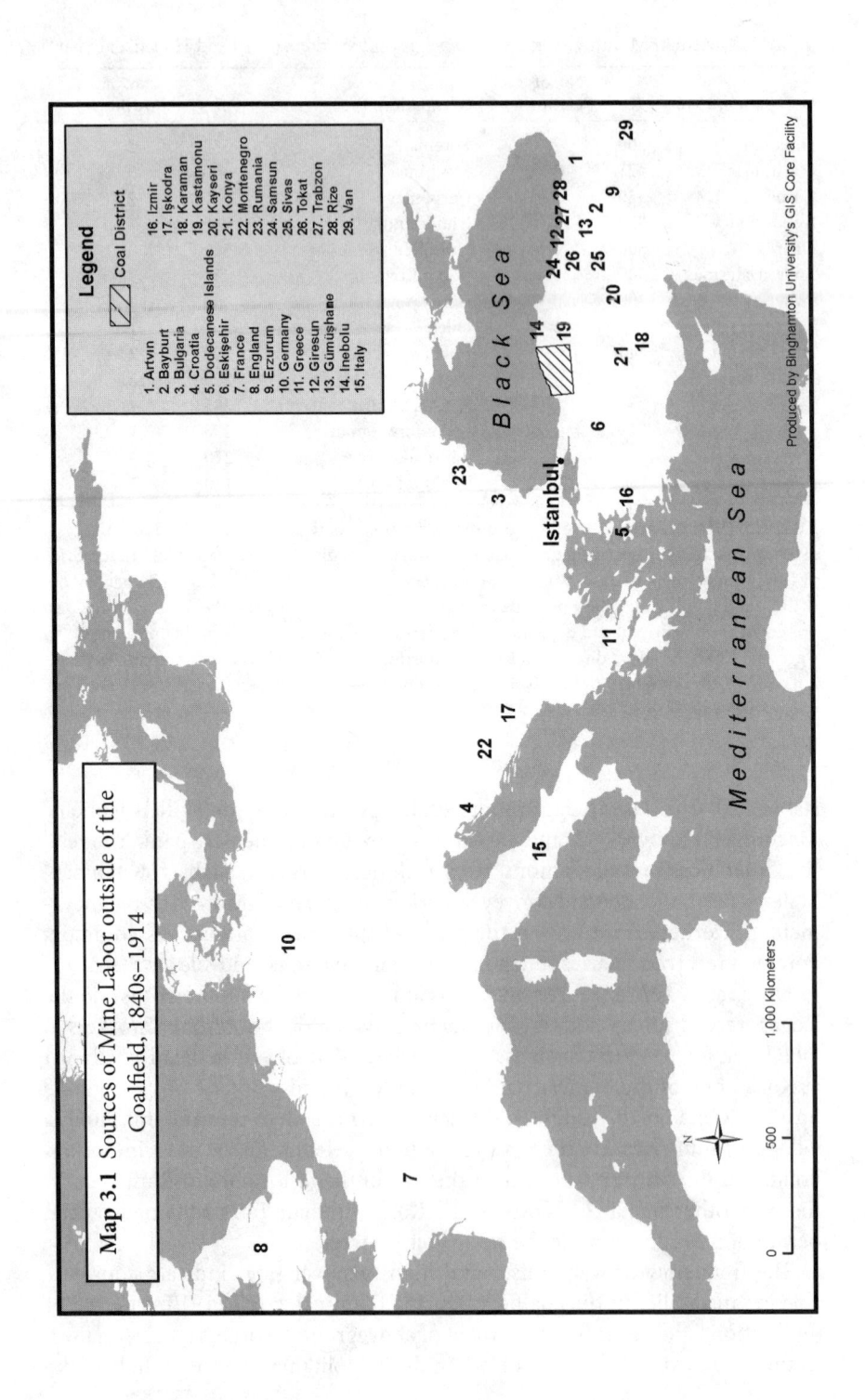

Map 3.1 Sources of Mine Labor outside of the Coalfield, 1840s–1914

Legend
- Coal District

1. Artvin
2. Bayburt
3. Bulgaria
4. Croatia
5. Dodecanese Islands
6. Eskişehir
7. France
8. England
9. Erzurum
10. Germany
11. Greece
12. Giresun
13. Gümüşhane
14. İnebolu
15. Italy
16. İzmir
17. İşkodra
18. Karaman
19. Kastamonu
20. Kayseri
21. Konya
22. Montenegro
23. Rumania
24. Samsun
25. Sivas
26. Tokat
27. Trabzon
28. Rize
29. Van

Produced by Binghamton University's GIS Core Facility

Table 3.4 Raises by Occupational Group (1911 fiscal year)

Occupation	Raise (in %)
Switchman	33
Conveyer worker	31
Foreman	20
Unskilled worker	16
Boiler fireman	11
Ironworker	15
Machinist	15
Carpenter	10
Railroad worker	6

Source: KU 158, 91–136.

out, more than 50 percent of the individuals in this same group received raises (table 3.4).[76] Altogether, two-thirds of the work force gained wage increments during these two years.[77]

The raises produced a certain leveling of wage differentials among workers in the same occupation. Conveyer workers overall won raises of about 8 percent in 1910. During the subsequent year, the two higher-paid conveyer workers in the group received no wage increase, another conveyer worker received an equalizing raise of 25 percent while yet another, the lowest paid among them, obtained a 42 percent increase. Thus, the wage gap among conveyer workers significantly narrowed. Among carpenters in the sample, two of the lower-paid received no raises, another obtained a 60 percent increase (likely a promotion) and three others respectively obtained 5, 8, and 17 percent raises. By contrast, the two highest-paid carpenters' raises averaged 6 percent, so their relative position deteriorated slightly.

The superintendent of the iron foundry obtained consecutive 8 percent raises in both 1910 and 1911, while apprentices there impressively gained successive 20 and 25 percent raises.[78] It is not clear if strikes or threats of work stoppages played a role in obtaining these gains. In 1908, strikes had won important wage gains for many workers, and there appear to have been additional labor stoppages that triggered increases. For example, in late November 1912, just after war had erupted, active reservists went to work in the Kilimli #113 mine. A month later, under the leadership of their foreman, Ahmed from Devrek, they went on strike, demanding 8,000 krs in unpaid wages, no small sum.[79]

In iron foundry work, dramatic wage gaps are displayed between apprentices, journeymen and masters: in 1910, apprentices' wages were two-thirds those of the journeymen and barely one-half the master craftsmen's. Overall, the raises of iron foundry workers in 1911 averaged 15 percent. Their relative ranking among all workers improved dramatically thanks to these raises, and in 1911 they were the best-paid group of aboveground workers (see the discussion of turnover below). Moreover, the raises in this group tended to reduce the wage discrepancies among apprentice, journeyman, and master iron foundry workers. Apprentices' relative wages improved the most, rising from two-thirds to three-quarters of journeymen's wages and from one-half to nearly two-thirds those of the masters'. By contrast, journeymen's wages rose modestly, barely gaining ground on the masters'. Boiler firemen as a group averaged a relatively modest 11 percent raise in 1911. As in the conveyer worker group, raises among boiler firemen tended to smooth out wage differences among them. Thus, the highest-paid received 3 percent raises while the lowest paid gained a 25 percent increment. Among machinists, four individuals obtained raises of 11 to 13 percent. Unusually, the highest-paid member of this group—the head machinist—won a 27 percent raise, which positions his wage relatively higher than before.

To summarize the wage increment data: during 1910 and 1911, the median wage rose from 300 to 330 krs.[80] The lower-paid workers among these, by a substantial margin, won relatively higher raises. Those earning below the median wage averaged wage increases of 21.8 percent while those making the median wage or above averaged 11.9 percent, nearly half that level. Moreover, in a number of occupations the raises reduced wage differentials among persons holding the same position. In the case of ironworkers, the wage gap separating apprentices from both journeymen and masters narrowed impressively. Only among machinists and carpenters, relatively highly paid groups, did the wage differentials not decrease.

The ledgers also provide a glimpse into the important issue of job stability—how long workers stayed in their posts. Turnover rates among these workers seem high for a period of relative peace, when military mobilization presumably was less of a drain on manpower sources. During 1910, fifty-two individuals occupied 36 different positions over the course of the year while in 1911 sixty-six persons occupied 50 different positions. Only rarely are causes given for the turnover. In one case, we learn that illness prompted the worker to leave.[81] In another, Yorgi, a boiler fireman on the railroad and a native of Safranbolu, routinely failed to show up for work and was fired on 28 August 1911.[82] Clearly, many workers quit to seek better fortunes or were fired for real and imagined grievances.

In the case of certain positions, the turnover was extraordinary. The job of switchman was occupied by eight workers during 1910 and 1911, when it was the highest paid position. During the first year, one worker quit after just two months. His replacement, a native of Kilimli, had barely arrived when his superiors appointed him to another job, that of conveyer worker. The native of Işkodra (in present-day Albania) who next accepted the position lasted six months before quitting, and the post went vacant for a month before a local worker, from Kozlu, filled the vacancy. In 1911, one worker hurt his foot and left but three others subsequently resigned later in the year without stated cause.[83]

Among the seven positions listed at the iron foundry (*demirhane*), there were two cases of extreme turnover during 1910. In the first instance, an apprentice quit for reasons not stated and his successor began work, at a wage raised 20 percent, from 8 to 10 krs, on 3 June 1910. But he walked off the job less than a week later, and his replacement also quit, before the end of the year.[84] Similarly, three different apprentices successively occupied another post at the iron foundry over just seven months in 1910, despite receiving very large raises. In May 1910 the first was removed, and his replacement, a Kozlu native, started work with a wage raised 20 percent above that of his predecessor, from 10 to 12 krs. But in September, Davud b. Ahmed also was fired and his successor began work just a few days later.[85] In 1911, for unstated reasons, turnover among iron foundry apprentices was equally rapid, three in less than a year. Thus, six different iron foundry apprentices came and went in just two years.

The ledgers also permit a comparison of wages of aboveground workers with those of compulsory workers, and also with the salaries of the administrative personnel who worked in the offices and, often, were their supervisors. Hewers were the best paid of the compulsory workers. In 1911, their median daily wage was triple that of basket carriers'. Overall, a hewer's daily wage placed him in the middle of the median wages earned by aboveground workers in 1911. Thus, the hewer's median daily wage in 1911 was 20 percent lower than that of foremen and carpenters and slightly more than machinists'. It surpassed, by at least 50 percent, the wages of conveyer workers, switchmen, and oilers, and fared still better when compared to the earnings of lower-paid aboveground workers such as guards and railroad bed workers.[86]

Generally, both compulsory and free aboveground workers' wages paled when compared to the salaries of the top administrative personnel in the region. Arif Pasha, who in 1906 was mine superintendent and thus the ranking official, earned twenty times more per month than the median aboveground worker. Similarly, the chief engineer at the time, Istilioyanos Efendi, likely the most highly trained technician in the coalfield, was earning fully eight times the median wage of the aboveground workers under his supervision.[87] Istilioyanos and his superior, the superintendent, respectively earned five and seven times the wages of the railroad and road foremen, the highest-paid workers in the 1910 ledger. On the list of professional job holders, I also found the office boy, inscribed in the payroll ledger accounts between an assistant secretary for documents and the mining engineer in charge of the Zonguldak locale mines, both, in very different ways, highly trained personnel. The office boy, by contrast, cleaned the administrative offices and provided the staff with coffee and tea. There were two of them—one at the central offices (probably at Zonguldak) and the second in the Ereğli offices. These positions, likely obtained through patronage, were quite unskilled, and the wage—7 or 8 krs a day—was about 10–20 percent below the median for all workers. In other respects, they more closely resembled workers than the officials with whom they were listed in the wage ledgers.

Meanwhile, the average skilled worker (nearly all those in table 3.3) was well off compared to most of the rank-and-file bureaucrats employed locally in the coalfield by the Mining Ministry. Ironworkers and machinists earned more than either the average accountant in the Zonguldak central office or the official in charge of weighing the coal in the port. Carpenters earned about as much as clerks in the accounting office of the port. The brick factory workers and workers in unspecified tasks drew median wages roughly equal to those of clerks and officials working in the various locale offices of the Mining Ministry.[88] And wages of most carpenters equaled or exceeded the monthly salaries of the sole weighing official at Çatalağzı and his four counterparts at Zonguldak.

Aboveground workers, moreover, enjoyed a number of advantages over bureaucrats, even those receiving higher salaries. They were not subject to a number of wage deductions endured by officials—for example, withholding for the 5 percent retirement fund (*tekaüd sandığı*), which nominally returned to the official upon retirement, or for the contributions, supposedly voluntary, to help finance building of the Hejaz Railroad. High rank did not spare officials from the fate of the many hundreds of workers who suffered from arrears in wages paid. Indeed, the salaries of numerous officials went unpaid, sometimes for many years.[89]

Notes

1. Spratt (1877), 529, publishing a March 1854 report. These Croats likely were from Bosnia. Quataert (1983), 45, n. 30.
2. Kahveci (1997), 36, and citing Naim (1934), 24. Also see Çatma (1998), 78–79. In September 1858, John Barkley helped supervise the construction of a 40-mile long railroad from Constanta on the Black Sea to Cernavoada on the Danube.
3. Quataert (1983), 54; Çatma (1998), 78–79.
4. Spratt (1877), 524.
5. *Bolu vs 1334*.
6. For example, in March–April 1902, there was a prolonged discussion, involving consultation of official maps, regarding taking labor from three villages that, as it turned out, were outside of the coal district. ED 3, 171 #42, 7 March 1902.
7. For example, see Faroqhi (1994), 462.
8. The term *amele* is used throughout the sources, sometimes designating unskilled worker, sometimes basket carrier and sometimes simply worker, skilled or unskilled. The exact meaning often is clear from the context. ED 4, 303, 1 Mart 1295/13 March 1879 is the only document of the many hundreds that I examined in this volume that uses the term *küfeci*.
9. Quataert (1983), 41–69.
10. Etingü (1976), 57, puts the weight of the baskets at 88–110 lbs, as compared to 84 lbs in Quataert and Duman (2001), 156.
11. See discussion in n. 8 above.
12. See, generally, Quataert and Duman (2001), and for the quotation 156. Thirty *okka* equals around 84 lbs.
13. Kahveci (1997), 285–286, referring to conditions in the 1990s.

14. In the 1990s, hewers were easily the most highly paid workers in the coalfield, accounting for 73 percent of the highest-paid workers. Kahveci (1997), table 3.24, 324.
15. Çıladır (1977), 42–43. He cites the dangerous work they performed as the reason for their special status.
16. Compare Articles 21, 22, and 23 of the Dilaver Pasha regulations.
17. ED 4, 201, 22 Temmuz 1294/3 August 1878.
18. ED 4, 56, 18 tl 1293/30 October 1877.
19. Article 53 of the Dilaver Pasha regulations.
20. These have been overlooked in most secondary accounts of the coalfield. At some date between 1867 and the outbreak of war in 1877, the state had prepared ledger books containing the names of those it considered eligible for mine service. Persons required to be noted in ledgers for service in the mines included *sütunkeş, kiracı, arabacı, felekeci*, and *gemici* as well as *kazmacı* and *amele*. These persons were to report to the village council (*kariye meclisi*) along with their relatives, and register themselves for mine duty. ED 4, 83, 8 ts 1293/20 November 1877.
21. İmer (1944), 43.
22. Articles 13–20 of the Dilaver Pasha regulations. Also, ED 4, 290, 18 ks 1294/20 January 1879.
23. ED 4, 345, 14 Temmuz 1295/26 July 1879.
24. In the empire overall, this tax was paid in cash, not kind, and the monies here came from nearby districts.
25. Quataert (1983), 57–58, and sources therein.
26. See, for example, Castles (2003).
27. Quataert (1983), 58.
28. KU KD 2, 457, 6 Mayıs 1328/19 May 1912 and 9 Mayıs 1328/22 May 1912.
29. Quataert (1983), 62–63, and Kahveci (1997), 102–103.
30. Quataert (1983), 63.
31. KU KD 2, 457, 9 Mayıs 1328/22 May 1912, #181/121 and #687/122.
32. Thobie (1977), 414–415 erroneously states that the number of underground workers employed by the Ereğli Company rose from 1,500 to 3,000 between 1899 and 1906.
33. CAMS file Pf3, Ereğli, informant, Ioakeim Yailaoglou; interviewer, Babis Nikiforidis, 12/3/1963. A native of Kozlu, in another interview, noted that these boatmen also sometimes brought along goods for sale: "From Ereğli *kayikçi* would also come with things to sell: fish, vegetables or fruits." CAMS file Pf5, Kozlu, informant, Dimitris Moisiadis; interviewer, Babis Nikiforidis, 25/4/1963. The Ottoman documents reproduced in Özeken (1944a) very closely agree with this expatriate memory.
34. Compare ED 4, 290, 18 ks 1294/20 January 1879 with *Kastamonu vs 1314*, 432–433.
35. KU KD 2, 490, 14 Mayıs 1328/27 May 1912,#745/133.
36. Özeken (1944a), 12–18, reproducing documents concerning the negotiations, January–June 1913.
37. Quataert (1983), 60–61.
38. ED 3, 2–250.
39. See Kahveci (1997).
40. Quataert (1983), 57. The Zonguldak mines were the personal property of the sultan and thus not subject to the regular mining regulations of the Ottoman state. Nonetheless, it may be worth noting here that in 1887, general mining regulations came into force permitting foreign nationals to work in the mines as engineers or foremen. The laborers for their part were from the surrounding villages of the mining region. Other articles of this regulation were similar to those of the 1867 mining regulations. Kahveci (1997), 26.
41. CAMS file Pf4, Zonguldak, informant, Evangelos Paslidis; interviewer, Babis Nikiforidis, 6/5/1963.
42. Seltzer (1985), for discussion of piecework and of the contract system.

43. Compare ED 4, 290, 18 ks 1294/20 January 1879 with *Kastamonu vs 1314*/1898, 432–433.
44. ED 3, 157, 16 Nisan 1316/29 April 1900; ED 3, 159, 23 Mayıs 1316/5 June 1900 and 28 Mayıs 1316/10 June 1900. Inflation rates at Zonguldak are unknown, and it should not be assumed they necessarily followed patterns set in Istanbul or elsewhere in the empire. See Pamuk (2000).
45. ED 4, 142, 3 Mart 1294/15 March 1878.
46. Quataert (1983), table on 60. It now seems certain to me that these wages are for basket carriers and unskilled workers, not for transporters as I mistakenly wrote.
47. For this assertion, however, there is no supporting documentary evidence.
48. Quataert (1983), 60 and Varlık (1985), 917–922.
49. Quoted in Quataert (1983), 60.
50. ED 3, 178, #6, 6 Nisan 1318/19 April 1902. He cut 216 meters of coal, at a contracted rate of 80 krs per meter.
51. The family of this headman, Karamahmudzadeler Mehmed Agha, remained powerful in the area, exercising a decisive impact on events many years later during the Turkish Republic. ED 3,179, #8, 10 Nisan 1318/23 April 1902. See chapter 1 for the role of Tiran in the early years of coal mining.
52. ED 3, 218, #12, 29 Mayıs 1321/11 June 1905.
53. ED 16, 476–478, #88, 23 Mart 1334/23 March 1919.
54. ED 16, 476–478, #88, 23 Mart 1334/23 March 1919.
55. Naim (1934), 21–131. This text is different from the one translated and presented in Quataert and Duman (2001).
56. Çıladır adds that this form of oppression continues down to the present day in the *sarma üsülü*, in which they have to fulfill a production quota to be paid; thus, they end up working more than the designated eight-hour shifts. Çıladır (1977), 32, note *.
57. Drawing here on KU 207, KU 71, and KU 76 for the years 1905, 1906, and 1907. See chapter 6 for further discussion of the limitations of wage ledgers.
58. KU 76.
59. During one month, August, he received four payments that equaled more than two months' salary. KU 76.
60. KU 143.
61. KU 76 and KU 207.
62. KU 207.
63. By contrast, the full names of such employees as the mine engineers, clerks, and other officials are routinely presented, which simplifies the task of tracing their job continuity.
64. Compare the reporting in KU 207, KU 71, and KU 76 with that in KU 143.
65. Weekly pay became a target of union demands in Western Europe and was adopted after 1870. Church (1986), 266. The testimony of Ethem Çavuş, probably from the period of the 1890s, can be read to indicate that his cohort was receiving semi-monthly pay, at the end of each twelve-day shift. But the larger text seems to suggest that payment actually came only at the end of the month. See Quataert and Duman (2001), 164–165, which is quoted in chapter 5.
66. For a fuller discussion, see Quataert (1993).
67. For example, see Behçet Bey's monthly work schedule for one month, table 2.9 in this volume.
68. KU 206 and 76.
69. Even with the recording problems discussed above, this pre-eminence is clear.
70. KU 207.
71. KU 207. These statements set aside the problem of the substantial amounts paid for unspecified labor, even though it is quite likely that at least some of these monies were paid to aerial-car and railroad labor.
72. The median wage for 1905–1907 was calculated for 408 entries (KU 76 = 65; KU 207 = 110; KU 71 = 233 entries). Entries were excluded from the sample either when their data were not statistically significant or when they clearly represented payments to groups of workers.

Most entries were for the individual workers, but some were debts or payments to several persons. Therefore, the median wage category includes at least 408 persons.

The category *amele*, as seen, contains wages of some skilled workers such as carpenters and boiler fireman and thus is not very helpful. In 1909, the sample totaled 36 positions, occupied by 52 persons over the course of the year. Because the 1909 sample is so small, most observations are drawn from the 1905–1907 reports.

73. Surprisingly, boat launchers appear in these ledgers and were relatively well-paid at a median wage of 243 krs for five workers.
74. Unfortunately, only 6 percent (23 cases) of the cases record the workers' places of origin. KU 76 = 6; KU 207 = 0; KU 71 = 17. Six persons were Kurds from Van while Gürün and Samsun each provided two workers. Seven of the twenty-three cases were local people from Ereğli, Bartın, and several villages.
75. KU 158, 99, 106, and 136.
76. Twenty-six persons received raises in 1911; 24 of these were authorized on 14 Temmuz 1327/27 July 1911.
77. KU 158. Five received successive raises in 1910 and 1911.
78. KU 158, 47–86.
79. ED 12, 203, 8 ts 1328, #1865/262.
80. The sample of enumerated workers consists of some fifty individuals.
81. KU 158, 77 for 1910.
82. KU 158, 103.
83. KU 158, 81, and 136.
84. KU 158, 72.
85. KU 158, 48.
86. Support workers could have earned as much as 200 krs in a thirty day period, assuming no days off. In this instance, their maximum wage still fell below that of a hewer's median wage of 240 krs per twelve-day shift. See sources in table 3.3 and Quataert (1983), 60, and Varlık (1985), 917–922.
87. The salaries of office employees, unlike the workers', were uniform month after month. Most officials received rations (*tayinat*); the engineer did not. But he did have an expense account.
88. KU 207, 76, and 71.
89. See KU 14.

4

"Like Slaves in Colonial Countries"
Working Conditions in the Coalfield

Introduction

In the present chapter, I describe the varieties of labor in the Zonguldak coalfield. Giving particular attention to the dangerous underground work within the mines, I discuss as well the supporting tasks that were necessary to bring coal to market. Often reading between the lines of documents, I offer glimpses into the daily lives of labor more than 100 years ago.

At the end of the nineteenth century, and likely throughout the coal-mining era, the aboveground labor force worked in better conditions than their underground colleagues. Much of this, of course, was due simply to location. After all, no matter how strenuous or difficult the job aboveground, it favorably compared to working in the dark, explosive, cramped, health-threatening, and dangerous conditions of underground work, especially those at the coal face. But better working conditions also owed much to the fact that aboveground workers, with important exceptions such as the transporters and support makers, were free labor. They worked more or less by choice, attracted by the availability of wage work or better-paying jobs. Since they could leave as they wished or at least at the end of their contracts, employers had to pay some attention to retaining their services by offering some amenities. Most underground workers, by contrast, belonged to the compulsory labor force. They labored because of the will of the village headman or council of elders. Operators likely felt less concerned about maintaining attractive working conditions for them. The free-labor underground workers recruited from outside, of course, did have a choice and thus, like the free aboveground workers, likely obtained better housing and medical care.

Notes for this chapter begin on page 93.

Aboveground Workers

The late-nineteenth-century construction of important infrastructural facilities, such as the coal scrubbers and repair shops near or in the growing town of Zonguldak, attracted large numbers of aboveground workers. By the early twentieth century, hundreds were employed at these facilities as part of a permanent work force. Many more found work on the railroads and in the port. Following construction of a railroad from important extraction centers such as Üzülmez to Zonguldak, "there was a train going all the way to the tunnels to bring coal to the port. It would go a one-hour distance to Üzülmez—that's where the coal was mined. There were cranes in the port. The crane would lift the coal from the train wagons and then drop it onto the ship."[1] These trains not only facilitated coal transport; they also eased the movement of workers between the mines and the town of Zonguldak. As an unintended and unwanted consequence, which drove both state inspectors and the Ereğli Company to frustrated distraction, it became possible (though not legal) to hop train rides between town and mine. The trains routinely were packed with hundreds of above- and belowground workers (see chapter 7). Daily commutes to housing and recreation in town became feasible for the first time. Also, the trains may have opened up the housing market in town, offering an alternative to company-built housing at the mine sites.

There is little doubt that the working conditions of aboveground workers improved at the end of the century as coal production mounted. Both the Ereğli Company and its Ottoman and foreign competitors built housing and other facilities to attract and retain free above- and belowground workers. Informed by its engineers that "the workers of the Ereğli region are neither indocile nor incapable, but they have little energy and few needs," the Ereğli Company recruited "more robust and more energetic workers," particularly favoring Montenegrins, Croats, and Kurds. To retain these workers they built lodgings, providing the various categories of employees and workers with a hierarchy of quite different accommodations. Workers who were Ottoman subjects were lodged in collective buildings of wood and stone, erected at the various production locales. Employees and Western Europeans (there were sixty French foremen in around 1914) obtained more spacious accommodations in individual houses. And top-ranking administrators and engineers lived in villas built high on the slopes overlooking Zonguldak (photograph 2.16). Thus, the town had a European enclave set apart from the rest, a feature it shared with many port cities and commercial centers during the age of imperialism. The Ereğli Company also opened shops that, as even a critic of the company acknowledged, sold goods at moderate prices. Yet it seems these shops were not open to rank and file workers but only to the professional and administrative personnel. Similarly, the Ereğli Company founded two primary schools—for the sons and daughters of administrative and professional personnel. Their language of instruction certainly was French: in the boys' school, the Oblates of the Assumption were the original teachers, replaced in 1906 by another order of Catholic brothers.[2]

Work Conditions at the Coal Face: An Overview

To gain entry to the coal, miners at Zonguldak mainly employed both the so-called drift and slope mining methods. Initially, since the coal literally was on the surface, they employed drift mining, in which miners simply followed the course of the coal seam from the ground level. In addition, slope mining soon came into use, in which a sloping entry was cut from the surface to the coal that lay not too far below. There also were some, comparatively few it seems, shaft mines, where vertical shafts were dug straight down for the transport of workers, supplies and the coal itself. Of these three methods, drift mining was the cheapest and shaft mining the most expensive. Even after the arrival of better-capitalized enterprises such as those of the Ereğli and the Sarıcazadeler companies, most entrepreneurs lacked sufficient capital. Thus, since production methods can be fairly characterized as comparatively labor-intensive and capital-extensive, we can assume that drift mining predominated. And yet after 1882, there were rising capital inputs and the employ of increasingly complex technologies. By 1900, for example, two companies had initiated extraction of coal beneath the seabed, joined by a third firm a few years later.[3]

Once they gained access to the coal seam, Zonguldak miners, during the Ottoman period, commonly extracted the coal via two methods, respectively the drift and the room-and-pillar systems. A third method, the long-wall system, commonly employed in nineteenth-century Europe but not the United States, apparently was not practiced at all at Zonguldak during the Ottoman years. Economics, geology, and the character of the workers helped dictate the form of extraction: "The economic feasibility of long-wall mining depended, therefore, not on physical and technological factors alone, but on market conditions and the availability of a peaceful and disciplined work force."[4] The local geology, inadequate capital, and lack of adequate and disciplined labor supplies, needed to maintain the uninterrupted work schedules that long-wall mining demanded, combined to preclude adoption of this method at Zonguldak during the Ottoman era.

At the outset of operations in the region, workers using the drift method followed the coal from the surface downward, propping when necessary. Since the room-and-pillar method was described in the 1867 regulations we can assume it also had come into widespread use sometime during the first two decades of mine operations.[5] Both systems remained commonly employed during the Ottoman era. For steeply sloped seams, workers tended to favor the drift method. Under such conditions, even baskets were of little use in transporting the coal from the face. Instead, workers shoveled the coal to the drift entrance, and only there was it loaded onto the available transport—the backs of basket carriers and animals or carts on rails. Because of the cramped spaces, the work crews in drift mining tended to be small.

The exploitation of larger, less tortured coal veins favored the room-and-pillar method (figure 4.1), in which work gangs were substantially larger and

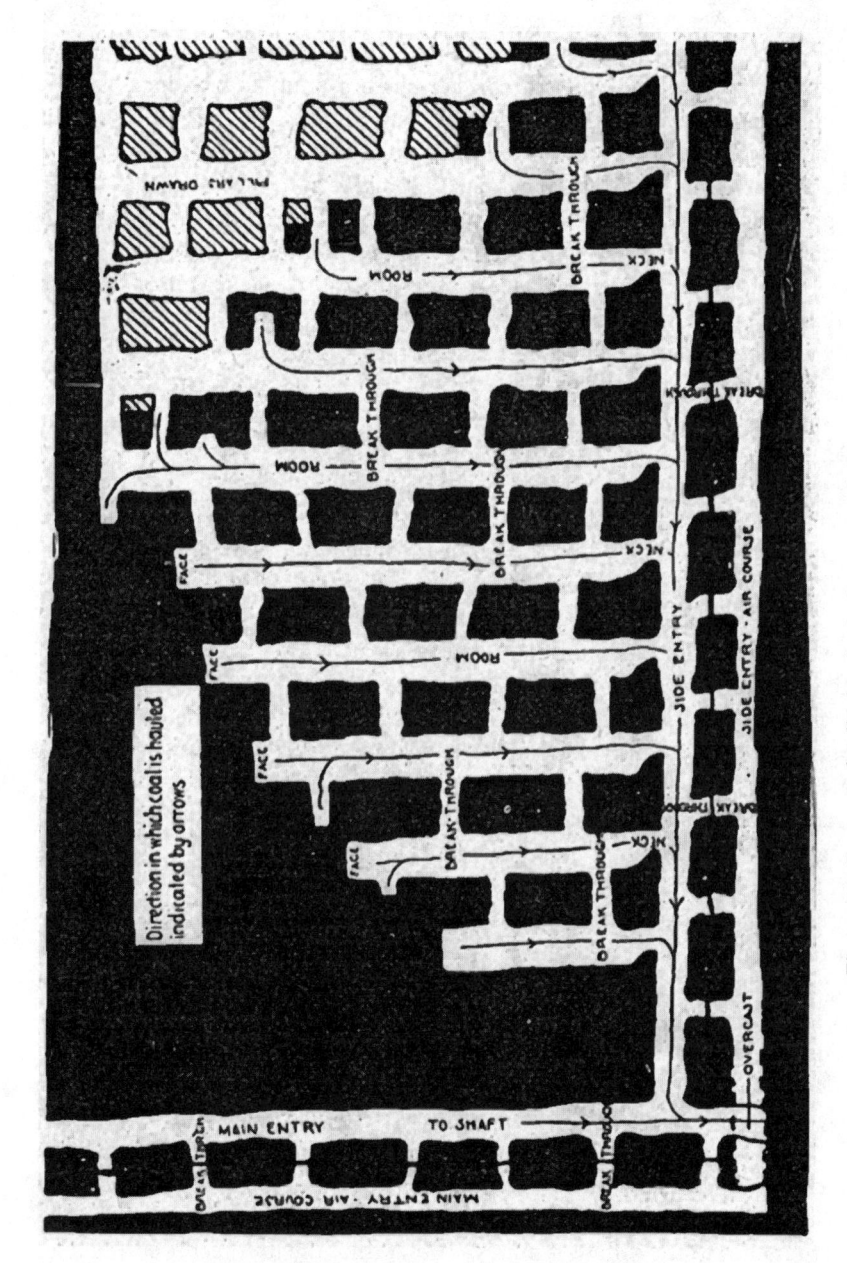

Figure 4.1 Room-and-Pillar Method of Mining. Source: Dix (1977), 5.

transport much easier. In this method, a main entry was driven horizontally into the coal seam from the bottom of the drift or slope opening, and from there, turning at a right angle, workers cut side entries of a certain length into the coal. Again at right angles to these side entries, workers cut lines of so-called rooms parallel to the main entry. Most of the mining took place on the advancing front of each room. Basket carriers, animals, and, increasingly, railroads hauled away the accumulated coal. The size of the rooms varied depending on the seams and overall conditions, keeping in mind the need to prevent the ceiling from crashing down. Rooms were connected to each other by "breakthroughs" in the coal, and walls of coal were left standing between rooms. When all the rooms in a section were worked out, the workers began retreating from the former coal face. In this process, they engaged in the very productive but highly dangerous process of "pulling down" the walls of coal that once had demarcated the rooms (see figure 4.1).[6]

Underground Work

Through the 1840s and until at least the mid 1850s in the Zonguldak coalfield, the coal seams lay exposed on the surface, visible to the trained eye on horseback. During these years, the readily available coal could be extracted with relative safety and ease. Small-scale ventures, as seen, were located as close to the coast as possible, and sometimes the coal was loaded directly from the mine on to the ship.[7] The newly imported miners from the Balkans dug horizontal tunnels into the hillsides, but because air entered solely at the mine opening the tunnels were not extensive. Using wooden braces only at the mine entrances, these workers depended on pillars of coal and schist for interior support. The extracted coal was transferred either by basket or by wooden mine cars pushed along wooden rails; ponies then hauled it from the gallery entrance to the rude port facility. The English company then in charge of the mines, like the Ereğli Company that became so dominant after 1896, neglected investment and concentrated on the most accessible and profitable operations.[8] These policies coupled with labor shortages and primitive production methods resulted in very low annual output levels of around 50,000 tons.[9]

Dissatisfied with these results, the state annulled the contract of the English company in 1851 and hired the English engineer John Barkley. At the outset of the Crimean War, there perhaps were 500 persons in the mines, working in very primitive conditions. Barkley led the most organized effort at the time. By 1854, the drifts extended 90 to 360 meters into the slopes, and a tramway traveled around five km up the valley from the beach at Kozlu, with branches to the different mines. At that time the first recorded accident occurred, an explosion "by which three native miners were rather severely burnt." Croats were working in areas outside of Barkley's control, such as Alacaağzı, but at Zonguldak these Croats had given up their work because of the twisted geology and "their want of capital to meet these difficulties."[10] Thirty-five years later, coal mined during the Crimean War era still lay piled in heaps "covered with moss and ferns."[11]

The earliest republican Turkish writer on the coalfield vividly described working conditions in this first period of exploitation, 1848–1865:

> During the 'Hazine-i Hassa' administration, Zonguldak villagers worked in the mines like slaves in colonial countries. Arbitrary working hours were set in two shifts namely 'sunrise shift' and 'sunset shift'. The ponies' stables were more hygienic than the workers' barracks. There were no first aid facilities or a doctor even around big coal pits. If a miner got injured or became ill, the company would throw him out. When a miner was seriously injured, the coal company would put him on a pony and send him to his village. This was a common practice.[12]

Working conditions in the 1870s differed slightly from those of the preceding decades, as we learn from a Belgian engineer who inspected the mines in 1876. He noted that in most mines, only picks were used to work the coal while wedges were absent. In just a few mines, he said, where the coal was solid and air circulation sufficient, workers used powder.

> As for interior transport: in all the mines it is done on the backs of men except for a few that have iron rails. The workers are 15–20 years and they carry the coal in small wicker baskets holding 15 kgs of coal strapped on their foreheads to their waists and they carry it to the depot situated at the entrance to the mine. There are no means of lighting given to the transport workers; occasionally there are some candles fixed on the walls of the galleries that illuminate the path they are taking.... Conditions are such that in some mines the height of the galleries is reduced to less than one meter and in these children of 15 years of age move about with loads of 15–20 kgs on their backs.... In some other galleries, conditions allow the use of small wagons holding 500–600 kgs and each wagon is pushed by a worker ... to the depot at the entrance to the mine.[13]

Productivity, deeply affected by irregularities in pay, averaged just one and one-quarter tons per day. To increase productivity, the Belgian engineer recommended dividing coal veins into "massifs," regular pillars of coal that are mined and then pulled down—that is, the room-and-pillar system. Another major problem at this time was water accumulation, which was compelling the abandonment of many mines. Only four or five mines were using mechanical pumps and the rest relied on bucket brigades or even hand pumps! The Belgian engineer also complained about the inadequate number of supports and the very poor lighting–indeed, mines were scarcely lit at all. The use of candles and fish oil lamps caused lots of smoke, contaminating the interior of mines and possibly, he speculated, damaging the constitution (*organisme*) of the workers: "Safety lamps are not at all in use." He closed by noting the generally dangerous conditions and reported a particularly grievous explosion in the mine of Hüseyin Mahmud that wounded many workers.[14]

During the 1870s, when the mines were not nearly as long as they would be later, basket carriers bore 300 kg of coal during each shift. They made eighteen daily trips down galleries that then were 200–300 meters long.[15] When considering the underground workers, both contemporary observers and later writers unanimously assert that conditions were horrendous throughout the coalfield, with some amelioration in the latter part of the period. One activist author labels the conditions medieval, by which he means exceedingly bad.[16] The workers, in his account, slept on the ground in barracks filled with rubbish, with just holes for windows and doors. The 1867 regulations called for proper housing but, he complains, to little avail. For heat and cooking, workers made a circle of small stones in each barracks and inside it built a fire from bits of coal and wood. Smoke escaped from a hole in the ceiling. Many mornings, workers woke up with burned skin because the cold had forced them too close to the heat. There was no escape, he concluded, from the bugs and filth.[17] Notably, he was describing conditions in the 1890s, after considerable improvements in the work environment had taken place.

Much depended on the particular mine operator and on whether the worker was free-market or compulsory labor. The better-capitalized operators, Ottoman as well as foreign, paid cash wages to the workers and built stone or brick dormitories. Everywhere in the coal district, operators had constructed "huts for the workers, offices, storage places, canteens."[18] In describing the population of his former hometown of Kozlu, a refugee Greek Orthodox Ottoman subject distinguished between the townspeople and the miners who visited the town: "There were, of course, thousands of Turkish workers, but those ones would come and go, they were not permanent residents. They were living in the workers' lodgings, which the companies had built for that specific purpose half an hour outside the village [of Kozlu]. The workers' shifts would rotate every fifteen days."[19]

Only the comparatively urbanized centers at Kozlu, Zonguldak, and Ereğli provided greater amenities for workers. To counter this lack of housing infrastructure, a number of operators built improved housing for their workers. In the early twentieth century, the Ereğli Company constructed a number of eighty-man barracks for rotational workers.[20] In June 1913, Mazlumzade Hacı Yakub Bey began building a dormitory for the inclined plane workers of his #158 mine at Kozlu, while at the same moment the Sarıcazadeler were building housing for their workers at the Ezbih/Enbih mine.[21] In these practices, the entrepreneurs were following patterns well established elsewhere, for example, in the northeast of England and Scotland, where colliery operators recognized that housing attracted and helped to retain the best hewers and better working conditions were readily understood to assure a more regular and higher-quality work force.[22]

Many Zonguldak operators persistently were trapped in cash flow shortages and, lacking sufficient capital, provided makeshift housing or none at all. These operators would sell their coal piecemeal to Istanbul merchants for low prices, so their workers had to wait for the wages to trickle in from Istanbul.

Many often returned to the villages without being paid in full. Workers laboring at the mine sites of such operators made do as best they could, often living in cave-like shelters they had made or cut into the hillside.²³ Here is Ethem Çavuş's description of such housing, at some point during the 1880s or 1890s.

> In those days, the employers did not provide shelter for the workers. Each work gang built one from this and that, and covered it with mud, thus creating a shelter during the period of rotation they worked in the mines.
>
> I was able to find accommodation in one of these. We would lie on the ground, place a piece of wood under our heads, and wait for the roosters to crow by the candle light.
>
> Those novice workers who could not build a shelter like the one I stayed in had to make one by digging out the slope of a hill, creating a place like a cave. And they stayed in these caves during the night.²⁴

On one occasion, he said, a cave shelter collapsed, trapping sixteen workers. In the end, thirteen were rescued but three had died in their sleep.²⁵

The workdays were very long, even in the best of circumstances. Consider the legally defined workday as set in the 1867 regulations, which frequently are credited with attempting to improve workers' lives.²⁶ These put legal limits to the workday of the hewers and the unskilled compulsory workers. Hewers were to be on duty from sunrise to sunset, alternating four-hour shifts at the coal face with other tasks inside and outside the mine. The unskilled workers' day was set at ten hours of actual labor in every twenty-four hours: this was set at four hours hauling coal; a two hour break outside, two hours of work outside at the direction of the foreman, and four more hours hauling coal. For the transporter, the regulations merely stated that there were to be two great shifts, with fifteen days of coal work for each shift.²⁷ Legal niceties aside, Ethem Çavuş complained about the lack of standards in regard to the hours of work. The notion of fixed "working hours did not exist," he said, "and [we began] to work very early in the morning and left it at sunset." The crowing of roosters cited above was to signal the start of work, but even this very early hour was advanced by mine operators: "[R]oosters around the mines crowed before the morning light [because] they were made to crow earlier by a candle lit in front of their cages."²⁸

Similarly, in a 1976 interview given when he was 74 years old, a former basket carrier described the conditions of his labor toward the very end of the Ottoman period. He spoke of working in the Çamlı mine, a seven or eight hour walk from his village, where he worked, he said, in twelve-hour shifts, bringing coal in baskets to a wagon at the mouth of the mine. From an employee waiting there, the worker receiving a coupon for each wagon that was filled.²⁹

At the end of the Ottoman period, the revolutionary government in Ankara formally reduced the workday to eight hours, but with little practical effect, according to one labor activist, because the introduction of piecework required workers to produce so much in a day that, in reality, the work shifts were longer than the designated eight hours.³⁰ Thus, during the Ottoman period, workdays of 10 to 12 hours and much longer were routine. Elsewhere in the mining world, similar conditions had prevailed earlier in the nineteenth century, about the time that the Zonguldak mines first opened. During the 1840s, the average miners' workweek in England totaled more than 60 hours. But then it fell sharply, thanks to labor action and state legislation, to 43 hours in 1913.[31] At this later date, Ottoman miners were averaging at least 20 more hours per week than their English counterparts.

No day of the week was set aside as a day off for compulsory workers. The 1867 regulations (Art. 56) stipulated that since Muslims formed the majority of the work force and Christians were "very few," Sundays were not holidays. Yet the article did not go on to make Friday the weekly day off. Instead, the workday on Fridays and Sundays was to begin only after the religious services were concluded—presumably the Friday noon prayer and Sunday morning mass.

The state, however, did recognize two days in the Muslim calendar and one in the Christian (Easter) as worthy of time off for the compulsory workers. For the overwhelmingly Muslim rank-and-file work force, the holidays surrounding the end of Ramadan were important social and festive events. During these times, workers expected to be back in their home villages, celebrating with their families. But their expectations clashed with the state's definition of the holidays as two separate one-day affairs. While specifically stating that Muslim workers had the right to time off on the two holidays (as Christian workers did for the Easter holiday), the state was vague about the duration of leave. For the workers, the holidays meant additional days off before and after each of the two particular holidays. The workers' and the mine administration's struggles over the definition of time off became especially acute during times of labor shortages, such as the wartime crises of the 1870s and the 1911–1921 era (chapter 9).

Rotational workers commonly brought their own food from the village, planned to last the entire shift. According to the testimony of a basket carrier who began mine work in 1919, staples included corn bread, dried curds and flour (*tarhana*), and bulgur.[32] Permanent workers, both above- and belowground, obviously had no village provisions to fall back on. When on the job, they depended on the company stores that "every mine operator had" for their provisions. Like company stores in many other coal-mining areas of the world, they too charged exorbitant prices for clothing, goods, coffee, sugar, rice, soap, and other provisions.[33]

The workers also shopped in the small towns of the region. A former resident of Zonguldak recalled how the town attracted villager-miners who, at the end of their shifts, stocked up before heading home for the "rest part" of their rotation.[34] A former resident of Kozlu vividly remembered payday in that small town, probably at the turn of the century.

> Everybody had their job in the mines or were self-employed professionals. Every fifteen days the wages the companies paid to the laborers, the skilled workers and the clerical personnel in the mines would amount to 2,500 napoleons. All this

money stayed there, in Kozlu. For a village with a mere three hundred houses that was a huge amount of cash. Thousands of workers would get their wages and then do their shopping in Kozlu—they had to spend some of that money in our market. You see, they used to buy their everyday food there—they paid for that with their own money—and also buy supplies to take home. It was those wages that kept business going both in Kozlu and Zonguldak.[35]

Payment of Workers' Wages

The above description implicitly paints a rosy picture, one in which workers actually received wages, and on a timely basis at that. It certainly is an accurate account, but, only for one moment in time–that is, it is not representative of the period as a whole. By contrast, it may be true that as late as the 1890s most workers, most of the time, did not personally pocket timely wage payments. (Thereafter, unfortunately, statistical evidence is still lacking.)

Before 1882, recall, mine operators were compelled to sell their production to the state. Unfortunately for operators and workers alike, the state, chronically short of cash, usually could not pay ready money for the coal that it demanded from mine operators. Instead, the Istanbul regime issued promissory notes to the provincial government, to be used as payment for the coal. In one estimate, of uncertain accuracy, only 10 to 20 percent of the owed monies actually ended up in the mine operators' hands. It is thus within reason to imagine that workers often went unpaid or received only a fraction of their wages, with predictable effects on absenteeism, flight, and production.[36]

Matters began to improve after 1882, when operators legally could sell 40 percent of production on the open market and output began increasing. Needing more workers, some began to offer cash wages, creating quite a stir among workers and the competing operators. When the owner of the Giurgiu Company began offering cash wages, the action threatened "a friend of his" in the government who had been manipulating the promissory note procedure to skim off 10 to 15 percent of workers' wages. To protect his scheme, the friend asked the mine superintendent to prevent other operators from paying wages in cash.[37] Ethem Çavuş, however, remembers the shift to cash more positively.

> The Gurci [Giurgiu] mine was in Kozlu. It was making payments to workers completely in cash at the end of [the] month. Because of this, workers began to come to the mines of this company in huge numbers. It was worth it to see the mine when workers were to be hired at the end of the month. About 2,000 workers showed up in front of the mine for 400 jobs and they gave innumerable presents to the foremen and gang bosses. After a few attempts which had ended without success, I had given up looking for employment that was paid in cash. [But] my late father came from the village like a God-sent figure. A basket of [prized] Safranbolu grapes which he presented to the foreman made me one of the happy workers making 6 piasters daily, one of those who was paid at least partly in cash.[38]

A former Zonguldak resident turned refugee remembered the arrival of the Ereğli Company and the impact on workers when it offered higher and more regularly paid cash wages.

> Before the French came, individual mine-owners used to pay their workers next to nothing: half an oka of petrol, one oka sugar, one hundred drams of coffee and one mecidiye for fifteen-days' work. The workers had to cover their food expenses from their own money. Following the arrival of the French, the other mine owners were forced to search the streets for workers. The workers, their eyes now opened, weren't willing to return, and answered "Now there's a foreign company here! [*Şimdi giavur kumpanya var*]."[39]

The basket of grapes from the father of Ethem Çavuş further illustrates that gift giving was a well established practice in the coalfield. The presence of this practice complicates our understanding of the role that mining played in the lives of the villagers. On the one hand, there is massive evidence documenting workers' flight and other forms of resistance to work in the mines. On the other hand, gift giving was a commonplace step toward gaining mine work, a custom that dated from the earliest days of Zonguldak mining until the end of the empire. In 1923, villagers seeking work offered the mine foreman some chickens, eggs, or even a little cash, just as their grandfathers and fathers had in previous decades: "If you didn't give, you didn't work."[40] Fifty years earlier, during the late 1870s, production had collapsed in the face of substantial worker resistance to mine work. And yet, at that very moment, villagers were bribing certain mine operators with olive oil, eggs, and lambs in order to be accepted into the mine work force.[41] Several explanations for this paradox come to mind. Perhaps the gifts were offered to gain entry into mines where work conditions were known to be better or safer, or mines where workers were paid cash rather than promissory notes for their toil. Or perhaps the villagers were seeking miner status as an escape from military service. It is certain that gift giving to get mine work and worker actions to avoid it coexisted in the coalfield.

Child Labor

Coal mining in many countries commonly was built on the foundation of cheap, pliable, child labor. In the British Isles, legislation supported by local unions prohibited, in 1842, the employment in coal mines of boys under the age of ten years and of all females. Until then teenage girls spent fourteen hour days dragging 77 kg of coal on their hands and knees and then up winding stairways and six-year-old boys hauled coal for their miner fathers through one meter-high tunnels. In the United States, similarly, mines employed boys until the early twentieth century, when the practice finally was outlawed. The state of Pennsylvania prohibited coal mines from hiring boys under twelve years only in 1885.⁴² In 1902, some 20,000 children were still working in the anthracite coal industry as trapper boys, mule drivers, and slate pickers.⁴³

Like their contemporaries, the Zonguldak mines routinely employed young children. The 1867 regulations, which aimed to improve conditions and remained legally in force until 1921, expressly permitted the employ of 13 year-old boys in underground work. During the final Ottoman half-century, legal definitions of childhood changed considerably, but without decisive impact on work in the coalfield. In one sense, males reached adulthood only at the age of 20, the age of eligibility for military conscription. But this definition clashed with the 1867 regulations, which specified that all males in the fourteen administrative districts aged 13 to 50 were eligible for mine work. In this different notion of adulthood, males between 13 and 19 thus were considered fit for hard labor in the mines but not for active military service.

Still other definitions of childhood and adulthood were afloat. Not later than December 1911, boys younger than 16 were expressly prohibited from working underground in the mines. Presumably, they could work aboveground legally. From May through December 1913, the superintendent's office actively campaigned to enforce the prohibition. Operators, the inspecting engineer complained, were being punished only in cases when underage children were injured. The superintendent urged the Commerce and Agriculture Ministry, then responsible for the mines, to more harshly punish operators who were out of compliance. While his insistence on punishment is commendable, it also reflects the state's more general refusal to treat workers and their families as capable of responsibility for their own actions. Instead of promoting policies that engaged workers to bring about changes, the superintendent turned to others, in this case the mine operators, as agents of change (see chapters 7 and 8 for further discussion).⁴⁴

In October 1913, the Zonguldak locale engineer Setrak, together with M. Rouvin, who was the engineer of the Çay Damarı mine, went on an inspection tour of the mine and found four boy laborers aged 14 and 15, all of them from Black Sea regions outside of the coal district.⁴⁵ In December, Setrak toured three different mines operated by the Ereğli Company and found fourteen underage workers. In their origins, these were about equally divided between local mine villages and areas outside the coalfield—that is, between compulsory and free labor workers. Most of the boys were 15; the youngest was 12.⁴⁶ Boys regularly formed part of the labor force, both as recruits from outside regions and conscripts from coalfield villages.⁴⁷

Diseases in the Coalfield

A host of diseases preyed upon workers, including pneumonia, tuberculosis, typhus, malaria, black lung, and syphilis. Prolonged exposure to damp and cold and the overall lack of proper housing surely accelerated the incidence of pulmonary diseases and generally weakened resistance. Black lung plagued miners and shortened their lives (see chapter 8). An 1897 imperial enumeration of medical facilities in the empire makes clear that the coalfield suffered particularly from disease. The presence of the coalfield surely accounts for the following, seemingly surprising, statistic for Kastamonu province: in the entire empire, the province held the third-largest number of hospital beds among all administrative units at the provincial level or its equivalent. Only the capital city itself and the rich, heavily populated province of Aydın in Western Anatolia contained more beds. Kastamonu province accounted for 3 percent of the empire's population but nearly 7 percent of its hospital beds.[48]

Syphilis was particularly widespread and its presence is noted in several accounts, but without elaboration as to its origins.[49] One account implausibly attributes its prevalence in Kastamonu province to the Crimean War and Ottoman-Russian War of 1877–1878.[50] In the literature on mining during the Ottoman era, there is no discussion of syphilis and its links to mine work. During the post-1923 era of the Turkish Republic, however, when very high rates of syphilis prevailed among miners, the connections are clear. In 1944, the Turkish Ministry of Health worried about miners laboring near the towns. There were many prostitutes working both in the towns and (illegal) brothels set up near the mines. The rotational labor system, which took workers away from their homes for weeks at a time, was held to blame.[51]

There can be no doubt that the local prevalence of syphilis during Ottoman times derived from the same combination of factors that spread the disease during the post-1923 era. Zonguldak as a boomtown surely attracted its share of prostitutes, likely from Istanbul and other Eastern Mediterranean cities, drawn by the presence of many hundreds of bachelors (*de facto* as well as *de jure*) living in or near the town. Their clients included not only the rotational workers but also the hundreds of miners and aboveground workers who lived in the area for months on end. Similarly, although not a shred of documentary evidence is presently available, brothels away from town at various mine sites surely played their own role in the spread of venereal diseases.

Notes

1. CAMS file Pf4, Zonguldak, informant, Yiannis Kaptanidis; interviewer, Christos Samouilidis, 19/2/1963.
2. Thobie (1977), 409–410.
3. At this juncture, I do not know if the Ereğli Company had undersea mines but assume this must be the case.
4. Dix (1977), 8.
5. Articles 46–47 sought to regulate and record the removal of pillars. For room-and-pillar methods in the 1920s, see Kahveci (1997), 124, quoting Yersel (1989). See Kahveci (1997), 131, for an interview with a worker who used both drift and room-and-pillar methods during his years of labor from 1934 to 1969. Therein the worker asserts that the long-wall system came into use only later on.
6. Dix (1977), 5–6.
7. Winkler (1961), 30–31.
8. Here I am following the argument of Kahveci (1997).
9. Kahveci (1997), 33–35, sometimes quoting Nichols and Kahveci (1995).
10. Spratt (1877), 529.
11. Cuinet (1895), 421–423.
12. Naim (1934), 100–101, as quoted and translated by Kahveci (1997), 84.
13. Credit Lyonnais, Series G2 A4.77.83. Affaires industrielles 1876–1891. Extrait 19–23. Rapport sur les Mines d' Heraclée, September 1876. Basket capacities are far less than as noted in chapter 3.
14. Credit Lyonnais, Series G2 A4.77.83.
15. Quataert (1983), 56–57.
16. Etingü (1976), 56.
17. Etingü (1976), 56–57.
18. CAMS file Pf3, Ereğli, informant, Ioakeim Yailaoglou; interviewer, Babis Nikiforidis, 12/3/1963.
19. CAMS file Pf5, Kozlu, informant, Dimitris Moisiadis; interviewer, Babis Nikiforidis, 21/4/1963.
20. Quataert (1983), 66. In 1880, a group of French investors unsuccessfully bid for a mining concession at Ereğli and in their proposal agreed to provide housing for the workers, suggesting that the 1867 rules were being enforced to some degree. Kahveci (1997), 95.
21. ED 10, 63, 30 Avril 1329/13 May 1913 and 183, 18 Mayıs 1329/31 May 1913.
22. Church (1986), 277–279.
23. İmer (1944), 50, might be the source for Çatma (1998), 108.
24. Slightly modified translation from Quataert and Duman (2001), 157–158.
25. Quataert and Duman (2001), 158.
26. Çıladır (1977), 125, argues that the 1867 and the 1920–1921 laws were impressive only on paper and had little impact on everyday life.
27. Articles 28, 29, and 32.
28. Quataert and Duman (2001), 157.
29. Kahveci (1997), 118, citing interviews in Çıladır (1977), 128–129.
30. Çıladır (1977), 132.
31. Church (1986), 254–255, table 3.9.
32. Çıladır (1977), 128–129. Another worker, Izzet Akman, who started in 1923 in the mines of Italian entrepreneurs at Kandilli, recalled bringing provisions in a bag as he began his work.
33. İmer (1944), 45.
34. CAMS file Pf4, Zonguldak, informant, Yiannis Kaptanidis; interviewer, Christos Samouilidis, 19/2/1963. See quotation in chapter 3.

35. CAMS file Pf5, Kozlu, informant, Dimitris Moisiadis; interviewer, Babis Nikiforidis, 25/4/1963.
36. İmer (1944), 45.
37. İmer (1944), 45–46.
38. Quataert and Duman (2001), 159. Also Çıladır (1977), 61, who may be depending on the memoir of Ethem Çavuş as a source.
39. CAMS file Pf4, Zonguldak, informant, Evangelos Paslidis; interviewer, Babis Nikiforidis, 6/5/1963.
40. Çıladır (1977), 128–129.
41. ED 4, 245, 18 tl 1294/30 October 1878.
42. Derickson (1998), 26.
43. Seltzer (1985), 24 and 29; also Derickson (1998), 26.
44. ED 10, 14–15, 23 Avril 1329/6 May 1913, referring back to 15 kl 1327 correspondence. When the emergent Turkish Republic passed its new labor law for the Zonguldak coalfield, it stipulated eighteen years as the minimum age for underground work. See Kahveci (1997), 113ff.
45. ED 16, 17 tl 1329/30 October 1913.
46. ED 16, Ottoman, 211, 7 kl 1329/20 December 1913.
47. In outlining his task to prepare an overall plan for the mines, one engineer commented on his employment of a worker who was required to present a worker's identity card (*carnet d'ouvriers*) so that he could write down the days which the worker worked. ED 16, 183, 11 Novembre 1329/24 November 1913. This is the only mention that has come to my attention of a practice that likely was common among the free-labor force.
48. Güran (1995), 53. It is not certain that the coalfield medical facilities noted in chapter 8 were included in this enumeration.
49. *Bolu vs 1334*, 285, and Etingü (1976), 59.
50. Yıldırım (1985), 1328–1329.
51. Correspondence with Erol Kahveci, 11 January 2004.

5

Ties That Bind
Village-Mine Relations

Introduction

A fascinating and increasingly thick web of relations bound together villages and mines in the Zonguldak coalfield. The central state, in fits and starts, imposed a relationship of obligation on the villages, requiring them to serve the labor needs of mines that soon numbered 100. Certain villages furnished the workers while others sent the food and supplies. Toward the end of the century some clear patterns had emerged, as several hundred villages and a handful of town quarters routinely sent boys and men to work the mines. Most villages furnished one particular kind of labor, and to only one mine. There were many exceptions, however, and some villages supplied several kinds of workers to a number of mines.

A village-mine nexus came to interlace the coalfield, binding villager-workers to the worksite in ties of obligation and indebtedness. As workers worked, flows of actual or promised payments bound the fate of the mine to that of the villages providing labor to it. When a mine failed to meet its financial obligations, villagers went unpaid, usually without recourse. Although workers not infrequently appealed to local courts for justice, arrears in wages nonetheless characterized the coalfield. When payments from operators actually did arrive, the amounts that workers pocketed often were but a fraction of their gross earnings since operators deducted sums for the taxes the workers owed and bread they had eaten while at work.

Besides the wages they paid, other monies from operators flowed into the local economy. Mines came to play an important role in supporting local charitable activities and were especially active in financing religious observances at key periods in the sacral calendar. Through these modest donations, the place

---

Notes for this chapter begin on page 123.

of religion in the social and cultural life of mining communities becomes visible on the historical stage.

Village headmen and labor bosses maintained, presided over, and profited from the village-mine nexus. Empowered by their access to the military forces of the state, they sent the workers, pursued shirkers and deserters, and in exchange received wages and political power. But the central state, aware of the dangers of tipping the scales too far in favor of the headmen and bosses, sought to reduce their powers later in the century—a chapter in the larger, continuous struggle between central and local authority. Labor bosses and village headmen nonetheless remained key figures in the lives of villager-workers.

The Origins of the Villager-Miner

Before the inauguration of coal mining, local village life presumably more or less resembled that elsewhere in the empire. As seen, the region was not well endowed agriculturally, and villagers eked out their living from subsistence farming and, frequently, work in the timber and shipping industries. Also, for centuries the Black Sea region had exported significant numbers of men to the capital. While there is no concrete information about chain migrations before the onset of mining, they likely were present in some of the local villages that later provided mine labor.

At the end of the Ottoman era, after just seventy years of coal work, mining villages were locked into patterns of survival unusual in both the empire and the world at large. Boys and men trekked great and small distances across mountains and hills, moving between village (or town) and mine in semi-monthly waves. On the road, they routinely met hardships, even death. Only sometimes did they actually receive the wages earned at the mines, but these sums certainly transformed relationships among villagers and among family members. The record trail, however, is too faint to allow for reconstructions of daily life.

As commercial exploitation of coal began in the years before 1850, villagers at first were able to avoid mine labor thanks to their lack of experience and their refusal to accept the work. Gradually, however, this kind of resistance faded as villagers observed the miners brought from outside and saw the cash incomes that mine work provided. From them they acquired new skills previously unknown in the region. Meanwhile, as villager willingness to participate in mining was increasing of its own accord, the state launched its coercive apparatus, the 1867 regulations that created the compulsory labor categories and the rotational labor system.

The carrot-stick combination began molding a rotational compulsory work force in patterns that would become well entrenched (and more visible) in subsequent decades of the nineteenth century and, indeed, persist to the present day.[1] By the 1870s, particular villages were already providing different types of laborers—mine support makers, or animal transporters, or basket carriers, or hewers. In April 1878, for example, the hamlet of Başir provided both basket carriers and hewers for the mine of Murad Şiiyan in the Ereğli district.² Similarly, this hamlet (which still was sending workers to the mines during World War II) provided labor for the mine of Kireneli Hasan Agha in Kozlu.³ At that time, several different villages would send workers to the same mine. Thus, in 1877 the Toma Müdiye mine in the Kozlu locale, in 1877, drew basket carriers from four different hamlets near Devrek (two of these appear in the compulsory labor rosters during World War II).⁴ In sum, during these early years we can observe patterns, such as the presence in one mine of workers from different villages, that continued into the 1890s—indeed, to the 1990s.⁵

During the 1870s, the emerging compulsory labor system erected in the 1867 regulations was still subject to considerable tinkering. In 1874, seeking to solve labor recruitment difficulties that had brought mine operations to a halt, the mine superintendent proposed a solution that violated the regulations passed just seven years before. Ignoring the restriction of recruitment to the fourteen administrative units, he suggested summoning workers from Trabzon province, with free passage on a government vessel.⁶ In another instance of experimentation with the emerging system, consider the example of the villages around Alacaağzı that had been providing workers for some mines at Kozlu. In January 1879, the superintendent noted that villagers near the Kozlu mines were traveling to work at Alacaağzı mines while Alacaağzı workers were working at Kozlu mines. Not illogically, he proposed switching villages and assigning them to the closer mines.⁷ In the same month, he suggested that it become a general practice to ignore assignments by shifting surplus workers from one area to mines with labor shortages.⁸

Several other examples of experimentation concern certain tax privileges that the compulsory force enjoyed during the 1870s. In 1879, for example, residents of the Bartın and Ereğli districts who worked in the mines were exempted from a special per capita tax levied to help the imperial treasury. Those who were not mine workers had to pay the tax and also were obliged to provision the mine workers.⁹ Also, several villages in Bartın district had been under the jurisdiction of a tax farmer but had been agitating for an escape from his oppression. In 1878, their headmen and councils of elders petitioned for a second time, on this occasion successfully, for the right to pay their taxes directly to state authorities. The petitioners argued they already were burdened with the duty of providing compulsory mine labor, so the double burden of a tax farmer was unfair. The mine superintendent concurred and ordered district authorities to permit the shift.¹⁰ In a third case of tax privilege, headmen in the district informed the Ereğli district official that they no could longer ask workers to pay a certain tax (*iane bedeli*) in cash because the workers were overwhelmed by debts. Workers had been receiving only promissory notes for their labors and had turned these over, at deeply discounted rates, to merchants and moneylenders. They were fleeing to escape their obligations to state and private creditors. If the state, the headmen asserted, insisted on cash payments for the tax, the remaining villager-workers would resort still further to moneylenders, flights would escalate, and coal production would suffer still further.[11]

The Compulsory Labor System in Action: A Snapshot from the 1870s

When the state assigned villages the task of providing workers for the mines, it placed these communities in a precarious position.[12] Overall, the mine districts were agriculturally poor and offered a fragile basis for subsistence. The fifteen days per month that villagers spent away obviously made it more difficult for the village unit to produce sufficient food for the subsistence of the entire collective. The compulsory labor system effectively reduced the amount of available male village labor for agriculture by a full one-half and that of the entire village by perhaps one-quarter. In theory, a village could reallocate the burdens to fulfill agricultural tasks but this meant restructuring intra-village relations. In certain cases, moreover, workers came from villages where grain was scarce and prohibitively expensive to buy. (Some villages reportedly abandoned agriculture altogether in favor of full-time mining, although this was very unusual.) In fact, many workers came to the mines expecting to be able to buy cheaper bread there.[13] On the whole, given the high social costs and great difficulty of restructuring village life around the task of feeding co-villagers engaged in mine work, the custom of workers bringing their own food along with them to the mines likely was less common in the 1870s than it would become later on.

During the 1870s, workers who did not bring their own supplies depended on at least two sources for the food that sustained them at the mines. First, mine operators of their own accord took the initiative, purchasing food and supplies from mine district villages that were not providing compulsory labor. Such provisioning was not a choice but an obligation for these villages. In such instances, local cultivators in principle were to obtain reimbursement.[14]

Second, the mine administration sought to organize a system for provisioning workers with the food and supplies they required while at mine labor. It argued that villagers assigned to mine work needed and were entitled to such assistance. Provisions flowed to the mines in the form of wheat, maize, barley, straw, candles, oil, and gunpowder.[15] This provisioning system depended, in the first instance, on local sources. The supplies sometimes derived from taxes in kind that local producers paid. Typically, a tithe was collected in kind in the Ottoman Empire at this time, and indeed, throughout the final Ottoman century. Cereals collected in kind to pay the cultivator's tithe obligation provisioned mine workers and animals through several different fiscal devices. In one case, proceeds from selling part of the tithe from the Bolu area provided monies for the provisioning of workers.[16] Sometimes, in the district of Ereğli, cultivators deposited their barley tithe in kind in warehouses of the mine administration.[17] The mine superintendent also purchased tithes in kind from certain areas adjacent to the mine districts, for the provisioning of animals and workers. For example, in November 1877, Kastamonu province sent to the coalfield some 2,600 *kiles* from its general barley tithe, while the Bolu administrator sent an additional 2,000 *kiles* from Akşehir, a small port area southwest of Ereğli with a fertile plain behind it.[18]

When supplies from the mine districts were inadequate, officials were required to purchase goods from any quarter. During the crisis years of the 1870s, local sources of grain—collected from the mining and adjacent districts—frequently proved insufficient. And so, in October 1878, barley was requisitioned from Istanbul, to supplement the barley tithes from Bartın and Ereğli districts that were already being furnished to the mines.[19] More generally, not only the capital city but also most of the Black Sea littoral—as far east as Trabzon—played a role in supplying the mines during the 1870s. In the provisioning procedures described here, the state organized the flow of supplies but the workers, in the end, paid for them. According to the regulations of 1867, these provisions were to be debited against the account of the mine operators. When operators made coal deliveries, the provisioning debts were deducted against the amount owed by the government. In turn, the mine operator, in the ledger books that each mine maintained, had noted not only the names, villages, and other vital statistics of workers, but also the monetary value of provisions each one had received from the mine operator. At the end of the pay period, this "bread money" and other sums were totaled and deducted from the wages paid (also see below).

Authority over the compulsory and rotational labor system filtered down from the mine superintendent and his staff, who oversaw operations in the entire coalfield via a chain of command, to district officials[20] and finally to hamlet or village officials on the spot. All these links were centrally appointed officials. Members of the first two links in the chain—the superintendent and the district officials—derived their authority solely from the fiat of the capital city, and usually hailed from outside the area. The hamlet/village headmen and councils of elders, however, were different, since their appointments by the central state rested on the local authority and prestige they had already possessed prior to their occupancy of the position. The sources of their authority and prestige surely varied: some were wealthier members of the community, others descended from locally prestigious families without a financial base. In the larger Ottoman world, headmen already possessed considerable responsibilities and authority. Charged with maintaining law and order, they channeled state orders to the village and were accountable for the behavior of the community. For example, when fights broke out among villagers, the participants were called to the house of the headman to explain themselves.[21]

The compulsory labor system, however, invested the headmen with a chilling amount of additional authority over their fellow villagers.[22] Overall, headmen supervised the flow of materials and manpower and were held accountable for shortfalls. Thus, in some villages they oversaw preparation and transport of the mine supports or delivery of the transport animals.[23] In other communities, they sent the basket carriers in a timely manner.[24] In addition, ledgers of these flows of supplies and labor passed through the headmen. After mine operators had recorded the gross and net amounts owed to the various basket carriers and mine support workers, "trustworthy basket carriers" delivered copies to the headmen.[25]

The superintendent's office determined how many workers were needed for each particular mine and accordingly informed the district official.[26] These district officials in turn determined the villages from which the workers would be recruited and the numbers of each particular kind of worker that each village would provide.[27] The headmen enforced the district officials' orders and organized the villagers for the work.[28] In one example, the headman arranged for certain quantities of mine supports. In another instance, an important mine in Zonguldak was in danger of flooding and collapsing during the winter season 1877 with the Russian war still raging and the coal desperately needed. To prevent this, the superintendent, via the district official, sent headmen "special instructions" to assure sufficient labor supplies.[29] More generally, the choice concerning who went to mine work and who did not rested in the hands of the headmen. Each village headman was responsible for organizing a steady flow of labor, arranged into two shifts per month, for all categories of workers except the hewers. These skilled, valuable, and scarce workers were left free to negotiate directly with the mine operators. All those eligible for mine work were expected to assemble, together with their relatives, at specified inspection sites. At one time during the 1870s, there were collective inspection sites for a number of hamlets. After the inspection, workers were ordered to return to their home village, report to the village council, and only then proceed to the mines. Assembling at such collective sites soon was abandoned in favor of inspection at the specific home village or hamlet. This decision may well have derived from an August 1878 assembly of village headmen and councils of elders held in the town of Bartın under the leadership of the district official. There, the assembled leaders had discussed sending the selected workers directly to the mines without collecting them together, a measure the superintendent thought would make it easier to supervise the headmen, that is, to watch the watchers.[30]

Here is Ethem Çavuş's account, likely dating from the 1880s–1890s, of the inspection and selection of basket carriers.

> I was fourteen when I came to the mines. At that time there were the Dilaver Pasha regulations. The mines under the operation of the navy were worked by workers who were recruited just like Janissaries. The village headman would assemble the kids and organize wrestling matches. Then he would choose the kids who were able to carry 30 okka baskets loaded with black stones on their back and put them on pay lists. At the beginning of each month he would order; 'ok, you, go to mine X'.

You had to go. Otherwise, a navy sergeant would come with two armed gendarmes and take you to the mines.[31]

More officially, those selected were to report to the village council of elders and prepare to leave for mine work. District officials, through village headmen and councils of elders, compiled detailed register books. These contained the names and surnames, by occupation, of all the workers assigned to a particular mine, and each worker's specific job. (In 1892, a new law specified that patronymics [künye] be included.)[32] The headmen and elders also completed the identity papers sent by the mine superintendent and forwarded by the district official. In the 1870s, when 6,000 persons were eligible for compulsory labor, the superintendent placed a request for 5,100 copies of the identity paper forms that workers were required to submit.[33] Village authorities then forwarded the register books, together with the identity papers (ilmühaber), either to their immediate superiors at the district level or directly to the mine superintendent.[34] On the appropriate date (and likely led by their foreman) the workers began their walk to the mines. Their fifteen-day shift included three days' travel time, so we must assume that some workers walked approximately that long in transit (see below). On arrival, their fellow villagers could leave off working at the mine site and begin their trek back home. No shift was allowed to leave the workplace until its replacement shift arrived from the same village.

In the meantime, district officials or the superintendent forwarded the register books to the official of the district in which the mine was located. For their part, these officials in the mine locale, with the assistance of the mine operator, noted the presence or absence of the listed workers, arranged by district and by particular occupation for each particular mine. They wrote down the names of those who had proper excuses for not leaving their villages. They also recorded the length of improper absences as well as the names of those who had never arrived in the first place. Moreover, in a policy revealing a principle of collective responsibility, they inscribed the names of the friends of illicit absentees. After the mine operators provided this information,[35] locale officials forwarded copies of the register both to the mine superintendent and to officials in the workers' home districts.[36] Mine operators must have been doing the actual recording of those present and absent and certainly were maintaining the journals noting the wages due to the various types of workers.[37]

When material supplies faltered, the enforcement system responded, sometimes quickly, sometimes not. Hence, when refugees from Balkan areas ceded by the empire began cutting firewood in forests reserved for mine supports, the headmen and local officials went out to stop them.[38] Workers who failed to fulfill their labor obligations soon encountered the formidable apparatus sent into motion against them. Thus, for instance, the Ereğli district official ordered the local headman to make sure that the local boatmen (sandalcı taifesi) provide support transport and stop their delaying tactics.[39] In another case, when ten workers from Karaca Viran hamlet assigned to the Toma and Luka mine went into hiding, the superintendent ordered the Devrek director to send labor bosses and a sub-district committee to the hamlet.[40] The superintendent also ordered officials from Ereğli, Bartın, and Devrek to curb absenteeism. Each official was to form a committee of military officers, civil officials, and others, who in turn organized the officials of their respective districts. Village headmen and councils of elders then were to take measures to fill in the manpower gaps and send to the mine administration the identity papers of the workers and transporters being sent to the mines.[41] Tellingly, it was the village headmen who were charged with organizing and carrying out punishments.[42]

Wage payments to workers during the 1870s followed patterns commonly present in the 1890s as well. In this earlier era, some workers were in a direct wage relationship with their employer, the mine operator. For example, in March 1879 mine operator Laz Hasan personally paid his individual workers in cash and provided each with a sealed document (*ilam*) attesting to the payment.[43] But, more commonly at this time, operators paid their workers with promissory notes.

During these early years of compulsory labor, the pay system functioned in ways that gave village headmen considerable power over the workers of their villages. Wages usually reached the workers in a roundabout manner, one that harmed workers and bolstered headmen's authority. First, the mine superintendent inspected the coal being stored by a mine operator, estimated its amount, and paid the operator for the coal that had been delivered. The operator received payment—usually and perhaps almost always during this early period—in the form of promissory notes, not cash. (As we will see, promissory notes also were a regular feature of mine life in the 1890s.) The operator first paid off his operating expenses. Then, before wages were paid, he deducted the debts owed to him by individual workers—for example, for bread, oil, flour, and other provisions that he (or others) had provided. Such patterns of indebtedness also remained common in later decades. Workers in the 1870s also paid for the gunpowder they used in blasting. In later years, they received allotments of gunpowder and oil for their lamps.[44]

Mine operators, while powerful figures in the lives of the miners, like them were caught in the vise of the state's financial distress. Repeatedly the state reneged on its debts or issued near-worthless paper. Because of this, the operators, themselves often near bankruptcy, issued their own devalued paper. And sometimes they cheated the workers altogether. In June 1878, the operator Hacı Omer Bey Zade Ahmed kept the money due to the workers of several villages. In another case, mine operator Yusuf at Kozlu maintained false pay accounts for workers in his mine who had been recruited from Senekir hamlet in the Alacaağzı locale. For some, he recorded a four, five or six-day work period, when in fact they had labored for the full twelve-day shift. The mine superintendent discovered the abuses and ordered the workers to appear before an investigative commission.[45]

Moreover, in the 1870s at least, the operators did not pay whatever balance they owed to the workers personally. Instead, operators turned over the total sum to the village headmen, either in the form of cash or promissory notes, to be paid to workers in a particular village. After the operators obtained a receipt from the headmen, they submitted it to the mine administration. The headmen in turn were to pay the workers according to the sums recorded in the register books.[46]

Workers thus were fixed at the bottom of a hierarchical chain that stretched all the way to Istanbul. Of more daily concern to them were the actions of those immediately above them, including the headmen, their home district officials, officials of the mine locale, the mine operator, and the superintendent of mines. Sometimes, the weakness of the workers' position subjected them to double jeopardy. Take, for example, the case of nineteen animal transporters from Alaplı who, in 1878, had committed some unspecified crime and as punishment had been ordered to work the mines with their animals. Instead, however, they had been put to work cutting wood for the personal profit of a regional merchant. In evaluating the case, the mine superintendent knew that the workers had labored to serve their sentences and had documentation to prove it. Yet, even as he acknowledged that his actions were unfair, he ordered them to undergo their prescribed punishment of work in the mines.[47]

The mistreatment of workers at officials' hands could be very brutal, as a later example vividly illustrates. In the summer of 1894, accumulations of methane gas prompted workers to abandon several mines and flee to their home villages. The mine superintendent at the time, Hasan Pasha, sent soldiers to the villages; they destroyed the homes of the workers who had fled and took them prisoner.[48]

Headmen possessed considerable police authority to force villager-workers into or back into the mines. Villagers, as we shall see, often refused to show up for work at all. Indeed, as one report put it in November 1877, when summoned to mine labor the villagers "naturally" fled. Others went off as scheduled to the mines but then returned home before completing, or perhaps even beginning, their work shifts. During the holidays, many workers left work to be with their families, official orders to remain notwithstanding. In such cases, the headmen were charged with finding and returning the workers to the mines. For example, in October 1877, the mine superintendent ordered the Ereğli district official to cooperate with the headman of Bulçuk hamlet to locate a mine deserter, one Bekrioğlu Ahmed.[49] In these cases, the headman summoned the friends of the deserter or absentee. The headman, recording their names in a register book, interrogated friends about the whereabouts of the missing. Moreover, the headman was empowered to inflict punishments, publicly in the village square, as deemed necessary.

The headmen's exercise of power in determining those who entered mine service sometimes seems quite cruel. For example, in February 1879, two sons of Ismail Ustaoğlu in Topal hamlet (of Ereğli district) were already laboring as transporters at the mines, while a third son was serving in the military. Nonetheless, the headman ordered the fourth brother, Hüseyin, into mine work. In this case the family successfully appealed, obtaining a special dispensation since taking the fourth son would interrupt the family's ability to farm and perform household chores.[50] On one occasion, when the "impiety" of the headman interfered with the flow of materials, he was removed.[51] But otherwise the records imply general support for headmen and their activities.

The Labor System during the 1890s

The historian's instruments for examining village-mine relations during the 1890s[52] are considerably different from those used for the 1870s. In the earlier period, they comprised a thick set of narrative reports from the superintendent's office. For the mid 1890s, however, the instrument is an accountant's ledger. On hundreds of pages and in many thousands of entries, therein accountants inscribed, respectively on the right and left sides of the page, both the credit (*matlubat*) and the debit sums (*tahsilat*) for every individual mine in the coalfield. The accountants organized the ledger by each of the six coal locales. Within each locale, the records of the individual mines were presented in rough numerical order.[53]

Nominally there were 122 mines in the coalfield, but only 97 actually were functioning during the mid 1890s, some at the most minimal level.[54] About one-third of all active mines were in the Kozlu locale while mines in the locales of Zonguldak, Kilimli, and Alacaağzı accounted for most of the balance. (Three mines were operating at Çatalağzı and Amasra at the eastern end of the coalfield.) Altogether, 231 named villages and five town quarters[55] in the coalfield provided labor at or in these mines—as hewers, basket carriers or general unskilled laborers, transporters, mine support makers, and boat launchers.[56]

Usually in a painstaking hand, accountants inscribed the sums that the mines owed and paid out to meet their various obligations. Alas, these records are an imperfect device for studying lives of labor, for they ultimately fail to provide a guide for re-creating the sociological reality of the miners' universe. Too often, as will be seen, the abundant statistics employ categories presenting the conceptual world of the accountants rather than the actuality of workers' lives. All too frequently, that is, they offer a world of record-makers, not workers. And yet, as will be shown, they provide otherwise unobtainable insights into workers' lives. Notably, they demonstrate the continued functioning of the compulsory labor system, set up a quarter-century before, during the decade of the 1890s.

Altogether, during about 1894 to 1895, the mines paid out a total of some 2.7 million krs for labor. These payments for mine labor fall into five different categories that collectively reveal the lives of workers and the connections between mines and villages (see table 5.1).

In the first category are the monthly lump sum payments to the particular village, hamlet, or town quarter for the different kinds of labor services its residents

Table 5.1 Mine Operators' Debts Incurred for Labor, 1894–1895 (in krs)

1. To all named villages	570,058
2. For the taxes of named villages	116,508
3. For the "bread money" of unnamed villages	673,655
4. For the "coal dug" by unnamed persons/villages	1,270,366
5. Owed to named individuals	48,904
Total	2,679,491

Note: Analysis is based on 231 named villages and three named quarters. It does not include the unnamed villages, for example, those receiving "bread money." Named quarters received 2,800 krs in direct payments and 2,826 krs in taxes. There were 1,312 entries; among these, 793 entries noted village names and 519 entries did not.
Source: KU 64.

provided. A few villages appear just once. For example, an entry in June 1895 is the only indication that the village of Acarlar provided any compulsory labor at all, when accountants noted a payment of 200 krs to basket carriers of that community. Most villages appear in the ledgers at least 3 or 4 times, and many—such as Tabaklar village—are noted on 10 to 15 occasions. Altogether, 231 different villages received 570,058 krs in lump sums from the various mine operators.

Other entries, forming the second category, note the amounts that mine operators paid for the taxes of villages and of individuals. Noted simply as "taxes" (*vergi*), this term likely refers to the various taxes levied by the Ottoman state rather than to any one specific impost. These may have included the tithe, a proportional (about 10 to 12.6 percent) tax on agricultural produce, usually collected in kind almost everywhere in the empire. There also was the animal tax, monetary levies per head of livestock. And finally, the term *vergi* also encompasses real estate taxes, collected proportionally, in cash, on the value of a person's real estate, in this case the villager's home as well as the land on which it stood and any surrounding gardens.[57]

In the accountants' reports of 1894 and 1895, mine operators made *vergi* payments to more than forty different villages, for a total of 116,508 krs, or about 4 percent of total labor payments. Mines rarely paid the taxes of individuals, recording only four different persons, at a sum total of less than 1,000 krs. For example, Kozlu #271 mine paid a rather hefty sum of 325 krs for the taxes of a hewer, one Buzoğlu Hüseyin. On another occasion, the owner of Kozlu #356 mine, Hasan Efendi, used 156 krs of his mine's revenues to pay his own taxes.

Significantly, operators usually used promissory notes to take care of their obligations. Thus, four separate bills of exchange between May 1894 and January 1895 paid out sums for the taxes of Sivriler village: the important Kozlu #5 mine issued three bills in the name of that village while another mine issued a fourth on behalf of the people of Sivriler.[58] Two mines at Kozlu issued bills of exchange to pay for the taxes of Kargarlar village,[59] while Alacaağzı #278 mine issued two different bills of exchange, exactly one year apart, for the taxes of Şamlar village. On another occasion, this same mine issued a single bill of exchange for the taxes of three different villages—Şamlar, Ramazanlı, and Kızılca Pınar.[60]

For decades local elites used these promissory notes to control and exploit village and town workers. Ethem Çavuş testified that, in his day, about the time of these ledgers, villagers were working in mines to pay off the tax debts they owed. The mine superintendent, Grammar Hasan Pasha, sent bills of exchange noting the wages earned to the district treasurer for credit against taxes owed. Thus, the money passed directly into the treasurer's hands and was never in the workers' pockets. His need to pay taxes, Ethem Çavuş reported, drove him back to a mine of the Giurgiu Company, even after a terrifying accident had killed sixty-seven workers. Also, he claims that bills of exchange from the mines often were used to pay for the taxes of the headmen and their cronies.[61]

The continuing use of promissory notes for tax payments from the 1870s to the 1890s powerfully marks the lack of capital plaguing the minefield throughout the Ottoman era, including the period well after the years being discussed here. The practice further suggests the complexity of the financial relationships in which state and capital—the local government and mine operators—worked together to control labor, the villagers. It affirms Ethem Çavuş's testimony that the taxes of mining villages collectively were levied on and paid by villages and town quarters. And they point to a form of state-organized debt peonage.

Literally hundreds of entries recorded the payment of sums, often in relatively large amounts, for a third category called "bread money" (*nan bahası*). About two-thirds (sixty-one) of the mines operating during these years made bread money payments, for a total of 673,655 krs. In no instance is any village, person, or other entity named as recipient of the monies. The payments are simply "bread money," for which no persons or groups is indicated.

At some mining locations elsewhere in the empire, the government compensated compulsory mine workers with both a cash wage and food rations and shelter. On some of these occasions, it paid a money equivalent for the food rations.[62] In the Zonguldak coalfield, Ethem Çavuş spoke of occasionally receiving bread as compensation. He related that sometimes, when the mine paymaster was late, he and co-workers waited for days at the mine site for his arrival. On such occasions, he said, they worked and were paid a loaf of corn bread for a day's labor.[63]

The key to the "bread money" puzzle, however, lies elsewhere. The 1867 regulations required the mine operator to record the daily wages owed to a worker, as well as the "bread monies and other sums they received."[64] During the 1870s, as seen, mine operators were making deductions from workers' wages for the bread and other provisions they themselves or merchants had provided. A wage ledger dated 1921—that records the individual names and wage information for many hundreds of workers—clearly illustrates this practice, demonstrating the impact of the 1867 regulations more than a half-century later.[65] In the ledger, against the name of each worker are the wages earned and also entries for *ekmek bedeli*, a more modern Ottoman Turkish rendering of *nan bahası*. Each individual worker's net wage was calculated by deducting the amount of *ekmek bedeli* from the gross wage.[66] The "bread money" of the mid 1890s thus represents the value of the bread provided to workers, sums deducted from their gross wages before payday.[67] In total, as table 5.1 shows, about one-quarter of all wages paid to workers during the mid 1890s bought the bread that kept them alive while at the mines.

Accountants also noted payments of 1.2 million krs, 44 percent of the total paid for labor for "the balance owed for the coal dug" (*kömür esmanına mahsuben*) a fourth category that is puzzling at first glance. After all, how can mine operators, who are in the business of extracting coal, be in the position of owing money for coal? As in the case of the "bread money" entries, there is no named village, person, or worker group recipient. All monies paid are anonymous entries, "the balance owed for the coal dug." The answer lies with the hewers, in their capacity as workers free to labor at mines of their choosing in exchange for negotiated wages. Mine operators owed these sums for the coal that hewers, quite literally, dug out of the ground. The 1.2 million krs represents the net amount, the balance that mine operators owed to hewers. From the gross salaries, operators deducted expenses incurred by the hewers, for example, for bread, or perhaps gunpowder and other supplies.[68] Artın Karamanyan, who operated the important Alacaağzı #131 mine, paid out the largest single sum for this purpose, about 157,000 krs. Many payments were quite small; for example, Reza Efendi and Hüseyin Agha, the operators of the #272 mine at Alacaağzı, paid out just 30 krs for this purpose.

Hewers saw little of the money they earned, even these net amounts. Cash payments (*nakden*) of wages were relatively unusual, accounting for only one-third of all payments for the coal dug. Mine operators paid two-fifths of their total obligations to the hewers in promissory notes (*havaleten*). They recorded another one-quarter on the books to be credited (*mahsuben*) against debts owed by the hewers to other parties, such as the state for taxes due.[69] No wonder, then, that the workers excitedly responded to the promise of cash wages at the Giurgiu mine, which spurred 2,000 workers to show up for 400 jobs.[70]

Finally, accountants reported a fifth category of sums, paid to fewer than fifty individual, named, workers. They represent just a tiny fraction (2 percent) of mine operators' payments to labor, a mere 48,904 krs. Most often, foremen or hewers received such individual attention, but sometimes so did basket carriers and hard rock miners. Thus, in September 1895, the Alacaağzı #340 mine paid 120 krs to the hewer Kor Ahmed while in January 1895, the Alacaağzı #21 mine paid 200 krs to the basket carrier Hasan, a rather hefty sum for the latter, representing the pay for several shifts of work.

The Accountants' World of Workers

As we have seen, individual workers are scarcely present in the accountants' version of the mining world. Reluctant to individuate in their record keeping, the clerks recorded more than 98 percent of all labor payments as made either to collectives or to anonymous parties.

And yet, as the following testimony from Ethem Çavuş makes starkly clear, mine-village relations hardly were impersonal or anonymous. Once, after waiting eight days for the paymaster and being paid in corn bread during this interval, he relates, payday arrived.

> Finally we were to get our money. Everything was prepared. The clerk Mehdi Efendi affirmed this. The expected signs of payday began to be visible. First, the village aghas came from the distant villages and tied their horses in the yard. The tax collector took his position opposite the pay window. Peddlers, meatball [*köfte*] sellers, spinach-corn pastry sellers, all were in front of the mine. Finally the accountant of the mine opened the window to make payments. And he began to ask;
>
> – 'What is your name?
> – Ercep.
> – Here, one, two ... etc.
> – Efendi, this money is short.
> – Go away, it should be right.
> – Boss, please, my village is far from here. Give exactly what I earned, then I will go.
> – I said leave. Is there nobody out there to take this guy away.'
>
> Raise your objections if you can and tell him that the money is short because he had embezzled it.
>
> After being paid along with being cursed and pushed around we had to pay the aghas our debts that had accumulated because of the seed and animals we bought from them. Then we would be able to take a deep breath.
>
> Many times we were left with no money after paying our debts and could not go to the village, leave aside eating a morsel of meatballs or spinach-corn pastry. I do not know why, either because we were young or we were stupid, we did not feel too sad about all these things. We joked around while making plans about the money we would be earning during the second part of the twelve-day rotation.[71]

In contrast to this world of personal struggle and conflict, the books of the accountants portrayed a collectivizing universe where individual workers are nearly invisible. These accountants only reluctantly individualized the record-keeping mechanisms and instead emphasized collective entities and collective identities. In their universe, villages and labor classifications (*amele, kiracı*, etc.) were present but scarcely any individual villagers or workers. The clerks were engaging in accounting practices drawn from an earlier age when the state categorized in groups and collectives at the expense of the individual. In these ledgers from the mid 1890s, the state scarcely considered individual labor as a category organizing production. Therein we do not find capitalism reproducing itself in its own fragmented, individualized image but instead we find conceptual collectives and anonymities.

Yet, at the same moment, in other parts of the mining bureaucracy, practices contrary to anonymity and collective identity were becoming evident (see chapters 7 and 8). At the very time these accounting ledgers were being prepared in their anonymity, mining engineers' accident reports offered increasing details about the person of the accident victim or witness and gave mounting attention to the notion of responsibility for the event. These safety records reproduce the logic of the individual, a person responsible for actions taken. Thus, one body of mining documents, the accountants' records, offers a vision of the workers' world as anonymous and collective, while another, the reports of safety inspectors, presents another universe, inhabited by identified individuals. Also, recall the strikingly different character of the 1921 ledger and its many hundreds of workers' names, together with their occupations and places of residence. Like the accident reports, these ledgers in their individualism starkly contrast with the account books and demonstrate the complexity of labor relations in the coal basin.

While the clerks' world of collective and anonymous categories of labor groups did not reflect workaday life, it was, in a certain sense, a real world. The workers, in their everyday lives, did need to confront and interact with the categories constructed by these bookkeepers of the state. They had to be concerned with whether or not they personally would actually receive payment for the coal cut, or credit for the taxes paid on their behalf. And, they were in fact inhabitants of the village in whose name the payments for labor were recorded. The bread payments were real sums that affected the pay they could take back to the village. Workers thus were compelled to inhabit the universe of the accountants.

The Mines in the Early 1890s

Notwithstanding their disappointing vagueness and lack of personal and geographic specificity, the account books of the 1890s[72] provide further, indispensable, insights into the world of the mines and villager-workers. They reveal that, although ninety-seven mines were open for business, nearly all were quite small-scale, badly capitalized operations. Take, for example, the Kasap Tarlası mine in Kozlu as representative of a very small-scale operation. Kasap Ismail Agha of the Kasapoğulları family had moved from Ereğli to Kozlu in around 1874 to provide meat to the maritime soldiers stationed at Kozlu. He bought some brush-covered land near the shore, 2 km northeast of the town, cleared it, and planted fields and gardens—hence the name *kasap tarlası*, the field of the butcher. While busy in his fields, Kasap Ismail Agha encountered coal, obtained a concession, and in around 1892 began working his mine. Most of the coal, however, ended up as coal dust, without market value. Forced to increase his capital to maintain production, he transferred one-third of the mine to his brother-in-law in Ereğli and in this way struggled along in the coal business until his death in 1912.[73]

On a somewhat larger scale, the merchant H. Hallaçyan was involved in a number of different mines, both solely and in partnerships. Many entrepreneurs similarly spread their risks and capital among several operations. Hallaçyan Efendi is prosperously seated before one of these mines, the so-called Domuz mine at Kozlu, in a photograph dated 4 July 1902 (photograph 2.4.). His wife, the third woman to the left, is present as is one of his younger brothers and his wife. Workers, including a hewer with his pick, stand at the back. This extraordinary picture also shows a mine directly on the seashore, with a short gangway leading from the mine out over the sea. Hallaçyan Efendi also acquired a 20 percent share in the so-called Kılıç mine at Kozlu in 1888, joining, among others, the bankers Sava Savidis and Avram Aslıoğlu in a venture called the Kılıç Mining Company (Kılıç Ocakları Kumpanyası).[74]

This Kılıç mine was one of a mere fifteen that together employed more than 50 percent of all the labor in the 97 mines open during 1895. Much of the story remaining from this time revolves around this baker's dozen of operators. Strikingly, given its later central role in the coalfield, the Zonguldak locale accounted for just one of these more important mines. In the middle rank of these more active mines we find the Kılıç (variously Kılınç) mine, also known as the #5 Kozlu mine, administered by Hallaçyan Efendi between 1888 and 1914. The following narrative briefly focuses on its payroll as a way of suggesting operations at an average active mine during the early 1890s.

The mine was set in the rich veins of the Kılıç Valley near Kozlu village. Many villages repeatedly sent the same kinds of labor to the mine, demonstrating that relationships between mines and villages had acquired a certain rhythm, pattern, and permanence since the 1870s.[75] The company payroll further illustrates that workers were pocketing barely half of their earned wages; and that hewers fared the best among these. In 1895, the mine made labor payments to an impressive number of different identified villages, twenty-two in all (table 5.2).[76] Nearly two-thirds of the wages paid to these villages went for taxes (35,000 krs) and thus were never seen by the workers. The balance (17,000 krs) flowed to the headman for distribution, commonly to transporters and basket carriers and to a few hewers and support makers. The Kılıç Company paid out another sum (68,000 krs) to hewers from unnamed villages for "the balance owed for the coal dug." This amount exceeded the total it paid to all twenty-two named villages for the various forms of labor. Hewers, whatever their villages of origin, thus earned more than all other categories of labor combined. And finally, the Kılıç Company paid an additional amount (37,000 krs) for the "bread monies" of unspecified workers, a sum about the same as it had paid for village taxes.[77]

Table 5.2 Labor Payments of Kozlu #5 Mine, 1895

Recipients	in krs
Taxes of named villages	35,000
To hewers directly	68,000
Via headmen to workers	17,000
For bread	37,000
Other	20,000
Total	177,000

Source: KU 64.

The company also paid two individuals for bringing workers to the mine. In July 1895, it made a substantial payment, 600 krs, to headman Ibrahim Agha. Perhaps he was the headman of Sivriler village, since a tax payment to that village is the preceding entry. This debt, however, had been incurred for services rendered in 1889, when the register recorded a promissory note to him in the amount of 600 krs. In 1889, the mine had paid out this sum to the headman of Kargarlar village, one Selim Agha, and slightly more to the just-mentioned headman Ibrahim Agha.[78] And, on three separate occasions, it paid the labor boss Ishak Agha smaller sums totaling 240 krs.[79] In 1893, by comparison, his payment had reached 260 krs. In addition, in 1893 the company made four very small monthly payments of 23 krs each, and one larger sum (186 krs), for the salary of an "English engineer," otherwise unnamed. In these latter two instances of the boss and the English engineer, the Kılıç Company shared in a cooperative payment scheme. Because the two persons provided services to the wider area and not just one mine, many different operators, including the Kılıç Company, made payments toward their wages. Such collective payments, commonplace in the wage ledgers, likely were set up and coordinated by the mine superintendent's office. Sometimes the different operators paid out identical sums; sometimes the amounts varied according to no readily visible criteria.

The Kılıç mine's connections to the community hardly stopped at its considerable payments to the villager-workers. The company, with its three Christian partners, also made a series of payments to support Muslim religious observances and institutions in the local area. During the sacred month of Ramadan, it contributed sums for the support of permanently stationed members of the ulema, such as a prayer leader (*imam*), Qur'an reciter (*hafız*), and religious teacher (*hoca*), either because they offered prayers and observances at or near the mine site or in support of the mosque in the nearby town of Kozlu. Exactly six months later, the company contributed an identical sum for another Qur'an reciter, a payment pattern suggesting an annual schedule of such contributions. In addition, the company contributed an amount to the religious school (*medrese*), presumably in the town of Kozlu, which equaled the combined donations for these three ulema members. Several years before, in 1893, the company had contributed a nearly identical total amount, half of which went for the minaret of the mosque in Kozlu and the other half to the religious teacher.[80]

Mines and Charity

As the Kılıç mine example illustrates, a network of charitable contributions linked the mines and mining communities. The earliest evidence of this dates back to 1877, when mine operators and wealthy residents at Kilimli financed a new mosque, erected at the quay of the village. Perhaps in recognition of their contribution, they were invited to play a decisive role in hiring the prayer leader and preacher for the mosque, named after Sultan Abdulhamid II.[81] Exemplifying the characteristic Ottoman blending of state and religion, the mine superintendent and the ranking ulema member at Ereğli (the Qur'an reciter) selected the candidate, who was to serve at the new mosque on a trial basis for one month. Then, if the congregation approved, the village prayer leader, the headman and the Muslim mine operators would send a letter of endorsement to the Bartın district government. We need to offer, the superintendent added, every possible assistance "because this is a matter of religion and of Islamic practices."[82]

In 1894 and 1895, nearly all operational mines together contributed a modest sum (totaling some 39,000 krs) to meet a wide variety of educational, religious, and charitable needs in the villages and towns of the coalfield.[83] Charitable contributions for ostensibly religious purposes outnumbered those for non-religious purposes by a margin of five to one (32,000 krs vs. 6,300 krs).

Mine operators thus provided aid to one accident victim, rugs for a mosque, and payments to ulema during religious festivities; they also funded religious instruction at local religious and state schools. Operators of six different mines contributed monies (about 2,000 krs) to repair cemetery walls in three different mining locales. In a widespread campaign, two-thirds (47) of all functioning mines forwarded monies to help the victims of a fire that had raged in the town of Bolu. Similar kinds of contributions were made in 1893, when, for example, two mines contributed 1,000 krs to maintain the minaret of the mosque in Kozlu and two others provided sums (800 krs) for the icehouse of the mosque. In that same year, another two mines contributed small sums (93 krs each) to repair the bathhouse in Kozlu.[84]

Contributions to various members of the ulema accounted for fully one-half (19,000 krs) of the total amount contributed (but see below). This included sums from a number of mines at Kozlu for religious teachers and for those who had memorized the Qur'an at both the primary and the secondary state schools in the small mining center. During the month of Muharrem in both 1894 and 1895, eight different mines contributed monies (totaling 2,750 krs) for the support of the Qur'an reciter Ahmed Efendi at the Kozlu state primary school, and during the Ramadan season they made additional gift payments to him. Two mines, one already a contributor to the primary school, gave money for the salary of an unnamed religious teacher at the Kozlu secondary school. Nimmet Hoca, who had memorized the Qur'an and thereby had won the title of Qur'an reciter, offered services at seven different mines at Alacaağzı and two mines at Kozlu between June and September 1895. In another case, a mine donated a total sum of 125 krs for a religious teacher in the village of Sufiler, which at the time was providing labor to two other mines as well.

In addition to the amounts just noted, twenty nine different mines in three mine locales (Alacaağzı, Kozlu, and Zonguldak) donated funds (12,800 krs) for "*medrese* assistance." The pious foundation of the religious school likely received these sums, to be spent at the discretion of its administrator (*alim*). With just one exception, payments were made in the form of promissory notes.[85] These religious school contributions were comparatively large, averaging more than 400 krs, and probably flowed to support teachers at schools located in the various mine villages and towns of the coalfield.

The important religious observances surrounding the month of Ramadan are reflected in the flow of contributions from mine operators to the ulema. Ramadan was the most significant holiday time in the Muslim calendar, the most active and important season of public life in the Ottoman world. It was a period of fasting, prayer, and intense socializing, with heavy demands on the services of the ulema. Throughout this month, ulema members continuously read the Qur'an, and, customarily during the late Ottoman period (and perhaps before), students who were studying to enter the ulema ranks left the larger towns and cities for the countryside, where they preached and taught. The month ended with a holiday, seen as time off by mine workers but not always by the mine administration. During Ramadan 1895, donations to ulema make clear that prayers, Qur'an recitations, and other religious observances were being performed at the mines themselves in support of the workers there, and perhaps also back in the mining villages. More than one-quarter of all payments made to ulema members in 1894 and 1895 occurred during Ramadan in the latter year.[86] Thus, twenty-seven different mines (in four locales) made cash payments to anonymous Ramadan teachers.[87] Many probably were the traveling students carrying out observances at the various mines and mine villages that provided labor to the particular mine making the contribution. Some may have come from Istanbul, Bolu, or Kastamonu and others from the town of Ereğli. In other cases during the month of Ramadan, the religious teacher Düzceli Osman Efendi obtained payments from six different mines in Alacaağzı and another two in Kozlu, likely for religious services either at those mines or the mine villages. Nine different mines in the Zonguldak locale offered contributions to anonymous religious teachers; again, many likely were the traveling students. The religious teacher at the administrative center at Alacaağzı, who probably was a permanent appointee, received 300 krs assistance (*iane*), again during the month of Ramadan. And finally, at Alacaağzı an unnamed prayer leader, a permanent ulema post, received offerings from seven different mines. All of the contributions to the ulema during this sacred time were in cash.

There were other contributions during Ramadan, likely timed to coincide with this special season. For example, in Ramadan 1895, one Balıkçı Ahmedoğlu Hacı Mehmed Ali Agha, the operator of the Alacaağzı #345 mine, donated a comparatively large amount (850 krs) to buy flat rugs for a mosque, likely at Kozlu. During Ramadan in the preceding year, one mine operator gave money (190 krs) to Hacı Mehmed Efendi, the victim of an unspecified accident, perhaps at his mine.

Another cluster of payments occurred around the month of Muharrem, a sacred time centering on three days of fasting and fast-breaking celebrations. Thus, the contributions by seventeen mines at Kozlu to Kadri Efendi, who had memorized the Qur'an, all were made during and just after Muharrem 1895.[88] Similarly, all ten of the contributions to the religious teacher Omer Efendi occurred in Muharrem 1895.[89] Further, 95 percent of the monies for the Qur'an reciter of the Kozlu primary school, Ahmed Efendi, arrived during the month of Muharrem and the balance during Ramadan. The first two but not the third ulema member received all of their payments in cash.

Mine operators' contributions could be quite small. Those for the fire victims, for example, averaged 57 krs. Overall, for all purposes, there were more than 200 different contributions, averaging 180 krs over the two-year period.[90] This finding seems consistent with the conclusion of a major study of Ottoman imperial philanthropy that noted the modest size of Sultan Abdulhamid's charitable contributions, dedicated to a wide variety of different purposes.[91]

The size of donations does not seem related to the output of the particular mine. Smaller mines often donated amounts much larger than their mere size warranted. Thus, some mines contributed 150 krs to the fire victims' relief fund while mines ten times their size donated 40 krs. The two largest donors to this relief fund donated amounts that, when the size of their mine operation is used as the basis of comparison, relatively were five times greater than the contributions of other mine operators. Consider the entrepreneur who gave 850 krs to buy flat rugs for the mosque—a sum equaling 40 percent of the monies he paid out in wages! Different mines contributed to the assistance (*iane*) of Kadri Efendi but without much correlation to output. Two mines, with nearly identical payrolls, respectively contributed 100 and 250 krs. In this case, multiples of 50 krs apparently were used as the basis of assessment, while for traveling teachers during Ramadan (and the fire victims), the sum of 57 krs frequently appears.

Overall, among donating mines, neither their size, productive capacity, nor profitability determined the size of contributions. Nor did their citizenship, religion, or ethnicity exempt mine operators from contributing to the various educational and religious endeavors. Recall here the donations by H. Hallaçyan and his two Christian partners to Ramadan activities and to the support of the town's religious school. Also, six mines operated by the Christian Armenian mine operator Artın Karamanyan contributed monies to the fire victims' relief fund and for religious teachers during the Muslim observances around Ramadan. Similarly, the four mines of the foreign Giurgiu Company gave sums for the fire victims, for the Ramadan preachers, and for the support of Kadri Efendi as well as several other teachers at Ramadan time. Indeed, these two operators were among the most important in the coalfield at the time, together accounting for nearly one-third of all mining activity. The presence of these Christian operators as supporters of events surrounding the Ramadan cycle is a measure of their integration into the social, cultural, and religious life of the Ottoman Muslim majority, and more particularly, of the overwhelmingly Muslim community of the coalfield region. By contributing to celebrations central to the lives of their workers, these entrepreneurs were aligning with them, eliding the differences, and bridging the gap between capitalists who were either Christian or foreign, or both, and their workers, who were Muslim. Thus, in a real sense, the celebrations belonged to the entire mining community. These mine operators' participation in joint philanthropic ventures with Ottoman and Muslim operators for the sake of the larger community attests to the ecumenical nature of late Ottoman state and society. It underscores the importance of an overarching Ottoman identity and the absence of religion and ethnicity as negative signifiers in day-to-day affairs.

And yet, a look at the ratio between giving and coal production offers a different picture of the integration of the Giurgiu and Karamanyan companies into local society. That is, given the large size of their mining operations, they comparatively gave very little (table 5.3). The two companies together gave about one-seventh as often as the other companies in the coalfield. On the average, the other mine operators—foreign and Ottoman, Christian and Muslim—donated 1 krs for every 87 krs they spent on mine operations. In other words, their charitable contributions accounted for slightly more than 1 percent of their total expenditures. The Giurgiu Company, however, contributed 1 krs for every 250 krs it spent for labor payments. And the Karamanyan Company gave far less, only 1 krs for every 845 krs spent on labor.

However, there does not appear to be any conclusion to be drawn from these patterns. The relative stinginess of the Karamanyan and Giurgiu companies was not without parallel. Twenty-eight mines with an aggregate payroll of

Table 5.3 Relative Rate of Donations (in krs)

	A (donations)	B (expenditures)	B/A
Karamanyan mines	750	633,487	845
Giurgiu mines	2,890	722,498	250
All other mines	34,431	2,996,083	87

Source: KU 64.

some 225,000 krs made no donations of any kind. It is true that twenty of these barely functioned and had payrolls of less than 10,000 krs each. There was a substantial difference between the size of mines making charitable contributions and those not contributing. On the average, payrolls of mines making contributions of any kind were six times larger than mines making no contribution. But some relatively important operators, Muslims and Christians, Ottomans and foreigners, made no charitable contributions of any kind. Thus, several mines of both Mustafa Çavuş and Yasıf Efendi, each with a total payroll of about 34,000 krs, gave nothing nor were donations made by Petrosky, whose five mines had a payroll of 80,000 krs. But a third mine of Yasıf Efendi contributed 153 krs, while his fourth mine, with a payroll six times that of this third mine, donated only three times as much. Clearly, the patterns determining charitable contributions are not mathematically evident and likely were a matter of personal choice and conviction.

With more certainty, we can speak of the impact of such charitable contributions, which served as a bridge between capitalist entrepreneurs and their workers. Through such contributions, the entrepreneurs affirmed that events affecting the community—whether fires or Ramadan celebrations—were of importance to them as well. Such donations were the equivalent of the mid twentieth-century American factory owners' gifts of Thanksgiving Day turkeys or Christmas hams to their employees, promoting the pleasant fiction of a united capitalist-worker world. Parsimony, on the other hand, whatever its cause, meant that the tool of charity was not used to mitigate the class differences dividing operators and workers.

Mine Villages during the Early 1890s

Ishak Agha, a labor boss in the Kozlu locale, the most important one at the time, must have been a formidable local presence. In this post, he made certain that the workers were duly sent to the mines. Over a nineteen-month period in the mid 1890s, Ishak Agha received 3,120 krs, a sum greater than the combined wages of a hewer and several basket carriers during that same period. Over these months, the monies dribbled in from twelve different mine operators in the Kozlu area, who made payments to him on 39 different occasions. The amount paid by a particular mine almost always was the same—60, 90, or 120 krs—indicating that he had reached agreements with the various operators to supply them with labor for each of the two semi-monthly shifts being sent.[92]

The power of village headmen, for their part, had remained formidable since the 1870s despite state efforts to undermine an important foundation of their sway over villagers. In 1892, legislation stripped headmen of the legal authority to collect and distribute mine wages owed to villagers (see above). In this measure, the central state gave another nod to free market capitalism and took another step to dismantle state control over coal mining. Henceforth, the people of the village (or quarter) who did the work were to be paid directly by mine operators. Headmen specifically were ordered not to accept the money for distribution.[93] Nonetheless, as indicated by the 1893 and 1895 ledgers, headmen retained wage-distributing authority over their fellow villagers. Thus, the collective payment system was still operating despite its legal abolition several years before.

Some headmen also were entrepreneurs. One member of the powerful Karamahmudzadeler family, Mehmed Agha, served as the headman of Tiran village. In 1902, he was leasing at least part of the operations of the nearby Alacaağzı #216 mine and there employing workers from his village.[94] Other headmen received payments from mine operators. Take, for example, the disbursements by the Kılıç Company to the headman of Kargarlar village. These equaled one-sixth of all the sums that the company paid to the village for labor during 1889. Notably, the headman obtained his in cash while the workers received their wages in promissory notes.[95]

At least until World War I, headmen continued to play a central role in the collection and discipline of labor in the coalfield. When labor was scarce, the state continued to rely on headmen despite its efforts to block their power. For example, in 1913, as mine operators in both the Kozlu and Zonguldak locales clamored for more workers, the superintendent ordered headmen to find a solution, pointedly ignoring legal provisions that should have exempted some individuals from work duty.[96]

Among the 231 named villages that provided mine labor in 1895, the majority specialized in the kinds of workers they provided. Most villages, for example Abdulmalik, Çaydere, Uluköy, and Akbaba, furnished only one kind of labor—either basket carrier or transporter or hewer or support maker. A substantial minority of villages—one in five—sent more than one kind of mine worker but fewer than 3 percent sent three kinds of workers. Among the latter, Ebegümeci and Beyat villages each provided basket carriers, hewers, and support makers, while Tabaklar village sent basket carriers, hewers, and transporters (see table 5.8). Only Tiran village, under the direction of the headman Mehmed Agha just mentioned, provided four different types of compulsory labor.[97]

Basket carriers formed the vast majority of the compulsory labor work force; between 58 and 74 percent of the villages providing just one kind of labor to a mine sent basket carriers.[98] When a village furnished several kinds of labor, basket carriers were present in 44 percent of the cases, followed by hewers (32 percent), transporters (17 percent), and support makers (9 percent). Similarly, in terms of monies paid for the various occupations, payments for the basket carriers formed the largest single category (see table 5.4).[99]

As seen, only 10–15 percent of area inhabitants lived in towns—mainly Ereğli, Devrek, and, following its emergence in the later 1890s, Zonguldak. The vast majority of coalfield residents subject to compulsory labor were villagers, living in hundreds of communities scattered throughout the coal basin and its hinterland, backing up to the mountain spine paralleling the Black Sea coast. Once upon a time, in 1867, the borders of the coalfield itself were precisely coincident

Table 5.4 Payments to Workers, 1894 and 1895 (in krs)

Basket carrier	235,067
Transporter	82,473
Support maker	27,904
Hewer	3,046
Basket carrier and hewer	55,070
Basket carrier and support maker	2,510
Sub-total	406,070
Unspecified	164,118

Source: KU 64.

with Ereğli sub-province. But, consistent with patterns elsewhere in the empire, administrative boundaries here also mutated constantly. Whereas Ereğli sub-province, itself a part of Kastamonu province, was once the administrative framework for most workers' lives, this entity disappeared from the organizational chart soon after 1867. Ereğli district, subsequently joined by Zonguldak district, within Kastamonu province served that function later on. Still later, Bolu province emerged from another administrative reorganization, again with new boundaries. The administrative shifts could be quite dramatic. For example, in an 1895 state publication, Ereğli district held 63 villages, while just a few years later, in 1898, it contained 137 villages, more than twice as many.[100]

The details of these administrative fluctuations are not of interest here. It is relevant to our story to note that, during the mid 1890s, most of the compulsory workers[101] came from two areas: the villages located in the areas quite near the town of Ereğli and in rural districts around Devrek, to its south, about a 6 to 12 hours' walk from the mines around Zonguldak.[102] At this time, the Ereğli and Devrek regions contained some 300 villages with a sum population of around 40,000 persons. During the mid 1890s at least one in three of these villages provided labor of one sort or another to the mines (table 5.5).[103] The area around Bartın, in the eastern part of the coalfield, furnished about one-fifth of the compulsory workers and the balance (about 18 percent) walked from villages in other areas of the coal basin.[104]

Compulsory workers flowed in rivulets from a large number of villages. More than two-thirds of all enumerated villages supplied workers to only one

Table 5.5 Population of Ereğli and Devrek Districts, ca. 1898

District	No. of Villages	No. of Village Households	Village Population	Ave. per Household
Ereğli	137	2,753	22,336	8.1
Devrek	169	2,194	18,476	8.4
Total	306	4,947	40,812	8.2

Source: *Kastamonu vs 1314*, 320–358.

mine (table 5.6). For example, the twenty-five households in Akça Hatipler village (in Ereğli district) sent basket carriers to Zonguldak #63 mine while twenty households in Karacaoğlu village (Bartın district) sent basket carriers to Zonguldak #281 mine. When these villagers worked side by side with one another at the mine site, as many surely did, village identities were reinforced, as they were when fellow villagers traveled together to the workplace. In villages that repeatedly sent workers to the same mine, season after season, the work experience became defined by that of the particular mine, rather than by mining in general. But nearly 30 percent of mining villages sent workers to more than one mine (table 5.6). Thus, Ortaköy sent workers to Kozlu #5 and #284 mines while Kırancık village furnished labor to eleven different mines, all of them also in the Kozlu locale. Drawing on the experiences of labor in 2, 3, 4, and more mines, these villages must have developed notions of work that were different and more generalized than single mine villages.

Table 5.6 Villages Supplying Labor to Mines, 1894–1895

Villages supplying labor	176	35	13	10	12
Number of mines	1	2	3	4	5 or more

Source: KU 64.

When viewed from the perspective of the mines receiving workers rather than villages sending them, the transformative possibilities appear somewhat differently. It is striking that the typical mine during the 1890s employed workers from at least 6 different villages.[105] Many mines drew on 10 or more villages for their labor needs, while a number employed labor from 15 to 18 different villages. Thus, the Kozlu #5 mine, which Hallaçyan Efendi and his partners operated, drew basket carriers, transporters, and support makers from 18 different villages, among them the villages of Yüzce, Kırancık, Alakilise, Aydın, Kulah, Sivriler, and Dereköy (table 5.7).

The mine work force therefore appears mixed, typically originating from at least half a dozen different villages and sometimes three times that number.[106] Thus, as seen in the example of Hallaçyan Efendi's enterprise at the Kozlu #5 mine, workers from many different villages met and shared on-the-job experiences that offered possibilities for alignment, solidarity, and identity formation along work rather than village lines. Considerable intermingling of workers from different villages certainly was taking place. Many villagers at the mine site worked only with fellow villagers, but many, after all, did not. The short, two-week work cycle, however, might have weakened this process of new identity formation.

The mingling of (mainly) underground workers from different villages also is reflected in accident reports in which more than one person was involved, either as victim or witness.[107] Significantly, two-fifths of accident participants

Table 5.7 Villages and Town Quarters Providing Labor to Mines, mid 1890s

Locale	Mine	No. of Villages	No. of Quarters	Locale	Mine	No. of Villages	No. of Quarters
AA	128	3		KU	356	4	
AA	131	6		KU	357	15	
AA	135	2		Z	56	3	
AA	138	17		Z	63	14	
AA	171	3		Z	69	1	
AA	204	2		Z	70	6	
AA	216	9	2	Z	74	1	
AA	263	2		Z	196	2	
AA	278	6		Z	241	3	
AA	339		2	Z	234	16	
AA	340	1		Z	265	5	
KU	5	18		Z	267	4	
KU	6	4		Z	280	2	
KU	7	2	1	Z	281	16	
KU	14	6		Z	292	3	
KU	17	1		Z	239	11	
KU	21	15	1	Z	299	1	
KU	22	4		KM	85	8	
KU	25	9		KM	93	5	
KU	33	11		KM	94	2	
KU	158	11		KM	100	4	
KU	167	5		KM	112	1	
KU	227	11		KM	113	7	
KU	233	12	2	KM	114	1	
KU	235	14		KM	226	3	
KU	245	5		KM	288	4	
KU	271	2		KM	341	2	
KU	284	10	2	KM	268	8	
KU	298	2		CA	285*	31	
KU	300	2		AM	143	2	
KU	342	8		AM	283	2	
KU	347	1					

Note: The reporting for CA 285* included two other unspecified mines run by the same operator. AA=Alacaağzı; KU=Kozlu; Z=Zonguldak; KM=Kilimli; CA=Çatalağzı; AM=Amasra.
Source: KU 64.

were laboring in the company of workers from other villages, that is, persons they likely first had met at the worksite. For example, a 1905 rockfall killed or injured seven workers in the Pavlaki #299 mine at Zonguldak. The victims included a foreman, basket carriers, and hewers who came from four different villages—Uzunköy, Kargarlar, Bigun Hatun, and Uzungünü.[108] This is impressive additional testimony to the number of those working side by side with laborers from other coalfield villages and even, in a number of cases, from places outside of the coalfield altogether.

The communities sending labor to the mines were small in size, averaging 250 residents. The villages of Firnik and Gevze, both in Devrek district, were among the largest, each with 51 households respectively containing 418 and 489 persons. At the other end of the spectrum, Hocalar village in Gerede district held just 73 persons in 13 households.[109] A weak correlation exists between village size and the number of mines it staffed: larger villages were somewhat more likely to send workers to multiple mines. Villages sending workers to five or more mines averaged about 20 percent more inhabitants than villages providing labor to four and fewer mines.[110] The 421 persons from Kırancık village and 454 residents from Beyat village, both large communities, respectively furnished labor to thirteen and fourteen different mines, while Ayvatlar's 356 residents (180 males) worked in five different mines. At the same time, smaller villages often supplied multiple mines with labor. For example, Ikse village (in Ereğli district), with only 23 households and 129 residents, sent workers to six different mines (table 5.8). Similarly, 187 Kabaca villagers (in Devrek district) who lived in 23 households furnished laborers to four mines, as did the 213 residents of Ebegümeci village. Some large villages, however, supplied labor to only one mine—for example, the 489 persons in Gevze village, the largest of all mining villages, and the 398 persons in Nizamlar village, both in Devrek district. Indeed, two of the five largest mining villages supplied labor to just one mine, while three of the nine smallest villages furnished labor to multiple mines (table 5.8).

Somewhat larger villages tended to have an occupationally more diversified labor force, sending more than one kind of labor. Villages providing two or three different kinds of labor averaged 282 inhabitants while those sending labor to five or more mines averaged 293 persons (recall the average village of

Table 5.8 Villages Sending Compulsory Labor to Multiple Mines

Village Name	Kinds of Labor				Total No. of Mines	Village Population	Mine Locale
	1	2	3	4			
Beyat	1	1		1	4	454	All AA
Birek	1	1	1		2		All AA
Ebegümeci	1	1		1	4	213	All KU
İkse	1	1	1		6	129	AA KU KM
Sufiler	1		1	1	3	227	Z KM
Tabaklar	1	1	1		5		Z CA
Tiran	1	1	1	1	3		AA
Üçköy	1	1		1	5	287	AA KU

Note: Kinds of labor: 1 = basket carrier; 2 = hewer; 3 = transporter; 4 = support maker. See table 5.7 for mine locale codes.
Source: KU 64 and *Kastamonu vs 1311*.

250 persons). Table 5.8 shows a stronger correlation between villages sending labor to multiple mines and those providing more than one kind of labor. The table presents villages sending three and more kinds of compulsory labor to two and more different mines. Indeed, all of the villages providing more than one kind of labor sent workers to more than one mine.

On the Road

Well-beaten paths crisscrossed the region, marking the journeys that began and ended the twelve-day shifts. And yet scarcely a word about the paths or the journeys appears in the written record. Over the years and the decades, many thousands and hundreds of thousands of treks from village to mine and back again marked mining village life just as surely as did mine labor and village life. Many villages were quite close to the mines in which their inhabitants worked. The village of Kızıl Elma literally was adjacent to the Çatalağzı #285 mine, to which it sent basket carriers. Others were over an hour away: Balıoğlu village provided workers to the #138 mine at Alacaağzı, just under five km away. Workers from many villages perched atop steeply sloped hillsides quickly walked down to mines in the Kozlu locale in about three hours. But longer treks were not unusual. Even in the early 1890s, when coal production was one-sixth its peak pre–World War I levels, workers' journeys exceeding 20 km were common. Indeed, recall that villagers around Ereğli and Devrek provided most of the labor for the mines. These were some 36–50 km distant from the mines they served, a trip of perhaps 5 to 7 hours on foot.

Most of these journeys to and from the village go unmentioned, even though from village to mine and back filled hours and days of the workers' monthly rotation. Only quite rarely do we begin to glimpse the hardships. Here is Ethem Çavuş's account of his first journey, some 50 km down the mountains.

> I'll never forget. The first time I came to work in the mines was one of the coldest days in the winter. I mean it; it was very cold. We descended from Çomaklar village in Devrek district to Zonguldak. Everywhere was covered by snow; because of the blizzard you couldn't see the hand in front of your face....
>
> We put on our rawhide sandals and snowshoes, packed our food, and got on the road. We did but our hearts were beating heavily as we were wondering whether we would come back home healthy and find it as we had left it. Would they beat us at the mines? I began to have a strange feeling. While walking, I was watching other kids. If one of them tries to run away, I will do the same. Some childhood.[111]

Villagers on their journeys to and from the mines encountered not only routine hardships but also danger and even death, both from natural and human causes. The violent storms that commonly wracked the area were noticed mainly for their impact on shipping. Hence, the infamy of the storm that, in 24 hours, destroyed the newly built breakwater of the Ereğli Company and cost shareholders half of their capital, or of the 1905 storm that sank five steamships and 70 sailing vessels seeking refuge in the harbor at Ereğli. But such storms surely endangered and took workers' lives as well, even if the casualties went unrecorded.[112]

Brigands were a familiar part of workers' journeys throughout the mining era. In the early Fall of 1877, a robber just released from a six-year sentence in Sinop prison preyed on workers traveling between their villages and the mines.[113] Around this time, transporters and basket carriers in the hamlet of Oğriler stayed home for fear of other bandits and, the following October, several thieves robbed workers from the Bartın region going and coming from the mines.[114] Forty years later, in 1912, workers around Zonguldak "on the road are violently seized and robbed by persons without conscience." The superintendent viewed the district as a "collection spot for persons capable of such misdeeds and especially of strangers." Combinations of gendarmes and military reservists repeatedly swept the region but were seen as too few to stop the violence.[115]

The following account, taken from an interview of a miner who worked from 1934 to 1969, vividly summarizes the dangers encountered on the road by generations of miners.

> We walked to the mines whether it was winter or summer.... But one winter it was extremely cold. I left Kozlu with a friend of mine for the village. Halfway through the journey my friend says, "Yahya, listen to me. We can't make it." We slept for the night at a village called Hoca. At night a çavuş [foreman] with his three workers came. They had some wine with them. The çavuş said "who fucks the cold weather?" and off they went. In the early morning we left the village. We hadn't walked about half a kilometre when we saw four bodies lying frozen. I saw so many frozen bodies and bodies beaten to death by bandits. There were many thieves. They usually were around on pay days. Many workers lost their money on the way back to their villages. Some were killed by the thieves in the forest.[116]

Notes

1. Kahveci (1997); Roy (1976); also see below.
2. ED 4, 153, 15 Nisan 1294/27 April 1878.
3. ED 4, 182, 29 Haziran 1294/11 July 1878.
4. Namely, Çukur Viran, Yakacık, and Dereli. ED 4, 20, 13 Ağustos 1294/25 August 1877 and 27, 23 Ağustos 1294/4 September 1877, two different documents. See also ED 4, 33, 6 Eylül 1293/18 September 1877 and ED 4, 182, 29 Haziran 1294/11 July 1878 for two villages providing labor for the mine of Kireneli Hasan Agha at Kozlu.
5. ED 4, 11, 31 Temmuz 1293/12 August 1877. The superintendent determined how many workers were needed for the mine, while the local government determined the number of workers from each hamlet.

6. ED 4, 370, 14 Mart 1290/26 March 1874. Five years later, he seems to have been pursuing the same plan, that is, recruiting workers from outside of the Ereğli region. See ED 4, 346, 27 July 1879.
7. ED 4, 287, 9 ks 1294/21 January 1879. Whether he had the authority to order the change is not clear. Forty years later, in 1912, he did not. See below, ED 12, 210, #1881/321.
8. ED 4, 288, 11 ks 1294/23 January 1879. Similarly, when shortages of animals threatened operations in September 1878, the superintendent bent the rules in another way. He ordered that the animals already at the mines work a double shift, that is, remain working for an additional fifteen days. ED 4, 234, 10 Eylül 1294/22 September 1878.
9. ED 4, 323, 18 Nisan 1295/30 April 1879.
10. ED 4, 202, 23 Temmuz 1294/4 August 1878.
11. ED 4, 12, 31 Temmuz and 1 Ağustos 1294/12 and 13 August 1877; similar problems in 39, 16 Eylül 1294/28 September 1877, and 48, 5 tl 1293/17 October 1877. Whether or not any of the tax privileges just noted were continued in later years is not known and the subject requires further study.
12. ED 4 provides an extraordinarily detailed look that, alas, is unique in the materials consulted for this study.
13. ED 4, 153, 11 Nisan 1294/23 April 1878 and 290, 18 ks 1294/30 January 1879.
14. In the state records that are the basis for this historical reconstruction, these provisioning patterns are scarcely visible but traces do remain.
15. In the years 1292–1295 (1876–1879), 36,000 *kiles* of barley were delivered to the mines. ED 4, 256, 26 tl 1294/7 November 1878.
16. ED 4, 40, 17 Eylül 1293/29 September 1877.
17. ED 4, 229, 2 Eylül 1294/14 September 1878.
18. ED 4, 72, 23 tl 1293/4 November 1877; also ED 4, 307, 10 Mart 1295/22 March 1879. By May 1878, Akşehir had provided 15,000 *kiles* of barley for provisioning the mines. ED 4, 155, 19 Nisan 1294/1 May 1878.
19. ED 4, 247, 12 tl 1294/24 October 1878.
20. ED 4, 177, 20 Haziran 1294/2 July 1878.
21. This example is from the 1890s but surely applies to the 1870s as well: ED 3, 15, 12 Eylül 1310/24 September 1894.
22. For a study of growing state power and its effect on village headmen in a sixteenth- to seventeenth-century south German region, see Rebel (1983).
23. Articles 16, 17, and 33 of the 1867 regulations.
24. Article 26 of the 1867 regulations.
25. Article 85 of the 1867 regulations.
26. In ED 4, 366, 22 Ağustos 1295/3 September 1879, the Ereğli district official asked the commission for a register book listing separately the *Rum, Bulgar, Ermeni* (Greek Orthodox, Bulgarian, Armenian), and other classes (*sınıf*) who were working in the districts of the mines.
27. Decades later, in 1912, the current superintendent insisted that neither his administration nor the special "worker commissions" then functioning to recruit labor possessed the authority to order particular villages to work at particular mines. Rather, he insisted, the workers (*amele*) themselves were to decide, and it was a matter of negotiation between them and the mine operators. ED 12, 210, #1881/32,13 ts 1328/26 November 1912.
28. ED 4, 21, 14 Ağustos 1293/26 August 1877.
29. ED 4, 35, 9 Eylül 1293/21 September 1877.
30. ED 4, 200, 20 Temmuz 1294/1 August 1878.
31. Quataert and Duman (2001), 156. 1 *okka* = 1.28 kg = 84 lbs.
32. The law also stated that if there are no other sons of the same father who are more than 10 years old, that son is not to be taken for compulsory service. *Kastamonu vs 1311*, 68, 11 Mayıs 1308/23 May 1892.

33. Assertion by the mine superintendent. ED 4, 83, 8 ts 1293/20 November 1877; ED 4, 69, 19 tl 1293/31 October 1877. Ereğli and Devrek district population in all quarters equaled 7,074 persons and in all villages, 40,812 persons during the later 1890s; see *Kastamonu vs 1314*. In 1877 and 1878, Sultan Süleyman quarter successively provided 200 and 377 persons; in 1877 Sultan Orhan quarter provided 143 persons. Çatma (1998), 95–96, citing original documents.
34. ED 4, 12, 31 Temmuz 1293/12 August 1877 and 235, 19 Eylül 1294/1 October 1878. Compare ED 4, 85, 21 November 1877 with ED 4, 200, 1 August 1878; also see ED 4, 11, 31 Temmuz 1293/12 August 1877.
35. ED 4, 33, 6 Eylül 1293/18 September 1877.
36. ED 4, 194, 14 Temmuz 1294/26 July 1878. "The very first duty of the locale officials is to personally investigate the shortages which occur in the changing of each shift of the basket carriers and transporters. They are to organize two copies [for the locale and the superintendent] of journals and on the page they are to show separately the district arrears of transporters, basket carriers, and hewers. With haste by special guard at once they are to send a copy to the government and at once print it, notifying the government by horse and by telegram that it is coming. And one copy is to be sent here to us. The commission and the locale officials were informed but without effect so far. Further studies by the government have been without effect. So, henceforth, be zealous in this duty. Henceforth, so that nothing will be left unsaid, for the last time do this with alacrity. The journal on the deficiencies in the transporters has not been sent. Examine this and communicate by telegram." Also see ED 4, 271, 30 ts 1294/12 December 1878.
37. The mine superintendent in turn sent monthly register books to the Marine Ministry. ED 4, 29, 26 Ağustos 1293/7 September 1877.
38. ED 4, 218, 14 Ağustos 1294/26 August 1878; and 37, 11 Eylül 1293/23 September 1877.
39. ED 4, 42, 20 Eylül 1293/2 October 1877.
40. ED 4, 289, 12 ks 1294/25 January 1879.
41. ED 4, 235, 19 Eylül 1294/1 October 1878.
42. ED 4, 27, 23 Ağustos 1294/4 September 1879, reporting on events in October 1878.
43. ED 4, 2, 28 Şubat 1294/12 March 1879.
44. For one example of workers receiving, on a monthly basis, gratis supplies of wicks and oil for their lamps, see ED 16, 355, 23 tl 1333/23 October 1917. The example is that of the Ereğli Company; it is unknown if this was a common practice.
45. ED 4, 287, 9 ks 1294/21 January 1879.
46. ED 4, 171, 1 Haziran 1294/13 June 1878, which refers only to transporter wage payments. In this case, the operator pocketed the sums.
47. ED 4, 198, 17 Temmuz 1294/29 July 1878.
48. OA, BEO 932, Kastamonu telgraflar, 48, #22/34360, 8 Ağustos 1310/22 August 1894, which is a protest sent under the signatures of Mustafa and Hüseyin from the Ereğli administrative headquarters.
49. ED 4, 42, 21 Eylül 1293/3 October 1877.
50. ED 4, 293, 28 ks 1294/9 February 1879. In this case, the superintendent supported the appeal.
51. ED 4, 50, 8 tl 1293/20 October 1877.
52. These years are seen as particularly difficult for the villagers and massive indebtedness passed from villager-miner father to son. Collection of the tithe at this time reportedly fell to Montenegrins, Greeks, and Armenians. See Etingü (1976), 56.
53. *Matlubat defterleri* were consulted for the years 1305 (KU 72), 1309 (KU 208), 1311 (KU 64), 1320 (KU 98), and 1321 (KU 206). That selected for analysis here, KU 64 for 1311, is the most detailed, by a considerable margin. The payment side of the ledger proved more useful than the collection side. The last registers in the series, KU 98 and 206, proved disappointingly general.

54. Most of the entries in KU 64 fall between March 1894 and February 1896. Some, however, date back three and four years, indicating payments made in arrears.
55. KU 64. Ten villages were excluded because their names were illegible. The town quarters were: Sultan Orhan, Sultan Süleyman, and Müfti in the town of Ereğli; Camicedid in Devrek; and Dışra, which could not be located in the population statistics given in *Kastamonu vs 1314*, 320–359.
56. There certainly were more villages than the number specified; see the discussion below. The names of 129 of the 231 villages were located in an approximately contemporaneous provincial yearbook, which provided population data. *Kastamonu vs 1314*, 320–359.
57. Du Velay (1903), 654–660. The tithe and the real estate tax accounted for two-thirds of all direct taxes collected in the empire as a whole. When made for the tithe owed, such monetary payments were exceptional since 90 percent of all tithes in the late empire were paid in kind.
58. KU 64, 157.
59. KU 64, 195 and 210, respectively mines #289 and #357.
60. KU 64, 138.
61. Quataert and Duman (2001), 159. Because of its date, this accident was not recorded the ledgers available for this study.
62. Murphey (2003).
63. Quataert and Duman (2001), 164.
64. Article 85.
65. KU 217, 1337–1339.
66. KU 217, 1337–1339. Some workers received no *ekmek bedeli*; others received it in amounts ranging from 17 to 100 percent of their gross wage earning. We need to consider that there may have been workers from villages not among the 231 enumerated in KU 64.
67. Whether mine operators or merchants were supplying the bread is not noted.
68. When two persons or entities owed each other money, accountants rendered the two amounts as just one transaction, instead of recording the gross salaries owed by the company in one column and the monies owed by hewers for bread and supplies in another.
69. More precisely, *mahsuben*—26 percent; *nakden*—34 percent; *havaleten*—41 percent.
70. Quataert and Duman (2001), 159.
71. Quataert and Duman (2001), 164–165.
72. See note 53 above. In 1893, when its operations were quite reduced compared to 1895, virtually all Kılıç Company payments were in cash.
73. People's House (1933), 161–162.
74. For the photograph and the information in this paragraph, I am very grateful to Arsen Yarman. Coal likely traveled over the gangway in the picture to small boats, but the photograph is not entirely clear in this regard.
75. Based on comparison of KU 72, KU 208, and KU 64. The repetition of village names suggests relatively stable flows of labor. While only four villages are recorded as sending workers during each of the three years, this does not mean the flows of only those villagers were stable. After all, most labor payments do not specify villages and are anonymous.
76. The 1889 register notes "x" *divan* (hamlet) while the 1893 register refers to the same place as *kariye* (village). It is unclear if, during these decades, there was any actual difference between *divan* and *kariye*.
77. KU 64. In addition, the mine paid out a lump sum of 20,000 krs for the taxes of basket carriers, support makers, and hewers in unspecified locations. And finally, the mine paid out a small amount, less than 3,000 krs, for imperial soldiers' wages.
78. Compare KU 72 and KU 64.
79. KU 208.
80. KU 208 for 1309.
81. So named, perhaps, because the Sultan had donated funds for its construction. Özbek (2001).
82. ED 4, 71, 22 tl 1293/3 November 1877 and 22 tl 1293/3 November 1877.

83. KU 64. The register nominally lists 122 mines: among these, 66 mines made contributions and 56 did not. Among the 56 non-contributing mines, 25 recorded no expenditures of any kind and thus were not operating at even a perfunctory level. From the number of functioning mines we also deduct another 22 mines that were functioning only minimally, with total payments of less than 10,000 krs. We also exclude two other mines for various reasons. Seven mines that did not contribute averaged more than 10,000 krs in total payments. These seven are included among the functioning mines. Thus, for purposes of this discussion, the number of functioning mines is 66 + 7 = 73 mines. Overall, the more active mines tended to contribute; see below for a fuller discussion.
84. For 1893 contributions, see KU 208, 134–211.
85. All were during the months of July through September
86. A sum of 19,272 krs was paid to the religious teacher or Qur'an reciter (*hoca* or *hafız*); of this amount, 5,364 krs were paid in Mart 1311, which begins on 16 Ramadan 1312.
87. All were in Mart 1311 (except for two arrears payments in Februar 1309 and Februar 1310). There were also single payments; in this case, no mine made two payments: 19 Kozlu mines, 4 Kilimli, 1 Zonguldak, and 3 Çatalağzı mines = 27 different mines.
88. One contribution to him occurred several months later, in September 1311, from an Alacaağzı mine.
89. One mine was at Alacaağzı, three at Zonguldak, and six at Kozlu.
90. The median contribution equaled 100 krs. The manner in which these amounts and the other contributions were assessed cannot be directly determined but likely followed established practices elsewhere in the empire. Namely, state authorities (perhaps the mine superintendent) set a gross amount to be collected and distributed the burden among the various contributors.
91. Özbek (2001); KU 2, ED 10, 12, and 16.
92. KU 64, entries in the Kozlu locale only.
93. *Kastamonu vs 1311*, 75–76, 22 Temmuz 1308/2 August 1892 cites Article 25 of a regulation concerning compensation of village and hamlet people who carry out compulsory labor duties. Per this article, the people who do the work should be paid the money, not the headmen.
94. ED 3, 179, 10 Nisan 1318/23 April 1902.
95. KU 72, 152–153.
96. ED 10, 198, 29 ts 1328/9 December 1912.
97. KU 64. The sample size is 231 villages. Fifty-two sent more than one kind of labor; and in these cases, the basket carrier-hewer combination accounted for 30 instances. None of the town quarters sent workers with specified occupations. Payments in these cases were either for unspecified purposes or for payment of taxes.
98. In the 231 villages, transporter labor was next in frequency, in 22 percent of the cases, while hewers and support makers accounted for the balance (4 percent). Most of the hewer labor was captured in the "payments for coal dug" category discussed above. In another counting of 252 villages, 145 villages sent basket carriers; 50 provided transporters; hewers came from 39 villages and support makers from 18 villages; see KU 64.
99. Sample is 252 villages. Recall that the accountant recorded only the name of the village and left unspecified the labor it had provided.
100. Compare Cuinet (1895), 405 and *Kastamonu vs 1314*, 320–358.
101. Sixty-one percent of the villages noted in the register were located in the two districts of Ereğli and Devrek.
102. For purposes of this discussion, I am using statistics from the districts of Ereğli and Devrek noted in *Kastamonu vs 1314*, 320–358. At this time, towns located in the two districts contained just over 7,000 inhabitants.
103. Sixty-five percent of all villages providing labor (KU 64) were found on the lists of villages in the region. *Kastamonu vs 1314*. Nearly two-thirds of these located villages were within the district of Ereğli or Devrek. It is likely that, if the remainder of the villages had been located, the representation from these two districts would have been higher still.

104. Confusingly, in more 10 percent of the cases, two to five villages from different areas have the same name, thus making it impossible, at this time, to determine which among them was the mining village. Again, recall the above discussion that emphasizes that most payments made for labor went to unspecified locations.
105. These are minimum numbers. As seen in the earlier discussion of, for example, "bread money" and payments "for the coal dug," considerable sums were being paid out to villagers but not in ways that allow us to trace those payments back to the village of origin. This table includes only those mines reporting named villages.
106. Similarly, in 1889, the important Kozlu #5 mine drew workers from eight different hamlets: KU 72, 152–153. Virtually all were paid in promissory notes.
107. KU 2, ED 10, 12 and 16. In the sample there are 43 such accidents involving 185 persons. Among these, 56 persons were of unknown origin and were removed from the sample, leaving 129 persons of known origins.
108. ED 3, 221, accident dated 21 Temmuz 1321/3 August 1905.
109. Thus, households in mining villages were slightly smaller than those in the two districts overall. In the average mine village, four in seven persons were male.
110. Thus, 250 persons lived in the average mine village, but the nine villages sending labor to five and more mines averaged 293 persons.
111. Quataert and Duman (2001), 156–157.
112. Naim (1934) and Thobie (1977); *Bolu vs 1334*, 162.
113. ED 4, 25, 21 Ağustos 1293/2 September 1877 and 40, 18 Eylül 1293/30 September 1877. In the summer of 1877, workers returning home to Devrek attacked and robbed villagers of cash and clothing. ED 4, 7, 26 Temmuz 1293/7 August 1877.
114. ED 4, 41, 243 and 320, various dates from 1878 and 1879.
115. KU KD II, 436, 6 Mayıs 1328/12 May 1912.
116. Kahveci (1997), 139. Part of interview with Yahya Gebes, aged 77, February 1993, at his home in the village of Kemallar.

Photograph 2.1 Kozlu Kılıç Mine, Workers, and Supports. Abdül Hamid Collection

Photograph 2.2 Armutçuk Mine of the Merchant Ahmed Efendi, Inclined Plane. Abdül Hamid Collection

Photograph 2.3 (Top) Gelik Mines Inclined Plane, Ereğli Company.
Orlando Carlo Calumeno Collection and Archives
Photograph 2.4 (Bottom) Domuz Mine, Kozlu.
Orlando Carlo Calumeno Collection and Archives

Photograph 2.5 (Top) Aerial Cable, Main Station toward Gelik, Ereğli Company, 1917.
Orlando Carlo Calumeno Collection and Archives

Photograph 2.6 (Bottom) Zonguldak Port View, Ereğli Company.
Arsen Yarman Collection

Photograph 2.7 (Top) Zonguldak Port. Orlando Carlo Calumeno Collection and Archives
Photograph 2.8 (Bottom) Zonguldak Port and Breakwater. Arsen Yarman Collection

Photograph 2.9 (Top) Second Ereğli Company Coal Scrubber, Zonguldak, Cornerstone Ceremony. Orlando Carlo Calumeno Collection and Archives

Photograph 2.10 (Bottom) Kozlu, Giurgiu Company Mine, Machine Room. Abdül Hamid Collection

Photograph 2.11 (Top) Kozlu, Çatal Dere, Ahmed Efendi Mine Tunnel.
Abdül Hamid Collection

Photograph 2.12 (Bottom) Kozlu, Giurgiu Company Mine, Machinery.
Abdül Hamid Collection

چتال اغزی نام موقعده سایۀ ترقیواېۀ حضرت پادشاهیېۀ مجدداً انشا و تمدید ایدیلان تیمور یولڭ رسم کشاد ی

Photograph 2.13 Çatalağzı Railroad, Opening Ceremony. Abdül Hamid Collection

Photograph 2.14 Zonguldak, Coke Production. Abdül Hamid Collection

Photograph 2.15 (Top) Zonguldak Street, Entrance to Market.
Orlando Carlo Calumeno Collection and Archives

Photograph 2.16 (Bottom) Zonguldak Plateau Quarter, 1917.
Orlando Carlo Calumeno Collection and Archives

Photograph 2.17 (Top) Ereğli Town, View from Sea. Abdül Hamid Collection
Photograph 2.18 (Bottom) Kozlu Town. Abdül Hamid Collection

Photograph 3.1 (Top) Muleteer at Mine Entrance, ca. 1926. Collection of the Author
Photograph 3.2 (Bottom) Muleteer at SA Mine Entrance (doctored photo). Collection of the Author

Photograph 3.3 (Top) Kozlu, Workers at the Petri Mine. Abdül Hamid Collection
Photographs 3.4, 3.5, 3.6 (Bottom, l. to r.) Boy Basket Carrier, Worker before SH (Ereğli Company?) Mine, Worker with Lamp (photo perhaps reversed). Collection of the Author

Photograph 3.7 (Top) Zonguldak, Boat-Launching Area. Arsen Yarman Collection
Photograph 3.8 (Bottom) Kozlu Coal-Loading Pier. Abdül Hamid Collection

Photograph 3.9 Armutçuk Mine of Ahmed Efendi, Workers, and Equipment. Abdül Hamid Collection

Photograph 3.10 Armutçuk Mine of Ahmed Efendi, Workers, Machinery, and Machine Shop. Abdül Hamid Collection

6

MILITARY DUTY AND MINE WORK
The Blurred Vocations of Ottoman Soldier-Workers

Introduction

Locally recruited, active-duty soldiers were part of the labor mix that state and capital relied upon to extract and deliver coal. Together with local compulsory labor workers and the free market labor recruited from outside the region, these soldiers routinely worked in the coalfield, filling in the persistent gaps in the civilian work force. They formed an integral part of the solution to the problem of chronic labor shortages.

When voluntary labor had initially proved inadequate back in the 1840s and 1850s, the 1867 regulations had created a compulsory labor force of local workers obliged to spend one-half of each month in mine work. In 1906, as production mounted, free labor from outside the coalfield was summoned to remedy the defects ascribed by officials to these village workers—insufficient numbers and a poor work ethic. These measures were not fully successful, however, and significant numbers of active-duty soldiers also routinely worked in the minefield. Indeed, since soldier-workers usually received a fraction of civilian workers' wages, mine operators actually may have preferred them as a source of labor. Moreover, because they especially suffered from non-payment of the wages owed them, they were a particularly cheap form of labor. Even by the already oppressive standards of the coalfield, soldier-workers were exquisitely vulnerable participants in mine work.

The compulsory labor provisions of 1867 in principle had divided the male population of the coalfield between those working in mines and those serving on active military duty; performance of the one duty was supposed to preclude service in the other. In reality, however, the lines between soldier and worker often were quite blurred. During peace and war, active-duty soldiers worked in

---

Notes for this chapter begin on page 147.

the coalfield, supplementing and sometimes replacing the civilian work force. In peacetime, soldier-workers mainly worked in transport, hauling coal from the mine head and loading it onto ships. During the Ottoman-Russian War of the 1877–1878, soldiers nearly completely replaced civilian workers in the coal mines. But forty years later, during World War I, soldier-workers were almost completely absent.

The differing levels of soldier participation during these two great wars derive from a number of factors. The Ottoman-Russian War—its severity and loss of life notwithstanding—was a relatively limited conflict in terms of both the manpower and the resources it drained out of the Ottoman economy and society. Thus, soldiers from the front could be spared for mine work. By contrast, total war engulfed the Ottoman world between 1914 and 1918, demanding literally the totality of all resources that could be mustered. The relative youth of the compulsory labor system, scarcely a decade old at the time of the first conflict, surely played some role. Potential workers may have evaded labor bosses and state officials more readily than they did forty years later and besides, soldiers were in comparatively abundant supply in the 1870s. The state may have found it easier to direct soldiers to mine work than to locate and coerce a civilian compulsory labor force. Moreover, during the 1870s the civilian work force still was relatively inexperienced in mining so soldiers, even if those without prior knowledge of mining, could be used with comparatively fewer losses to efficiency than during World War I, after four long decades had created a skilled and experienced cohort of mine workers. Also, these four decades of experience with compulsory labor had deepened the disciplinary channels and inured villagers to mine labor.

The presence of these soldier-workers again highlights the powerful position in mining society enjoyed by village headmen. In this context, headmen emerge as powerful figures, determining who would mine and who would enter active military service. A headman's decision to accord a young man the status of miner protected him from service in distant lands, for example, the notorious Yemeni battlefields from which so few soldiers returned. The headman, literally, held the power of life and death over his fellow villagers. As I will show below, the continuous presence of active-duty soldiers as workers dramatically underscores the failure of state and capital to solve the labor problem in the Zonguldak coalfield.

Soldiers in the Mines

Military service played a vital role in the lives of Ottoman subjects everywhere, especially the men conscripted and their families, who lost breadwinners, sometimes for years and sometimes forever. With the implementation of (theoretically) universal conscription, which began in earnest in 1848, men between the ages of 20 and 40 years and in good health were called to military service.

In the Ottoman world, this was a severe obligation that legally could last for twenty years. In reality, near-lifetime conscriptions were not uncommon. Over the decades, the precise terms of military duty varied but generally included between 3 and 5 years of active-duty, followed by intervals of 2 to 6 years in the active reserve, and 4 to 7 years in the inactive reserve, and another 2 to 8 years in the home guard (see table 6.1). While on active-duty, a soldier might serve at the front or elsewhere but legally, after his tour of active-duty, the remainder of service was performed in the home district, except in wartime. As active reservists, the soldiers were to provide a disciplined, trained corps around which to build the inactive reserve. The inactive reserve, for its part, aimed to police the local countryside and handle local law and order issues.

Military personnel played an important role in the initial development of the coalfield and in these first years may have been the only persons extracting coal. In subsequent decades and throughout the remainder of the Ottoman period, active-duty soldiers regularly worked in mining operations. Thus, by 1867 they had been in steady use as workers during the decades between the site's initial exploitation and its formal organization as a coalfield (*havza*). During the Crimean War years, soldiers from all over the empire worked in the mines, some reportedly laboring throughout the entire term of their military service.[1] The 1867 reorganization brought about an important legal change. Universal conscription was in the process of becoming an Ottoman reality when, in 1867, coalfield residents fell under a second obligation, to serve in the mines. Thereafter, as seen in chapters 3 and 4, all male residents of

Table 6.1 Terms of Military Service, 1843–1914 (in years)

	Active Soldiers (*nizamiye*)	Active Reserve (*ihtiyat*)	Inactive Reserve (*redif*)	Home Guard (*mustahfız*)
1843	5		7	
1838–1848	5	2	7	8
1869	4	2	6	8
1879	3	3	6	6
1886	4	2	8	6
1886	3	6	9	2
maritime service		8 total	4	0
1914		20 regular	abolished	5
1914 maritime service		12 regular		5

Sources: (1) 1843, 1886 maritime service, 1914 and 1914 maritime service: Çatma (1998), 30–31. On 39–40, Çatma notes a 12 May 1914 law that changed the 1909 law. It abolished the inactive reserve and established 25-year military service—twenty years of regular service and five years of home guard. Zürcher (1999) simply says that the inactive reserve was merged with the regular army, adding that the merger should have happened in 1912 but was delayed until 1914. (2) 1838–1848, 1886: Shaw (1977), 100 and 246. (3) 1869, 1879: Zürcher (1999); over 32 years of age for inactive reserve and 32–40 years of age for home guard.

the coalfield between 13 and 50 were eligible for mine work, and their names were inscribed in special registers for that purpose. Nowhere do the 1867 provisions themselves state or imply that mine work would substitute for the military obligation. But clearly this was the case, since during the Ottoman-Russian War of 1877–1878 (also see chapter 9), the presence of separate labor pools for mine work and for active military duty guided administrators' decisions. Workers from the fourteen coal-mining districts who were registered in the rosters as subject to the compulsory labor requirement apparently were exempt from the duty to bear arms in active military duty and fight for the empire. Instead, the military authorities considered compulsory mine laborers to be inactive reservists and members of the home guard.

Thus, as an important study on the soldier-workers of Zonguldak correctly asserts: "[Y]ouths of military age in the coalfield, for the length of the time they were eligible for military service, worked in the mines as compulsory labor in inactive reserve divisions."[2] Significantly, this finding ties together the obligations of mine work and military duty. Men in the fourteen districts fulfilled both their soldierly duties and their compulsory labor obligations by working in the mines.[3] Left unresolved, however, is a certain lack of fit between the two duties—mine work and military service—that deserves attention. For military service, males were eligible between the ages of 20 and 40 years, while inactive reservists were to be over 32 years of age, and those in the home guard, between 32 and 40 years. For mine work, however, the age range of eligibility was much greater, between 13 and 50 years. Large numbers of boys and men both above and below the conscription age limits routinely worked in the mines. The records abundantly document the presence of teenagers belowground, both legally and then illegally, as laws redefined child labor and outlawed the work of boys under the age of 16 (chapter 4). Moreover, there were many men in their forties and even fifties working in the mines (chapters 7–9). Thus, even in theory, mine labor could not have been a simple substitute for military service since compulsory mining work included those both too young and too old for military duty.

A key to resolving the apparent contradiction lies—again—in appreciating the vital role that village (and hamlet) headmen played in designating the mine labor force. Headmen provided lists of those actually doing mine work. As long as the persons listed kept working in the mines, they were not to go into the military. When, as numerous documents from the mine superintendent's office make clear, the record keepers noticed absences from mine work, the absentees immediately were conscripted (at least in wartime). Thus, once inscribed in the registration books as mine workers, these boys and men supposedly could not be conscripted as long as they actually did the work. They now theoretically belonged to a manpower pool separate from those required to serve in the military.

This principle, at work in the 1870s, clearly was reiterated in May 1912, as the empire struggled to find manpower during the mounting crisis surrounding the

Tripolitanian War with Italy and the Balkan Wars. When mobilization immediately caused labor shortages in the coalfield, the district official, under orders from the mine superintendent, called together mine operators, including the director of the Ereğli Company. In the meeting, the district official tried to assure his listeners that labor supplies would remain available. He reminded them of the ongoing policy regarding the rotational labor force. Regularly employed mine workers who were in the inactive reserves and home guard previously had not been eligible for active-duty and, he pledged, would not be. He defined the conditions of exemption. And he sought to protect those who had been working in the mines for years and to screen out those who would "lie outrageously,"[4] pretending to be mine workers or seeking mine work to avoid military duty. To these ends, mine operators were to provide the superintendent with labor force rosters. The ledgers would list the names, places of origin, and occupations of all persons who in the past and at present were part of the rotational labor force, with an established work record of 150 days per year. Further, the operators needed to certify, with appropriate revenue stamps, the accuracy of the ledger, formally attesting that those recorded within were "real, genuine, authentic" workers.[5] Several days later, the superintendent, clarifying an apparent confusion, reminded all parties that workers who were back in the home villages on the rest part of their rotation were to remain exempt from active military service.[6]

The distinction between mine workers exempt from military service and soldiers was intended to ensure sufficient labor for the strategically crucial coal industry. Miners would mine and soldiers, when present in the mine district, would provide security. The reality, of course, was somewhat different, since in fact, miners soldiered and soldiers labored at mine work. The War Ministry repeatedly intervened in mine affairs and, despite strident protests from the mine superintendent, commandeered mine workers for military duty. Villagers inscribed on the list of miners thus were dragged off to fight on faraway front lines against foreign enemies such as Greece in 1897, or quell domestic uprisings, like the one in early twentieth-century Macedonia. Meanwhile, since mine labor remained in chronically short supply and because the coalfield remained under military administration until 1910, active-duty soldiers formed a frequent and sometimes crucial source of manpower for the mines.

Fragments of evidence in the existing secondary literature testify to the use of soldiers as mine workers. Former miner Erol Çatma wrote a very useful 1998 book, *Soldier Workers*, powerfully influenced by the Turkish Republic's draconian measures to maintain a mine labor force during World War II. Often quoting extensively from Ottoman state documents, he argues that soldier-workers dominated the coalfield work force during the Ottoman period as well. That is, Çatma seeks to demonstrate that soldier-workers, a brutal reality in his own lifetime, were a characteristic element of mine work during the Ottoman era as well. The following seeks to determine the actual extent to which soldiers were used as mine workers during the Ottoman period.

Soldier-Workers in Peacetime

The question that Çatma raises—the participation of active-duty conscripts in above- or belowground mine work—is a crucial one because it addresses the essential nature of the mining labor force. His vigorous assertions about their central role notwithstanding, Çatma offers only a few examples of soldier-workers as concrete evidence for their presence. He presents the following cases: in July 1896, a soldier from the Ereğli area was paid for unspecified mine work while elsewhere a soldier deserted his job while at the mines and in December 1898, rations were being provided for soldiers working the semi-monthly shift.[7]

Accident reports and the accountants' ledgers from the superintendent's office provide enriching and suggestive evidence of mining labor by active-duty soldiers. The accident reports, for their part, almost never indicate the presence of soldier-workers. The scope of these reports encompassed underground and aboveground work, including the movement of coal and workers between the mines, the loading facilities and residential centers (see chapters 7 and 8). The port of Zonguldak itself occasionally is included, but not very often. There are hundreds of reports of accidents belowground that had thousands of victims or witnesses. Importantly, not one of these records the presence of soldier-workers (or soldiers) working underground during peacetime. Aboveground, soldiers are mentioned in a number of accident reports but almost always in their capacity as military personnel guarding trains, train stations, the port, or serving in garrisons at various locations. In the accident reports, they repeatedly are featured, for example, as disciplinary forces in the stories of workers illegally hitching rides on (or more accurately, falling off of) coal trains moving between the mines and the port. Hardly ever do the aboveground accident reports note soldiers' presence as workers during peacetime. Among the hundreds of accidents reported between 1893 and 1907, there are just two cases involving soldier-workers. The first concerns Osman b. Mustafa, a native of Ereğli, who was enrolled as a marine soldier. Serving as a boat launcher chief in the Zonguldak locale, he contracted an unspecified disease and died in the military hospital at Kozlu in May 1894.[8] Later on, in 1905, ten anonymous imperial soldiers are noted as repairing the railroad at the Kozlu and Kilimli locales.[9] Are these the tip of an unreported iceberg, or should we take soldiers' low involvement in accidents as an indicator of scant participation in the aboveground work force?

To probe further into the question of how often soldiers were utilized as workers, I have examined three different sets of accountants' ledgers. These are, first, several annual accounts of individual mines between 1889 and 1896; second, a debit ledger dated 1906; and, third, a ledger of debits and credits from 1907.

In one ledger, accountants monthly itemized the debits and credits of 136 separate mines between 1889 and 1896, including payments to workers of all kinds, both named individuals and anonymous groups. During this period, when production was not markedly different from the two previous decades, output averaged only some 150,000 tons, about one-sixth its subsequent peak. These accounts show soldiers present at only a few mines. In this comprehensive accounting of 136 mines, soldiers are recorded as present at just seven mines. In another ledger, for 1894–1895, soldiers appear in the accounting of a different seven out of a total of 121 mines. They usually were present in the ledgers of the most important companies of the era, those providing the majority of the coal—the mines of the Karamanyan, Giurgiu, and Karamahmudzadeler companies.[10] In most instances, the labor they performed in the particular mine is not clear: they are itemized only as "imperial soldiers" (*asakir-ı şahane*), without further elaboration. Since these soldiers are recorded in the ledgers of only a few mines, we can safely assume that the payments were not for their military services. If that had been the case, "imperial soldier" entries arguably would have appeared in every mine's account, since military forces were scattered throughout the entire coalfield for disciplinary purposes.

In a very small minority of cases, the ledgers specify sums spent for the mining labor by soldiers and not merely for "imperial soldiers." In January 1895, "soldier-workers" (*asker amelesi ücreti* or *asker amelesi*) received payments at two Zonguldak mines, while a third Zonguldak mine in October 1895, and an Alacaağzı mine in 1894, made payments to soldiers who were boat launchers. On a larger scale, the Kozlu #232 Giurgiu mine made payments in 1893 to soldier boat launchers that equaled one-third of all the labor wages paid by that mine. At the same #232 mine, an 1895 "imperial soldiers" entry noted, without further details, payments approximately equal to those made for the boat launcher work of soldiers during the preceding year, 1894. This documentation suggests that when "imperial soldiers" appear in ledgers, they are working, not soldiering. At mine #232, in 1894 and 1895, soldier-workers' wages again formed one-third of the total sums paid for labor.[11]

Even at the larger mines where most soldier-miners were working, they formed a small portion of the total work force present. The #131 Karamanyan mine at Alacaağzı in 1895 paid "imperial soldiers" a sum equaling 20 percent of all monies it paid in wages during the year.[12] At the #299 Pavlaki and Vasil mine at Zonguldak, monies for "imperial soldiers" equaled around 9 percent of its total expenditures for labor. Other examples yield broadly similar results. Between 1889 and 1896 at the #131 Giurgiu mine, accounts indicate about 4,000 man-days of labor. Soldiers provided an estimated 1,356 man-days while non-soldier-workers, to call them that here, worked twice as many, about 2,600 man-days. In yet another example, from the #299 mine in 1894, the contribution of soldier-workers is still smaller. At this mine, while all types of labor performed a total of about 5,800 man-days of work, soldier-workers provided only about 800 man-days of labor. Civilian workers, for their part, contributed the balance, approximately 5,000 man-days.[13] Thus, in the final examples of these two mines, soldiers provided about one-quarter of the labor.

Altogether, these account books, which record wage payments by the individual mines, show some variation in the contribution by soldier-workers to the total labor needs of a particular mine. Even among the larger mines, where their contribution was the greatest, soldier-workers usually accounted for roughly 10 to 25 percent of the total labor requirements. In sum, soldiers as workers steadily contributed to the aggregate peacetime work force in the coalfield, but in relatively small numbers.

These mine accounts illustrate that the line between soldier and miner indeed was blurred and easily crossed, an elision readily made by contemporaries. The account ledgers note soldier-workers at mines on nearly fifty separate occasions between 1889 and 1896. Clearly, their presence was routine and without need of explanation or justification. Nor, as the following demonstrate, are the accounting ledgers the only place where I found the blurring and crossing of lines. Other records, noting the appointment and departure of workers, illustrate how readily workers moved from their civilian jobs to military duty and back again. In some cases, the workers' military service was in the active-duty reserves. Take, for example, Mustafaağazde Hüseyin, the head carpenter at Kozlu. He left his job on 18 December 1910 to enter the active reserve, but just three days later the official in charge issued orders so that Hüseyin could return to his job on 28 December 1910. During that ten day absence, moreover, he continued to draw his carpenter's wage. But on other occasions, the service apparently was active-duty, not just a stint in the active reserves. Again, the carpenter Hüseyin was involved. Six months after resuming his civilian job, Hüseyin set out for military service (askerlik), which the records treat as distinct from active reserve duty (ihtiyat). At this time, the official specified that Hüseyin would return to his regular work duties after only forty-five days of service. The official ordered a native of Devrek to fill the post in the meantime, at the same wage. In another example, a carpenter returned home on leave from military service on 20 September 1911 and just twelve days later resumed his civilian job. In yet another example, a road foreman went to military service on 30 August 1910 but returned and went back to work on 1 December 1910.[14] The ease with which Hüseyin and his fellow workers moved between their civilian tasks and discharging their varying kinds of military duties seems remarkable and underscores the fluid nature of the division between soldier and worker in the coalfield.

Another set of ledgers (düyun defterleri), which monthly recorded various kinds of debts or payments to the mine personnel, also illuminate the role of soldiers as coalfield workers. These records exclusively concern aboveground employees and workers. Transactions involving soldiers (asakir-ı şahane) are documented several different ways in these accounts. Significantly for my argument, the records of military personnel in these ledgers makes clear when they were soldiering and when they were laboring as mine workers.[15] For the period 1905[16]–1907,[17] I can offer a number of conclusions about soldiers in the coalfield, unique insights into the role of military personnel as mine workers.

A note of caution, however, is in order before comparing the wages received by soldier-workers, compulsory workers, and free-market labor. In looking at wage levels comparatively, I first needed to consider non-monetary contributions to the livelihoods of the three different groups. Soldier-workers received housing, uniforms, and rations from the state in addition to wages. The situation for compulsory laborers was not totally dissimilar. Much of their food came from their own farm plots and thus was "free" in a certain, strictly monetary sense of needing no cash to be actually laid out for food. Also, their housing at work often was without monetary cost—some enjoyed company-provided barracks, while others fashioned quarters in caves or hovels that, however miserable, were rent-free. If their clothing was market-made and not homespun, workers bore some monetary burden for it. Free-market workers lived better but endured higher-out-of pocket maintenance costs than either soldier-workers or the compulsory labor force. They had access to better company housing, certainly on a more frequent basis. But they garnered neither state nor household support for their housing, clothing, or shelter needs. Thus, the nominal differences among the wages of soldier-workers, compulsory laborers, and free workers noted below must be read and analyzed with these factors in mind.

Having spotlighted these differences in expenditures, I turn to a comparison of soldiers' and soldier-workers' wages with those of the other two groups from the debt records. First, in the coalfield overall, the sums spent on soldiers carrying out military duties (57,585 krs) surpassed that paid for soldiers performing labor tasks (39,001 krs). Elsewhere, we will see, the coalfield suffered from a shortage of soldiers enforcing discipline.[18] Second, the overall sums spent for aboveground civilian workers' wages vastly exceeded that spent on soldier-workers. In 1906, wages of civilian workers were more than ten times greater, equaling 145,443 krs, than soldier-workers' wages. The disparity in wage totals is only partially due to discrepancies in the respective sizes of the civilian[19] and soldier-worker work forces, 874 and 402 persons, 1,276 in total. Civilian aboveground workers thus outnumbered soldier-workers by a margin of more than two to one. Put another way, soldier-workers in this case formed 32 percent of the aboveground work force but accounted for only 9 percent of the payroll. The average wage of each soldier-worker totaled only about one-fifth that of a civilian worker (34 vs. 167 krs).[20] As another example, consider three soldier-workers who labored full-time throughout the year. Each received a daily wage of only about 5 krs—a very low figure, below that of any category of compulsory labor, including basket carriers. Soldier-workers, obviously, were poorly paid.[21]

Only thirty-four soldier-workers are individually named (between four and nine monthly), and nearly all of them were locals. They worked mainly at the harbor and the town of Ereğli provided the largest single contingent.[22] Thus, Ismail b. Hüseyin and Hasan b. Mehmed Ali from Ereğli joined Zonguldak natives Nuri b. Ali and Yusuf b. Ismail in harbor work, while Mehmed b. Mustafa from Bartın labored at the Kilimli locale. Named individual soldier-workers earned a median monthly wage of 80 krs. By contrast, soldier-workers whose monthly wages were recorded anonymously in groups earned just 24 krs each.

Given their comparatively high wages, soldier-workers who are individually named presumably were so indicated because of their high military rank or, less likely, the relatively skilled occupations they held (the ledger does not present either piece of information). Long-term work seems to have been rare among these better-paid soldier-workers. Fewer than 10 percent of them labored month in and month out, while several others worked only during three or four months of the year.

At each mine locale (for example, Zonguldak or Kozlu), the vast majority of payments to soldier-workers were recorded only as going to anonymous groups that collectively received a certain sum of money. For example, there were groups of unidentified soldier-workers whose labor was reported during the months of June, August, and November. In these months, anonymous soldier-worker groups respectively numbered 93, 110, and 123 persons and earned an average wage of 25 krs for work periods of unknown duration during the reported month.[23] The similar levels of the aggregate payroll over the course of the three months suggests that the duration of the work was similar for each of the three months. During the other nine months, no such work groups are recorded.

The wages noted in this ledger thus make clearer the varied experiences of soldier-workers during the peacetime year of 1906. Workers on active military duty remained in their home district, where they were called to labor in the coalfield, often in its port facility. These statistical data reinforce the impression gained from literary sources that soldier-workers often served as boat launchers and in other areas of surface transport. A minority of the soldier-workers labored full-time, but most worked for just a few weeks during the year. Finally, soldier-workers accounted for about one in every three aboveground workers.

There is yet another wage ledger, for the fiscal year 1907, of use when considering soldiers as workers.[24] In a different format from that above, it often corroborates the evidence just presented. In a sample (table 6.2) taken from one month of the ledger under examination, 98 percent of the recorded soldier-workers were locals. The few who were not from the coalfield came from quite close by, for example, from Çarşamba, just east of its legal boundaries. Thus, virtually every soldier-worker whose place of origin is noted was a coalfield native.[25] A sample from another ledger spanning April 1906 through March 1907 offers similar results: except for three who came from Çarşamba, all named soldiers were locals.[26] From this evidence, the following larger observations can be made. Upon military conscription, soldiers served at least part of their tour of active-duty within just a few kilometers of their birthplaces. It is noteworthy that all aboveground soldier-workers were from towns of the region, unlike the belowground workers who, without exception, were villagers. This reinforces the impression that a division of labor existed in the coalfield, in which most boat launchers (and perhaps stevedores as well) were active-duty conscripts from its few urban centers, while the underground labor came from the villages, which held the vast majority of the local population.[27]

Table 6.2 Origins of Soldiers Working in the Kozlu Locale, October 1907

Alaplı	5
Bartın	8
Çarşamba	2
Cide	17
Devrek	22
Ereğli	6
Zonguldak	21
Total	81

Source: KU 71.

In 1907, not only were soldier-workers paid far less than civilian aboveground workers, but they also were less likely to be paid promptly. During the year overall, the superintendency incurred debts for labor totaling 148,748 krs, of which 19 percent was owed to soldier-workers and 81 percent to civilians (see table 6.3). Payments actually made, however, were much less than the amounts owed. The difference between the amounts recorded as owed and the sums actually paid to the two groups equaled about 45,000 krs,[28] a sum that likely constituted arrears in wages. Thus, more than one-third of all wages owed went unpaid in 1907. Soldier-workers fared far worse than compulsory civilian labor. In this case, 56 percent of their owed wages were in arrears compared to a 25 percent arrears rate for compulsory civilian workers (see table 6.3).

Table 6.3 Wages of Workers and Soldier-Workers, 1907 (in krs)

	Workers	Soldier-Workers
Owed	121,036 (81%)	27,712 (19%)
Paid	91,227 (88%)	12,540 (12%)
Percent in arrears	25	56

Source: KU 71.

Ledgers: A Source for the History of Soldier-Workers?

At first appearance, the presence of a ledger with the names of workers and soldier-workers would seem a real boon to the labor historian. And yet, the character and inconsistent nature of the accounting procedures limits its utility. The nature of the reporting disguises the activities and numbers of soldiers and soldier-workers in aboveground work in several ways. (See chapter 3 for a similar discussion of civilian workers.) First of all, the ledger is inconsistent in its reporting procedures. During some months, the ledger records the full name—father's, son's, personal name and city of origin, for example, Zonguldaklı Hasanoğlu Hüseyin b. Ahmed is Hüseyin Hasanoğlu, the son of Ahmed, from Zonguldak. But in another month, we read just the personal name or part of the full name, for example, Hüseyin. For a few months, the register notes the name of every single person. But during other months, we find only payments for unnamed individual soldier-workers. Thus, it is hardly ever possible to trace the work activity of an individual from month to month over the course of the year.

Equally problematic, the ledger presents lump sum amounts paid to groups of unnamed workers or soldier-workers of undetermined size, without any means of determining the number of persons to whom wages are due.[29] Moreover, when individuals (both named and unnamed) are paid, the sums recorded fluctuate quite sharply. The wages owed to a single soldier-worker for unspecified labor fluctuate between 12 and 31 krs. These variations certainly reflect differences in the time worked and the task performed that cannot be known from the source used here.

Also, the gross monthly totals of wages recorded as paid during a certain month do not accurately reflect the labor actually performed in that month. For example, the total wages paid in February are greater than those paid in July.[30] This cannot be correct given the known seasonal nature of mine work, which often shut down operations during the winter months. The amounts recorded arguably reflect accounting procedures or time lags in payment rather than actual work activity. Thus, there can be no precise determination of the actual monthly presence of soldier-workers.

Bearing these limitations in mind, I again turn to the wages and numbers of soldier-workers in the aboveground work force. Table 6.4 seeks to take advantage of the occasional practice of recording the names and paid wages of individual workers and soldier-workers. In the sample, from one month in the Kozlu locale, just thirteen workers collectively received more wages than 81 soldier-workers— that is, they received an average 159 krs while their active-duty soldier-worker counterparts earned about 12 percent of that amount, just 18 krs.[31]

Given the wild disparities in reported wages of the aboveground work force, I turned to the device of median wages to better understand the wage structure and more effectively compare wages received by workers and soldier-workers. Thus, there were eight workers at the port, among them Mustafa from Devrek district within the coalfield and Mehmed from Kayseri, far away in southeast Anatolia. The eight received a median wage of 115 krs in July 1907; by contrast, seventeen

Table 6.4 Wages of Soldier-Workers and Workers in the Kozlu Locale, October 1907

	Persons	Total Wage	Ave. Wage (in krs)
Soldier-workers	81	1,377	18
Workers	13	2,063	159

Source: KU 71.

anonymous soldier-workers at the port in that September obtained a median wage of 29 krs, just one-quarter the median wage for civilian workers at the same locale. At Kozlu, twenty-six workers received a median wage of 209 krs in September 1907, while at the same locale in October, eighty-two soldier-workers' wages equaled 22 krs, only 10 percent of the civilians' wage. In this instance, the workers are recorded anonymously but we learn the names of all eighty-two soldier-workers. Thus, in October Ahmed b. Mehmed from Devrek received 15 krs while Osman b. Mehmed from Zonguldak earned twice that amount but Hüseyin b. Ali from Bartın just 10 krs. In February, the seventy-nine soldier-workers at Kozlu who received a median wage of 29 krs are listed without names. In each respective month, soldier-workers' median wage was a fraction—25 percent, 11 percent, and 14 percent—of civilian workers' at the same locations.

Altogether, 321 civilian workers and 345 soldier-workers were recorded individually, often anonymously with a particular wage, but infrequently by name and place of origin. In most instances, the workers' origins are not noted. Thus, the carpenters Kadıoğlu Rasim and Mustafoğlu Hüseyin worked at Kozlu and the master building repair worker Manug at Kilimli, but we learn nothing more about them. However, from the minority of those named together with their places of origins, the diversity of the work force becomes clear. General laborers called Kurban Ismail and Ali from Gürün and Van in eastern Anatolia joined Abdi Aziz from Eskişehir in the western part of the peninsula and Ahmed, a railroad worker from Samsun on the Black Sea. The median wage for the 321 workers listed individually in 1907 equaled 200 krs. By contrast, the wages of soldier-workers who were noted individually totaled 28 krs, just 14 percent of the median wage of workers. Like the workers, many were listed anonymously, simply as "soldier-worker." Unlike the workers, the places of origin are noted for virtually all named soldier-workers, among whom nearly everyone came from within the coalfield or quite close by, from places such as Alaplı, Zonguldak, Bartın, Ereğli, and Cide.

In addition to the individual workers who received wages are some 110 other workers whose payments were recorded collectively and anonymously in lump sums. Thus, from the 1907 ledger I can piece together a composite record of 431 workers and 345 soldier-workers in the aboveground work force during 1907, a total of 776 persons.[32]

In summary: the various ledgers (but not the accident reports) demonstrate that in peacetime soldier-workers regularly accounted for a not-insubstantial proportion of the aboveground work force. Their numbers were in the several hundreds, and in 1906–1907, they formed between one-third and two-fifths of the aboveground work force. Some soldiers were more or less permanently assigned to coalfield work, while others were intermittently employed, likely used for only weeks or even days at a time. In all cases, the evidence shows unmistakably that they were poorly paid, earning 85–90 percent less than civilian workers. The ledgers also show, importantly, that the everyday presence and indispensability of soldier-workers in peacetime is an indisputable fact.

Soldier-Workers in Wartime

During the Ottoman-Russian War era (also see chapter 9), soldiers were the major source of mine labor as the state vacuumed up virtually all the available manpower for military duties. Despite the formal division of the local manpower into separate pools for mine work and for military service, around 90 percent of the male population of many mine districts had been mobilized into the military, leaving only 10 percent to be assigned as workers.[33] To fill the gap, soldiers drafted into the military immediately were turned over for work in the minefield, thus serving their active-duty time in mine labor, receiving workers' wages.[34] In these difficult days, the state conscripted townspeople of the mine districts who normally were exempt from compulsory mine service and sent them as soldiers to work in the mines.[35] The soldiers most commonly worked at relatively unskilled tasks, notably launching boats, loading coal onto ships, and cutting wood.[36] Fewer labored as hewers at the coal face.[37]

In September 1911, more than forty years after the end of the debilitating conflict with Russia, the Ottoman state embarked on a decades of wars, from the Tripolitanian War of 1911 and the Balkan Wars of 1912–1913 through World War I, 1914–1918, and the Turkish War of Independence, 1919–1922.[38]

On 14 October 1912, less than a week after the First Balkan War began, the Karamahmudzadeler Company and other mine operators at Kilimli complained of labor shortages as foremen, hewers, and workers began to take up arms and coal production fell off sharply. The Marine Ministry asked the War Ministry to exempt mine workers from active military service.[39] That same day, the Commerce and Agriculture Minister, who was responsible for the mines, assented to the exemption request. Coal for the fleet was understood to be vital to the success of the war effort and more important than the presence of a few additional soldiers at the front. Complaining of his inability to find non-conscripted miners, the minister ordered all coal workers who had been drafted to remain at their mining tasks.[40] Shortages simultaneously developed in the Kozlu mines. Since the Bartın brigade could not provide men, the superintendent—unusually—took recourse to the Devrek and Çaycuma brigades, ordering them to turn over their inactive reserves and home guards for mine work.[41] Except for the Amasra mines, where there were sufficient numbers of workers, labor shortages plagued the entire coalfield in the fall of 1912.

In response, the superintendent sought to obtain mine labor both from those listed in the military rosters as members of the reserves and home guard as well from those inscribed in registers as mine workers. These two groups supposedly were distinct, but the lines between them essentially disappeared during this wartime labor shortage crisis. He sent identical directives, on 22 October 1912, to mine officials in each of seven different mine locales, listing the communities that were to supply villagers who were mine workers but who were attached to the brigades of Bartın, Ereğli, Devrek, and Çaycuma. In other words, the brigades were to turn over experienced workers to the mine operators.[42] To identify the workers, furthermore, the superintendent checked the headmen's lists of registered workers and the mine operators' lists of those actually at work. Thus, a month after hostilities had begun, the soldiers remained at work in the mines, even after their mobilization.[43] For example, on 23 November 1912, the Ereğli Company asked the Ereğli, Çaycuma, and Devrek brigades to provide a list of foremen, machinists and other craftsmen, as well as workers, who had been assembled and dispatched for work at its mines.

These efforts reaped numbers sufficient to produce an overabundance of workers, at least temporarily. And so the superintendent asked the Ereğli Company to reward workers for their willingness to show up at the mines, even though they had performed no labor, rather extraordinarily requesting half pay for all those who were returning to their villages because they were unneeded at the mines.[44]

Less than two months later, in early December 1912, the superintendent less favorably reported on manpower supplies in the region (table 6.5). Altogether, the three brigades of the coalfield reported that 6,928 men were on their rosters either as unassigned soldiers, inactive reserves, or home guards.[45] The superintendent pleaded that the men not be sent off to fight but rather kept locally to mine coal. He said that 800 of them were allotted to the mines in the Ereğli locale and that the War Ministry had assigned the remainder to work at the Zonguldak locale mines. A commission, headed by the superintendent and a general staff officer lieutenant colonel (*erkani harbiye kaymakamı*) had been scouring the countryside to find workers. District officials at both Ereğli and Devrek had gone out to the villages, looking "day and night" for workers. Despite their best efforts, they had gathered only 1,499 persons (22 percent of those nominally present on the brigades' rosters). Since 335 of the 1,499 available conscripts were to be sent off for military duties, only 1,164 men (17 percent) remained available for mine work (table 6.5). To fill the gaps, the commission sought to find and bring to the mines: (1) unassigned soldiers who were not working in the mines; (2) those eligible for but not already in military service; and (3) permanent workers, not part of the compulsory labor system, who were on vacation.[46]

Table 6.5 Potential and Actual Conscripts, 1912

	(a) On brigade rosters	(b) Actually collected	(b) as a % of (a)
Ereğli brigade	1,957	300	15
Devrek brigade	2,491	621	25
Çaycuma brigade	2,490	578	23
Total	6,928	1,499	22

Source: ED 12, 251–252, 23 ts 1328, #1924.

Later in December 1912, the superintendent reported that he had received eight register books from the most important companies in the region: the Ereğli Company, Rombaki, Pavlaki, Ahmed Ali, Boyacıoğlu, and Giurgiu. The registers noted the names and total numbers of inactive reservists and home guards who were registered as workers in their mines but not present in those mines. The superintendent informed the Zonguldak district official that such persons henceforth were stripped of their status as workers and were required to bear arms. They at once were to be dispatched to the war zones.[47]

The superintendent reviewed the situation for his superior, the Commerce and Agriculture Minister, in May 1913. Earlier labor shortages had developed, he said, because workers from Ereğli, Zonguldak, and, to a lesser extent, Bartın, had been sent off to war. As coal supplies dwindled, the state decided against shipping out conscripted workers and instead retained them at the mines. Using these soldiers indeed had a favorable impact on coal shipments. Moreover, he stated, during the winter "unemployed" workers from neighboring areas just south of the coalfield—such as Kangiri—had found work in the mines and consequently, he no longer needed to resort to soldiers. But as spring had approached, many of the workers who had come "of their own free will" returned to their villages for agricultural work. The number of workers at the mines fell 50 percent. And so, the War Ministry issued orders to again employ soldiers in the mines.[48]

Other documents from the Balkan War era demonstrate that critical labor shortages meant shuffling scarce soldier-labor power from one location to another in the coalfield. Many soldier-workers had been working at mine repairs and shoveling coal at the depots located near the mine heads at both Kozlu and Kilimli locales and were seen as especially valuable in preventing the collapse of various mineshafts. But they had been withdrawn from this vital maintenance work and sent off to work in mines at Zonguldak. This decision was seen as especially harmful to operation of the Kozlu mines because agricultural needs had already reduced the numbers of workers available in that locale. The director of the Ihsaniye mine at Kozlu requested the return of the soldier-workers, arguing that extra workers weren't needed at Zonguldak since lots of coal readily was available there for shipment.

The superintendent responded favorably. Soldier-miners were very few in number, he indicated (incidentally affirming the conclusion I presented above). But, he noted, their repair work was playing an essential role in protecting workers inside the mines. Safe workers meant productive workers and more coal for the state's strategic needs (see chapters 7 and 8). Therefore, he ordered the return of the soldier-workers to Kilimli and Kozlu and to the Ihsaniye mine in particular.[49] On the same day, the superintendent reminded his superiors at the Commerce and Agriculture Ministry that he needed more than just the assigned workers to meet the government's needs for coal, then estimated at 2,000 tons per day. If the fleet, the Naval Ministry, the ferryboat service at Istanbul, and the government factories were to be supplied, the military must yield up its unassigned soldiers, inactive reservists, and home guards for mine work.[50]

The situation prevailing during the Balkan Wars surely deteriorated still further during World War I. The manpower shortages already evident during the Balkan Wars clearly became much worse. As mobilization for World War I began, most of those available for mine work were "children, old men, malingerers unfit for military service and those who never worked in a mine."[51] Coal production plummeted. In 1916 it was scarcely one-quarter the 1913 levels, and it fell still further in 1917 and 1918. Few miners—whether as workers or soldier-workers—were present in the mines.

In the absence of more direct testimony, accident reports can help to determine whether there were workers eligible for military service in the mines. Since the reports sometimes include the ages of victims and witnesses in their descriptions of accidents, they afford a means of determining if these workers in the mines were of military age, that is, between the ages of 20 and 40 years. Overall, between 1893 and 1914 (before the Sarajevo crisis) the accident statistics show a remarkably consistent age distribution pattern, with a blip in 1912 and 1913. Between 1893 and 1907, when there were no major wars, 56 percent of all accident victims or witnesses were in their twenties and thirties.[52] But then, during the first year of the Balkan Wars, in 1912 and early 1913, the involvement of workers who were 20–40 years old and thus eligible for military service increased remarkably. Indeed, 82 percent of all accident victims or witnesses at this time were between 20 and 40 years of age; the rest were a mix of teenagers and workers older than forty.

Given the manpower demands of the wars, this seems anomalous, and there is no documented explanation at hand. It might well be due to changes in accident reporting that had occurred between the end of one set of accident reports, in 1907, and the resumption of the new set, in 1912. During the interval, there had been important improvements in accident reporting procedures (see Appendix on the Reporting of Accidents). Thus, it is possible that the accident rates of 1912–1913 more truly reflect age distribution patterns of mine workers than the 1893–1907 data and that the 1893–1907 reports underreported the presence of 20- to 40-year-olds in mine work. As the Balkan Wars continued into 1913 and 1914 (before the Sarajevo crisis), the percentage of 20- to 40-year-olds appearing in accident reports dropped sharply, back to the levels of the peacetime era between 1893 and 1907. This drop in the presence of draft-age miners at accident sites during the later days of the Balkan Wars era suggests that the wars were more and more a drain on Ottoman society and, that in the coalfield, the 20- to 40-year-old cohort increasingly was being conscripted and taken away from mine labor. Thus, 54 percent of workers involved in accidents were of conscription age, in their twenties and thirties, while 12 percent were 40 years or over.[53]

Several different pieces of evidence from the later years of World War I confirm this picture of the growing strain that the demands of war put on local manpower sources. First among these is the precipitous drop, compared to previous periods, in the proportion of draft-age persons who were involved in mining accidents. (There are no statistics for the Ottoman-Russian War era.) The age distribution pattern of victims or witnesses of accidents at the end of World War I is radically different from all preceding periods, whether of the Balkan Wars or peacetime. Between 1917 and 1919, only 21 percent were of normal conscription age; most were older. A full 71 percent of all accident victims or witnesses were 43–45 years of age, too old for military service and or even for the inactive reserve or the home guard.[54] Thus, while one-half and more of all victims or witnesses were of draft age during the various decades before 1917, this group's share falls steeply, to less than one-quarter, between 1917 and 1919. The sample thus suggests that few soldiers or persons eligible for military induction were present in the mines during World War I[55] (table 6.6).

The impression provided by accident reports of the late World War I era—that few men of normal conscription age worked in the coalfield—is reinforced by a completely different kind of data, a payroll ledger for the period 1915–1920 where the superintendent's office carefully recorded employees' and workers' names, occupations, wages, and duration of service. More than 200 persons were listed: the professional staff numbered 61, while aboveground workers, skilled and unskilled, respectively totaled 52 and 101 persons. Each record noted the individual's length of service and when he assumed or left a position. It specifically noted resignations that had been tendered in order to enter military service. In this enumeration, 19 percent of the skilled workers and 8 percent of the unskilled workers in the register had left their jobs to perform military service. Thus, by all accounts, skilled workers were twice as likely to be drafted as were their unskilled colleagues. After all, it is quite likely that more unskilled than skilled workers already had been conscripted to meet the manpower needs of the long, deadly war. In sum, during this wartime era in which military manpower demands peaked, a surprisingly scant 12 percent of the combined skilled and unskilled workers quit their jobs because of conscription. This low figure attests to the severity of the wartime crisis; it seems fair to surmise that most draft-age men had already been taken away to the front lines. Payroll records reinforce the evidence from the accident reports that relatively few men of draft age were doing aboveground work during the World War I era, just as the accident reports indicate their absence belowground.

Table 6.6 Ages of Accident Victims and Witnesses, 1893–1919 (in %)

	Under 20	20–40	Over 40
1893–1907	44	56	0
1912–1913	11	82	7
1913–1914	34	54	12
1917–1919	7	21	71

Source: ED 3 and ED 16.

Within the context of this single payroll register, soldier-workers are present in comparatively large numbers. Indeed, they form about one-fifth of the unskilled workers present. Most worked for four months or less, temporarily filling in gaps, but a few did longer-term labor. While their tasks generally were not specified, many are noted to have performed railroad work, helping to rebuild or maintain the beds on which the rails ran. Others loaded coal onto ships. Strikingly, the wages of soldier-workers now equaled those of the unskilled workers whose jobs they were filling—that is, they obtained market wages for their work. Thus, in July 1918, soldier-workers daily earned 15–20 krs, the same wages being paid to various categories of civilian laborers, including the general workers and roadbed workers whose places they were taking.[56] In sum, during this wartime crisis, market pressures seem to have shattered the long-standing differential between the wages of soldier-workers and civilian-workers.

Notes

1. Çatma (1998), 81. In 1875, some 500 *soldats de marine* transported the coal from the mines to the coast by mule, and the pay for this service was deducted from the price the government paid the operator. Quataert (1983), 56–57.
2. Çatma (1998), 81.
3. Çatma (1998), 107.
4. KU KD 2, 491, ca. 14 Mayıs 1328.
5. KU KD 2, 477, 12 Mayıs 1328.
6. KU KD 2, 478–479, 2 Mayıs 1328; 491, 14 Mayıs 1328; 477, 12 Mayıs 1328, 475, 11 Mayıs 1328; 478, 12 Mayıs 1328; 479, 12 Mayıs 1328 and 490, 14 Mayıs 1328.
7. Çatma (1998), 106; *Belge* 8 and 9.
8. ED 3, 11, #65, 6 Mayıs 1310 and also 10, #65. There is only other exception to the absence of soldiers as victims or witnesses in accidents; in a document dating from 1917 is an accident that occurred in front of a military depot when a passing train injured a soldier. Otherwise, soldiers are fully absent from the accident reports.
9. ED 3, 203, #23, 15 Haziran 1320/28 June 1905.
10. In two-thirds of the 51 entries noting soldiers, they are working for large companies.
11. Based on analysis of the ledgers KU 64, 1304–1311 and KU 208, 1309–1310.
12. In this case, there were credit payments in arrears to imperial soldiers stretching over a seven-year period between 1888 and 1894.
13. Based on an assumption of five krs per man day. See chapter 9.
14. KU 158, 51, 64, 95, and 96.
15. KU 207, 147–149. Sometimes the names and wages of individual soldiers appear; sometimes only a total number and aggregate wage of unnamed persons is noted. Elsewhere, only the total amount paid appears, without names or numbers of soldiers.
16. KU 207, 147–149: in 1905, the figures are 23,639 krs vs. 13,525 krs. Only the total wages and not the numbers of soldiers doing military duty are recorded whereas both the number of, and the amounts paid to, soldier-workers is noted.

17. KU 76, 145–155: in 1906–1907, soldiers were paid 33,946 krs and soldier-workers 25,476 krs. Soldiers' median wage equaled 29 krs; the median wage of named individual soldier-workers (all local persons) was 76 krs, and the average wage for workers in anonymous groups was 34 krs between April 1906 and March 1907.
18. KU 207 has a format different from that of KU 71 below. The 1906 ledger notes only debits (*düyun*), the higher-ranking administrators received their own separate entries and there were separate entry pages for workers and soldier-workers listing the debts on a monthly basis.
19. On the pages captioned *Amele üceratının hesabı* were included administrative personnel, such as the district engineer and clerks. These were deducted from the calculations regarding "workers," which thus included skilled workers such as machinists and carpenters as well as unskilled labor and railroad construction workers. KU 207, 152–156 and 168–179.
20. Caution, however, is required here since highly paid machinists and other skilled workers were included, thus pushing up the average civilian wage. As in the case of other ledgers, the specific work period is unknown and presumably was some fraction or all of a month.
21. The three received wages of 100–134 krs per month for each of the twelve recorded months. Given this consistency over time, it seems fair to assume they were working full-time. This 5 krs amount is consistent with the information presented in chapter 9. Soldiers working in the mines were to receive a daily wage of 6 krs during the Ottoman-Russian War. Whether or not this practice continued into the subsequent peacetime decades is not known at this time.
22. Thirty-one percent worked at the harbor.
23. The payrolls equaled 2,615 krs, 2,616 krs, and 2,803 krs.
24. KU 71. In this ledger, the accounting is by month, not by individual or category. Each month, both the credits and the debits are noted. The credit (*tediyat*) side provided the itemized lists of workers and soldier-workers and, generally, was far more detailed than the debit (*deyn*) side. The accounts do not balance, either monthly or for the year as a whole.
25. KU 71. They numbered more than 144.
26. KU 207, 147–149. The sample is twenty-seven persons.
27. The towns—Ereğli, Kozlu, Zonguldak, Devrek—likely were too small to have provided most of the conscripts for the military, who also must have come from the villages of the coalfield.
28. Following standard accounting procedures, the ledger monthly presented both the amounts that the mine superintendency owed for labor (debit) and the amount that it actually paid out for the purpose (credit). On the credit side of the ledger, payments actually made to workers equaled 88 percent of all wages paid while soldier-workers received just 12 percent of the total paid.
29. By contrast, KU 207 lists the number of (anonymous) soldier-workers and the total wage paid.
30. Again, the KU 207 monthly wage amounts by contrast are more uniform and consistent with expected labor flows.
31. KU 71.
32. KU 207, in a different recording system, notes the presence of 874 aboveground workers and 402 soldier-workers, for a total of 1,276 persons. Thus, using quite different recording systems, the two ledgers noted the presence of 874 workers in 1906 and 431 in 1907. The number of soldier-workers in those years was approximately the same, respectively 402 and 345. Whether these differences are apparent or real cannot be known with the present evidence.
33. ED 4, 193, 12 Temmuz 1294/24 July 1878.
34. ED 4, 83, 8 ts 1293/20 November 1877. Also see ED 4, 290, 18 ks 1294/30 January 1879 for descriptions of the tasks.
35. ED 4, 274, 10 kl 1294/22 December 1878; 279, 20 kl 1294/1 January 1879; ED 4, 57–68, Eylül 1293/15 September 1877, individually notes the names and residence of some 365 home guards and absentee conscripts given over to mine work.
36. ED 4, 196–197, 16 Temmuz 1294/24 July 1878.
37. ED 4, 349, 24 Temmuz 1295/5 August 1879, reflects concern that persons drafted as soldiers who had mining experience should not be sent to mines where they once had been assigned

Military Duty and Mine Work 149

as workers. Clearly, there was some "double dipping," that is, using drafted soldiers in mine work. "Since there are no inactive reserve officers, this is a response to the 7 ts 1293 telegram sent from the telegraph office to the mine administration. The Ereğli mines are worked in several kinds of service. Some of the people of Ereğli and Bartın districts are mine support workers and some of those working with the coal are transporters and wagoners [*arabacı*] and boat launchers and boatmen [*gemici*] and the rest are hewers and basket carriers. In the towns which do not send people assigned to mine work, some run grocery stores and other kinds of shops. At Bartın, besides Kuruca and Tekke Önü sub-districts, there are no other villages. These shopkeepers are exempt from the need to register and are among the rare people who have not been assigned work in the mines. On the average, in the two districts there are about 6,000 skilled persons in favorable weather. In case these [6,000] people come to the village councils along with their relatives to be investigated."

38. The sources available do not document the era of the Tripolitanian War of 1911.
39. At this time, the Marine Ministry no longer administered the mines, but it remained interested because of the coal needs of the arsenal and the fleet.
40. ED 12, 64, 1 tl 1328.
41. ED 12, 91, 9 tl 1328 #1789/281.
42. ED 12, 93, 9 tl 1328 #1692/78. Also, ED 12, 195, 6 ts 1328 #1854/320.
43. ED 12, 185, 3 ts 1328. Such persons, the commander stated, did not have permission to travel for the holiday.
44. ED 12, 204, 5 ts 1328 telegram in 10 ts 1328 #1867/178.
45. This figure is quite close to the 6,000 persons registered in ledgers dating back to the 1870s. ED 4, 349, 24 Temmuz 1295/5 August 1879. ED 12, 251–252, 23 ts 1328 #1924.
46. ED 12, 251–252, 23 ts 1328 #1924.
47. ED 12, 324, 9 kl 1328 #2021/30 and 354, 16 kl 1328 #2062/192.
48. ED 10, 68, 25 Avril 1329 #20827/40.
49. ED 10, 109, #520/69, Mayıs 1329. The same case is reported in ED 10, 198, 20 Mayıs 1329; ED 10, 199, 20 Mayıs 1329.
50. ED 10, 199, 20 Mayıs 1329.
51. Quoted in Quataert (1983), 67.
52. ED 3, 203. Among accident victims, the ages of only 16 were given, in the percentages stated in the text.
53. ED 16.
54. During World War I, the accident reports continued in their often-exquisite detail. ED 16. The ages of fourteen such persons are presented in the accident reports. One was a 14 year old boy; another was in his twenties and two more in their later thirties. Strikingly, ten of the fourteen persons were between 43 and 45 years of age. In sum, only three of the fourteen individuals were of military age. Admittedly this is a small sample.
55. Zürcher (1996), 241–242, notes that eligibility for active-duty steadily broadened as the war progressed. By 1916, males 15–55 years could serve on active-duty, while in 1917, 12 percent of those serving were 16–19 years old.
56. KU 143, 51–84. Journeymen ironworkers also earned this same wage.

7

METHANE, ROCKFALLS, AND OTHER DISASTERS

Accidents at the Mines

Introduction

By international standards, accident rates in the Zonguldak mines were appallingly high. Overall, Ottoman workers were five to twenty times more likely to encounter work-related injury or death than their counterparts in Western Europe and the United States. While the twisted and narrow nature of the coal veins of coal at Zonguldak may have played some role, human factors were more important. The undercapitalization of the coalfield often meant insufficient safety procedures and equipment. Particularly in the smaller mines, the lack of ventilation shafts and fans, alongside inattention to safety lamps, aggravated already dangerous working conditions. For most of the period, moreover, medical care also was inadequate. Many workers had no access to a doctor, much less a hospital bed. Additionally, the fact that workers had to pay for their medical care surely kept many from seeking help. As I will show as well, free-market workers recruited from outside received better treatment than compulsory rotational laborers.

Reported accident rates worsened later in the period, despite improvements in the safety infrastructure of the mines and the greater availability of hospital care. Better reporting surely played some role. But so too did the greater length and depth of the mines. Exits became more distant and the release of methane gas more commonplace, sometimes exposing workers to dangers previously not encountered in the coalfield. Also, the greater heterogeneity of the work force following the employment of outsiders in underground work may have been a factor.

Besides telling of death or disfigurement, reports on accidents and mine safety offer often-unique insights into the composition of the labor force. In

---

Notes for this chapter begin on page 180.

increasing detail, the reports narrate the names, occupations, ages, marital status, and number of children of workers who either fell victim to or witnessed mine accidents. In this way, faces and identities become tangible, and a picture of everyday life in these mining communities begins to emerge. The impact of accidents on workers' families and communities comes into relief, for example, in learning that an accident created two widows and six orphans, affecting every fourth home in a particular village.

In many respects, the accident reports present our best view of the actual working environment. Thus, fellow villagers often were found at the same site, working (and dying) together. But commonly enough, former strangers from different coalfield villages labored side by side, as did coalfield village workers with miners from other regions of the empire and occasionally with workers from abroad. Onsite job experiences eroded local identities and helped mold new ones.

Mine safety also was a mechanism through which the state sought to discipline the work force and, more broadly, create a pliant, obedient citizenry. Increasingly stringent safety regulations did not merely aim to protect workers' lives. They also were part of the larger Ottoman state effort to implement change from above, a process in which the Istanbul government intended workers to be passive recipients of reforms inaugurated for their benefit. In the inspector's view, workers could not be trusted to initiate or even adopt the safety reforms. To oversee the reforms, ensure their implementation, and create safer working conditions, the inspector believed, officials and bureaucrats were necessary, indeed essential. In this way, safety legislation mirrored the larger patterns of nineteenth-century Ottoman reform as envisaged by the government: a top-down process in which elites introduced change and guided the rest of society down its path.

Mine Safety in Comparative Perspective

The mining of coal is a notoriously dangerous and deadly occupation that worldwide has killed many scores of thousands who have dared to dig for it in the earth. At the end of the nineteenth century, among coal miners in the United States, United Kingdom, and France, those in America were the most likely to die while at work. This assertion is true in both absolute and relative terms. In the United States between 1884 and 1912, nearly 43,000 miners died at their jobs.[1] Estimates of fatalities in England vary. In one count, more than 1,000 workers annually were killed between 1850 and 1913, while another notes that almost 13,000 died between 1851 and 1913.[2] Fatalities, of course, tell only part of the accident story, for there are the wounded and chronically sick as well. For every fatal accident in England, nearly 100 workers were injured while on the job.[3] Some injuries led to lingering deaths; others crippled their victims and left them dependent on family members for survival. Some of the wounded returned to mine work.

Many who, through skill or luck, neither died nor were wounded in accidents suffered gravely nonetheless. Mining produced enormous quantities of dust that workers inhaled, hour upon hour, day after day. Hewers picking at the coal face and those assisting them spent hours breathing in the dust produced by their blows or when the coal undercuts fell down. Similarly, the task of coal breaking, in which workers separated schist from coal and broke up the coal into manageable pieces, generated huge amounts of dust. These and other tasks caused a host of respiratory diseases that slowly crippled and killed many tens of thousands. Lumped under the term "pneumoconiosis," they notably included black lung, the miner's asthma. A black sputum triggered by inhaling coal dust produced anthracosis, which gradually weakened its victims and prematurely ended the lives of a great many workers. The "bad air that killed" was recognized as early as 1708 in Britain. By the mid nineteenth century, most European medical literature linked mine dust to workers' ill health, and by the turn of the century, a number of U.S. state and federal bodies had connected work conditions to the disease. In addition to anthracosis, a plethora of other respiratory diseases afflicted and shortened miners' lives. Prominent among these was silicosis, caused by inhaling hard rock particles.[4]

In order to address the issue of relative safety in the various coal-mining countries, some specialists measure the frequency of mining accidents by the number of deaths per 1,000 workers employed. In this way, they seek to avoid problems encountered when comparing countries with vastly different levels of coal production. For example, the U.S. alone accounted for one-third of world coal output around 1900 and employed 500,000 coal workers. By this measure, the dangers of U.S. mining again stand out: a U.S. miner who worked for 27 years had a one in eleven chance of dying while at work.[5] Nationally, the U.S. averaged 3.12 deaths per 1,000 coal-mining workers in the period from 1884 to 1912. By contrast, there were 1.7 mining fatalities per 1,000 mine workers in both France and the UK during the 1880s and 1890s. Thus, fatal accident rates among miners in the U.S. overall were twice as great as in these two Western European countries.

But within national averages reside considerable regional variations in safety. In the U.S. case, state-by-state figures exist for coal-mining safety. The safest states, according to one survey carried out in 1907, charted 2.47 deaths per 1,000 workers while the worst averaged 9.49 per 1,000 workers. A coal miner in Utah, for example, was three times as likely to die as one in Montana.[6] Comparing these state rates to European countries' national rates shows that U.S. workers in the least safe states were nearly six times more likely to encounter a fatal accident than their counterparts in the UK or France.[7]

Over the nineteenth and early twentieth centuries, accidents on a horrifying scale occurred routinely as the great industrial powers frantically sought coal to fuel their extraordinary economic growth. Almost unbelievably, 1,230 miners died in a single day in 1906 in Courrières, France. In another example, in 1907 in Monogah, West Virginia, 361 miners died in a single explosion—in a methane-free mine.[8] Just a few years later, in 1910, 344 men died in a single accident in Lancashire, England. In the U.S. and French cases, coal dust was the culprit; only after the 1906 accident did the French authorities become convinced that coal dust alone could explode. American specialists remained skeptical until 1914.[9]

The unsystematic recording of Ottoman data makes difficult a direct comparison to U.S. or Western European coal-mining safety records. There are no reliable statistics regarding labor force size or accident frequency, and so we cannot compile a table showing accident or fatality rates per 1,000 workers employed. Because output in the Zonguldak coalfield was miniscule compared to that of the great industrial powers (see chapter 2), the Ottoman accident rates, at first glance, appear moderate.

Table 7.1 summarizes all of the data that are known to have survived on accidents in the Ottoman period. Between 1893 and 1907, 121 persons died and another 102 were wounded in recorded mining accidents, above- and belowground. During these years, between 2 and 33 workers were hurt or died in mine work annually. To a significant degree, the considerable annual variations in the number of dead and wounded reflect reporting deficiencies. There is, for example, no other explanation for the total absence of recorded deaths or injuries in 1896 and 1898. The two worst reported Ottoman accidents—in which 14 and 8 workers died—occurred in 1906, a time of important changes in labor recruitment procedures.[10]

In addition to the 1893–1907 data, there are additional accident statistics culled from mining inspectors' reports during 1912 and 1913. In 1912, an estimated 63 workers died and another 78 were wounded, the highest annual number of recorded victims.[11] During the subsequent year, when production remained steady, 29 workers died and 57 were wounded (see table 7.1).[12] In 1913, workers experienced the worst single reported accident, in which 30 of them were killed or wounded.

At first glance, when compared with the raw numbers of accident victims in the U.S., Great Britain, or France, the Ottoman fatality and injury rates appear quite modest. This appearance, however, is misleading. Quite the contrary, by contemporary British, French, and American standards, work in the Zonguldak coalfield was extraordinarily dangerous, as seen in the comparison of accidents per 1,000 tons of coal extracted.[13] Moreover, since Ottoman accident reports are very incomplete, the actual fatality and injury rates surely were far higher than noted here. In 1906, when 31 Ottoman workers died digging 600,000 tons of coal, Ottoman fatality rates per 1,000 tons of extracted coal were at least ten times higher than in Britain and France. By comparison with even the most dangerous states in the U.S., Zonguldak miners still were 50 percent more likely to die. Even in 1907, when mine work killed a reported five Ottoman miners—a seemingly tiny number—the death rate per 1,000 tons was three times that suffered by British and French miners and at least five times the rate endured by American workers.[14] By 1912, when Ottoman

Table 7.1 Mining Accidents of All Kinds, 1893–1907, 1912–1919

	No. of Dead and Accidents		Total Dead and Wounded
1893	7/7		23
1894	7/7		22
1895	6/6		27
1896	0/0		6
1897	4/4		6
1898	0/0		2
1899		no reports	
1900	13/13		14
1901	3/3		6
1902	10/7		14
1903	8/8		13
1904	9/9		17
1905	18/12		28
1906	31/19		33
1907	5/5		11
Total	121/100		222
	Dead	Wounded	Total
1912 (partial)	21	26	47
1913 (partial)	29	57	86
1914	5	10	15
1917 (partial)	6	5	11
1919 (partial)		5	5
1927–1932		300–600/year	25–50/year

Sources and notes: (1) Not available: 1908–1911, 1915, 1916, 1918. (2) ED 3 for 1893–1907. (3) 1902: first occurrence of reported multiple-death accidents, on three occasions, killing 3, 2, and 2 persons. (4) 1905: two multiple-death accidents, killing 2 and 5 persons. (5) 1906: four multiple-death accidents, killing 14, 8, 2, and 2 persons. (6) 1907: incomplete, last report dated in June. (7) 1912: 21 dead and 26 wounded in 17 weeks of reporting; thus 17/52 weeks = ca. 63 dead and 78 wounded in the full year, if the rates are extrapolated. Among the missing months are June through August, the busiest of the mining year. Source: KU KD 2 (3 Mars–14 Mayıs 1328); ED 10 and ED 16. (8) 1913: 29 dead and 57 wounded reported; missing are the months of January and December, likely among the least active months. Eleven killed and 19 wounded in a single accident. Source: ED 10; ED 16. (9) 1917: reports from sporadic periods in later March, October, and November only, relatively inactive months. (10) 1919: reports from mid January to later March, relatively inactive months.

coal production had increased by one-third over the past half-decade, death rates per 1,000 tons were more than double those of the 1893–1907 era. Fatality rates in the Ottoman coalfield in 1912 thus were twenty times greater than in contemporary France and Great Britain.

Virtually all the killed or injured were workers-hewers, basket carriers, other transport workers, and hard-rock miners cutting out the tunnels. Hewers were the most likely to die, accounting for nearly one-half of all fatalities (see chapter 8).[15] Sometimes, for all their experience, foremen suffered death or injury.

The rare occasions when administrative or managerial personnel were killed or injured almost always involved freak accidents on the surface. Even more rarely, high-ranking state or company officials became fatality statistics. For example, in 1893, the director of the Giurgiu Company, the French subject M. Alfred Elzur, died as a result of a methane fire in the Incir Harmanı mine. Forty years old at his death, M. Elzur was buried locally, in the cemetery for foreigners. More than three years later, his brother was still completing the complicated arrangements for having the body exhumed and returned to France.[16] In another case, on a Wednesday evening in December 1903, the owner of the Murad mine in Kozlu descended to the 380 meters level accompanied by a worker. But their lamps went out, and in the darkness of the mine interior, the obese owner kept falling down and was unable to continue. His worker brought in a wagon but Murad died, just outside of his mine. The engineer, on investigating the incident, reported that "in some spots a fat person can't breathe because of the difficulties [the narrowness of the shaft] and the fear." This assessment notwithstanding, he did not determine an official cause of death.[17]

The worst single accident recorded in the 1893–1907 period occurred in July 1906. Frustratingly, there is but scant information although the accident killed fourteen workers. The mine was a small one, operated by Sila Bey near the town of Kozlu and, and it suffered from numerous "defects in operations and procedures." The fourteen died in some kind of panic, as the "workers [sought to] leave the mine by rushing and crowding one another at the mine airshafts."[18] By contrast, a 1913 accident caused by an explosion of coal dust and methane, which killed and wounded 30 persons, is well documented (see below). A still more devastating accident in the 1890s killed 67 workers. The miner Ethem Çavuş recalls this accident in his memoir, but it does not show up in the accident reports available to this study.[19]

Death and injury came in many guises to the Zonguldak workers. Most often they were crushed by falling coal or rocks, seared by exploding coal dust and gas, caught between runaway wagons and shaft walls, run over by wagons, or drowned. Some died in unique ways: for instance, a 19-year-old ascending a vertical shaft in a basket was struck and killed by a falling stone.[20] Table 7.2 summarizes the major causes of fatalities among the Zonguldak coal miners during several decades around the turn of the twentieth century. Rockfalls are indicated as the leading cause of death, annually accounting for between 41 and 52 percent of all known fatalities. Explosions of gas or coal dust usually ranked second, followed by accidents involving the transport of coal. This table, admittedly based on incomplete data and concerned with a small number of fatal accidents, nonetheless reveals patterns of death strikingly consistent with those in the coal mines of the UK, France, and the U.S. During the period from 1885 to 1912, rockfalls constituted 47 percent of all American mining accidents.[21] Similarly, rockfalls caused 40–45 percent of all deaths in the UK over the course of the nineteenth century. There, for every 1,000 killed in a given year, 840 died in "isolated occurrences," in other words,

Table 7.2 Frequency of Accidents, 1893–1907, 1912, 1913

	1893–1907 Accidents		1912 Accidents		1913 Accidents	
	no.	%	no.	%	no.	%
Rockfall	92	41	16	52	15	41
Explosion	57	25			5	14
Transport	17	8			9	25
Water	12	5				
"Crowding"	14	6				
Misc.	33	15	15	48	8	20
Total	225	100	31	100	37	100

Sources: See table 7.1.

in rockfall accidents that one observer characterized as "disaster in installments."[22] By contrast, explosions are the most infamous of mine accidents since they often produce truly massive fatalities. Because explosions were so spectacular and brought so much notoriety, mine operators more actively sought to reduce their occurrence. Thus, for example, gas and coal dust explosion accidents declined in the U.S. during the early twentieth century. But deaths from rockfalls and work involving the haulage of coal persisted as the major sources of accidents.[23]

There are no accounts of, or statistics on, black lung or other respiratory diseases afflicting Ottoman miners in the sources consulted for this study. This may be due partly to the slow-working nature of these diseases and the difficulty in tracking them. Though in most other mining centers, such as Western Europe and the United States, the connection between mine work and respiratory disease had already been well established, statistical data still were lacking.[24] Nowadays in the mines of Zonguldak, black lung is considered one of the most important health issues concerning coal miners. On the one hand, compared to other eras, various factors actually lessened its prevalence during the Ottoman period: black lung derives from coal particulates suspended in the air, which greatly increase when mechanized equipment is brought in to chew away at the coal face.[25] The local geology and the lack of capital meant that such equipment was rare (and perhaps completely absent) in the Ottoman Zonguldak coalfield. The hewing, undercutting, transporting, and breaking of coal, on the other hand, all produced vast quantities of coal dust, and the cramped nature of many Ottoman-era mines and the decades-long absence of ventilating equipment rendered these particulates even more deadly. There can be no doubt that black lung and other respiratory diseases attacked Ottoman miners. Despite the Ottoman sources' complete silence on black lung, we must assume this killer was present at Zonguldak, along with other respiratory diseases.

Accidents Aboveground

Aboveground accidents could and did happen everywhere. Istefan Veled, described as tall and able-bodied with a black mustache, was fatally injured in May 1897 when he slipped under a coal car, just fifteen days after arriving from Istanbul.[26] In 1897, a Kurdish worker in the developing port of the Ereğli Company was crushed between a locomotive and a beached lighter boat that had pulled up too near it. He was admitted to the Ereğli Company hospital but died there of his injuries twelve days later.[27] Çerkes Hasan Hüseyin, the 26-year-old father of a 3-year-old daughter, was loading coal near the coal scrubber in May 1913. He went to help others push some wagons when he slipped, fell between cars and broke his leg.[28] Not quite a year later, in March 1914, Agop Kazazyan, a 51-year-old doctor tending the workers at the coal scrubber, lost his leg: returning from a house call in the Soğuk Su area, he was walking along the tracks in the dark and failed to notice an oncoming locomotive until it was too late.[29] In another railroad accident, three cars crushed the life from a 20-year-old worker near the Ereğli Company administration building in Zonguldak at five in the evening in early October 1913 (see figure 7.1).

Here are the testimonies of several witnesses and the report of the engineer from the mine superintendent's office. These and other accident reports offer the rare opportunity to hear workers' voices—as reported, however, by state officials.

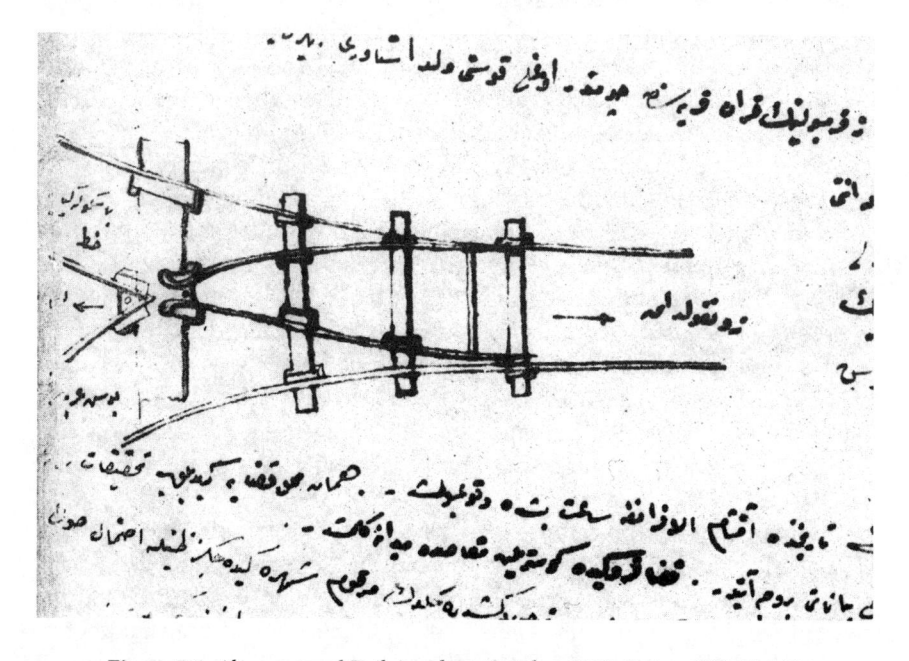

Figure 7.1 Aboveground Rail Accident, October 1913. Source: ED 16, 143.

The man in charge of coupling said: "I was in the last wagon in order to maneuver the train. I went to get a drink. The accident took place somehow."

The worker in charge of the rail switching said: "He passed over the track of the train. He gave a signal to me. I threw the switch. Suddenly, a man who was underneath the wagons cried out. And at once I called to the engineer, stop! The machine stopped. But I didn't see anything."

Another witness added: "He was walking along the train line and tried to come behind the wagons. But, he wasn't paying enough attention. I called out. But the last car struck him and he fell. He was very badly injured from his hands and feet to his face.

He was dead one-half hour after the accident. At first, it was not possible to determine who he was. But, later on it was. It is understood that he came to Zonguldak a while ago and found this work; and that he was a Greek Orthodox Ottoman subject."[30]

Trainhopping: Hitching Rides outside the Mines

With the development of railroads to haul coal, an alternative to walking—trainhopping—became available to workers in some areas of the coalfield. For workers, the issue was simple—the coal trains afforded a faster and less tiring way of moving back and forth to work and to the towns that had become a magnet for workers' leisure activities. Depending on location, trains also could ease workers' travel between mine and village. For the state and the companies, the matter was somewhat different. First of all, the Ereğli Company intended train transport to remain the prerogative of the upper and middle echelons of company personnel, a privilege not available to workers. It was insistent on this point despite pressures from the mine administration. While the Ereğli Company and the state agreed that trainhopping by workers could be a source of injury, death, and far worse (for them), undisciplined behavior, they split over the solution to the problem: the mine administration demanded transport cars for workers on the grounds of economic efficiency and morality but the company refused to provide them. Thus, although trainhopping became commonplace, it remained generally illegal for workers, at least until the eve of World War I.

Take, for example, the coal wagons that moved between a mine of the Karamanyan Company and a dumping area for coal debris. A bridge en route proved to be a popular spot for trainhopping in the Zonguldak-Acılık area: workers waited on the bridge for the train to come along with its (mostly) open coal cars and jumped aboard.[31] During the crises of the Tripolitanian War and Balkan Wars of 1911–1913, the mine superintendent's office began to push for special trains for workers transport, proposals that met with stubborn resistance from the Ereğli Company.

Trainhopping became a focus of official attention as of April 1912. By that date, workers had already developed the custom of hitching rides aboard the trains that hauled coal between the production center of Üzülmez and the town of Zonguldak, some nine kilometers. Today, the journey is an automobile ride of about fifteen-minutes but on the coal trains of late Ottoman days, it took about sixty minutes, a very short trip compared to walking the distance. The coal wagons on this railroad were "of a type that can be used as workers' wagons," and the workers caught rides on both the coal cars and the flatbed cars that carried supports for the mines and tunnels. A struggle, visible in the documents for just over one year, ensued between the insistent workers, the mine superintendent, and the Ereğli Company. As workers illegally grabbed the free rides, the state fought with the company to provide proper transport trains for them. And until those trains were provided, the superintendent sought to prevent illegal trainhopping.

Was official attention on trainhopping at this time a function of high mortality rates? In the preceding year, illegal rides had cost four workers' lives, and in the 17 subsequent months caused three additional deaths and ten injuries among workers. While these losses are terrible, the determination of the superintendent's office to halt the practice at this particular time derived from other causes. Beginning in September 1911, the Ottoman Empire became embroiled in the Tripolitanian War against Italy and then the First and Second Balkan Wars in October 1912 and June 1913, respectively. With the mobilization, active military forces and the ready reserve were called up and sent off to war, leaving the region stripped of the personnel who normally made up the bulk of the local law-and-order forces. Deeply fearful of unrest, district authorities worked with the superintendent to fill the gap, using a combination of gendarmes and the few remaining soldiers. The mines, they said, provided the livelihood for thousands of workers, and discipline was essential. But by May 1912, they reported, strikes had erupted and discipline had vanished from the region. Inventorying their disciplinary resources, they noted the presence of prisons in thirteen different locations in the coalfield, with a total of 19 gendarmes and 55 soldiers available to maintain order.[32] The superintendent and district authorities already had noted that a gendarmerie station had "been established to maintain discipline" and for a time successfully kept workers off the trains. But soon, they conceded, "discipline again [had] been neglected" and workers were back to riding the rails.[33]

As the mine superintendent explained to his superiors in Istanbul, there were insufficient numbers of gendarmes and military personnel in Zonguldak district. Both he and the Ereğli Company worried about the mounting disorder of recent months. In a classic formulation, the superintendent transferred responsibility for the disorder away from those under his supervision to strangers in the region.

> The workers in the mines in exchange for their lives earn little compensation, and return to their villages with 5–10 krs.... Sometimes some of them on the road are violently seized and robbed by persons without conscience. We generally need to prevent such deeds and excesses; these bring fear in the mining districts which are gathering places for persons capable of such misdeeds and especially for strangers who are moving around.[34]

The gendarmes had carried out their duties and maintained order until "those who dared to transgress did so in large numbers." In the face of what they considered a continuing crisis, the Istanbul authorities called for extraordinary measures.[35]

In December 1912, the superintendent wrote again to his Istanbul superiors, reviewing the situation as it had developed over the seven months since his May report. Retracing the earlier decision to commit more gendarmes and military forces, he complained that these still were not present in sufficient numbers and concluded that discipline remained lacking in the coalfield and on the railroad.[36]

An accident that happened just a week after the above report offers a close-up view of one trainhopper, a 20-year-old operator of the huge ventilating fans named Ayvaklı Yanni Kurduç. In his own words he described his efforts to avoid detection and how he was injured.

> I got on a loaded wagon from Asma to Zonguldak. I stopped at the Firun neighborhood in order not to be caught at the Zonguldak station seeking to go directly to the Çay Damarı mine. I wanted to ask for information about a wagon in the neighborhood of the station. Somehow or other I slipped. A part of the wagon passed over my left leg.[37]

Another accident, in April 1913, revealed tensions between the superintendent's office and the Ereğli Company. Each of two workers lost a leg in attempting to hitch a ride from the Zonguldak station to the mines at Üzülmez. As the train waited in the station, a crowd of workers had piled into coal wagons and onto a flatbed car (intended to carry mine supports) hooked between them. As the inspector described it, "the two wounded were among the many of the comrades who were seated on the flatbed, which was between the wagons," not realizing that the flatbed was to be uncoupled and left behind. When the train began to move to separate the flatbed from the wagons, the two workers—a 12- to 13-year-old from Zonguldak and a 20-year-old from Trabzon—lost their balance and fell underneath. Traveling on the wagons long had been prohibited to the workers because of accidents, the engineer added, but "the railroad supervisors don't have the means to force workers to get off and can't be faulted here." The reporting engineer then turned against the Ereğli Company. "These kinds of accidents will always occur [he warned] because of the company's refusal to act even though 90 percent of the workers who hop rides work for the firm." The engineer recommended that the Ereğli Company be required to provide "about twenty covered wagons" to transport workers and attach these to the coal trains when needed. The company should understand that it would profit, he wrote, since the workers would arrive rested and ready for work and "would do their hard work with pleasure." Even if such economic motives are put aside, "compassion" required such action. Then, he concluded, the accidents would cease.[38]

But problems persisted. Setrak, the Zonguldak locale engineer, became very frustrated. A grave accident occurred in the early evening of 14 June 1914 as a loaded coal train of twenty wagons derailed at Baştarla, on the way from Üzülmez to Zonguldak. Overloaded coal wagons had caused a wagon in the middle to jump the track on the curve, derailing all but the engine and six cars directly behind it. Three workers died, one of whom had a pregnant wife and young child, and another three were wounded. All had been illegally hitching rides. Rescue workers, including Setrak, worked through the night but found no more fatalities under the wreckage. Some of the wounded were treated in the *gazino* of the Kaçakcı Company while other victims were sent to the Ereğli Company hospital. When the gendarmes were present in force, Setrak again told the superintendent's office, trainhopping ceased. Suggestions to increase the number of gendarmes at each station and to have 5–10 others roving the line had been to no avail. A few days ago, he added, there suddenly were only two gendarmes present at the Zonguldak station and they were powerless to deter the trainhoppers. And he betrayed a sense of frustrated resignation over the current state of affairs.

> Some 100–150 workers force their way onto the coal wagons, either at the station or as it gets underway, using pistols or knives and two gendarmes can't do anything at all! The workers are traveling on trains from morning till night from Zonguldak to Üzülmez and Üzülmez to Zonguldak. Gendarmes and the Ereğli Company both have the duty to stop this practice. These kinds of accidents need to be prevented. But the truth is, it still goes on. I am forced to say that it is still possible to hop trains from Zonguldak to Üzülmez. This situation cannot be allowed to continue.[39]

A week later, the chief engineer once again ordered the Ereğli Company to provide trains designated for workers at all times.[40]

To conclude, let me return to a couple of points that seem of interest here. First of all, the Ereğli Company routinely provided train transport between Zonguldak and Üzülmez for its supervisory personnel and salaried employees but, at least until late June 1913, denied these services to the rank-and-file workers.[41] And second, the assumption that the workers were incapable of self-discipline and would become disorderly in the absence of military forces became only too evident as international war erupted in late 1911. Thus, the administration's belief that safety could come only from above was paralleled by its fears about what workers would do if not properly controlled and regulated.

Accidents inside Mines: Inclined Planes

Accidents occurred as humans on foot, animals, and wagons hauled coal from the face to the larger shafts and finally to the surface, in journeys that sometimes covered thousands of meters. The inclined planes along which the various transport modes moved wagons proved particularly dangerous. These were the places where full wagons from the coal face rolled to transfer points, dumped their loads for transport to the surface, and were turned about for refilling. In these sometimes very narrow confines, there was little margin for error. In 1895, after a piece of iron became entangled with a support in the Giurgiu mine at Kozlu, Gazzaroğlu Issin b. Hasan from Devrek hamlet, whose job was to stop the wagons at the inclined plane, ended up in the hospital.[42] A 14-year-old from the city of Samsun died in 1900 because he had been assigned a task beyond his experience. On a Friday morning in mid June, Kumaşlıoğlu Ahmed b. Hüscyin was changing wagons at the bottom of an inclined plane 600 meters inside the Tamoğlu mine of the Ereğli Company when a car rushing down the steep incline crushed him. The engineer blamed the Ereğli Company and the French foremen present for negligence on at least four counts, including employing a youth for such a complicated and difficult task.[43] A similar accident at the Kozlu #298 Pavli mine killed another worker in August 1902, when the cables holding the wagons suddenly let go without warning, sending one careening into the worker.[44] A month later, two workers from Akbaş village in Ovacık sub-district were killed at the bottom of an inclined plane. They were turning the emptied cars around to send them back up to be filled when a third worker, improperly climbing on the wagon for purchase, inadvertently released the hook holding the car, causing it to roll back onto the victims.[45]

Workers died in both unavoidable and preventable accidents. Through no one's fault, the spot on the inclined plane where full wagons were emptied in the Ereğli Company's Karamanyan mine proved deadly, in March 1903, for Demircioğlu Mustafa from Trabzon province.[46] Similarly, Hüseyin Onbaşı, a 25-year-old father of four from Devrek district, died in 1913 while making repairs on an inclined plane within the important Gelik mine of the Ereğli Company. His misfortune was simply to flee in the wrong direction when a wagon broke loose and ran out of control.[47] By contrast, Topaloğlu Ahmed b. Yusuf died from his own mistake. At an inclined plane 600 meters inside the Rombaki mine at Zonguldak, before coupling a just-emptied wagon, he prematurely gave the signal to release the full cars from above. When the full wagons rolled down and struck the empty wagon, it careened into him and killed him.[48]

The bottom of these inclined planes so often proved a deadly site because of the congestion of empty and full cars. Take the 1904 death at an inclined plane in the Üzülmez mine of the Ereğli Company at Zonguldak. While affixing the coupling, the worker gave the signal to release the wagons above. Full and empty wagons crashed together, shattered the coupling, and rolled over the victim.[49] In December 1905, two foremen—one a French national and the other from Zonguldak district—were carrying out inspections 250 meters inside the #390 mine at Zonguldak. At that moment, coal was passing from the second to the first inclined plane when an empty wagon derailed. As they worked to right the wagon, a full wagon rolled down from above and crushed the arm of the Zonguldak foreman, who was caught between the two cars.[50]

Methane, Rockfalls, and Other Disasters

At the Tünel mine at Karadon in June 1907, the hewer was taking "excessive amounts" of coal from the ceiling. "With the idea of completing his shift as soon as possible, he was about to pull down some supports." But two coal wagons appeared and bumped into the supports, causing them to fall over on the hewer, killing him.[51]

The following accident report, valuable for its voices of workers, also presents an unusually thorough description of inclined planes and coal transport operations. The accident occurred in February 1914, where they were tunneling to gain access to the coal veins within the Pavli mine of the Ereğli Company.

First, hear the testimony of accident victim Hasan b. Ahmed, age 22, a carpenter's assistant, married, from Trabzon:

> This tunnel serves as an inclined plane. There are brakes on the plane that are used to clear away the excavated material taken from the tunnel. The full wagons from the top of the tunnel descend to the bottom of the inclined plane by means of brakes. And at the same time, an empty wagon comes to the top of the plane. Each time that a wagon comes forward on one side of the inclined plane, another comes from the other side on brakes.... The full wagon was at the bottom of the plane. To bring more empty cars for the remnants of the excavated material, I released the brakes. One of my friends, the tunneler Ali Şakir, from the middle of the plane, and another two friends from the bottom of the slope, released the ropes. At that moment, the empty wagon, which had drawn near to the excavated material, broke from the ropes. We at once called out, "flee." Osman Mehmed was in front of the full wagon and Hüseyin bin Ahmed fled towards the bottom of the empty wagons. We [also] began to flee towards the road.
>
> To keep the excavated material out of the tunnel, some tools had been brought up. These collided with a flatbed that had broken loose and fell. On the one side, it destroyed the inclined plane ropes. It came towards the bottom.... Between the walls and the railroad was a place of eighty centimeters.

Here is the testimony of Hüseyin Çamlıoğlu Hasan:

> I was in front of the full wagons (that is, in the place where the two lines came together) and my friend Pazarlıoğlu Ali was behind them. We were pushing. There were some twenty cars on the line for the empty cars. And behind them was a flatbed. We were pushing along the full wagons. Suddenly an empty wagon derailed. The empty wagon struck the full ones [on the other track] and then all of the empty ones. And the flatbed that was at the back of these empty ones was pushed into the road which joined the two lines. I was eighty centimeters away. The flatbed also went off the rails. The poor wretch was caught between the walls and the iron rails. That's how the accident occurred.

Then there is the testimony of Zonguldak mine engineer Setrak:

> The statements of Hüseyin Çamlıoğlu Hasan are reasonable. The poor wretch had nowhere to flee since there were only 80 cm between the walls and the rails. Behind the flatbed and near the walls is always a dangerous position to be in. It is not correct

to seek safety behind wagons. Two workers were pushing twenty wagons, one in the front and the other in the back. It is natural that they could not notice at the time. The responsibility for this accident lies with no one.

Unusually, at the bottom was a comment in French to the superintendent, signed by the assistant head engineer, Ştronuz:

> The responsibility cannot be placed either on the inspectors or on the Company, the accident was caused solely by the inattention of the workers. It is necessary to order the Company to rearrange the rail bed, to enlarge it a bit.[52]

In this assessment, improvement was not to be found in educating the workers; rather, change once again would come from above, and in this way discipline and safety could be assured.

Transport Accidents Elsewhere inside Mines

Accidents involving coal transport were not always what they seemed—or were they? In May 1912, M. Robert, a company engineer working for the Ereğli Company, reported on the death of 18-year-old Salim Mustafa, from the town of Gümüşhane.

> Salim Mustafa was in mine 109. He and another worker finished there. While his friends were pushing one of the coal wagons, it struck Mustafa who was sleeping. They informed me that Mustafa, who was working nights, came to our office towards the morning hour and was given a certificate for admission into the hospital. After several days there, he died. Here are my personal views of the event. None of the above was corroborated by the friends of the deceased. If the deceased had been struck by a coal wagon, he would have had certain kinds of wounds. However, because these kinds of wounds don't appear in the report of the hospital doctor, I am thinking that the workers, while in the mine or while leaving the mine, possibly had a fight and at that time the deceased was hurt.

But when a fellow worker from Gümüşhane, 20-year-old Ali Osman, offered a different version, another 20-year-old from the same town, Hüseyin, corroborated the account.

> While I was pushing the coal wagon, my friend had his lamp several meters away from his person; he went to sleep; he couldn't be seen and was run over by his friend's wagon.

The mine superintendent's office concluded:

> Here is my considered opinion of the incident. This was no mining accident. Either it occurred because the deceased went into the mine to sleep; in that case, responsibility for the accident rests solely with the deceased. But, if the workers had a fight and he died in that way, then a court case is necessary.[53]

A serious accident at the Ikinci Makas mine of the Ereğli Company occurred around midnight on a June evening in 1913. Unusually, there were no witnesses. A 16-year-old named Hurşid Mehmed Kopurcu, described as a bachelor in the report, was a doorkeeper at one of the two air doors in a ventilated gallery. His job entailed opening the door on seeing the lamp hanging from the first of the approaching wagons. Hurşid, carrying out his job, suffered serious head injuries. His condition did not permit questioning, so to solve the mystery the inspecting engineer summoned nearby workers to the administrative building for questioning (figure 7.2).[54]

In February 1914, Kumoğlu Hüseyin, whose 50 years made him an unusually old worker, died when he was trapped between the mine wall and a flatbed wagon. According to witnesses, workers driving loaded coal cars toward the outside of the mine moved the flatbed, used to haul supports, off the line to a side track. But the distance between the two sets of tracks was too narrow. As the back part of the flatbed drew nearer to the full wagons, other workers jumped off but the 50-year-old was caught and crushed.[55]

Quite unusually among recorded fatalities, one worker, a horse driver who died in an accident, remained anonymous. The accident took place in 1912 in the Hacı Mehmed mine in Kozlu when the drover, leading an animal pulling a wagon, slipped and was run over by the animal and wagon.[56]

Another horse drover, named Ömer Ali, was gravely wounded when he stepped on a winch cable in the darkness. The victim was twenty-eight years

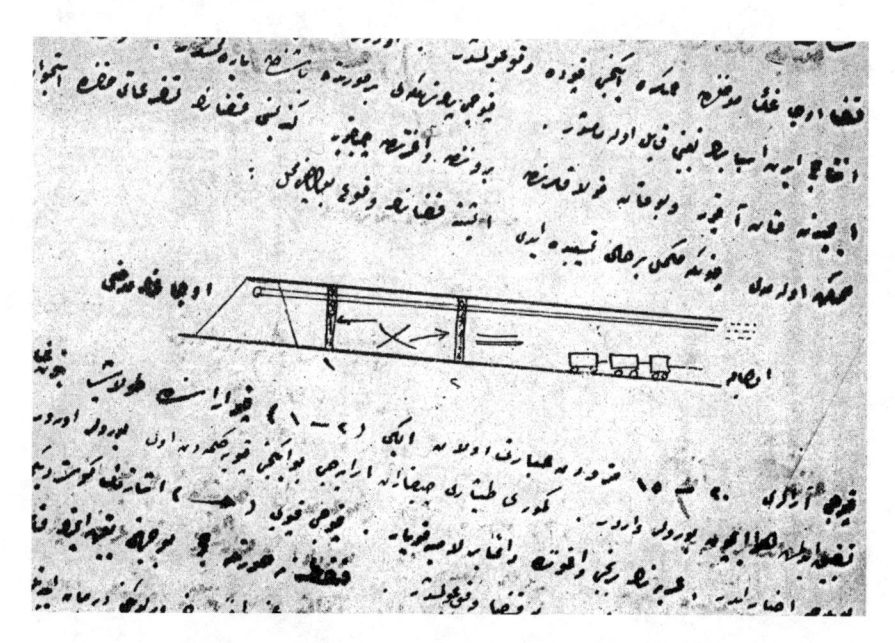

Figure 7.2 Accident at Air Door, Ikinci Makas Mine, June 1913. Source: ED 16, 350.

of age, married, with two children, from the village of Hocaoğlu in Bartın district. He and five others had been leading horse-drawn wagons in the Tünel mine of the Ereğli Company in October 1917. Hewers and other workers had finished work for the day and were preparing to leave. The six horse drovers wanted to leave with them but the foreman ordered the six to await the empty wagons scheduled to arrive from outside. The mine clerk arrived on the scene and, wishing to leave, overrode the foreman's directive. As they left, the lamp of Ömer Ali went out, when they were about 5–10 meters from a winch. At that point, the accident occurred, for which the head engineer blamed the drover's carelessness. Here is the statement of one drover:

> I was walking behind Ömer Ali for a while and his lamp went out. I heard a noise. I went forward at once.... But he wasn't visible. I went forward with my lamp lowered. I examined the line of the full wagons. I saw that Ömer Ali was in the ditch. I cried out saying, 'Ömer Ali has fallen into a ditch.' From among the drovers came Ahmed Yusuf, Ali Osman and Ismail Recep. They took him from the ditch; he didn't say anything.

The engineer noted the presence of two narrow-gauge lines parallel to one another, each taking half the room available. Because his lamp had gone out, the engineer concluded, the victim was unable to see the moving winch cable. He stepped directly on it and was thrown into the ditch (figure 7.3).[57]

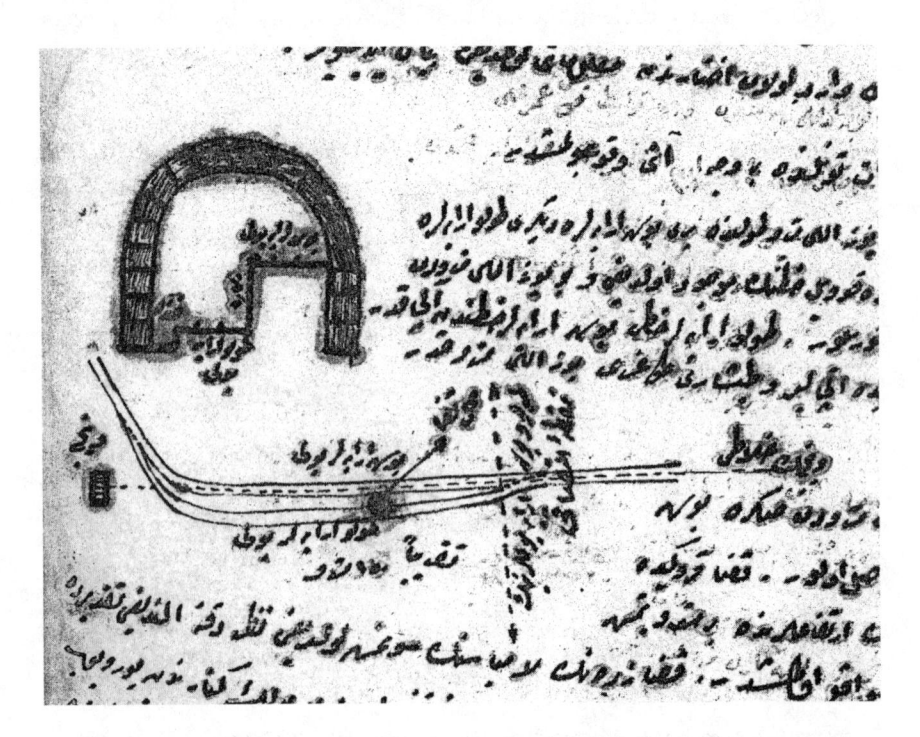

Figure 7.3 Accident on Winch Cable, Tünel Mine, October 1917. Source: ED 16, 348.

Illegal Carhopping inside Mines

As mining developed, the lengths and depths of the shafts increased. And as distances from mine entrance to coal face increased, so too, therefore, did the travel time of the work force. For example, at the Murad mine at Kozlu in 1900, a railroad covered the distance between the points of coal extraction and the surface in 16 (going down empty) and 27 minutes (coming up full) and made as many as nineteen daily trips.[58] Or, take the case of the Ereğli Company mine at Kerpiççilik, in 1907, where railcars traveled 3,000 meters between mine entrance and coal face.[59] At the Boyacıoğlu #69 mine at Zonguldak in 1917, rail lines ran 2,000 meters inside and another 500 meters outside.[60] For workers, especially those tired after completing a shift, the appeal of hopping onto a coal wagon was obvious.

Carhopping was legal in times of emergency. One crew, in 1914, was working far from the mine head when the alarm bell sounded, warning that a "very dangerous" situation had developed within the mine and that the workers needed to leave at once. After responding by ringing a bell, the crew climbed inside an empty coal wagon and began their ascent to the surface. They had been riding up for fifteen minutes when their wagons were derailed in a collision. One of the crew—a married 23-year-old hewer from Devrek district—died in the arms of a coworker.[61]

But this case is exceptional. All other recorded trainhopping accidents inside mines resulted from actions illegally taken. Thus, take the June 1903 example of a worker from Abide Cabakumcu village, who hopped on a coal wagon some 300 meters below sea level in mine #348 at Incir Harmanı. The wagon dispatcher sent the wagon, unaware of its human cargo, and when the car was not properly captured at a turning point it fell over and wounded the worker.[62] Similarly, when a group of workers in February 1907 hopped into full wagons on an inclined plane in the #299 mine at Zonguldak, one of them, Çürükoğlu b. Ibrahim from Uğurlar village, died when his wagon fell over.[63]

An accident in 1919 reveals the scale of illegal trainhopping taking place inside of mines. The site was the Tünel mine of the Ereğli Company, one with especially long distances between the coal face and the surface. A 43-year-old wounded worker who was interviewed in the Ereğli Company hospital at Üzülmez testified, not wanting to admit that he had been trainhopping, that he had been

> walking along the side of the wagons which were going from the Tünel to the outside of the mine. The wagon overturned. I was frightened. I went back but it struck my head [and parts of the body].

The foreman, however, offered a different view, placing the workers not alongside but inside the wagons:

> With the last train we went outside. All of us boarded the train. A few meters from the second gate, the train that the wounded had boarded fell over. He jumped. His head hit the edge of the tunnel and he was wounded. I saw everything because I was

behind him in the third wagon. The number of wagons going outside was 35 and more than 100 workers had boarded them. All the workers were frightened by the sounds that the fallen wagon made in the emptiness of the tunnel. They all got out of the wagons. The wagons again continued on their way. In order to get out of the mine we walked and did get outside. In spite of the warnings that the workers on the last shift in the Tünel mine made, paying no attention to anyone, in order to get out as soon as possible, he boarded the wagons and got out of the mine. Because the tunnel is approximately 1,200 meters long, the coming and going of wagons and sometimes the derailment of wagons is a normal event. Many times the wagons derailed because they fell apart as the workers got on.

To this statement, the Zonguldak locale engineer added:

Nowhere in the coalfield are workers permitted to board wagons in order to enter or to come out of the mines. To the contrary, this is prohibited. Thus, the Ereğli Company is not responsible.[64]

Technically, of course, the company was correct—it did not provide transport from work areas to the surface, even when the distance was 1,200 meters and more.

Drowning

Ethem Çavuş offers a touching account of a youth who died of drowning, a story that also illustrates the determination of coworkers in rescue operations.

A young kid came to the mine that morning from my village.... While we were digging upwards, the smell of moldiness was getting heavier. I took a sample of mud and smelled it. Water sitting in a place for a long time has a peculiar smell. That was the smell.
 There might have been a gallery on top of us that had been worked and abandoned years ago. Water veins must have been uncovered while working in this gallery. It was likely that water filled the gallery over time turning it into a cistern....
 After midnight the pit grumbled. It grumbled again. As people began to run away, the water burst forth. Those who managed to run away were safe but there were six workers left behind.
 Once there is an accident in the mines, there is no distinction between the night and day shifts. Everybody goes to work. I also rushed into the mine on hearing about the accident. Is it possible to go into the gallery where the water broke out? Water as large as a huge plane-tree trunk is running from the entrance of the gallery. We went through the back vent-hole.
 I called;
 – 'Boys!!...
 – We are here Ethem Çavuş.
 – How many of you there?
 – Five.'
 There were six workers who were trapped by the water. One of them was not there. The water calmed down towards morning. Five workers were able to survive

in a gallery out of the water's way, clinging on supports of the ceiling. A basket carrier kid was not among them. We searched every corner of the mine. He was not anywhere.

When I got out of the mine it was almost morning. I walked to the bank of a stream to wash my hands and face that were all black. While I was washing my face, my eyes caught something. I looked at it carefully. It was a clean pair of soles washed by the stream waters. I grabbed the feet and pulled out a kid's corpse that was buried upside down in the mud. This was the corpse of the child worker swept by the water that had burst forth in the gallery.

A pair of clean soles washed by stream water was the first present of the rising sun that day.[65]

Drowning was a rare cause of death but not unheard of in the Zonguldak coalfield. Overall, there were few reported water-related accidents, some 5 percent of those recorded in the 1893–1907 sample. For example, in March 1901, a group of five workers was cutting a tunnel in the #385 mine at Zonguldak, exploited by Şakir Beyler. When water burst from the ceiling, two were trapped underneath the debris and Yanni, from the island of Mytilene, died.[66] In a brutal accident in April 1906, ten were cutting coal 200 meters inside another mine when water suddenly exploded into their work area. In the ensuing mayhem only two escaped.[67]

Water was an ongoing problem, at least in part because of the porous sandstone formations surrounding many coal veins. Water in mines caused accidents, stopped work, and could even halt ongoing exploitation of mines. For example, in the 1880s the Pavlaki Company dug 275 meters into a rich coal vein but then abandoned the mine because it filled with water. Fifteen years later the mine remained closed because there were not the necessary resources to drain it.[68]

In September 1877, in the midst of the Ottoman-Russian War, the superintendent, discussing the importance of two mines operated by Ahmed Ali and his partner, Mustafa Çavuş, warned that the winter season was fast approaching and with the coming rains, measures ought to be taken against expected increases in water within the mines. His following remark reflects more concern for profits and production than workers' lives: "If water comes in, death and destruction will result and both the public treasury and the mine operators will be hurt." Therefore, he insisted, the local authority must make certain of the prompt arrival of the allotted 179 workers; otherwise, he warned, "there will be punishments."[69] Eight months later, he confessed, "mining depends on continuously favorable weather." Indeed, the intervening winter had been a difficult one, lasting until May 1878. In later June most mines still were flooded, as were many of the roads to them. Hence, little coal had been extracted over the months.[70] The situation persisted; in January 1879, the mines remained full of water.[71]

During the crises of World War I, the routine but critical maintenance tasks similarly went undone in the face of chronic labor and parts shortages, hampering efforts to control water in the mines. For example, several shafts of the Kozlu #33 mine were filled by rains in May 1917 and remained submerged for months.

In November 1917, water remained in two—the Milopere and Lockcha—of the mine's three veins, suspending work. The third vein was being worked, thanks to one larger pump that extracted 12 tons of water per hour and two smaller ones each pumping 6 tons of water hourly.[72] The #35 mine also had standing water, although three American-made Worthington steam pumps and one hand pump of the same name were available.[73] To control its water problems, the Boyacıoğlu mine in Zonguldak, in 1917, used two hand pumps, respectively extracting 8 and 4 tons per hour and one American (Worthington) steam pump handling 12 tons per hour.[74] In the #379 mine at Zonguldak, by contrast, no water pumps were available although heaps of coal and schist lying about the main passage had produced considerable accumulations of standing water.[75]

Rockfalls

Rockfalls occurred for all kinds of reasons, ranging from fundamental geology to dangerous work practices. Foliating schist peeled off unpredictably and fell on workers, causing numerous deaths and injuries. These kinds of accidents often were not preventable, but others certainly were. In common with miners in many regions of the globe, Zonguldak workers often pulled down the coal pillars that supported the ceiling, letting them collect large quantities of coal from the fallen pillars and collapsed ceiling. But this practice was perhaps the most common cause of rockfall accidents.

Some workers should never have been in the place of their misfortune. In June 1878, the hewers Yakub and Yusuf were working side by side when the ceiling collapsed. Yusuf, whose body was crushed below the waist, died; Yakub was injured in the foot. Yakub sued the mine operator, claiming that he and Yusuf had not been not classified as hewers and should never been compelled to do such work. He brought his case before the Ereğli court, where he confronted the operator's claims of innocence. Despite the power imbalance, Yakub won the case.[76] At the beginning of the new century, a 20-year-old worker died of inexperience in a very similar case. Although he was doing hewer work, he technically was a basket carrier. Lacking training, he cut the coal improperly and died in the resulting rockfall. In this case, his foreman was faulted for not directing the work in the proper manner.[77]

Rockfalls could come in consequence of the most routine tasks. In July 1894, a 30-year-old worker with a "yellow and white complexion" from the village of Yayılacık in Ebegümeci hamlet was on the morning shift with two hewers when rocks weighing 9 kg fell on him. After a coworker from the same area spread news of the accident, the mine director brought a prayer leader who said prayers over the site while the fellow laborers, without success, "struggled to save the man."[78] Death came slowly to worker İsbeyoğlu Halil, described as a 20- to 22-year-old without beard or mustache, from Çamlıoğlu hamlet. Wounded on the right side of his head by a rockfall, he entered the hospital on the evening of 1 August 1895, bleeding from the mouth and nose. There he lingered for a week before succumbing to his injuries.[79] In December 1900, the hewer Reşid and his foreman were inspecting a gallery just 100 meters inside a mine. When Reşid tested the ceiling by tapping it with his pickax, it collapsed and buried him. Four days later they had not yet retrieved the body.[80] Two brothers, Akif and Tevfik, were doing cleanup work for a hewer in the Çay Damarı mine of the Ereğli Company in February 1901. When Akif went outside to transport some debris, the ceiling fell on Tevfik. Despite the grieving brother's complaints about the hewer, no fault was assigned.[81] Death came in 1902 to three workers doing piecework under contract to the Tiran headman, Karamahmudzadeler Mehmed Agha (chapter 3). The three were more than 200 meters below sea level, 650 meters inside the mine, when a 100-kg rock fell and killed them all.[82] At the Ereğli Company mine at Üzülmez, a worker was wounded in 1904 as the support timber he was carrying on his shoulder struck a ceiling support and triggered a rockfall.[83]

In January 1906, a foreman's quick action saved his workers' lives but not his own. In the Giurgiu Company #348 mine at Kozlu, he saw dust begin to fall from the ceiling and acted immediately to protect the two workers under his supervision, ordering them to flee. They all did but, when he returned to pick up his lamp, the ceiling fell in and killed him.[84]

Hüseyin, a 20-year-old bachelor, and Osman, a 44-year-old father of four from the same Yenice village in Devrek district, died together in December 1912. The eyewitness, from the same village, stated:

> In order to come out of the mine sooner, we wanted to fill the baskets with coal faster for the basket carrier Osman. Three workers brought the coal in baskets to the wagon that was on the pit road. We left them inside the mine. All of us hewers quickly filled the wagon in order to go out of the mine together and waited on the pit road for the wagon boss. After a few minutes, we heard debris fall down.... Two workers remained trapped under the stones that fell from the ceiling. Three frameworks had broken; and we witnessed the really difficult situation in which only the fourth remained.[85]

Kozluoğlu Ali, who was an 18-year-old bachelor from Karabahçe in Devrek district, died from a rockfall while sitting "quite near" his co-workers in March 1913. The gallery where he died had been cut into hard rock, and in conformity with regulations, there was no support framing. There are cases, the inspecting engineer concluded, when careful examinations simply do not reveal any fissures in the rock.[86] A month later, Ali Ömer, a 23-year-old-hewer and father of two from the Trabzon area, died in a rockfall even though the strata at the site were considered solid and secure.[87] In June 1913, the 40-year-old hewer Giresunlu Bağcı Ismail, married with three daughters, was leveling the ceiling before placing a frame. The foliated schist causing problems in other locations suddenly fell away and wounded him on the hand and leg.[88] A month later, a 13 year-old basket carrier from a village in Devrek district died under a rockfall in the Giurgiu mine #9 (figures 7.4 and 7.5). The hewers were undercutting coal from a pillar and passing it back to the basket carriers when a stone fell on the boy. The hewers and other carriers, among them his cousin, rushed to his aid and dug him out, but found him already dead.[89] In November 1917, Mustafa, a hewer with a 2-year-old son and a 3-year-old daughter, died in another common type of rockfall accident, while cutting coal from the ceiling.[90]

Workers sometimes died or were injured in rockfalls because they ignored procedures.[91] In May 1894, a foreman and hewer were improperly pulling down pillars when the roof fell in and injured the latter. In this case, the two were using support columns of the wrong dimension and, it seems, not leaving coal pillars of sufficient size.[92] In April 1906, a hewer ignored the orders of his foreman to reinforce the ceiling with additional timber supports and died shortly thereafter when a 1,800-kg stone crashed down.[93] Similarly, several months later, the French foreman Bernard, paired with the Ottoman foreman Izzet, ordered Ömer, a hewer from Trabzon, to place reinforcing timbers in an inclined plane. Ömer instead gave priority to dispatching a coal wagon. When he later turned to the reinforcement work, the ceiling collapsed and killed him.[94]

In March 1912, departing workers informed the nightshift that a section of the frameworks needed replacement. A 28-year-old hewer, Dimitri from former Ottoman Bulgaria, said they first needed to prop up the ceiling. Thirty-year-old Yanni, from Limnos, who formally was in charge of the group, ignored the warning. As the two bachelors began to repair the timbers, a falling stone killed Yanni. The head engineer, Wilhelm Hühner, was harsh in his

Figure 7.4 Rockfall in Giurgiu Mine, July 1913, I. Source: ED 16, 72.

Figure 7.5 Rockfall in Giurgiu Mine, July 1913, II. Source: ED 10, 327.

assessment. "The cause of the accident consequently has been determined—as always—it is caused by the ignorance of the workers and one cannot accuse others of being responsible."[95]

In April 1912, eighteen workers on the morning shift were cutting coal from a pillar in the Sarıcazadeler #227 mine at Kozlu when a sudden collapse surprised and killed four of them. The victims' ages ranged from 15 to 45 and three of them—a foreman and two workers—were from the same village.[96] During that same month, two brothers, twenty-eight and twenty years of age, along with a third 50-year-old worker, died on the job in the Serafim Efendi #174 mine in Kilimli. The witness, who had been outside the chamber where the deceased were working, offered this account.

> At the accident site, the three persons killed were my friends who were working on the ceiling; at that time, while I was filling up a coal basket a few meters outside of the mine in which they were working. I didn't want to go into that mine because I heard several pieces of coal fall from the ceiling. I figured there must have been a cave in and that my friends had escaped. But they weren't expecting danger and after a brief moment something happened and my three friends couldn't escape. The coal which was being dug was very soft and was flowing like water.... Only I myself escaped.[97]

In July 1913, two brothers were doing tunnel work when a rockfall seriously wounded the younger, who was sixteen years of age. In this case, the engineer faulted the brothers for improperly spacing the supports. All frames should be one meter apart, he said, insisting also that stone, not coal, must form the floor and ceiling in the tunnel. The engineer called for increased inspections since "most workers don't attach enough importance to framing. The carelessness of workers is the principal cause of accidents."[98]

A hewer with twenty years' experience was injured in May 1914 as he worked without the supervision of his foreman. As he put it:

> At about 12 in the morning I began to work in the shaft which had been left by the evening shifts in such a state that it needed support work done.... For twenty years I have been an illiterate worker ... until the foreman comes I dare to do shaft work and cut a little coal.

But then a chunk of coal fell on him.[99]

Death sometimes came because those entrusted to protect the lives of workers failed in their duties. In 1904, three transport workers hauling coal were trapped when the coal pillars collapsed because the Ereğli Company had ignored existing regulations about their spacing.[100] Durmuş Mehmed, a 25-year-old hewer and the father of two children, died in December 1912, despite extra precautions that had been taken to shore up the ceiling of a particularly unstable mine. Two co-workers gave their eyewitness account.

> Five or six days ago, we went down with him, went to work.... The framework which had been one of the duties assigned to Durmuş Mehmed suddenly collapsed. A big stone had fallen on him. From the last frame to the hole was a meter. There was a two-support framework made with 107 frames which until now had not failed. From the ceiling, there was no sign of stones previously falling; they fell without leaving any time for escape.

In his report, the engineer noted the fundamentally unstable nature of the ceiling, made entirely of schist, and said that the accident could happen again in the future. He concluded by blaming not the worker but the procedures themselves.[101]

Kurtoğlu Hüseyin, a basket carrier in his late forties who was married with three children, died in a rockfall in the Pavlaki mine because a foreman failed to do his job. The preceding night shift of hewers had not set the timber frames, and the engineer had ordered foreman Şaban Çavuş to personally take care of this before the coal was transported. Instead of overseeing the workers, Şaban went to find the necessary timber. In his absence the now-unsupervised basket carrier went to work loading coal and died when a 30-cm piece of schist fell on him.[102]

Another basket carrier who died due to his supervisor's inattentiveness was a 13-year-old from the village of Himmetoğlu, who had been working with two hewers from the same village (figure 7.6). Coal had piled up 4.5 to 5 meters deep at a spot from which it was to be taken outside. The boy had filled

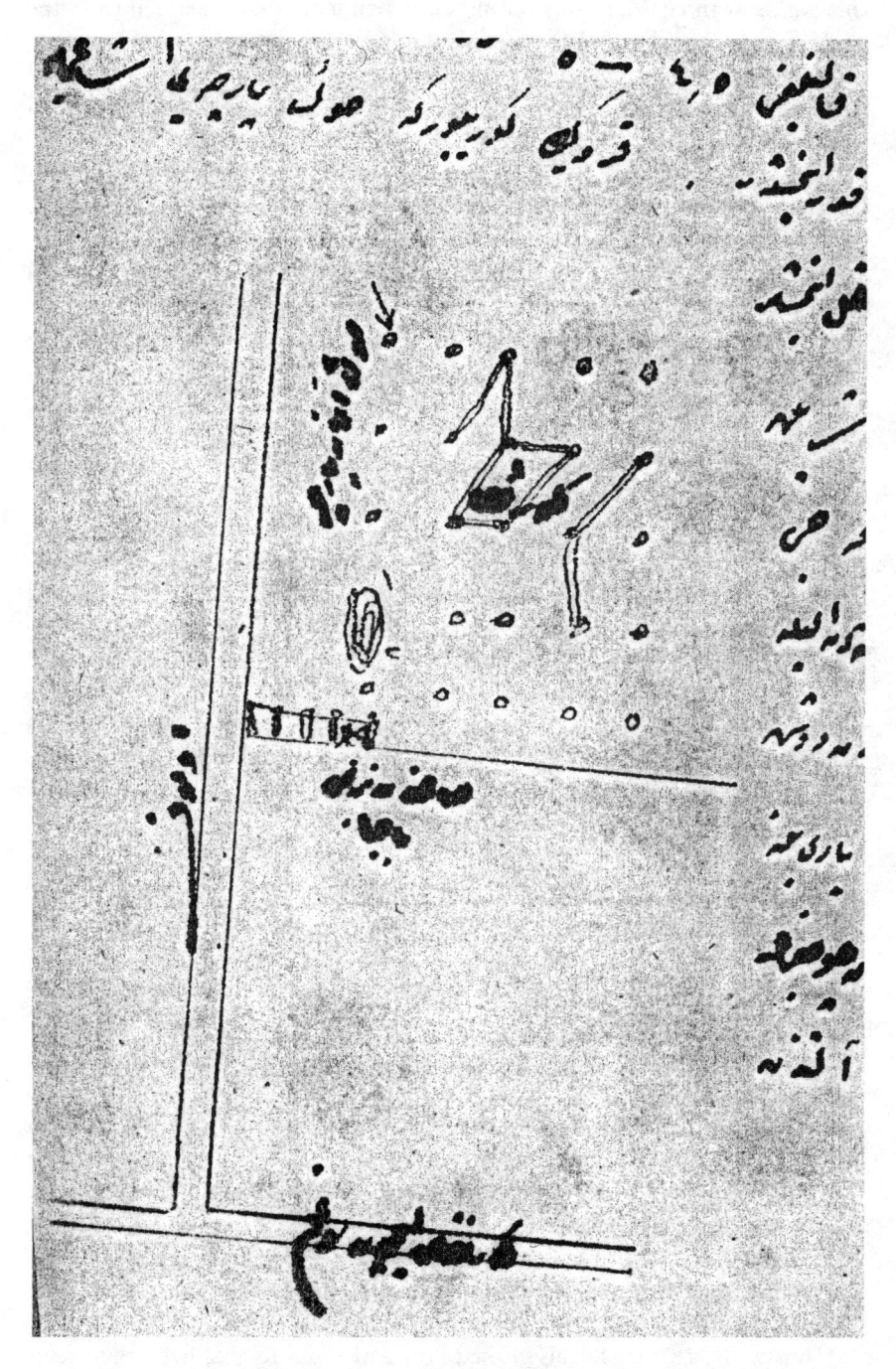

Figure 7.6 Rockfall in the Boyacıoğlu Mine, June 1913. Source: ED 10, 399.

his basket with coal and was setting out when a chunk of coal fell from the ceiling and covered him. Others "rushed to pull him out" and "whoever could take out coal did so." The boy nonetheless suffocated. The inspector concluded that the foreman had not recently inspected the site; had he done so he would have seen the danger and prevented the boy from working there.[103]

In one case, around 1915, a group of workers were placing supports to hold up the roof of an inclined plane. Normally, the hewers did the work of smoothing the ceiling and their assistants dug the holes into which the supports were inserted into the ceiling and walls. But in this case, an unskilled worker attempted the skilled task, even though both the head foreman and foreman were quite nearby. Careless work and careless supervision killed the 15-year-old boy.[104]

Fires and Explosions

Death and injury by fire and explosion came in many forms. The incorrect setting of fuses for explosive charges in hard rock areas, such as entrance or transport tunnels, only rarely appears as the cause of a recorded accident. In August 1893, rotational worker Kapakoğlu Ismail b. Mustafa, assigned to the Çatalağzı locale, was cutting a rock tunnel with an iron augur. A fuse that he set failed twice, but it flashed the third time and caused first-, second-, and third-degree burns.[105] A similar fate befell Pascal Fidancolu, an Italian subject, in 1903 while he was making a fuse hole in a rock tunnel: the gunpowder caught fire and burned him badly.[106] In November 1912, Mela Osmanoğlu Arif, who was helping cut a rock tunnel, lit the dynamite fuse and "waited a long time" for the explosion. When it didn't occur, he returned to where he had set the charge and, to his horror, found a very short, burning fuse. The ensuing blast injured him but the investigation absolved him of any responsibility.[107]

Similarly few were the accidents caused by the practice of shot-firing—using explosives to loosen coal. Among the hundreds of accident reports filed between 1877 and 1919, only one, dated late March 1913, refers to this practice. Several workers and the shot-firer Yorgi Lara had prepared charges throughout the Çay Damarı mine of the Ereğli Company. The shot-firer's carelessness set off a methane explosion that injured two hewers, one a 22-year-old bachelor and the other a 33-year-old father of two.[108]

Most accidental fires and explosions resulted from the ignition of coal gas (*gaz*), coal dust, or methane, also called firedamp (*grizu*). A mine's coal itself, once ignited, could burn for a very long time. In 1913, a fire had been burning for two full years in the Kandilli mine of the Sarıcazadeler, forcing the owners to abandon a good part of the mine with considerable losses.[109]

During the 1870s, officials viewed fires and explosions as naturally occurring events but sought "to eliminate whatever deficiencies there are in operations and prevent these tragedies from occurring." To this end, in August 1878, the Bartın district official telegraphed orders to keep workers from reentering a mine where a coal gas (*gaz*) explosion had occurred. The same official, however, asserted that a work stoppage was intolerable regardless of the danger.[110] In November 1877, hewers and workers were at the face when one worker arrived with an open lamp. A explosion "went off like a cannon and flames completely enveloped the mine. Coal wagons inside the mine were thrown outside." Two hours later, seven rescue workers sought to reach the accident site but fell back; two workers died in the explosion and six were wounded.[111]

These and many other workers died following a dangerous procedure that was standard practice for many decades in Ottoman mines, those in the U.S. and France, and likely elsewhere. Namely, workers routinely entered mines with open flames for the purpose of deliberately igniting (hopefully small) quantities of accumulated gases. For example, in the American state of Ohio during the 1870s, a "fire-viewer" was sent in the morning, before any miners were allowed entry, to walk through with a "naked light" to detect methane.[112] In the Zonguldak case reported here, workers went into a work area with an open flame to burn off the gas because, as the reporting engineer stated, "usually nothing would happen."[113]

Here is a description of the practice offered by the miner Ethem Çavuş.

> In order to avoid pit gas concentrations in the mine, burning lamps were left in suspected locations during the night. There were not any safety lamps like those used presently [ca. 1930]. These lamps burned pit gas slowly during the night, preventing its concentration in the pit.
>
> In the suspected pits where it was not possible to leave burning lamps during the nights, the pit gas detection workers were sent.... Their job was very crucial and dangerous. Before they set off for the work, they wore wet sacks on their backs and took the precautions necessary to protect their faces and hands. Then they took a long stick and used it as a torch to detect and get rid of the pit gas in the mine before other workers went below. By checking the ceilings and walls with the torches, these suicide workers got rid of any pit gas concentration while it was in a small quantity in the mine. Sometimes the gas concentration turned out to be stronger, and workers saved their lives by falling facedown on the ground. Since their heads and backs were covered with wet sacks, these workers warded off explosions with minor injuries. Nevertheless, as I remember, the workers who were killed during this dangerous task were quite numerous. Currently [ca. 1930], it is possible to avoid "fire-breath" danger, thanks to the safety lamps and the equipment that measures the concentration of pit gas. It is possible, yet we are not short of "fire-breath accidents."[114]

Thus, in 1894 in the Çay Damarı vein at a place called Acılar in the Zonguldak locale, a foreman entered to burn off coal gas (*gaz*). At one place where framing work had been suspended for 30–40 hours because of gas accumulations, his open lamp ignited the gas, burning him slightly. In the aftermath of this accident, the mine superintendent ordered the exclusive use of safety lamps.[115] Dangerous practices were in use on a Saturday morning in 1902, when three workers in the İncir Harmanı mine at Kozlu stopped to drink some water. They were just a few meters inside a new shaft and were burning off gases. However, because the mine had not been worked the day before, gas had accumulated, and it caught fire when the workers approached with their open lamps.[116]

The illumination of worksites with open lamps often caused explosions and fires. In June 1893, the rope used to haul coal wagons at the Hallaçyan mine at Üzülmez broke, and while awaiting a replacement rope, the foreman dispatched workers to repair and clean up the road inside the mine. A 30-year-old worker carrying an open lamp triggered a fire and suffered first- to fourth-degree burns on "his head, eyelids, ears, face, chest, hands and arms." He lingered for nearly two weeks in the Zonguldak hospital before finally yielding to his injuries.[117] Carrying an open lamp had been an acceptable practice at that location because previously there had been no fear of fire. In his report, the engineer faulted no one, neither the foreman nor the workers. Nonetheless, he henceforth required the use of safety lamps.[118] Three weeks later, a second fire erupted in the same mine, again caused by the open lamp of a worker.[119]

State inspectors repeatedly blamed fires and explosions on workers' carelessness, often marked by their refusal to use safety lamps (chapter 8). Not once, in the available reports, did they hold companies responsible for lamp-related accidents. In only one case did the inspecting engineer lay blame on a company not for a fire per se but only for failing to promptly notify the superintendent of a fire, in March 1913, in an Ereğli Company mine.[120]

An explosion triggered by open lamps and coal gas (*gaz*) swept through the Abdulrahim mine at Kilimli on a Sunday evening in mid September 1895. A group of hewers, after finishing their shift by pulling down coal pillars, left the mine. When seven workers came to the spot five hours later, their open lamps ignited the accumulated gas. They tried to flee but four were burned and two eventually died. All were from the same sub-district, Peşenbe, and two were only fourteen years old. One of them, after treatment at the Kozlu hospital, suffered for five weeks before dying.[121] Two workers died in a similar fashion in September 1900, in the Ihsaniye mine at Çatal Dere in Kozlu. At every branch, an air chamber had been constructed and "the greatest care" taken to assure good air circulation. Nonetheless, at a branch 1,000 meters inside, no air was flowing and the two died when they mistakenly entered an area full of burning coal gas.[122] Ethem Çavuş, when he was young, witnessed one of the worst mining disasters of the Ottoman period, a methane explosion that killed 67 workers in a mine of the Giurgiu Company.[123]

Sometimes workers died because they or their fellows violated known safety procedures. At the Karamanyan mines located at Zonguldak, in November 1895, six workers in a ventilator shaft were hauling mine supports on two wagons. On their third trip in, following the directions of the lamp bearer, they came to an area supplied with air pumps, where they previously had worked. But that day, the pumps were not operating, and the coal gas ignited as the six were gathered around the open lamp. All six were burned and three died—slowly—respectively, one, six, and eight weeks after the accident.[124]

Willful violation of regulations was commonplace. For example, two workers at the Süleyman Efendi mine in Kozlu disregarded specific orders and were burned in July 1902 because they used open lamps (see chapter 8).[125]

Methane gas explosions appear more common in documents from the post-1912 era, in part, certainly, because of better reporting. But there is more to the explanation, for as experiences in the U.S. and elsewhere suggest, the deeper the mine, the greater the presence of methane.[126] As mounting production after 1896 brought new dangers, including the increased likelihood of encountering methane, precautionary measures proliferated, such as the more extensive use of safety lamps and methane measurement devices (chapter 8). An October 1912 explosion that killed one worker and wounded another from the same village occurred in a mine known to have severe problems with methane gas accumulations. The two had been engaged in a kind of work known to release methane gas from the coal. The engineer's report faulted the two for not using the required safety lamps and for violating procedures concerning work in blind alleys, where methane was known to collect.[127]

Despite the self-evident dangers, cigarette smoking inside the mines not uncommonly caused explosions. For example, several workers, including the culprit, were burned on the face during one night in late April 1913 when 23-year-old Temel Hüseyin from Trabzon lit up a cigarette, igniting a pocket of methane in the Çay Damarı mine. The angry Zonguldak mining engineer brought the miner to court, invoking 1911 orders that demanded harsh punishments for workers causing pit gas explosions. He praised the Ereğli Company for its measures to avoid such methane explosions "not just to comply with the orders but for the sake of their own lives." The mine superintendent's procedures called for regular searches of workers to stop anyone from taking tobacco and matches into the mines.

> Nevertheless, the workers still manage to slip in tobacco and matches by hiding them in unimaginable places, in their hair or secret pockets of their clothes. As a result, all these efforts remain fruitless and pit gas explosions take place. That is why this specific explosion took place. Fortunately, it did not cost many lives this time. But it is most likely that a similar accident would take hundreds of lives.[128]

Notes

1. Derickson (1998), 2; Whiteside (1990), 74-75.
2. Church (1986), vol. 3, table 7.8, 586, for the lower figure; Tenfelde (1992), 1026-1029, for the higher.
3. Tenfelde (1992), 1026-1029.
4. Derickson (1998), 2-21; Seltzer (1985), 93-94. A huge controversy unjustifiably raged in the U.S. between about 1900 and the 1960s, when many medical authorities and mine operators refused to agree that coal dust produced lung disease, despite vast evidence to the contrary.
5. My thanks to Tom Dublin, Binghamton University, State University of New York, for this information.
6. Graebner (1976), 138, argues that the organization of labor or its lack played a crucial role in determining the level of safety. The more organized the labor, he asserts, the safer the work. "Death was due to a lack of organization." Whiteside (1990), 132-333, for Utah and Montana.
7. Whiteside (1990), 132-133; Tenfelde (1992), 1026-1029; Church (1986), vol. 3, table 7.8, 586.
8. Graebner (1976), 1.
9. Graebner (1976), 44-45.
10. The 1893-1907 data might be a consistent data set, reported by the same mine inspector.
11. KU KD 2 and ED 12. These figures are extrapolated from the recorded 21 dead and 26 wounded in 17 weeks of available reports during 1912, namely, late February to late May and then mid October to late November. My assumption is that if reports had been available for the entire 52 weeks, at least 63 dead and 78 wounded would have been reported. This estimate seems conservative since reports were not available for the busiest mining months of June through September.
12. ED 10; ED 16. The only missing months are January and December, normally inactive in mining.
13. The data permit comparison of Ottoman and British coal-mining accident rates on the basis of accidents per 1,000 tons of coal mined. These figures in turn permit indirect comparisons with French and American accident rates.
14. Graebner (1976); Whiteside (1990); Reid (1981); and Church (1986). Also, sources cited in table 7.1.
15. Based on data in table 7.1. There were 187 workers of known occupation, 28 percent were hewers and hewer assistants. There were 123 fatal accidents, in which 52 hewers died.
16. ED 3, 35, no no., 12 ts 1312/24 November 1896; ED 3, 35, #162, 31 kl 1312/25 December 1897. He was buried in a lead coffin; the superintendent inspected the second coffin, made of pine and walnut.
17. ED 3, 196, #56, 26 ts 1319/9 December 1903.
18. ED 3, 236, #19, 3 Temmuz 1322/16 July 1906; 237, #21, 15 Temmuz 1322/28 July 1906.
19. Quataert and Duman (2001), 161-162.
20. ED 16, 148, 12 Eylül 1329/16 September 1913.
21. Whiteside (1990), 74-75.
22. Tenfelde (1992), 1026-1029.
23. Graebner (1976), 1-6.
24. Only in 1962, many decades after the disappearance of the Ottoman Empire, did the Turkish Republic formally acknowledge black lung as a disease. Correspondence with Erol Kahveci, 11 January 2004; see also *Yurt Ansik* 10, 7784.
25. Whiteside (1990), 136-138.
26. ED 3, 37, #173, 22 Nisan 1313/4 May 1897.
27. ED 3, 37, #185.
28. ED 10, 116, #519/59, 6? Mayıs 1329/19 May 1913. ED 16, 48-49, for French version.
29. ED 16, 251-252, 6 Mart 1330/19 March 1914.
30. ED 16, 143-144, ca. 25 Eylül 1329.

31. ED 3, 139, #34, 20 kl 1310/1 January 1895.
32. KU KD 2, 435, 7 Mayıs 1328/30 May 1912 and for a table presenting prisons, gendarmes, and soldiers. Also, ibid., 434, 17 Mart 1328/March 1912.
33. KU KD 2, 283, 12 Nisan 1328/25 April 1912.
34. KU KD 2, 437, 12 Nisan 1328, #407/43. The first mention of these incidents in 1912 is in KU KD 2, 105, #175, 4 19 Mart 1328.
35. KU KD 2, 436, 6 Mayıs 1328, #658/91, a response to 29 Nisan 1328/12 May 1912, #26239/85. For other examples of illegal trainhopping, see ED 12, 163, second document: *suret*, #1797/206, 28 ts 1328/10 November 1912; ED 12, 166, a *suret*, without date but surely 28 tl 1328; ED 12, 166, third document, #1802/306, 28 tl 1328.
36. ED 12, 272–273, 26 ts 1328/9 December 1912. Since May, only two accidents of this nature had been reported; see ED 12, 163, second document, suret, #1797/206, 28 tl 1328/10 November 1912; and ED 12, 166. Next, a *suret*, without date, but surely 28 tl 1328; and ED 12, 166, third document, #1802/306, 28 tl 1328. All five workers injured between May and December were aboveground workers, and all of them had non-Ottoman surnames.
37. ED 12, 420, 28 tl 1328/10 January 1913, #82; ED 12, 419, 29 kl 1328/11 January 1913, 2156/196: 29 kl 1328, 2157/197; 2 kl 1328/15 December 1912, #1978/188; 25 kl 1328.
38. ED 16, in French, 28 Mars 1329, 18–19; Ottoman version in ED 10, 45, 27 Nisan 1329/10 May 1913. Also, ED 10, 46, #420/28, 28 Nisan 1329.
39. ED 16, 65–66, 3 Haziran 1329/16 June 1913.
40. ED 16, 65–66, in Ottoman and 67–70 in French. ED 10, 310–311, 3 Haziran 1329/16 June 1913. ED 10, 339, 11 Haziran 1329; ED 10, 341, 11 Haziran 1329; ED 10, 285, 2 Haziran 1329/15 June 1913, #730/73.
41. ED 16, 78–79, date blurred, in French, perhaps 2 Juin but more likely 8 Juin 1329/21 June 1913. I believe the practice long predates this document. ED 10, 341, 11 Haziran 1329/24 June 1913.
42. ED 3, 141, #43, 5 Mart 1311/17 March 1895.
43. ED 3, 159–160, #8, 5 Haziran 1316/18 June 1900.
44. ED 3, 181, #14, 1 Ağustos 1318/14 August 1902.
45. ED 3, 181, #16, 3 Eylül 1318/6 September 1902.
46. ED 3, 184, 17 Şubat 1318/2 March 1903.
47. ED 10, 359, 13 Haziran 1329. ED 16, 92, for French version.
48. ED 3, 187, #22, 11 Haziran 1319/24 June 1903. This is the first accident in the register since Şubat 1318, a full three months earlier. ED 3, 181, #14, 1 Ağustos 1318/14 August 1902.
49. ED 3, 202, #20, 25 Mayıs 1320/7 June 1904. For similar cases, see ED 3, 181, #14, 1 Ağustos 1318/14 August 1902 and ED 3, 184, 17 Şubat 1318/2 March 1903.
50. ED 3, 227, #36, 4 kl 1321/17 December 1905.
51. ED 3, 247, 20 May 1323/2 June 1907.
52. ED 16, 240–241, 17 Şubat 1329/2 March 1914; ED 16, 24 Mart 1334. #24.
53. KU KD 2, 376, 26 Nisan 1328.
54. ED 10, 350, accident dated 7–8 Haziran 1329; ED 16, 86–88, for the French version.
55. ED 16, Ottoman, 242–243, 18 Şubat 1329/3 March 1914, #118.
56. KU KD 2, 255, #367, 61,11 Nisan 1328/24 April 1912; KU KD 2, 256, 369/18.
57. ED 16, 347–349, #26, 21 tl 1333/21 October 1917.
58. ED 3, #1, 157, 12 Nisan 1316/25 April 1900; ED 3, 158, #4.
59. ED 3, 247, #11, 16 May 1907.
60. ED 16, 383–386, 30 ts 1333/30 November 1917, #47.
61. ED 16, 276–278, 23 Nisan 1330/6 May 1914. #10.
62. ED 3, 188, #26, 12 Haziran 1319/25 June 1903.
63. ED 3, 240, 2 Şubat 1322/15 February 1907.
64. ED 16, 472–473, 13 Mart 1334/13 March 1919.
65. This translation differs somewhat from that originally offered in Quataert and Duman (2001), 167–168.

66. ED 3, 167, #32, 19 Şubat 1316/4 March 1901.
67. ED 3, 232-233, #7, 8 Nisan 1322/21 April 1906. For a water-related injury, see KU KD 2, 415, #631/105, 3 Mayıs 1328/16 May 1912.
68. ED 3, 170, #37, 22 Mart 1317/4 April 1901.
69. ED 4, 35, 9 Eylül 1293/21 September 1877.
70. ED 4, 184, 7 Haziran 1294/19 June 1878.
71. Çatma (1998), 98-99, Belge 53, 19 ks 1296/19 January 1879.
72. ED 16, 380-382, 30 ts 1333/30 November 1917, #46.
73. ED 16, 387-392, 5 kl 1333/5 December 1917, #48.
74. ED 16, 383-386, 30 ts 1333/30 November 1917, #4.
75. ED 16, 418-421, 21 kl 1333, #58.
76. ED 4, 170 and 173, 31 Mayıs 1294/12 June 1878 and 10 Haziran 1294/22 June 1878; and 171, 3 Haziran 1294/15 June 1878.
77. ED 3,168, #33, 19 Şubat 1316/4 March 1901.
78. ED 3, 11, #67, 8 Temmuz 1310/20 July 1894.
79. ED 3, 25, #121, dated 1 Ağustos 1311 and 27 Ağustos 1311/8 September 1895.
80. ED 3, 166, #29, 3 kl 1316?/16 December 1900.
81. ED 3, 167, #31, 31 ks 1316/13 February 1901.
82. ED 3, 179, #8, 10 Nisan 1318/23 April 1902.
83. ED 3, 202, #21, 8 Haziran 1320/21 June 1904.
84. ED 3, 230 #46, 31 ks 1321/13 January 1906.
85. ED 12, 450, 9 kl 1328/11 December 1912, #59; 29 kl 1328/11 December 1912, #59; ED 12, 451, a translation of a 2 kl 1328, #19 report dated 3 ks 1328.
86. ED 16, 7, French, 10 Mars 1329.
87. ED 16, 30-31, French, 14 Avril 1329.
88. ED 10, 326, 10 Haziran 1329/23 June 1913, #33789/89: ED 16, 72-73 for versions in Ottoman and in French. ED 10, 326, same date, #790/80, 327.
89. ED 16, 115-117, French; ED 10, 444-445, 29 Haziran 1329 and 30 Haziran 1329/12 July 1913.
90. ED 16, 375-376, 19 ts 1333/19 November 1917, #42.
91. ED 3, 134, #14, 28 Nisan 1310/10 May 1894; 6 Mayıs 131/18 May 1894. ED 3, 134, #15. ED 3, 134, #15. ED 3, 134, #14 and #15, 7 Mayıs 1310/19 May 1894. ED 3, 134, #16.
92. ED 3, 134, #14, 28 Nisan 1310/10 May 1894. ED 3, 134, #15.
93. ED 3, 232, #5, 17 Nisan 1322/30 April 1906.
94. ED 3, 234, #10, 20 Mayıs 1322/2 June 1906.
95. KU KD 2, 117-118, 26 March 1912, French. KU KD 2, 240 19 Mart 1328, #4, is the Ottoman version of the same accident.
96. KU KD 2, 188, #274/38, 31 Mart 1328/13 April 1912. KU KD 2, 443, 8 Mayıs 1328, #669/69. KU KD 2, 444, Ottoman translation of a 29 Mart 1328/11 April 1912, #97, in French. Also, KU KD 2, 446 contains the same document copied a second time.
97. KU KD 2, 226, #329/35, 8 Nisan 1328/21 April 1912; KU KD 2, 228, #330/52, 8 Nisan 1328. KU KD 2, 472, 12 Mayıs 1328/25 May 1912, #21.
98. *Kazaın başlıca sebebi amelenin kayıdsızlığı.* ED 10, 499, 2 Temmuz 1329/15 July 1913 and copy dated 9 Temmuz 1329. ED 10, 500, 9 Temmuz 1329.
99. ED 16, 279-280; 28 Nisan 1330/11 May 1914.
100. ED 3, 201, #15, 20 Nisan 1320/3 May 1904.
101. ED 12, 384, Ottoman translation of 24 ts 1328/7 December 1912, #85.
102. ED 16, 110-112, French version of the Ottoman document in ED 10, 427-428, 25 Haziran 1329/8 July 1913.
103. ED 16, 99-102, 17-18 Haziran 1319/30 June 1913. ED 10, 399, for the French version.
104. ED 16, 208-209, 28 ts 1329.
105. ED 3, 5, #30.
106. ED 3, 187, #23, 11 Haziran 1319/24 June 1903.

107. ED 12, 193, #84, a translated copy of report 77, dated 8 ts 1328/28 November 1912.
108. ED 16, 9–11, French, 16 Mars 1329/29 March 1913; and ibid., 14–15, French, 29 Mars 1329/11 April 1913.
109. ED 16, French, 83, 9 Juin 1329/22 June 1913.
110. ED 4, 204, 27 Temmuz 1294/8 August 1878 and compare with ED 4, 205, same date. ED 4, 264, 12 ts 1294/24 November 1878.
111. ED 4, 78, telegram of 3 ts 1293/15 November 1877.
112. Roy (c. 1905), 116–120.
113. ED 4, 78, 3 ts 1293/15 November 1877. ED 4, 197, #14, 17 Temmuz 1294/29 July 1878.
114. Revised translation of Quataert and Duman (2001), 163.
115. ED 3, 136, #27, 7 Ağustos 1310.
116. ED 3, 180, #11, 30 Haziran 1318/13 July 1902.
117. ED 3, 2, #12, 2 Haziran 1309/14 June 1893.
118. ED 3, 24 Mayıs 1309, 129, #1.
119. ED 3, 15 Haziran 1309, 129–130, #2.
120. ED 16, 9–11, French, 10 Mars 1329/23 March 1913 and 17 Mars 1329, 14–15.
121. ED 3, 26, #124, 3 Eylül 1311/15 September; also, ibid., #125 and #131 on 28, 15 tl 1311/25 October 1895. ED 3, 145, #56.
122. ED 3, 163, #18, 11 Eylül 1316/24 September 1900.
123. For his vivid description, see Quataert and Duman (2001), 161–162. This accident is not recorded in the accident reports available for this study and thus is not included in the tables of chapters 7 and 8.
124. ED 3, 29, #135, 20 tl 1311/29 November 1895; 30 #141, 25 ks 1311/6 February 1896.
125. ED 3, 180, #11, 30 Haziran 1318/13 July 1902.
126. Graebner (1976), 72–73.
127. ED 12, 200, 1 tl 1328/14 October 1912, #67. The work in question was termed *trikaj*.
128. ED 16, 32–36, French; see ED 10, 50 for the same report in Ottoman. Also, ED 10, 132–134, 20 Juillet 1329; ED 10, 49, #424/40, 27 Nisan 1329/10 May 1913; ED 10, 50; ED 10, 48–49, #423/43, 27 Nisan 1329/10 May 1913.

8

VICTIMS AND AGENTS
Confronting Death and Safety in the Mines

Introduction

The present chapter focuses first on the individuals who died or were injured in myriad accidents plaguing the coalfield. The accident reports offer a look at individual workers that is unprecedented in Ottoman labor history. In them, we learn not only the workers' names but also their occupations and origins, ages, marital status, and sometimes even the sex and ages of their children. Next, the chapter discusses the medical care available to the work force. The quality and number of medical personnel and hospitals surely improved over the decades but left much to be desired. Moreover, since it was the workers who paid for the care received, many compulsory workers instead returned to their villages and others simply endured their injuries alone. Next, the chapter examines the safety programs of the Ottoman state and the agendas it pursued in striving to make the mines safer, healthier work spaces. These programs were part and parcel of nineteenth-century reform programs with dual aims: (1) to discipline Ottoman society and make it more amenable to administrative control, and (2) to create a healthier, more informed, aware citizenry to better serve the state. The chapter concludes by assessing the workers' frequent refusal to accept these mine safety programs.

Profile of Accident Victims: 1893–1907

rge mine operations sometimes were the site of the deadliest accidents.[1] The known accident of the Ottoman era, which killed sixty-seven workers, in the Giurgiu mine, one of the biggest in the coalfield. It would seem

r begin on page 203.

self-evident that at bigger mines, since they employed larger numbers of workers, there would be more potential victims for any mine disaster. Yet the data available for this study reveal that workers laboring in the pits of small firms were more likely, by a considerable margin, to encounter injury and death than those working in the mines of larger companies. Strikingly, nearly half (46 percent) of all accident victims found misfortune in the mines of small operators, those accounting for as little as 10 percent of total coal output in 1900. For example, two of the gravest single accidents, which killed fourteen and eight persons, occurred in the tiny operations of M. Sila Bey and Hoca Stefan. Mines run by four of the largest companies claimed 54 percent of all the victims. Giurgiu Company workers were the second-largest group, 15 percent, of all victims. In around 1900, the Ereğli Company accounted for only 22 percent of the accident victims but alone furnished three-quarters of aggregate coal production. Indeed, twice as many workers died or were injured in small mine operations than in the pits of the Ereğli Company, and its share of accident victims is remarkably small when compared to its proportion of overall output. Thus, the 1893–1907 sampling of accident indicates, mines of larger operators were safer workplaces than those of small entrepreneurs and safest of all were the mines of the Ereğli Company.

This pattern may not be particularly surprising, since small-time entrepreneurs could least afford the improvements and procedures that saved lives but cost money. Moreover, because they were so small, they may not have received as much attention from the state inspectors who perhaps focused their energies on the larger mines, which held more workers and produced more coal. The Ereğli Company, for its part, was comparatively well financed and could better afford to install and implement often-costly safety procedures. But there may be an additional reason for its better accident record. The concession leading to formation of this French company had been a controversial one within state policymaking circles, a decision the Ottoman regime had reached only when indigenous means to extract coal had seemed futile.[2] State inspectors may have given special scrutiny to Ereğli Company procedures not merely because of the company's size but also because the firm seemed poised to endanger Ottoman economic autonomy. In this argument, therefore, the better safety record derived both from company procedures and extra-careful government vigilance.

Hewers, whose jobs placed them at the coal face where the risks of rock falls, fires, and explosions were the greatest, pursued the most dangerous occupation among the workers. They constituted perhaps one-quarter of the total work force but accounted for 43 percent of all fatal accidents, a disproportionately large number. Basket carriers and unskilled workers died in relatively small numbers: they formed two-thirds of the underground work force (in this sample) and accounted for only two-fifths of all fatalities. In the case of nonfatal accidents, by contrast, the various categories of workers were injured in numbers proportionate to their participation in the work force, as enumerated in this sample (table 8.1).

Table 8.1 Distribution of Accidents by Occupation, 1893–1907

	Kind of Worker		Accidents Fatal		Accidents Non-fatal	
	no.	%	no.	%	no.	%
Basket carrier	118	63	48	39	65	64
Hewer	52	28	52	43	36	36
Other workers	17	9	22	18		
Totals	187	100	122	100	101	100

Source: ED 3.

Profile of Accident Victims: June 1912–May 1914

In common with the earlier 1893–1907 era, the mines of the Ereğli Company during the 1912–1914 years continued to provide a safer work environment.[3] Furnishing at least three-quarters of the coal, its mines accounted for 36 percent of all reported accidents, fatal and non-fatal. The mines of all other operators, who altogether furnished about one-quarter of the coal, accounted for two-thirds of the accidents. The conclusion seems inescapable that workers in Ereğli Company mines less often encountered death and injury at the worksite.[4]

In a number of other respects, however, the profile of accident victims between 1912 and 1914 differs from that of the 1893–1907 era. Several factors may be responsible. Production jumped from an average 150,000 tons during the mid 1890s to 800,000 tons and more in the final pre–World War I years. There were more mines, deeper mines, more workers, and a more heterogeneous work force. In addition, reporting certainly improved as increased numbers of inspectors oversaw safety operations. Vastly greater attention was given to safety; note, for example, the increasingly specific information about the identities of the victims and the witnesses. There can be little doubt that in this later period, fewer accidents escaped reporting than during the years between 1893 and 1907. In these earlier reports, moreover, we learn much about the accidents but far less about the humans involved in them. Later, while information about the accidents continues to flow, it provides considerably more details about the victims and sometimes even the witnesses.

The correlation between occupation and accident frequency during 1912–1914 (table 8.2) is different from that for 1893–1907. In the earlier period, hewers were involved in accidents twice as often as their share of the work force warranted. By contrast, in 1912–1914, hewers' involvement in fatal accidents was about proportional to their share of the total work force, about a quarter of the total (compare with table 8.1). This seems surprising, given the inherently more dangerous nature of their occupation.[5]

Table 8.2 Occupational Distribution of Accident Participants, 1912–1914

Occupation	Victims				Witnesses Fatal and Non-fatal	
	Fatal		Non-fatal			
	no.	%	no.	%	no.	%
Basket carrier	27	44	21	37	10	17
Hewer	18	30	22	39	21	36
Other occup.	12	20	11	19	21	36
Unknown occup.	4	7	3	5	7	12
Total	61	101	57	100	59	101

Sources: KU 2, ED 12, ED 10, and ED 16. Database differs slightly from that of table 6.6.

The accident statistics also reflect the growing importance of workers from outside the coalfield. In the 1912–1914 sample, 20 percent of all victims were Ottoman subjects from outside the coal district. Most came from Black Sea coastal areas to the east, notably Bartın and Trabzon as well as Giresun and Inebolu while others were from the interior, such as Kastamonu, Tokat, Karaman, Bayburt, and Erzurum.

The workers who were hurt or killed in accidents from 1912 to 1914 were comparatively young (table 8.3). Most injured or killed workers were 25 years old or younger. Indeed, boys and young men between the ages of 12 and 25 made up a full three-quarters of accident victims.[6] Teenagers, some as young as 12–14 years, were one-fifth of all victims during this period. More than half were young men in their twenties. Older men, in their forties and fifties, by contrast, accounted for only one-tenth of accident victims.[7]

Table 8.4 denotes the correlation between age, occupation, and death or injury. Between 1912 and 1914, there were twice as many victims among unskilled workers who were twenty-five years and younger than among hewer victims. The younger unskilled workers often were in their early teens, while most hewers were at least 20 years old.[8]

Thirty-six percent of all basket carrier accident victims were in their teens, while an equal proportion were ages 20–25; in all, nearly three-quarters of unskilled workers were 25 or under. In contrast, only one hewer victim was in

Table 8.3 Ages of Accident Victims, 1912–1914

	Teens	20s	30s	40s	50s	
Nov. 1912–July 1913	2	14	4	2	1	
Aug. 1913–April 1914	14	25	7	3	1	
Total (no./%)	16/22	39/53	11/15	5/7	2/3	73/100

Sources: KU 2, ED 12, ED 10, and ED 16. Database differs slightly from that of table 6.6.

Table 8.4 Age and Occupation Distribution of Accident Victims, 1913–1914

	\multicolumn{6}{c}{Number Aged}	
	12–19	20–25	26–29	30–35	36–40	over 40	Total
Unskilled worker	11	11	4	0	1	3	30
Hewer	1	11	6	8	1	1	28

Sources: KU 2, ED 12, ED 10, and ED 16. Database differs slightly from that of table 6.6.

his teens, while more than half were older than 25. Thus, the difference in accident rates for the various types of workers in 1893–1907 and 1912–1914 seems attributable to the youth and inexperience of the workers (table 8.4).

Experience, of course, was no guarantee of safety. Take the example of Yusuf, a 45-year-old foreman who, on an early spring day in 1912, died along with two hewers and one worker as the pillar supports collapsed on eighteen workers. Yusuf, as his years suggest, had long mined and for seven years had been a foreman in the mine that took his life.[9]

And finally, table 8.5 includes both the victims of accidents and the workers who witnessed accidents but did not suffer death or injury themselves. The witnesses' inclusion gives us a fuller picture of the work force within and outside the mines. Teenagers formed 24 percent of all workers involved in accidents as victims or witnesses and another 54 percent of victims and witnesses were in their twenties. In sum, 78 percent of all involved workers were under the age of 30.

Each accident, whether it brought death or injury, was felt acutely on the personal and economic level. Families back in the village suddenly confronted new realities. The sudden disability or death of sons, husbands, fathers stand beyond the measure of documents and can scarcely be imagined. These were crucial losses in every respect.

Looking at the size of the victims' villages can help suggest the impact of a miner's injury or death upon the communities. Overall, the villages of worker victims were quite small. In the following three cases, the victims' villages ranged

Table 8.5 Ages of Accident Victims and Witnesses, 1912–1914, 1917

	Teens		20s		30s		40s		50s		Total	
	no.	%	no.	%	no.	%	no.	%	no.	%	no.	%
Nov. 1912–July 1913	7	16	26	59	7	16	3	7	1	2	44	100
Aug. 1913–April 1914	13	33	19	49	2	5	4	10	1	2	39	99
Total	20	24	45	54	9	11	7	8	2	2	83	99
1917	1		0		2		9				12	

Sources: KU 2, ED 12, ED 10, and ED 16. Database differs slightly from that of table 6.6.

between 25 and 31 households and averaging fewer than seven persons each. In September 1903, two workers from the village of Akbaş died together in a single accident. Thus, the accident killed men from one in every 13 of its households.[10] In August 1905, a foreman and a worker died together in a rockfall; the two were from the village of Kargarlar, with a population of 120 males and 104 females living in 31 households. Between August 1904 and November 1905, two workers from the village of Tabaklar died in accidents and a rockfall crushed the face of a third. These numbers may seem small, but for a village such as Tabaklar, the three accidents were disasters. In a short space of fifteen months, they had directly afflicted 10 percent of all households in the community.[11] Even for a larger village, such as Fırnık with 244 inhabitants in 37 households, losses like these were keenly felt: two accidents in the early twentieth century meant that 5 percent of Fırnık families suffered lost income as the injured workers returned home.[12]

The accident reports that yielded these statistics thus also hint at the impact of the accidents on workers' communities and families. The patterns of work, life, and death were hardly abstract but full of intimacy and familiarity. When two workers from the village of Isa Beyler died together in May 1913, the accident removed a person from every fourteenth household in this community of 282 souls. That same month, catastrophe befell the village of Süleyman Beyler, which contained 227 inhabitants in perhaps 25 households. In a single day, one in five households lost family members in a methane gas explosion. Even a single death was no trivial event. There were only 23 households in the village of Çayırköy; so the May 1914 loss of the 20-year-old hewer Yukub b. Ahmed must have been keenly felt in many homes, and not merely that of his widow.

As the preceding suggests, accident statistics confirm that persons from the same village often worked together in the same mine. More precisely, 40 percent of the victims or witnesses were standing next to a neighbor, a fellow villager, when the accident struck.[13] In the terrible May 1913 accident (described further), the thirty workers who suffered death and injury came from only seventeen different villages.

Sometimes the bonds between workers were yet more intimate and personal than a common village of origin: many died or endured injury in the presence of family members. Thus, on 19 May 1913, rolling coal cars near a coal scrubber crushed the leg of 26-year-old Hasan Hüseyin as his brother-in-law looked on. In mid July 1913, 29-year-old Şamlıoğlu Mehmed and his younger brother Yusuf were tunneling when a stone fell from the ceiling, trapping Yusuf. As his brother pried at the stone, a chunk of it rolled over and smashed the leg of the 16-year-old.[14] In early July 1913, Arikoğlu Hasan, a skilled hewer, was cutting away a supporting coal column with two other hewers, one from his village. The three were passing coal back to basket carriers, among them his 13-year-old cousin Mehmed, from a different village. Chunks of the ceiling fell in, fatally crushing the boy.[15] Or consider the unskilled worker Kedaroğlu Ismail, who was working together with his hewer father, Satılmış Kurmanoğlu, when "a big chunk of coal" fell down and wounded the 35-year-old hewer.[16] In an accident involving criminal negligence by the mine operator, a hewer named Laz Ibrahim b. Mustafa died before the eyes of his cousin.[17]

There is little information about the families of accident victims (or witnesses). Thirty-six workers were reported as married and another fourteen as single. Since there is no marriage information for the remaining two-thirds of the group, the small size of the sample allows few meaningful comments. It may be worth remarking that there is no recorded case of a married worker in his teenage years. Two-thirds of those noted as married were between the ages of 20 and 35. Among those few persons (14) specifically noted as single, six were in their teens, four were 20–25 and another four were 25–30 years of age.[18] When workers are 12–15 years old, there is no reference to their marital status. But at 16 years, the reports sometimes note bachelor status while at other times confer no designation. It seems that the cusp of adulthood was 16 years.

There are similarly few data about victims and their children. Only twenty-five cases record the presence of children (table 8.6). All but two of the twenty-five fathers were older than 25 when they fell victim to accidents. Yet even these few stories clearly indicate the suffering brought upon mining families. When the 38-year-old worker Kadrakoğlu Satılmış Mustafa was injured in November 1917, the mining inspector absolved the company of any fault. Without financial recourse, the accident immediately jeopardized the lives of his wife and five children back in Sandallar village.[19]

Table 8.6 Size of Families of Accident Victims, 1912–1914, 1917

No. of Children	Accident Victims
1	5
2	9
3	7
4	3
5	1

Sources: KU KD 2, ED 12, ED 10, ED 16.

In the small sample that records them, accidents befell the fathers of sixty-one children, of whom twenty-six lost their fathers in fatal accidents. Among the worst was the case of a 25-year-old hewer named Fransevi Izzet, who had been enlarging a hole to replace support timbers. He undercut the rocks too much and they collapsed on him, ending his life and leaving behind a widow and three children.[20] In a similarly disastrous event, a 30-cm piece of schist fell from the ceiling and smashed into a 45- to 50-year-old-basket carrier, Kurtoğlu Hüseyin. The report, which faulted the carelessness of his foreman, cannot have been of much comfort to his widow and three children back in Kum Tarla village.[21]

Medical Care in the Coalfield

In the Zonguldak coalfield, mortality rates certainly were worsened by the poor medical care available, notwithstanding steady improvements in its quantity and quality. Ottoman miners were hardly alone in suffering from a lack of adequate medical support. In the United States, sporadic medical coverage and substandard care offered by company doctors were overcome only in 1945, thanks to action by the United Mine Workers.[22] Still worse, Zonguldak miners who received medical treatment did so at their own expense and were obliged to provide reimbursement for the care received. Again, this was a practice common in many other areas of the globe.[23] How the Zonguldak miners paid for their treatment is not entirely clear. During the Ottoman era, across-the-board wage deductions for medical care are not visible in the pay ledgers. Injured or sick workers apparently were billed after treatment for the individual services received.[24] The obligation to pay for medical care surely discouraged many workers from seeking it and likely contributed to the low percentage of accident victims who obtained hospital care.

A mine administration hospital already existed at Kozlu in 1871, joined by a second at Ereğli in 1876.[25] During the 1870s, the medical personnel present had many responsibilities besides the care of mine workers. In 1877, for example, one "mine doctor" tended both mine workers and soldiers.[26] In another case, the "mine doctor" aided not only the Muslim refugees from the Balkans who then were flooding into Anatolia, but also seamen from the imperial merchant marine.[27] The Kozlu and Ereğli medical staff were joined in 1878 by a surgeon and a doctor assisting him, stationed at a third location in the Zonguldak district. At first working without a dedicated facility of any kind, they were promised a proper hospital, which indeed was constructed.[28] A fourth medical facility for the care of miners appeared in June 1878, when an experienced surgeon arrived to aid workers at the mines of the Kilimli locale. Until then, injured or sick workers at these mines had relied on the Kozlu hospital for care, some 2.5–3 hours distant (the fortunate ones were sent by boat, but others, even when wagons were not available, were sent there by land).[29] In addition, sick and injured workers repeatedly obtained treatment both at the naval hospital at Ereğli and the Naval Arsenal Hospital in Istanbul.[30]

During the early 1890s, mine administration hospitals at both Kozlu and Zonguldak were treating accident victims.[31] The naval hospital at Ereğli served marine officers and the rank and file, and continued to aid miners.[32] At this time (and until at least 1906), the mine administration had a "health committee," consisting of a doctor (holding military rank), two surgeons, and one pharmacist.[33] During the mid 1890s, the medical staff, in addition to treating mine workers, carried out many scores of physical examinations, mainly to determine the fitness of young men for military service. Sometimes they examined on-duty soldiers and sent them to the naval hospital for treatment.[34]

The opening of the Ereğli Company hospital at Zonguldak, in May 1897, is the first documented instance of a company-operated hospital facility.[35] Over the years, this hospital treated not only company workers but also accident victims who were not employees. During the final decades of Ottoman rule, there were a number of other company-run hospitals or dispensaries for immediate worker care. But overall, the medical support was tiny compared with the need. Government regulations required companies to take active measures against diseases, including the hiring of at least one doctor and constructing special barracks for quarantine purposes.[36] In June 1913, the Rombaki Company, one of the larger operators, maintained its own three-bed hospital.[37] By 1917, the Ereğli Company was operating a hospital at Üzülmez, in the heart of its operations.[38] This likely was an addition to its Zonguldak-based facility which in 1922 held fifteen beds.[39] Overall, the company simultaneously employed the services of four physicians.[40] The Sarıcazadeler mines, in 1918, operated a six-bed hospital and employed a Doctor Vakiyadis to care for the injured and sick. When these beds were full, he customarily sent patients to the Ereğli Company hospital in Zonguldak.[41]

Many workers remained without direct recourse to medical care, even at the very end of the Ottoman era. In 1917, workers in the Gregovich #33 mine, for example, were brought for treatment to any doctor who happened to be available.[42] The Kilimli #114 mine, operated by Mrs. Hiristofilis, similarly did not employ a full-time physician. Instead, Dr. Vakiyadis of the Sarıcazadeler Company traveled to the barracks of workers and, if unable to solve the problem, sent them to whatever hospital had free beds.[43]

Thus, the availability of medical care and facilities had expanded considerably over the years. By 1918, it consisted of a mix of state and company-run facilities and staff. There can be no doubt that the improvements were considerable. While much of the care was on an outpatient basis to the walking wounded, victims sometimes were hospitalized for extensive periods of time. For example, in 1893, a burn victim received six weeks of hospital care. The expansion of medical facilities notwithstanding, the medical infrastructure treated only a small fraction of those needing assistance. Comparatively few workers, about one in nine officially reported accident victims, received hospital care during the period 1893–1913 (table 8.7).

Table 8.7 Hospitalization of Accident Victims, 1893–1907, 1912, 1913

	Died in Hospital	Died out of Hospital	Injured with Hospital Care	Injured without Hospital Care
1893–1907	5	121	22	101
1912	1	21	5	26
1913	0	29	8	57

Sources: ED 3, ED 16, ED 10, KU KD 2.

Most fatally injured workers died outside the hospital. Indeed, only 4 percent of all those who died in mine work did so inside a hospital. This is hardly surprising since the vast majority of fatalities occurred instantaneously or nearly so, at the time of the rockfall, explosion or fire. Nineteen percent of workers in hospital care died while hospitalized. Among persons injured in mine accidents, only 18 percent received care at a hospital. The low proportion of injured workers using hospitals is a clear indication of the dearth of sufficient care and the reluctance of workers to seek medical assistance (table 8.7).[44]

In 1912, 11 percent of recorded fatalities or injured received hospital care, a proportion identical to that for the period 1893–1907. Only 4 percent (1 in 27) of those admitted in 1912 died while in the hospital. Hospital dead formed 5 percent (1 in 22) of all who died in mine work that year. The injured who were treated in hospitals were 16 percent (5 of 31) of all persons recorded as wounded in mine work. During 1913, hospitalized persons formed a somewhat smaller proportion—9 percent (8 of the 94) of the killed or wounded—than in 1893–1907 and in 1912. None of the 29 mine accident fatalities in 1913 died while in the hospital. The hospitalized wounded were 12 percent (8 of 65) of the total injured during that year (table 8.7).

The inadequacy of available care thus is strikingly evident. Ninety percent of all *reported* victims did not receive hospital care or, for that matter, medical treatment on the spot. Officially reported accident victims, moreover, certainly were but the tip of the iceberg. An overwhelming majority of victims likely went unrecorded, never showing up in the accident reports or receiving any professional treatment. Among all workers, those locally recruited under compulsory labor conditions were the most neglected and only a small proportion of the injured among them received medical aid. In 1912 and 1913, one-quarter of the hospitalized victims (of known origins) were local workers, that is, from the coalfield proper.[45] Yet it was these workers, recruited under conditions of compulsory labor, who accounted for the vast majority of the total work force and provided the overwhelming majority of the underground labor force. Since they made up the numerical majority of all workers and labored in the most dangerous jobs, there can be no doubt that local workers were hurt or killed in numbers much greater than workers from outside the district. Their scant presence among hospitalized victims reflects the neglect that they suffered over the decades of the Ottoman era.

By long-standing practice, injured local workers commonly were sent back to their villages for recuperation (or death). In a charitable view, these workers were not far from home and the care they would receive from family members. Less kindly, compulsory labor workers were badly treated because they had no choice but to work at the mines. The hospitals and medical care that were insisted on in the 1867 regulations were more absent than present. Ethem Çavuş succinctly summarized the situation. "Since the mine had neither hospital nor doctor, the injured were sent back to their villages on mule back. The mine regulations of the time cared about us that much."[46] By contrast, workers from outside—usually in safer jobs and a smaller percentage of the work force—were hospitalized in disproportionately high numbers. They had no family network to fall back on and so had no alternative to mining hospitals. And since they had been recruited to the region, the companies, to retain them, offered preferential treatment, both in housing and in medical care.

The place of health care issues among workers' demands when they repeatedly went on strike during the fall of 1908 is an open question. Led by the railroad workers, miners on all of the worksites of the Ereğli Company walked out. Contemporary newspapers and official accounts report only wage demands and the company, largely, met these.[47] But a leading authority writing in the 1930s states that in September 1908, striking workers made a series of demands, including higher wages and removal of the obligation to pay for their own hospital care in case of injury on the job. In the negotiations that followed, he says, the company accepted the workers' demands and the strike ended.[48]

But events transpiring after World War I seem to contradict this account and make it all but certain that the Ereğli Company did not concede free medical care to its workers in the pre-war era. In September 1921, the Ankara government passed a law governing labor relations in the mines. One provision (repeating the 1867 regulations) required mine operators to provide hospitals, certified doctors, and pharmacies for the workers. To pay for these facilities, workers were required to contribute 1 percent of their wages to a reserve fund set up under the administration of the mine operator.[49] Some observers have hailed this provision as a great improvement over Ottoman practices, while authors more sympathetic to workers have criticized the 1 percent tax. But none have argued that the law represented a step back from already existing, company-financed medical care. Rather, their discussions implied that workers of the post-war era had been paying out-of-pocket for medical treatment received. Thus, it seems likely that in 1908, the Ereğli Company probably had conceded only to wage demands, not to any relating to issues such as medical care or worker control.[50]

The Campaign to Adopt Safety Lamps

Introduction

The mine administration's campaign for improved safety in the coalfield, including the promotion of safety lamps, can be understood on several levels. It certainly was concerned with saving lives and in this way can be seen as a humanitarian endeavor. There can be do doubt that many state officials and mine operators were appalled when death and injury befell workers. But mine safety very much was a business venture as well. Safer mines protected entrepreneurs' profits, a factor that likely became more powerful after the 1882 state decision to allow open market sales. Although safety required considerable investments, mine operators stood to make net gains. Safe mines encouraged worker retention and fewer accident-related work stoppages; in this sense, they were more efficient operations. Thus, safety might be a humanitarian program, one supported by a rational economic calculus. In this way, the state benefited as well: the more stable work force and better profit potential for mine operators could result in greater production to meet military and government factory needs for coal.

Mine safety, however, was not merely a humanitarian, business, or military enterprise. Another dimension underlay the state's remarkable concern for mine safety. Safety involved the administration's effort to control the work force of the mines and, by extension, mining society and Ottoman society as a whole. Programs to impose safety on the coalfield aimed to educate, discipline, and control those whom the state sought to rule. As such, these mine safety programs were quite consistent with the broader programs pursued by the nineteenth-century Ottoman government. During the first quarter of the century, for example, the imperial Ottoman state mounted impressive efforts to spy upon and control its citizens. It carried out this surveillance and control through spies it placed in the coffeehouses of the capital to overhear and report the conversations of citizens. Somewhat later, it registered its citizens in the provinces in ledger books that noted their whereabouts and movements.[51] Throughout the post-1850 era, it also initiated and expanded a massive new school system designed to form a citizenry educated in the values of the state and not merely those of religion. And to create and support a healthier citizenry who could be of greater service to the regime, it simultaneously instituted hospitals, medical facilities, and charitable organizations.[52] In this atmosphere, the mine administration increasingly viewed worker discipline as the key to safety.[53] Its reverse, the absence of order and control was considered a cause of accidents. Mine safety more and more became the purview of professionals, of experts, and in the story of the Zonguldak mines we see the emergence of the science of expertism.

At the core of the state's mine safety program stood the effort to impose safety lamps on the workers. The search for safer means of illumination within coal mines dates back to at least early nineteenth-century England. Open flames were enormously dangerous when brought near coal dust, gas, methane gas, or some combination of the three. The Davy lamp, first developed in 1815 in England, sought to seal the flame off in such a way as to make it impossible to ignite the combustible materials surrounding the lamp. The Davy lamp offered insurance against such ignition, but at a high price. Namely, it gave off very little light and thus endangered the miner. Consequently, better safety lamps generating three times the light of the Davy lamp, such as the Marsault or Muesler, soon were developed and adopted widely.[54]

The mine administration's calls to adopt safety lamps and better ventilation form major themes in Zonguldak accident reporting and are found in the first available documentation, dating from the era of the Ottoman-Russian

War. After an 1878 explosion, the mine superintendent reminded his reader that a special commission formed to enhance coal production had called for the adoption of safety lamps.[55] A familiar sub-theme regarding safety lamp usage emerges in an 1893 report of a gas (*gaz*) explosion in a Hallaçyan mine where gas previously never had been found. In a refrain that became a mantra between 1912 and 1914 (when there are abundant records), the mining inspector insisted that safety lamps be adopted even though, he said, explosions were not likely in this particular mine. Better to err on the side of caution: henceforth, all workers in the mine were to use safety lamps.[56] A somewhat different case revolves around a deadly September 1895 accident that occurred in a small mining operation in the Kilimli locale. The explosion occurred at a crossroads in the mine where engineers then detected substantial quantities of methane. They banned the use of open lamps and ordered the exclusive use of safety lamps.[57] Similarly, when an accident suspended work at the Izzetlu Halil Bey mine in Alacaağzı during the summer of 1903, the superintendent ordered the installation of ventilator fans, a permanent prohibition on open lamps, and the exclusive use of safety lamps.[58] And following a non-fatal October 1912 methane gas explosion in the Alacaağzı locale, the superintendent reminded the Sarıcazadeler mine operator of standing orders regarding safety lamps and their proper use.[59]

During the spring of 1912, administrators and engineers argued over which kinds of lamps were suitable. In mines where methane was not present, the Zonguldak district official stated, workers were using small open petrol lamps. But when they found themselves working veins only one meter wide, ventilators were hard pressed to provide sufficient air. In these close quarters, the fumes of petrol-burning lamps were "like poison." Mine operators, inspectors argued, needed to discard them in favor of safety lamps or, at least, adopt lamps that did not pose ill effects on the workers' health.[60] At this time, the superintendent was pressing the Ereğli Company to make it impossible for workers to employ safety lamps unsuitable for use in the particular conditions of some of its mines. The company, he said, needed to provide the workers exclusively with *mandallı* lamps, which workers could not open.[61] The chief engineer, however, took a different position on the matter of open lamps. In Europe, he inaccurately asserted, workers long had been breathing the smoke of these oil lamps without ill effect.

> If the smoke had caused harm to the workers, this would be known by now. On the contrary, the use of these lamps is not harmful and moreover, this kind of open lamp gives more light and works for a longer period of time.... Since, in relation to the safety lamps, there are more of these open lamps, the workers in the mines and shafts see better and are in a cleaner environment. And, thus, they are better protected from accidents.

And, he concluded, in mines with methane, the administration must use the *mandallı* lamps in both the Zonguldak and the Ereğli regions.[62]

The State's Safety Campaign and the Çamlı #188 Mine Explosion

State efforts to promote safety lamps gained new urgency after a mine disaster in May 1913.[63] Methane and coal dust had worked in deadly combination to kill eleven and wound nineteen workers at the Çamlı mine in Kilimli. The site was the #188 mine operated by Karamahmudzade Halil Pasha, which he had contracted out to one Yohannes Efendi.[64] The dead included a foreman, two hewers and eight workers; all but one of the injured were workers. Five of the dead and one wounded came from the same village, Süleyman Beyler. And two of the wounded were related, perhaps brothers or father and son. The mine engineer, Arnaud Berlis, offered this assessment, based on eyewitness testimony.

> I was in the mine the very same morning, 1.5 hours before the accident. During my inspection I did not see anything deficient. When I came back to my residence, I saw that the ventilator fan had stopped suddenly. I instructed the necessary persons to start it. At the same time, it came to my mind that something might have happened inside the mine. As soon as the fan was started, black smoke poured out of the air pipe. At once, taking the head foreman with me, I entered the mine to discover the site of the accident. I found twelve corpses in the gallery at +4, and eighteen wounded in the gallery at -6.[65] I had them taken out of the mine. As for the cause of the accident: there must have been an area in front of the vein where pit gas was concentrated. After this area was filled with coal, the pressure must have increased inside the shaft. From the statements of the eyewitnesses, I think that because of the pit gas pressure, the safety lamps of the workers working at the accident site went out. Once other workers came to help their fellows with oil burning lamps, the explosion took place caused by these very lamps.

In the ensuing rescue operations, the ventilator fan was run at high speed to clear the remaining gas. The following day, engineers tested the pit gas ratio in the air being sucked out. Concluding there was no gas remaining in the mine, they divided into two groups and entered, keeping thirty to forty paces apart. After measuring the ratio of pit gas in the air every forty steps, they found it ranged from 0.5 to 1 percent, an amount considered safe so long as safety lamps were used. But at the accident site itself, ratios reached 4–5 percent, so they closed the site and the entire mine.

The accident report blamed a procedure that allowed open lamps in some parts of a mine but only safety lamps elsewhere in the same mine. In fact, workers cutting tunnels in solid rock properly had been using the open lamps but "for some reason" went to their colleagues whose safety lamps had gone out. There, in the gallery where the accident took place, conditions were extremely dangerous, a combination of very low ceilings, poor air circulation, and coal veins full of methane. The would-be rescuers' open lamps set off the methane, which then ignited coal dust circulating in the mine to produce the explosion. The black smoke the engineer saw pouring out of the ventilator after the explosion was key to this assessment. If methane alone had been involved, he said, only yellow smoke would have resulted.

In fact, the mine had been operating according to fairly strict safety standards, including the use of high-speed electric air pumps. But the miners had run into a methane gas accumulation previously not encountered in the Çamlı coal vein or, it seems, in the Zonguldak coalfield generally. When the workers hit this pocket, the methane rushed out and extinguished their safety lamps, triggering the sequence of events. In the eyes of the report's authors, the accident occurred because the workers with the open lamps were insufficiently disciplined and had gone into forbidden areas to help colleagues. Prohibitions against carrying open lamps into areas of potential methane concentration had proven insufficient. Effective immediately, the superintendent ordered the exclusive use of safety lamps in that mine and, within two months, in the other mines at Kandilli and Alacaağzı where the same or similar veins were being worked. Additional safety measures included the installation of meters (*enzimetro*) to measure the composition of the circulating air, and of hand-operated ventilators to supplement the main ventilators. And finally, workers were to be searched two or three times a week to deter them from taking cigarettes and matches into the mines. Proper supervisory work could now begin, the superintendent concluded, since a new administration building at Kandilli had just been completed to watch over the regions of Kandilli, Çamlı, Alacaağzı, Teflenli, and Çavuşağzı.[66]

To improve safety in areas of potential methane concentrations, the mine superintendent sent identical orders regarding these dangers to the Kozlu, Zonguldak, and Kilimli mine engineers.[67] The superintendent repeatedly pressed mine operators to follow regulations closely. The #364 mine at Alacaağzı, for example, had a reputation for producing lots of methane. After his visit in June 1913, the engineer reported that air circulation was "primitive" and the electricity poorly installed; to boot, nearly half of the workers had open lamps. Moreover, he noted, the lamp shop where miners picked up their lamps when going on shift was located within the mine, so workers walked in and out of it carrying lighted, open, lamps. The engineer offered a four-part recommendation to the superintendent, focused chiefly on the relocation of the lamp shop to a site outside of the mine and the exclusive future use of safety lamps. In addition, to improve air circulation, he urged the enlargement of the return airshaft and the use of hand air pumps in the dead-end passages where accumulation problems were likely (figure 8.1).[68]

During a one-week inspection tour of the mines in the Ereğli locale in late June 1913, the engineers found that only the mines at Çamlı, among five locations inspected, were using safety lamps unsatisfactorily. The workers there were using safety lamps as he previously had ordered but were opening them improperly. To permanently remedy this problem, he ordered new lamps with magnetic locks to replace the old safety lamps, which were to be disposed of. During the few days it would take for the new lamps to arrive, the Çamlı administration was to assure that workers properly closed the existing lamps.[69]

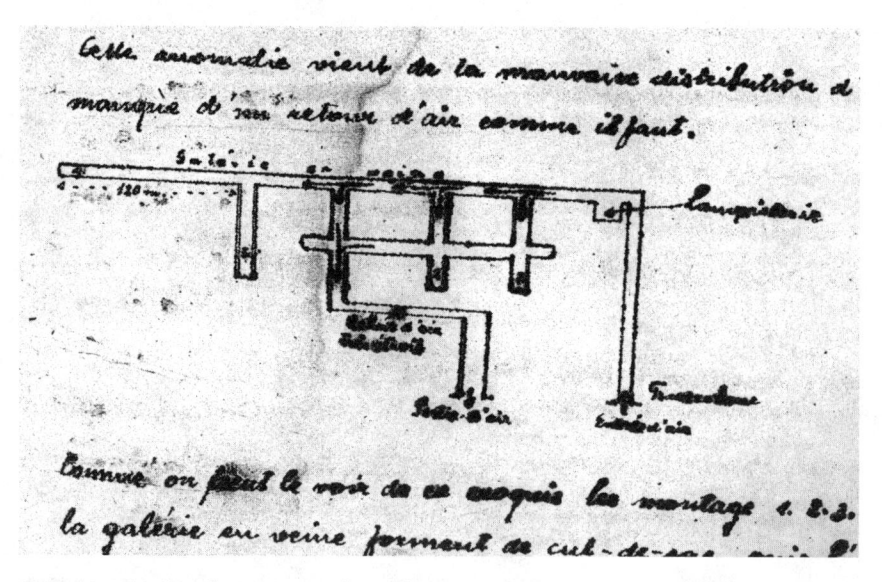

Figure 8.1 Air Ventilation Proposals, at Alacaağzı #364 Mine, June 1913. Source: ED 16, 76.

The plethora of regulations sometimes had little or no impact. For example, in June 1913, both the engineer and another official were inspecting the Alacaağzı #340 mine but failed to notice a small gap in one of their safety lamps. This ignited the surrounding methane, which they knew to be there, and both were burned badly.[70] Inside the Pavlaki #299 mine in May 1913, there were good air flows overall but faulty air returns in certain galleries. Therefore, workers were ordered to stop using open oil lamps and, as already directed, employ safety lamps.[71] Two months later, in July 1913, "the impudence of a single worker," who was smoking at a methane site, caused a burn injury. The engineer angrily reported his frustration. "The Ereğli Company has furnished safety lamps with lead rivet fastenings but the workers here always leave without [closing them]: encouraged by the state of things, they indifferently light cigarettes." The frustrated chief mining engineer added his own assessment: "Methane explosions generally are the result of the stupidity of the workers."[72]

Such powerful denunciations and admonitions notwithstanding, fires and explosions persisted. In December 1913, a gas (not methane) fire erupted in the Ikinci Makas mine of the Ereğli Company and the locale engineer traveled there to help. He directed the construction of barriers to flood the mine, with eventual success. In his opinion, workers at the coal face had caused the fire by using an open lamp, found at the site of the accident. The use of such lamps, he demanded, must be discontinued at both the Çay Damarı and Ikinci Makas veins.[73]

More tellingly for the ineffectiveness of the safety campaign, serious difficulties with fire continued to plague the #188 mine at Çamlı (figure 8.2). Approximately seven months after the fatal explosion in May 1913, a month-long fire

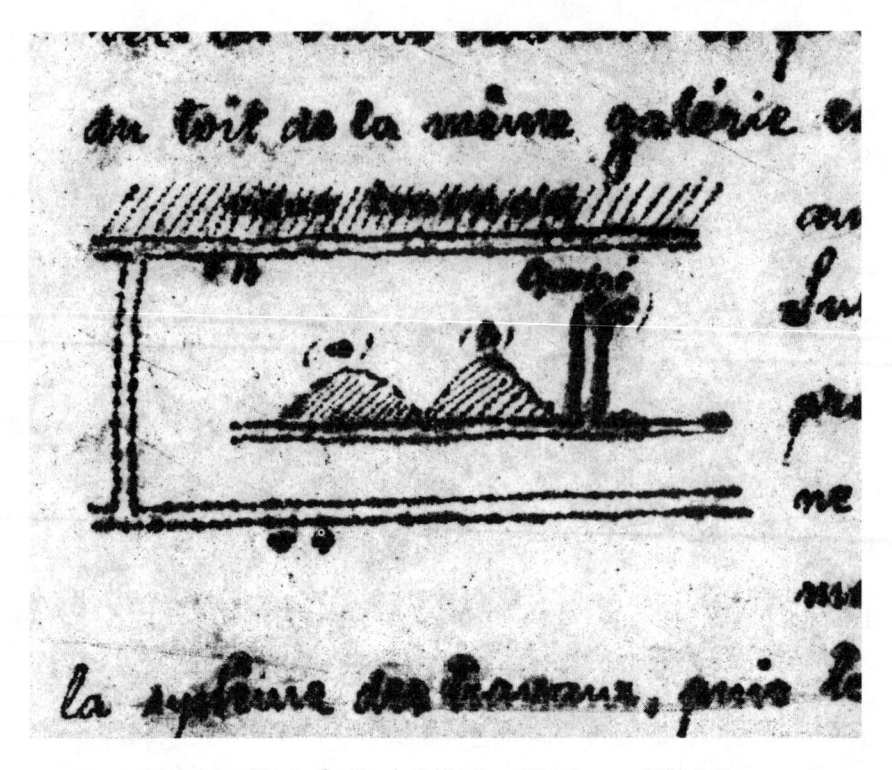

Figure 8.2 Fire in the Çamlı #188 Mine, 1913. Source: ED 16, 214.

ravaged this same mine. The real culprit, according to the engineer in charge, was lack of attention to routine and attainable safety procedures. In this case, he was referring to the practice of filling in cavities created by coal removal. In this mine, he said, if the now-empty coal chambers were left unfilled, a fire "ordinarily" would erupt. Despite his earlier orders, the necessary filling-in work had not been done for two months preceding the fire, accounting for the many empty chambers that resulted from this neglect. Barriers now had been erected to choke off the flow of air; flooding of the mine had begun but would take 3–4 weeks. Only then could they complete the refilling and retimbering tasks necessary for the resumption of coal extraction.[74]

Workers' Resistance to Safety Measures

How are we to understand miners' repeated reluctance to use safety lamps, since at first glance it was self-evidently in their interest to accept the new technology? And how can we explain obviously dangerous practices such as smoking inside of mines? Part of the answer seems traceable to workers' resistance to the discipline that accompanied increasing safety measures. This was common among all workers, both free and unfree. The disciplinary burdens, however, must have fallen most heavily on the compulsory labor force. For decades the central state had been compelling villager-workers into the mines and increasingly regulating the conditions of their lives. There can be no doubt of the radical impact the mines had upon villagers of the Zonguldak region. Refusal to use safety lamps might well have represented their refusal to accept the centralizing discipline of the mine administration, which offered more safety but also more regulation.

Across the globe, more generally, discipline meant workers' compliance with state mining laws and state and company regulations. More particularly, discipline embodied two, quite different, concepts of responsibility. In the first, miners were seen as able to make good decisions about safety on their own initiative and be unsupervised most of the time. Education, as well as prosecution and even dismissal, were tools to help workers internalize safety values and act upon them. The second notion of responsibility, on the other hand, argued that the miner would make such good decisions only when subject to good supervision. This supervision-oriented notion of discipline gave primacy of place to mine officials and inspectors. Discipline thus derived from management and bureaucracy, and not from labor. Western Europe was the model for this latter kind of "military discipline," that is, "operations under strict police surveillance."[75]

Both models of discipline were present at Zonguldak although the latter model prevailed overall. Sometimes an accident report embodied both models. A striking example of this blurring lies in a 1909 engineer's report on a methane explosion caused by unsafe lamps. Mining engineers, he writes, provide safer and better work procedures. More boldly, "mining engineers have the qualities which are to the general welfare." That is, they impose better safety procedures leading to a healthier, stronger, more effective citizenry. But the goal, he continued, could be achieved only if the work force were disciplined—via punitive measures—into adhering to the new procedures that he had just outlined. For example, to assure that workers observed the rule on using only safety lamps, the engineer recommended a one-year prison term for violators! This draconian response aimed to produce a desirable work force and citizenry, one presuming that workers could take charge of their own fate.[76]

But more generally, the mine superintendency personnel at Zonguldak embraced a model of change from above, a perception of reform that closely corresponded to the imperial Ottoman state's notion of itself as the only source of positive change. In most accident reports, inspecting engineers and their staff assigned fault as they deemed fit. Sometimes worker or company carelessness was blamed; more often, no fault was assigned. But the reports, when they called for action, rarely if ever addressed the workers directly to demand change. Instead, they relied on company personnel—the engineers and the inspectorate staff. In the May 1913 accident report, the superintendent's office blamed the mine operator, insisting that safety could only come from above.[77] In the numerous cases of open vs. safety lamps, the superintendent's personnel repeatedly called upon engineers to take the necessary steps to assure safety. That is, they did not address the workers or ask them to take any actions; they assumed that the engineers would supervise workers into safety.

The belief that discipline and safety percolated down to the workers partly explains their apparent indifference to such obvious dangers as smoking in a mine. In an environment where administrators rather than workers bore responsibility for safety, the labor force at Zonguldak, like others elsewhere in the world, lost a sense of accountability for their actions. Regulations from above, in a miner's view, meant that administrators were taking care of safety. Supervisors would protect workers from injury since they were charged with that duty. Thus, safety lamps adopted by administrative fiat were understood to bring protection from explosions caused by open lamps or any flame, including a cigarette's.

The nature of the safety lamps, even the improved models, also helps to explain the Zonguldak workers' casual attitude toward their use. Despite all the improvements, the use of safety lamps remained risky because at best, they offered half the light of a single candle. This poor illumination, according to several specialists in European and U.S. mining, decreased fatalities from explosions but may well have increased deaths from rockfalls.[78] Thus, naked lights remained the norm in Scotland and parts of northeast England until as late as 1913. Indeed, several major pieces of safety legislation in Great Britain in 1872 and 1887 did not compel safety lamp usage, this occurred only in 1911.[79] "The defects of the lamps were … real, and the inadequacy of the light they radiated continued to check the speed of work without removing the danger."[80] Open lamps gave better light and lasted longer than safety lamps.[81] Moreover, in some mining regions of North America, miners believed that open lamps made mines safer because they burned off small accumulations of gas. For this reason, in 1916, 20,000 Indiana miners walked out to protest the use of Edison electric safety lamps.[82] Thus, Zonguldak workers' continued use of open lamps, even in seemingly dangerous situations, might not have been because of their "stupidity," as the head engineer had charged, but it may well have been owed to the workers' better sense of safety. Resistance to safety lamps may also be tied to the growing frequency of piecework in the Zonguldak mines (see chapter 3): the more abundant light shed by open lamps facilitated a faster pace of work.

If safety lamps were so dangerous and had these obvious disadvantages, why did the superintendent, his officials, and so many company officials continue to demand their adoption? Part of the answer must lie in the spectacular nature of gas and methane explosions. In the U.S. and the UK, major pieces of safety legislation regularly followed explosions that caused numerous fatalities. Surely the larger explosions in the Zonguldak coalfield discouraged workers from entering mines and worsened already-severe labor recruitment problems. In the view of one specialist on American mining, explosions were a greater concern to mine operators than rockfalls because the former damaged more property and could bring operations within an entire mine to a halt. So even though rockfalls caused more fatalities than explosions, these accidents usually were small-scale events involving one or two workers. Explosions were more costly to management, and in addition were more likely to disrupt coal supplies, a concern of both operators and the Ottoman state, especially in wartime. And even though the Ottoman explosions involved relatively few fatalities compared to those in Europe and the U.S., the superintendent, his engineering staff, and the company engineers were European-trained and thus profoundly shaped by the catastrophic accidents that killed hundreds at a time in European mines.

Notes

1. This discussion is based on ED 3 and a sample of 223 cases of accidents.
2. For details, see Thobie (1977), 406–412.
3. Sample consists of 199 persons for whom biographical data such as ages, marital status, and children are available. One hundred twenty-five persons were victims—61 dead and 64 wounded; the balance of 74 were witnesses. KU KD 2, ED 10, ED 12, ED 16.
4. For purposes of this analysis, I put aside the possibility that the company was suppressing evidence of accidents.
5. Workers with other occupations were 12 percent and 11 percent of all fatal and non-fatal accidents, respectively, perhaps reflecting better reporting and the development of more extensive rail and aerial transport and other support facilities to carry on with the vastly greater production of this era.
6. There were, as the table indicates, twenty teenagers. The data also show that twenty-eight of the forty-five workers in their twenties were younger than 26.
7. Inclusion of those witnessing but not harmed in accidents does not change the age distribution profile discussed here.
8. Of the 50 workers between 12 and 25 years old in the sample, 23 were workers, 12 hewers, 11 had other occupations, and 4 had no occupation listed. One unskilled worker was 12 years old; only one hewer, who was 18, was under 20.
9. KU KD 2, 189–192.
10. ED 3, 181, compared with *Kastamonu vs 1314* village data.
11. ED 3, 205, 226, and 240, compared with *Kastamonu vs 1314* population data.
12. ED 3, 201 and 223, compared with *Kastamonu vs 1314* village population data.
13. The sample here is 168 persons from named village or town locations; in 37 instances, there is no location noted.
14. ED 10, 499.
15. ED 16, 115–117.
16. ED 16, 235–237.
17. ED 16, 264–265; Rombaki and Panopolos operated the mine.
18. The sample here is for the years 1912–1914 and 1917.
19. ED 16, 379.
20. ED 16, 208–209, December 1913.

21. ED 16, 110–112 and ED 10, 427–428, July 1913.
22. Seltzer (1985), 56.
23. Whiteside (1990), 52, for western U.S. mines.
24. Özeken (1944b). I presently have no court records of the company taking workers to court for compensation.
25. The size and staff are unknown. Kıray (1964), 182. ED 4, 358, 25 Ağustos 1295/6 August 1879; and Winkler (1961), 32.
26. ED 4, 25, 24 Şaban 1294; ED 4, 245, 6 tl 1294.
27. ED 4, 36, 10 Eylül 1293; ED 4, 38, 14 Eylül 1293.
28. ED 4, 19 Mart 1294.
29. ED 4, 186, 10 Haziran 1294. In 1879, the mine administration allocated funds to support a pharmacy and pharmacist for one year. ED 4, 320, 10 Nisan 1295.
30. ED 4, 362, 13 Eylül 1295.
31. ED 3, 3, 9 Temmuz 1309; 5, 25 Ağustos 1309; 25, 1 Ağustos 1311.
32. The yearbooks for Kastamonu province do not list the presence of a hospital in the coalfield in 1894 and note just one, at Ereğli, during the years 1896 and 1899. *Kastamonu vs 1312*, 352–355; *Kastamonu vs 1314*, 484–485; and *Kastamonu vs 1317*, 352–353. Thus, the yearbooks seem to be recording only state-run hospitals for the general public.
33. *Kastamonu vs 1310*, 205; and *Kastamonu vs 1311*, 203. KU 199, 1322/1906. The doctor's salary was at least a third higher than the surgeon's.
34. ED 3, 1–38, ks 1308–Temmuz 1312 (February 1893–August 1897).
35. ED 3, 37, 22 Nisan 1313.
36. By 1910, an unnamed company had its own doctor, a pharmacist, and even a special barracks for the treatment of diseases, cholera in particular, which was erupting among workers at the Kandilli and Çamlı mines. OA DH.ID.C.I Sira: 3169, Dosye 48-1; Gömlek 34, 23 Ramadan 1328/28 September 1910.
37. ED 10, 73, 326–327, 10 Haziran 1329; ED 16, 383–386, 30 ts 1333.
38. ED 16, 342, 11 tl 1333; and ED 16, 479, 24 Mart 1334 for treatment of patients in 1919.
39. Cemal (1922), 23, incorrectly states that the facility treated only workers and employees of the company.
40. Özeken (1944b), 22.
41. ED 16, 458–461, 12 Şubat 1334.
42. ED 16, 380–382, 30 ts 1333.
43. ED 16, 474–475, 16 Mart 1334.
44. That is, 27 of 222 persons. ED 3. In addition, 5 persons who later died in the hospital were admitted.
45. The sample is drawn from thirty-one workers of known origins.
46. Quataert and Duman (2001), 163.
47. In response to the strikers, the government, urged on by the Ereğli Company, at least twice sent warships to maintain order. For example, *Tanin*, 14 Eylül 1324/27 September 1908, 7 and 12 tl 1324/20 October 1908, 7; *Sabah*, 29 Eylül 1908; also KU KD 2, 434, 7 Mayıs 1328/20 May 1912.
48. Naim (1934), 13–14, and Özeken (1944b). *Yurt Ansik* 10, 7791, follows Naim (1934), who may be the source of the account, in stating that workers demanded higher wages and abolition of the wage deductions made to compensate for their hospital care, and that the French Company accepted these demands.
49. If workers already had been receiving company-paid medical care (as a result of the 1908 strike), some comment to this effect should have appeared in the literature reporting on the 1921 law.
50. Naim (1934), 13–14, is the source for Özeken (1944a), 11–12, and Savaşkan (1993), 44.
51. Kırlı (2000), and Abdulkadiroğlu (1998).
52. Deringil (1998); Özbek (2001); Kırlı (2000).

53. Discussion based mainly on Graebner (1976), 157–172.
54. Church (1986), 326–327 and 583.
55. ED 4, 264, 12 ts 1294/24 November 1878.
56. ED 3, 129–130, #2, 24 Mayıs 1309.
57. ED 3, 145, #56, 15 Eylül 1311.
58. ED 3, 191, #37, 8 Ağustos 1319/21 August 1903.
59. ED 12, 200, 1 tl 1328/14 October 1912; ED 10, 334 and ED 10, 326, 11 Haziran 1329/24 June 1913. ED 10, 337, 11 Haziran 1329 and ED 16, 75–77.
60. KU KD 2, 307, 17 Nisan 1328/13 April 1912. Also KU KD 2, 423, #644/110, 5 Mayıs 1328/18 May 1912.
61. KU KD 2, 20 Mayıs 1327; KU KD 2, 298, #425/71, 15 Nisan 1328/28 April 1912. These lamps perhaps are similar to the modern-day Coleman lamps favored for today's outdoor sports.
62. KU KD 2, 424, 7 Nisan 1328 and KU KD 2, 307.
63. ED 10, 179, 16 Mayıs 1329; ED 10, 142–147, #22, 1 Mayıs 1329. ED 10, 171–175.
64. After a methane gas accident killed 21 workers, the superintendent expelled Halil Pasha, who personally had signed the agreement, from the district. But later Halil Pasha again rented this mine to the French group that took possession of the Çamlı mine. In World War I, the mine again passed back to Halil Pasha's administration. Savaşkan (1993), 35–38, and for details of the post-war era.
65. In the formal report, however, only eleven names are listed. One of those initially reported dead must have survived.
66. ED 10, 142–147, #22, 1 Mayıs 1329. The French version is in ED 10, #22, 15 Mai 1329/28 May 1913, 171–172. ED 10, 179, 16 Mayıs 1329; ED 10, 180–181, 16 Mayıs 1329; ED 10, 169–170, 16 Mayıs 1329/29 May 1913.
67. ED 10, 180–181, 17 Mayıs 1329, #597/18, #598/6, #599/30.
68. ED 16, 75–77, French, 6 Juin 1329/19 June 1913.
69. ED 16, 80–81, ED 10, 347, 9 Haziran 1329/29 June 1913.
70. ED 4, 84, French, 9 Juin 1329/1913.
71. ED 4, French, ca. 24 Avril 1329/8 May 1913.
72. ED 16, 32–36, French, and ED 10, 50, Ottoman; also 132–134, 20 Juillet 1329.
73. ED 16 Ottoman, 197–198: 27 ts 1329.
74. ED 16, 214–219, French; ED 16, 225–226, French, 4 Janvier 1329/17 January 1914. Air/methane ratios of 14:1 were considered safe but 9:1 or 10:1 had a high explosive potential. Roy (ca. 1905), 121.
75. This argument closely follows Graebner (1976), 123–124.
76. OA DH.MUI.C.II (22f-2) Sira 552; Dos 17-2, 18 Ramadan 1327.
77. ED 10, 142–147, #22, 1 Mayıs 1329 and ED 10, 171–175; ED 10, 169–170; ED 10, 179, 16 Mayıs 1329/29 May 1913.
78. Church (1986), 583; and for the U.S., Graebner (1976), 1–6, who states that between 1907 and 1920, rockfall fatalities rose, while those from gas and dust explosions declined. Also see Whiteside (1990), 60.
79. Church (1986), 326–327 and 583.
80. Church (1986), 326.
81. KU KD 2, 424, translated copy of report dated 7 Nisan 1328; see also KU KD 2, 307.
82. Graebner (1976), 135.

9

WARTIME IN THE COALFIELD

Introduction

From the perspective of the Ottoman state, wartime was the fundamental reason for the exploitation of the Zonguldak coalfield. Its goals in the pursuit of the black stones that burned were quite different from the mine operators'. For the operators, the mines were intended to be sources of financial gain, of profit. Many had a variety of other interests, often as merchants; others, such as the Giurgiu Company, maintained a fleet of commercial vessels; still others, notably the Ereğli Company, focused solely on the coal business. The Istanbul regime, for its part, wanted to lessen its dependence on foreign sources to supply its fleet and factories. Since its earliest days, coal mining had been connected to the strategic needs of the Ottoman navy and state industrial establishments. In the minds of state planners, Zonguldak was to provide uninterrupted coal shipments independent of foreign suppliers.

Indeed, in the decades after the mines opened, the Ottoman state and economy became ever more dependent on coal. Coal imports mounted impressively: annually averaging some 193,000 gold liras between 1878 and 1882, they quadrupled to over 400,000 liras by 1913.[1] The fleet continued and completed its transition to steam power while state arsenals and factories making military equipment and uniforms similarly became based on steam-powered technologies. Parallel developments occurred in the private sector. Many municipalities, such as Salonica, Izmir, and Istanbul acquired electrification. Hundreds of coal-consuming factories opened in the towns, cities, and villages of the empire. In peacetime, coal could flow from the Zonguldak mines as well as from foreign suppliers. Some economists and planners clucked about the cost of imports to the national treasury, but the mix of foreign and local coal fueled economic growth and met state needs. When wars erupted, foreign supplies fell into jeopardy and the Zonguldak coal became more important than ever. War was thus the litmus test that determined how well state and capital had organized and disciplined the work force and built the infrastructure of the Zonguldak coalfield to meet domestic military and civilian needs, perhaps without help from abroad.

Notes for this chapter begin on page 224.

The two case studies presented below examine the coalfield in times of war, namely, the Ottoman-Russian War of 1877–1878 and World War I, 1914–1918. During the first conflict, just after the major reorganization of the mines in 1867, Ottoman coal production and consumption were far less than they would be later. Output averaged 150,000 tons or less annually, and the mines were severely undercapitalized; meanwhile the main burst of factory building and utility construction still lay in the future. Coal needs were small compared to later decades. In the 1870s war, moreover, foreign supplies were not nearly as vulnerable to disruption as they would be in 1914–1918. By World War I, however, coal output at Zonguldak had increased to around one million tons. New capital had flowed in, and extraction and transportation technologies were vastly better than before. Labor presumably was more disciplined, having been under the thrall of the compulsory labor system for nearly fifty years, and further enmeshed in a cash nexus to boot. The very successes marked by the fleet's conversion to steam, the increasing number of factories, and the generally growing use of coal, of course, meant that the Ottoman economy had become more susceptible to disruption of the coal supply. Also, the earlier war had involved just two antagonists, and Russia was no real threat to coal shippers outside of the Black Sea. By contrast, nearly all European states participated in World War I, and seaborne supplies were throttled by the British navy.

The Ottoman-Russian War

Introduction

The Ottoman-Russian War formally began in April 1877. Following a series of catastrophic defeats, the fighting stopped with an armistice signed in January 1878. When Russia imposed the harsh San Stefano accord in March 1878, the Great Powers intervened. Even so, the resulting Treaty of Berlin, signed in July of that year, was among the harshest in Ottoman history and resulted in the loss of almost all remaining territories in the Balkans.

The war disrupted mining village life and mine operations in nearly every possible way. During the fighting, war needs sucked already scarce manpower from the coalfield and, to boot, drained away animals, foodstuffs and monies. At the same moment, it brought on a human crisis of vast proportions as hundreds of thousands of Muslims arrived as refugees on Ottoman shores, having fled from or been expelled by the conquering Czarist armies in the Balkans and the eastern Black Sea region.

The Refugee Crisis

Because of their geography, the shores of the mine districts were important destinations for the refugees. Many were ferried on official Ottoman vessels to coalfield ports while others, also in substantial numbers, walked around the eastern shore of the Black Sea shores. Within a five-month period in 1877, for example, more than 19,000 refugees arrived in the coal districts. From there, the government planned to move them south for permanent settlement in central Anatolia and the Syrian provinces.[2]

The effort to meet this humanitarian task injured mining operations in many different ways. Refugees on shore, desperate for fuel to warm their bodies and their foods, cut down trees from the forests of Ereğli district that were reserved for the supply of mine supports.[3] Far worse, the flood of refugees logistically overwhelmed these small mining communities. Government ships assigned to bring provisions to the mines and to transport coal back to the capital and other locations instead were repeatedly diverted to rescue refugees. For example, on 1 September 1877, eight coal ships lying off Ereğli were ordered away to pick up some of the 9,000 refugees awaiting transport on the Balkan shores.[4] Three weeks later, other coal ships transported 400 Abaza refugees, who already had arrived at Ereğli, eastward to the Bartın area for further trans-shipment.

Once ashore, the transport of refugees often was entrusted to workers whose animals or carts normally carried coal or mine supports.[5] In the Bartın region, basket carriers and post makers, already in chronically short supply, were taken away from their mining tasks and ordered to transport the new arrivals. When the Abaza refugees arrived in Bartın, 200 mine transport workers met them instead of using their wagons to haul supports or coal.[6] Nine months later, basket carriers and animal transport workers and wagoners assigned to mine labor in the districts of Bartın and Ereğli instead transported 5,000 refugees over the mountains to Ankara province.[7] This was not a choice destination because just four years before, it had been a center of a killing famine that swept Central Anatolia.

The care, feeding, and transport of refugees strained and often broke supply systems of workers and animals. So many refugees poured in needing transport that mining operations in several locations were halted completely for months. Clearly, the resources of these small places were inadequate to the task. Hence, there were no ships to haul coal though there often was little coal to be had in any event, because there were no workers, animals, or mine supports. Nor did the refugee crisis end with the war. In April 1879, the mine superintendent wrote to the governor of Trabzon province, complaining that the refugee problem still had not been resolved and continued to burden his district.[8]

Did the mining authorities use refugees to solve the labor shortages plaguing the mines? Officially, at least, the answer is no. In a telegram to the Bartın administration, the mine superintendent at length discussed the most efficient means to guarantee delivery of the needed mine workers. At the end of his memo, he specifically stated that refugees were not to be used for mine labor and were not to be included in the labor recruitment procedures he had just outlined.[9]

Provisioning Shortages

Severe shortages of just about every commodity prevailed throughout this period, bringing operations to a halt, sometimes at a particular mine and sometimes in an entire locale. In November 1877, operations shut down in Bartın district for want of candles to illuminate mine work.[10] Gunpowder, used to open tunnels and sometimes to blast coal loose from the face of the mine, was well known to be absolutely essential. And yet in August 1877 the superintendent noted that the lack of gunpowder had halted operations and asked authorities in Istanbul to immediately forward some on the first possible ship. Shipments arrived, but by mid October, supplies again had been exhausted.[11]

Similarly, the grain supplies on which both workers and animals depended routinely were inadequate and sometimes totally lacking. "Only one or two days of flour, which is the lifeblood of mine operations remain although, generally, there is a lot of flour available. The steamship Batum is waiting."[12] This shortage existed despite a flurry of orders in early August 1877 that frantically had sought to locate supplies of barley anywhere on the Black Sea littoral, for the provisioning of the workers.[13] The mine administration also repeatedly sought to buy wheat from tax farmers to feed the boat launchers.[14]

As the above makes clear, shortages often were artificial. Profiteering and hoarding in wartime repeatedly disrupted supply lines. In the wheat example cited, nearby tax farmers had more grain in their possession than workers at the time required. In November 1877, the superintendent ordered the Bartın district official to assure bread supplies for workers employed at M. Broski's mine in Amasra.[15] At this same time he arranged for a similar transfer of wheat to a second mine, operated by Haci Ismailoğlu Ahmed Bey.[16]

In the following months, Bartın district authorities bought and shipped 5,000 *kile*s of maize—to be ground into flour for the miners—from the warehouses of a local tax farmer. But in May 1878, flour shortages still were disrupting operations.[17] In August, the mine administration, not for the first time, turned to Istanbul for flour.[18] To improve the quality of the bread, it built a new mill in November 1878. Since, it said, locals typically used maize for bread, and because it was cheaper than wheat, the administration planned to provide workers with bread made from maize mixed with a little wheat.[19] In January 1879, the mine administration opened a bakery, exclusively for the mine workers and operators at Tarlaağzı, where it sold the bread at fixed prices.[20] In the depths of winter 1879, the mine superintendent sharply critiqued a district official of Unye (eastward on the Black Sea coast) for failing to assure the shipment of 2,000 *kile*s of maize to the coalfield.[21] A month later, the superintendent turned to Trabzon merchants for workers' maize.[22] Even in late July 1879, more than a year after the war had ended, food and flour supplies for workers ran out completely while for soldiers working in the mines, only a few days of flour remained.[23]

State Fiscal Crisis

The actual harvests in the area certainly influenced grain, flour, and bread supplies. Yet no official cited crop failures or other natural problems to excuse shortfalls. Moreover, the profiteering and hoarding that normally accompany wartime alone were not sufficient cause for the continuing shortfalls. Rather, the fundamental cause of the provisioning shortages lay in the chronic financial crises of the central state and its reliance on precarious fiscal tricks to maintain operations. In 1875, the Ottoman state, unable to meet its domestic and international financial obligations, effectively declared bankruptcy. Shortly thereafter, the Ottoman government resumed the issue of paper money (*kaime*) as a means of keeping financially afloat. The public quickly lost confidence in these notes, however, and their value at the end of 1876 had fallen by half in Istanbul. Nonetheless, further issues of the paper money followed, compounding the crisis and by May 1879, the value of this paper money against gold had collapsed to less than 8 percent of nominal value. By then, the government had begun withdrawing paper money from circulation, restoring some measure of monetary stability.[24]

This imperial crisis profoundly affected the mines. In 1874, for example, the mine administration, which shared in the general indebtedness of the imperial government, owed a total of 8 million krs to mine operators and workers. Against this amount, the province of Kastamonu was to have paid the mine administration some 3.5 million krs but had failed to do so.[25] And so, the central state routinely issued promissory notes (variously called *maden senedi* and *kaime*) rather than cash to pay off mine operators and workers, and to obtain foodstuffs and other supplies. In the coalfield, the mine superintendent sometimes issued promissory notes to administrators of neighboring districts. For example, in spring 1879, he used the notes to buy barley obtained from the tithe of Bartın district.[26] He regularly issued promissory notes to workers. Indeed, during these years, workers received only notes, not cash, in exchange for their labor.[27] The value of a note fluctuated when cashed. They sometimes were backed by the value of the tithe to be collected, the tithe being the surety for the note issued. In 1878 alone, these notes totaled more than 6 million krs. Since the grain harvest that year was small, so too would be the forthcoming tithe; hence it was feared that the value of notes would fall.[28]

Everyone knew about the depreciated value of the notes. Coal operators were unhappy because the system required them to accept notes as payment for the coal that they delivered to the state, in effect deeply discounting the price. From the perspective of workers, payment in notes meant wages were lower than those stipulated officially. In April 1878, for example, it readily was acknowledged that payment in promissory notes spelled a 60 percent reduction in actual purchasing power.[29] In November 1878, animal transporters in several areas refused the notes and instead demanded cash from mine operators.[30] At the beginning of the next Ottoman fiscal year, March 1879, the superintendent notified the mine villages that use of promissory notes was being suspended. The workers had flatly refused to accept them. A ship was arriving to take on coal, the superintendent warned his superiors, but there was no coal because of the workers' inaction. And so, he asked for an infusion of cash to pay their wages. Local merchants, for their part, were buying notes on the cheap from disgruntled workers. Moreover, they refused to accept notes from workers in payment for goods. Kozlu merchants, for example, would not take the notes as payment for tobacco.[31]

In January 1879, the Istanbul government announced a new ruse and, with an imperial decree (*irade*) raised by 33 percent the price that mine operators would receive for each unit of coal. The payment, however, was to be in notes. Istanbul also raised the wages of mine workers. Basket carriers received a 17 percent raise, while animal transporters and those making and transporting supports obtained (presumably equal) raises as well. Nonetheless, the mine superintendent protested, the wage increases were totally inadequate. Inflation, he said, had driven up the price of commodities purchased by workers well beyond the raises just granted. The bread consumed by a single worker, he noted, cost more than two times the basket carrier's new daily wage. These basket carriers, he said, slogged through the mud and water in rawhide sandals during the twelve days of their shift. Not a single one was without debt. Equally bad, the animal transport workers lost three or four days per shift because of mud and snow and thus went unpaid, so they too were deeply in debt. Mine support makers, the superintendent said, earned a pittance—only half the wage of a basket carrier—and in private business, could be making ten times as much.[32]

Holidays in Wartime

Regardless of the war, workers planned to spend the important holidays surrounding the sacred month of Ramadan with their families. The superintendent for his part took measures to heighten the sense of festivities and, in advance of the Ramadan season, ordered the procurement of sheep for use in the rituals. Unfortunately for several mine operators, however, he used funds owed to them to purchase the animals.[33] But he also worried about coal production. After the outbreak of war in 1877, the superintendent warned that war was raging day and night and mine operations should never suffer because of the holidays. Therefore, he ordered, officials at the mines were not to permit workers, no matter the pretext, to return to their villages for the celebratory festival at the end of Ramadan. He also directed headmen in the villages to return all workers who came home against orders and to make certain that the new shifts be sent promptly regardless of the holiday. Yet when the holidays came, most workers and transporters abandoned the mines and went home, the superintendent's measures notwithstanding.[34]

The same problems surfaced during the next Ramadan season, in 1878. Fearing shortages, the superintendent ordered animal transporters to work two shifts in succession. But they resisted. The transport workers of Ereğli and Alaplı believed that the holiday entitled them to a week off. Despite the superintendent's assertion that their actions were "completely illegal" and that it was inappropriate for workers to use holy days as an excuse not to work, transport came to a complete halt.[35] By the actual onset of the festival, workers and transporters had vanished altogether from the mines, and operations had ceased. The superintendent ordered officers, officials, and soldiers to go to the home villages and, together with the headmen and councils of elders, send a full shift of workers.[36]

War and the Compulsory Labor System

During the wartime crisis of the 1870s, how effective was the elaborate and, in so many ways, thoroughly military, labor recruitment system? Not very, as the evidence so far suggests. Three additional bodies of evidence that will be highlighted to support this negative assessment: (1) chronic shortages of animals, (2) worker flight, and (3) the use of soldiers as coalfield workers. Each leads to the same conclusion: that more workers avoided rather than fulfilled their mining labor obligations during the period from 1877 to 1879.

Despite a normal abundance of local livestock, the coalfield suffered a chronic shortage of animals that curtailed the transport of mine supports from the forests and docks and the shipment of coal from the mine or storage area to the shore. In 1877–1878, compulsory labor workers in Alaplı and Devrek sub-districts typically were to provide some 800–900 animals and the mine operators personally were to add another 300 head. But by November 1877, most of the animals had died; many had been destroyed because inflated barley and straw prices had made their maintenance prohibitive.[37] Outside sources proved inadequate: the arrival of straw from Istanbul[38] and of barley from nearby Havza failed to resolve the shortages. Barley, for example, was totally lacking in October 1878.[39] Without fodder, transporters from Alaplı provided just one-quarter of their July quota of 130 animals, while only one-half of the 80 allotted animals arrived from Devrek sub-district.[40] In October 1878, a mere 15 percent of the 110 animals allotted from Alaplı arrived for mine work in the Ereğli locale.[41] Over the space of two shifts, fewer than 30 percent of the animals allotted from Vekile hamlet had arrived at the Alacaağzı mines.[42] In December 1878, the Ereğli district official personally toured the villages of his district to obtain 400 animals. Hoping for good weather at this brutal season of the year, he dispatched them from Devrek to load coal already mined.[43] Since coal was said to be stored in abundance at mines in the more remote areas, for example, on mountaintops, local residents in areas not normally tapped for mine work were ordered to send animals.[44]

The war occasioned a rare recorded appearance of female labor in the coalfield. At this time, the entire work force recruited through the compulsory labor system was Muslim; of this there is no doubt. As for gender, officially, all the workers were males. But a series of documents from August to September 1878 clearly indicate that at the time women were employed both outside and inside mines, against the preferences of state officials but with their consent. When looking for transport animals, officials in a particular district found them only in the possession of women since the men were away, either at mine work or in the military. Local officials sent these animals (250–300 in number), led by the women, off to mine work. When the women arrived with the animals, some officials at the mine were horrified and sent them back home with their animals, ruling that the employment of women was inappropriate. But the mine superintendent intervened, demanding that the animals and the women return and reminding his subordinates that a war was on, factories were working day and night, and the coal these women would transport was desperately needed. Moreover, he made clear in his orders that the particular case was not unique. Rather, he grudgingly admitted, women already were being used in various tasks within and outside mines. Hiring females, he pragmatically concluded, was preferable to delays in coal deliveries.[45]

During this wartime crisis, workers evaded mine labor on a massive scale. In the documentation of its efforts to combat labor stoppages, we clearly see the mine administration's meticulous attention to the whereabouts of mine workers and animals. In scores of reports, the superintendent lists the numbers of workers from each village who have failed to appear at the particular mine and hectors subordinates to redouble efforts to locate the missing. Sometimes he demands to know the whereabouts of, say, five individuals who are due to report to a mine. Elsewhere he seeks single individuals from three villages who have failed to report, and orders the dispatch of a missing fifteen animals.[46] Only one of eight and two of twenty workers assigned from two villages arrived for work in late August 1878, he complained.[47] In one typical document, he berates a Devrek official and enumerates the missing workers—ranging from four to twenty-two persons—from each of twenty-six different villages. On the same date, he castigates the Bartın district official because more than twenty-one villages in his jurisdiction were failing to send their allotted workers. In November 1878 he berates this official for a second time, making a new listing of 182 missing workers from twenty-one villages.[48]

In addition to the workers who totally evaded mine labor, there were others who entered the registration system, joined the village shift that marched off to work, and then fled from the mine. In January 1879, for instance, the superintendent mobilized officers and a special committee to pursue ten workers belonging to the village of Karaca Viran in the Devrek directorship who had fled from their assigned mine.[49] The day before, he had commanded the Ereğli district official to send an officer to find three missing workers who had disappeared before completing their shift.[50]

The absences are impressive. At one mine, in September 1877, only one in four workers assigned from two villages actually showed up. At two other mines, in the same month, one-half and slightly less than one-half of the assigned workers arrived. During one week in late October 1877, 1,344 workers were assigned to the mines in one area but nearly half never came. Also, some 400 of 898 workers assigned to another set of mines similarly did not appear.[51] During this same month, so many workers failed to arrive from Bartın district that mines dependent on their labor halted.[52] "These assignments [of unskilled workers, transporters, and mine support workers] are not sufficient for the mines. At the present time, in no corner of the Ottoman Empire is there anyone remaining who is not a soldier. So that mine operations not be interrupted, all who are not in the reserves, or conscripted, or on inactive reserve have been turned over for mine work."[53] Despite this directive, shortages persisted. In July 1878, only 50 percent of the 446 workers assigned from twenty-six villages actually were present.[54] Only 600 of the 1,200 workers allotted from Bartın district arrived for work. Still worse, by October 1879 those who came to work represented a mere 18 percent of 990 workers assigned from Bartın district.[55] The production and delivery of mine supports suffered as well. Between May and August 1878, just 26 percent of the 65,000 mine supports contracted from the Alaplı area, one of the major sources, were actually delivered.[56]

Some workers in mine service sought out personal profit while technically in mining service. In July 1878, for example, large numbers of workers cutting mine supports and engaging in transport slipped away to cut firewood in the forests reserved for mine supports.[57]

To make up for the dramatic shortfalls in the compulsory labor supply, soldiers drafted into the regular military service provided most of the mine labor during the Ottoman-Russian War. The mine districts thus suffered greatly during the 1870s as the state ransacked the region to find both mine workers and soldiers among the male inhabitants. Throughout, military authorities and the mine administration competed to tap into these human resources for their own different needs. In one sense the military won out, since most local residents entered the armed forces. Yet as we will see, a large proportion of conscripts ended up in mine work anyway. In many mines, moreover, military personnel labored alongside workers brought in through the compulsory labor system, or alternated with them in shifts.[58]

As the Ottoman-Russian War continued into the summer of 1877, the mine administration vied with military authorities for manpower, claiming, for example, that it needed the inactive reserves and home guards of Bartın district. The state clearly was caught in a double bind, needing the scarce manpower of the region for both military service and mine work.[59] In October 1877, for example, the superintendent warned of the approach of the season for military conscription, a process that normally caused the mines to shut down. The state must avoid this eventuality, he said, and ensure that conscription in the coal districts did not interfere with mining operations.[60] But these warnings went unheeded. By July 1878, as seen, only 10 percent of the eligible male population of Bartın district had been mobilized as workers; the rest had gone into the military.⁶¹ In the end, following practices dating back to the Crimean War, authorities systematically resorted to using active-duty military personnel from the coal districts for mine work. As early as September 1877, the superintendent had ordered the use of inactive reserves and home guards to fill in for Kozlu-locale workers who had not appeared for work.⁶²

More generally, in the conscriptions of 1878 and 1879, Ereğli district enrolled 1,050 persons in military service but turned over all of them for work in the coalfield. Some 10 percent of them served in a military capacity at the mines, as guards. The remaining 90 percent earned mine wages.⁶³ To put these figures into proportion, we need to recall that the territory of the coalfield held approximately 6,000 workers eligible for mine work, presumably not in the same pool of labor as the military conscripts. During the conscriptions of 1877 and 1878, the military routinely relinquished significant numbers of individuals normally exempted from mine work to the mine administration. It also turned to the townspeople of the region, who in their civilian capacity normally were exempt from compulsory labor service. In September 1877, for example, a ranking military officer relinquished to the mines several hundred residents of the towns of Ereğli and Alaplı.⁶⁴ Nearly two years later, however, when peace again prevailed, the superintendent admitted that it had been a misuse of "patriotic soldiers" (*vatanperver asker*) to employ these townspeople in the mines. Rather, he confessed, townspeople legally could be subjected only to boat launching mine work.⁶⁵

In principle, no one allocated to mine work could be conscripted into the military. In other words, there was to be no "double-dipping" into the same manpower pool to serve military and mining needs.⁶⁶ But as it turned out, workers who as civilians had labored in a particular mine found themselves, as active-duty soldiers, performing the same tasks in the same mine.

The military's accountant maintained careful records of military workers. He kept separate and detailed books, an individual volume for each locale, and after wages had been paid he turned these over to the local administration. All military personnel who had done mine work were to be paid properly, including those who subsequently had died, become POWs, or been transferred out the region.⁶⁷ In theory, soldier-workers received better rations and care than their civilian counterparts. During the early months of the war, soldier-workers received meat rations, mainly from sheep, purchased in several nearby districts.⁶⁸ Their grain needs were met by the imperial warehouses in Istanbul as well as local suppliers. When soldiers were used as workers, the military authorities paid them their soldiers' salary and provided their uniforms (*maaş* and *tayınat*). The mine operators, for their part, paid soldier-workers an additional daily wage of 6 krs. If these conditions actually had prevailed, soldiers would have profited from mine work. But as in the case of the civilian workers, the soldier-workers suffered from the fiscal and financial chaos of the 1870s. Their wages, food, clothing, and bedding—whatever the source—routinely failed to arrive on schedule and sometimes never appeared at all. In March

1878, for example, the superintendent wrote that, "for three years soldiers employed in the mines have not been given clothing; the bedding and clothing that exists is unacceptable."[69] Similarly, their military salaries went unpaid, sometimes for long periods. Soldiers loading coal onto ships in February 1879 had not been paid for seven months.[70] Food supplies were in equally short supply. Although the soldier-workers were entitled to provisions from the imperial warehouses in Istanbul, even these were failing.[71] In July 1879, the foodstuffs and flour for workers were exhausted, while only a few days' flour remained for soldier-workers. Despite pleas, fresh supplies did not arrive, and nearly a month later no flour of any kind remained at the mines for either soldiers or workers.[72]

In July 1878, most of those laboring in Ereğli district to carry baskets, transport coal, and cut supports were military personnel (both inactive reserves and home guards).[73] Most commonly, soldiers loaded coal onto ships and cut wood. In July 1878, for example, they formed a full two-thirds of all workers who were cutting mine supports in the forests.[74] Less frequently, but still often enough that it does not appear to have been uncommon, they labored as hewers at the coal face. In at least one instance, these soldier-hewers had been hewers in civilian life.[75] The conscription of such highly prized workers speaks to the victory of the conscription officials over the mining administration.

In some areas, even as late as eight months after the formal peace had been signed, all those on general conscription rosters as well as inactive reserves and home guards were still being assigned to the mines in the Devrek directorship.[76] Even later, in June 1879, the superintendent continued to hunt down deserters from the 1877 (1293) conscription so that he could assign them to mine duty.[77]

World War I

Introduction

For several months after the assassination at Sarajevo, the Ottoman cabinet remained fiercely divided over whether to join the camp of the Entente or the Allied Powers. After Great Britain rejected alliance overtures, choosing the Russians over the Ottomans, the proponents of Germany won out, and in late October 1914, the Ottoman fleet suddenly shelled Odessa and several other Russian Black Sea ports.

World War I placed enormous strains on every facet of Ottoman life—indeed, it helped to end the life of this 600-year-old empire. The number of soldiers who served is not precisely known. According to one estimate, 1.2 million soldiers continuously remained under arms, while over the four wartime years, as many as 2.9 million Ottoman subjects altogether were mobilized for military service.[78] Another estimate places the peacetime military at around 150,000 men and wartime strength at around 800,000. The proportion of Ottoman mobilized forces to the total population was above the average for all combatant states. Yet because of the many exemptions from service, and other factors, Ottoman subjects were less likely to serve than the French, Germans, or Russians. For example, about 10 percent of French citizens served, compared to about 4 percent of Ottoman subjects mobilized for war (and France had double the population of the empire).[79]

Mortality was horrendous, among both the general population and those serving in the military. Altogether an estimated 785,000 soldiers died. Most perished not on the battlefield but rather from disease (400,000) or their wounds later on (60,000).[80] There can be no doubt about the utterly devastating human impact of the war on the Ottoman world.

The government shifted gears to a wartime economy, to controlling the production and consumption of most goods and directing men and materials to the front lines.[81] Promissory notes, so much a part of financial and economic life in 1877–1878, similarly flooded the marketplace during World War I. In Istanbul, the exchange rates of the notes jumped from 120 to 500 per gold lira between 1916 and 1918. During the war years in Istanbul, the cost of a food basket of fifteen items soared nineteen fold.[82]

The impact of World War I on the coalfield was immediate: war came to the coalfield the very next day after the shelling of Odessa. A Russian cruiser arrived off the port of Zonguldak and fired a warning shot. In the hour before the all-day bombardment began, the townspeople piled into railroad wagons designed to carry mine supports and hid for safety inside the mines. In the ensuing shellfire, none were killed.[83]

Economic conditions around the mines became quite bad. This region was not self-sufficient in cereals, and since the war created near-famine conditions in many areas of the empire, the lack of adequate local supplies was particularly dangerous for residents. Indeed, a number of factors had been increasing local dependency on outside sources since the Ottoman-Russian War.[84] As the number of villagers working in the mines for cash wages increased, they may have bought more food and grown less. More certainly, the rising numbers of miners who had been migrating to the region depended completely on purchased foods. Residents of the new urban center of Zonguldak had been relying on food imports from the imperial capital, which itself suffered chronic shortages of food throughout the war. Istanbul had always enjoyed a privileged place in the provisioning policies of the Ottoman state, and its population fared better than most during crises. Yet even capital city residents found it very difficult, sometimes impossible, to obtain foodstuffs. Despite rationing programs, prices of basic commodities in the capital city soared. In 1918, bread cost 27 times more than it had in 1914, and as seen, there was an overall nineteen-fold increase in foodstuff prices. The situation in the coalfield urban areas can only be surmised. In 1914, a basket of twenty-six food items cost a bit more in Zonguldak than in Istanbul—92 krs vs. 86 krs. Over the course of the war years, the provisioning situation at Zonguldak and Ereğli—the urban centers of the coalfield—surely became much worse than in the capital, and food prices probably increased even more than in Istanbul.[85]

In 1915, the first full year of hostilities, coal production fell more than 50 percent from its 1911 peak of 904,000 tons. Total output declined another 50 percent in 1916, to 208,000 tons, and hit a nadir of 158,000 tons in 1917. During the final year of the war, production reached only 186,000 tons. Overall, annual output during World War I approximately equaled that in 1875, just before the state's last major war, the Ottoman-Russian War of 1877–1878.[86] These low production levels are shocking. There had been many capital investments and improvements in transportation and labor supply during the intervening decades. The number of mines operating all had increased sharply during the intervening forty years, and by all accounts many of the newer mines were comparatively very rich. Transportation improvements had been notable; added kilometers of railroads and aerial tramways as well as the port at Zonguldak bolstered productivity. And finally, operators had gained access to supplies of underground workers from outside of the coal district. Given the new inputs that should have boosted output, declines back to the level of the 1870s denote truly devastating conditions in the coalfield during World War I.

In sum, the Zonguldak mines had failed, abysmally, to fulfill the mission set out for them by state planners more than a half-century before. Imperial factories, the fleet, the merchant marine, and the imperial capital could not rely on the mines for their needs. Indeed, in 1918, as the war ended, the capital city turned to Germany, not Zonguldak, to relieve its critical coal shortages!

Workers' Wages and Turnover

The impact of World War I was unevenly distributed among the various kinds of workers in the coalfield. Administrative personnel were the least affected, while those under the compulsory labor system, especially the unskilled workers and basket carriers, were hit hardest by the war. There were so few compulsory workers of draft age still working in the mines that military recruiters could hardly find any to conscript. Skilled aboveground workers, for their part, were less likely to be drafted than the unskilled (usually belowground) workers.

Persons serving in professional administrative posts during World War I enjoyed higher wages and greater job stability than either the skilled or unskilled workers. Personnel here included the director of the entire mine district, mining engineers, clerks and, among others, officials in charge of the coal weighing scales. On the average, salaried officials monthly earned nearly three times as much as the average aboveground worker.[87] Moreover, the average official held his post for 33 months, twice as long as the longevity rates of skilled workers and nearly four times longer than the unskilled workers remained in their positions. Another benefit of these better-paid posts: only 2 percent of their occupants were drafted into the military. By contrast, skilled workers were six times and unskilled workers three times more likely to be drafted than administrative personnel. Unlike their less well-paid counterparts, however, officials received few of the wage increases that, after June 1916, might have helped to offset the rampant inflation of wartime.

The payroll records reflect an extraordinary turnover of aboveground labor during the war. Skilled workers—including ironworkers, carpenters, boiler men, switchmen, and foremen—held their posts for an average of 16 months. Machinists, the most highly skilled, held their jobs for a full 4 years. By contrast, unskilled labor—workers (*amele*), road workers, or conveyer workers—stayed at their jobs for an average of only eight months. In a number of cases, they quit after only one or two months, for unspecified reasons but not for military service.[88] The war, however, does not seem to be the variable explaining this extraordinary turnover because during the peacetime years of 1910 and 1911 (see chapter 4), turnover was comparably great. Worker turnover cannot be blamed for the wartime production declines.

Nor can the mines' inability to provide the coal be traced to the Russian bombardment in 1914, as one author argues.[89] To the contrary, Hüseyin Fehmi Pasha, the mine superintendent who was present during the bombardment, specifically stated in his memoir that operations had not been disrupted. Indeed, he said, port operations quickly reverted to normal after pulling some equipment out of the mud.[90]

Thus, neither worker turnover nor Russian attacks brought mining to a near halt. Rather, the mines failed to produce coal because of a fundamental breakdown of the mechanisms so carefully developed during the decades after the Ottoman-Russian War. The rotational compulsory labor system did not deliver the men, and the provisioning system bringing food, materials, and animals collapsed.

A Glimpse inside the Mines

As the mines completed their third full year of the war, 1917, two high-ranking members of the technical staff made an inspection tour with an eye to bolstering sagging production. The head engineer, Setrak Efendi, and the Zonguldak locale engineer, Mustafa Fazıl Efendi, separately and collectively visited a number of mines.[91] They probably inspected operations in most mines; serendipitously about twenty of their reports survive, offering a bleak picture of wartime conditions. As seen below, most mines were vastly understaffed. On the one hand, conscription drained away many villagers. On the other hand, those who had escaped the draft often then refused mine work. Workers present at the mines sometimes were malnourished and under-equipped with supplies of even the most essential items. Basic foodstuffs often were lacking. Oil for both lamps and lubrication, and even mine supports—key elements of safety and mine exploitation—remained in gravely short supply.

Their inspections trace falling levels of production in individual mines and make real the production decline that is less vividly seen in the aggregate data.

Their graphic observations also illustrate more general patterns of work within and outside mines and reveal many details of everyday work life. For example, during the first two years after military mobilization, the Boyacıoğlu Zonguldak #69 mine, part of which tapped into a coal vein 12–18 meters thick, monthly yielded 1,800 and 1,200 tons. By 1917, output had dropped to 550 tons.[92] In many instances, the engineers monitored production over a period of time (often twenty-five days), measuring daily output and exploring ways to increase output. Four of the mines they visited in October to December 1917 together were employing 1,297 workers, one in five of whom worked aboveground. In the important Asma mine of the Ereğli Company, there were 406 workers, 52 outside and 354 workers underground—an outside/inside ratio of one to seven workers. Among those, 128 hewers were working at the end of October, making them about one-third of all underground workers in that mine.[93]

In almost every instance, the engineers reported that the labor present was a fraction of the work force allotted to a given mine through the rotational system. The engineers minutely examined operations within each mine, usually ending their report with a call for more workers as a means of increasing output. For example, Mustafa Fazıl Efendi made a two-day inspection of the Rombaki mines at Zonguldak, together with the company engineer, M. Anasatas. In his four-page report, the inspector focused on the amount of coal being extracted and ways to increase production. He noted the presence of work gangs—totaling 335 hewers and other workers—who were cutting new shafts, doing cleanup work, and extracting coal from a number of veins. He fretted that workers who were clearing away accumulated debris instead should be working the coal. But the basic problems, he said, lay elsewhere. The size and character of the work force were defective. Villager-miners were not showing up for work, and labor supplies had become irregular. Moreover, he critiqued the rotational labor system in principle, claiming that it promoted an itinerant lifestyle among workers, making them soft. Turning back to the specific situation, he noted that the villager-miners who actually were present were being overworked. They were improperly rested, fed, and cared for and were not even being allowed time to wash themselves. Lighting in the mines was poor, and there were too many accidents.[94]

Similar conditions prevailed in the mines of the Ereğli Company, which accounted for most coal production. A full one-third of the assigned rotational work force had never shown up, and many of those who had were walking off the job. Worse still, workers on the rest rotation back home in the villages suffered from daily hunger. And finally, the engineer complained, lighting was very bad. As a result, the Ereğli Company mines were yielding about one-third of their previous production. Moreover, he added, production could never be increased to needed levels so long as workers were being dragged off forcibly into the military.[95]

On another inspection of the Ereğli Company's Gelik mines two months later, the engineer, Setrak Efendi, remarked on the "extraordinarily rich" coal veins. But, he said, on inspecting some of the veins he encountered no workers, none.[96] Similarly, the lack of workers essentially had halted operations in the rich Milopero vein of the Kilimli #114 mine.[97] And when Setrak visited the Kozlu #200 mine, no one at all was working within the mine. Only ten of twenty-five rotational workers had actually arrived for work, and all of them, plus six full time workers were outside loading coal or making supports. And, he noted, not a single worker for the second shift had reported for work.[98]

The juggling of labor at the Zonguldak #379 mine likely illustrates the general state of affairs in late 1917. Only twelve of the twenty workers allotted from the villages of Ikse and Avaslar actually arrived. Worse, they were mule drivers, and not laborers suited for underground work. Casting about to find the needed labor, the mine operator made a two-for-one swap with another operator who needed transport workers, exchanging the twelve mule drivers assigned to his mine for six basket carriers assigned to the other operator. But then these six workers "decided to go back to their village without permission."[99]

In the early spring of 1918, Mustafa Fazıl submitted another detailed report on one of the largest mines in the region, the rich and productive Asma mine of the Ereğli Company. He carried out the inspection over a six-day period, examining the work force at different locations within the mine (table 9.1 brings together some of his findings). His report illustrates the absences that plagued work at the various veins. Within the mine, depending on the particular location, between 40 and 80 percent of the labor force was absent. Overall, 1,242 of the required 2,157 workers were absent from the mine in April 1918, and three-quarters of the wagons once available were not in use, either needing repair or lacking animals to pull them. Thus, while normal mine operations required 3,004 wagons, only 743 were available (table 9.1).

As has been seen, shortages in most mines were limited not merely to the supplies of manpower and wagons. In the Gelik mines, in December 1917,

Table 9.1 Labor Shortages in the Asma Mine, April 1918

	Workers		Wagons	
Vein	Normal	April 1918	Normal	April 1918
Piriç	121	70		
Domuzcu	172	39	176	41
Acılık floor	188	75	304	64
Acılık ceiling	132	30	240	0
Acılık west	384	170	612	164
Acılık west	288	156	672	202
Piriç	872	375	1,000	272
Total	2,157	915	3,004	743

Source: ED 16.

proper lubricating oils were nearly completely unavailable. This shortage was particularly serious because the most productive mines made heavy use of steam engines to ventilate shafts and pump water, as well as to power locomotives and aerial tramways. With oil unavailable, workers in the Gelik mines abandoned the railroad engines and at first resorted to animals to pull the coal wagons. But then animal shortages blocked this stratagem. Workers dropped their assigned coal extraction tasks and instead hauled coal themselves, teaming up to pull chains of cars, sometimes 50–60 wagons, along the tracks within and outside mines.[100]

Mine supports similarly disappeared from the market. Until the war, contractors had been supplying different mines with supports of specified sizes at agreed-upon prices. The Sarıcazadeler #349 mine, for example, had contracts with two different suppliers, each for annual delivery of 5,000 supports.[101] This system generally fell into disarray during the war because of persistent labor shortages. Compared to pre-war levels, the supply of mine supports at the Kilimli #174 and #278 mines dropped by 50 percent, from 100 to 50 daily. At the Kilimli #114 mine, support shortages triggered production declines of 80 percent. The Zonguldak #69 mine managed to sustain the delivery of mine supports at pre-war levels through 1915 and 1916, but it then fell by 95 percent in 1917 when the supplying contractor "didn't do his duty."[102] Some mines continued to rely solely on contractors. Others maintained their contracts but blended in new sources of supply. In one case (the Kilimli #174 and #278 mines), a contractor provided most of the supports but the mine operators ordered sixteen coal face workers to the task of monthly delivering 60 additional supports.[103] At a number of mines, operators relied on open-market purchases of supports, wherever they could be found. At another mine (Kilimli #114), local women provided some of the supports while small boats (*kayık*) brought others from outside. Neither Mustafa Fazil, who prepared the report, nor Setrak Efendi, who endorsed it, made any comments about the presence of these women. To me, this lack of further commentary suggests that such activities by women were not unusual. Their contribution to the functioning of this mine—which was operated by a woman, Hiristofilis Hanim—was not presented or regarded as a unique or noteworthy phenomenon.

Shortages of materials made mine work more difficult and risky. Underground workers increasingly spent their hours making mine supports, once supplied by others. Shortages of lamp oil meant poorly illuminated and hence very dangerous worksites. Many, perhaps most, workers failed to receive the prescribed ration of oil. Also, as seen, the lack of motor oils meant shutdowns of railroads and other transport facilities, and of the pumps and ventilating fans that preserved life within the mines.

To provide adequate food supplies, the state arranged monthly deliveries of wheat flour rations to each mine. In taking these actions, it anticipated that supplies would be exhausted toward the end of the month, and that operators would buy bread from local bakeries and sell it to the workers at heavily subsidized prices. While the supplies lasted, mine operators distributed flour rations to each worker. In 1917, operators apportioned to each a daily ration of around 600 grams, about enough for a single loaf of bread. But in 1918 and 1919, the ration increased to 750 grams.[104] By comparison, during the war, soldiers theoretically were entitled to a daily ration of about 1 kg of bread.[105]

The provisioning of wheat flour is noteworthy, since breads made mainly or exclusively from corn were the local workers' staple diet. Wheat flour was a prized commodity in the region. Food supplies of any sort were very scarce in the coalfield, so assured rations of wheat flour were meant to attract workers to the mines. By showing up for work, the villager could obtain food, and that of a sort rarely available. The extraordinary step of offering larger rations in 1918 and 1919 suggests how scarce labor had become.

But neither the engineers' zeal nor the promise of wheat bread could overcome the basic problems of human and material shortages that plagued the wartime mines. These deficits did not merely reduce the number of workers, animals, and mine supports; they also meant that the workers who were on the job were poorly supplied and underfed. Consequently, productivity per worker declined sharply at most mines (table 9.2). Before the war, daily output levels of 400–500 kg per worker were considered normal and they occasionally approached 600 kg. Toward the end of the war, however, average per capita output fell in the meager range of 200–300 kg. Compared to pre-war levels, per-worker productivity had fallen a full one-third by the last months of the war.

Thus, the collapse of coal production derived from shortages of manpower, animals, and virtually every kind of material—from mine supports to lighting, and lubrication oils. The material shortfalls in turn triggered further declines in productivity among the malnourished, badly supplied, scarce laborers who still remained at mine work.

Table 9.2 Per Capita Productivity Levels at Various Mines, 1914–1919

	Pre-war	Wartime	
Mine	Kg/Day	Kg/Day	Date
Asma	400	230	Oct. 1917
Ikinci Makas	450	400	Oct. 1917
Rombaki	400	213	Oct. 1917
Ikinci Makas	500	330	Mar. 1918
KM 174 & 278	590	490	Mar. 1918
Z 349	414	222	Feb. 1919
Total	2,754	1,885	
	Tons/Mo.	Tons/Mo.	Date
KM 114	1,000	200	Mar. 1918

Note: KM=Kilimli, Z=Zonguldak.
Source: ED 16.

Notes

1. Pamuk (1995), 48–52.
2. ED 4, 24, 20 Ağustos 1293/1 September 1877.
3. ED 4, 218, 14 Ağustos 1294/26 August 1878.
4. ED 4, 24, 20 Ağustos 1293/1 September 1877.
5. ED 4, 24, 20 Ağustos 1293/1 September 1877.
6. ED 4, 36, 11 Eylül 1293/23 September 1877.
7. ED 4, 166, 22 Mayıs 1294/3 June 1878.
8. ED 4, 314, 24 Mart 1295/5 April 1879.
9. ED 4, 200, 20 Temmuz 1294/1 August 1878.
10. ED 4, 81, 12 Zilkade 1294/6 ts 1293.
11. ED 4, 18, 9 Ağustos 1293/21 August 1877; 33, 6 Eylül 12945/18 September 1877; and 49, 7 tl 1293/19 October 1877.
12. ED 4, 23, 18 Ağustos 1293/30 August 1877.
13. ED 4, 5, 24 Temmuz 1293/5 Ağustos 1877; 11, 29 Temmuz 1293/10 August 1877.
14. ED 4, 45, 28 Eylül 1293/10 October 1877; 22, 17 Ağustos 1293/29 August 1877; 18, 9 Ağustos 1293; and 19, 12 Ağustos 1293/24 August 1877.
15. ED 4, 81, 6 ts 1293/18 November 1877.
16. ED 4, 71, 22 tl 1293/3 November 1877.
17. ED 4, 156, 22 Nisan 1294/14 May 1878. The weight of a local *kile* is not certain, and therefore conversions to kg were not attempted.
18. ED 4, 222, 19 Ağustos 1294/31 August 1878.
19. ED 4, 253–255, 25 tl 1294/6 November 1878.
20. ED 4, 279, 21 kl 1294/2 January 1879.
21. ED 4, 294, 31 ks 1294/12 February 1879.
22. ED 4, 309, 15 Mart 1294/27 March 1879.
23. ED 4, 344, 14 Temmuz 1295/26 July 1879.
24. Eldem (1994), 132–140.
25. 8 ts 1295/1878, as cited in Çatma (1998), 92.
26. ED 4, 307, 10 Mart 1295/22 March 1879.
27. ED 4, 314, 24 Mart 1295/5 April 1879.
28. ED 4, 283, 29 kl 1294/10 January 1879.
29. ED 4, 151, 2 Nisan 1294/14 April 1878.
30. ED 4, 258, 20 tl 1294/11 November 1878.
31. ED 4, 308, 13 Mart 1295/25 March 1879; 316, 22 Mart 1295/3 April 1879; 314, 24 Mart 1295/5 April 1879.
32. ED 4, 290, 18 ks 1294/30 January 1879. In August 1879, to meet a severe shortage of basket carriers and wagoners from Erzene, the superintendent ordered the Bartın district official to pay cash wages. See ED 4, 350, 21 Temmuz 1295/7 August 1879.
33. ED 4, 199, ca. 20 Temmuz 1294/1 August 1878.
34. ED 4, 21, 14 Ağustos 1293/26 August 1877; 37, 13 Eylül 1293/25 September 1877; 24, 20 Ağustos 1293/1 September 1877 and 30, 2 Eylül 1293/14 September 1877; 25, 20 Ağustos 1293/1 September 1877; 31, 2 Eylül 1294/14 September 1877.
35. ED 4, 224, 25 Ağustos 1294/6 September 1878; 334, same date; 233, 10 Eylül 1294/22 September 1878.
36. ED 4, 235, 19 Eylül 1294/1 October 1878.
37. ED 4, 211, 5 Ağustos 1294/17 August 1878 and 241, 1 tl 1294/13 October 1878. ED 4, 253–255, 25 tl 1294/6 November 1878; ED 4, 81, 6 ts 1293/18 November 1877; ED 4, 271, 29 ts 1294/11 December 1878.
38. ED 4, 365, ca. 20 Ağustos 1295/1 September 1879.
39. ED 4, 44, 27 Eylül 1293/9 October 1877.

40. ED 4, 194, 13 Temmuz 1294/25 July 1878; 177, 22 Haziran 1294/4 July 1878; 188, 24 Haziran 1294/6 July 1878.
41. ED 4, 240, 26 Eylül 1294/8 October 1878.
42. ED 4, 241, 1 tl 1294/13 October 1878.
43. ED 4, 271, 29 ts 1294/11 December 1878.
44. ED 4, 211, 5 Ağustos 1294/17 August 1878; 236, 23 Eylül 1294/5 October 1878. These were Safranbolu district and Nalınca and Milaş sub-districts.
45. ED 4, 221–222, 19–21 Ağustos 1294/31 August–2 September 1878.
46. ED 4, 182, 29 Haziran 1294/11 July 1878; 182, 29 Haziran 1294/11 July 1878; 191, 10 Temmuz 1294/22 July 1878.
47. ED 4, 220, 16 Ağustos 1294/28 August 1878.
48. ED 4, 244, 4 tl 1294/16 October 1878; 259, 1 ts 1294/13 November 1878. The two lists were separate inventories of the missing, not a repetition of the same command. The second listing contained seven villages from the first list, one of which had the same number of missing workers on both lists.
49. ED 4, 289, 13 ks 1294/25 January 1879, the Toma and Luka mine.
50. ED 4, 288, 12 ks 1294/24 January 1879; see also ED 4, 358, 25 Ağustos 1295/6 August 1879.
51. ED 4, 72, 24 tl 1293/5 November 1877.
52. ED 4, 164, 14 Mayıs 1294/26 May 1878.
53. ED 4, 196–197, 16 Temmuz 1294/28 July 1878, referring to Alaplı but reflecting general conditions.
54. ED 4, 195, 15 Temmuz 1294/2 July 1878.
55. ED 4, 366, 21 Eylül 1295/3 October 1879.
56. ED 4, 196–197, 16 Temmuz 1294/28 July 1878; therein the dates are stated as May–August 1878.
57. ED 4, 190, 5 Temmuz 1294/17 July 1878.
58. ED 4, 26, 22 Ağustos 1293/3 September 1877.
59. ED 4, 14, 6 Ağustos 1293/18 August 1877.
60. ED 4, 69, 19 tl 1293/31 October 1877.
61. ED 4, 193, 12 Temmuz 1294/24 July 1878.
62. ED 4, 33, 6 Eylül 1293/18 September 1877.
63. ED 4, 83, 8 ts 1293/20 November 1877. Also see ED 4, 290, 18 ks 1294/30 January 1879 for descriptions of the tasks.
64. ED 4, 274, 10 kl 1294/22 December 1878; 279, 20 kl 1294/1 January 1879; 57–68, 2 Eylül 1293/15 September 1877, individually noting the names and residences of some 365 home guards and absentee conscripts given over to mine work.
65. ED 4, 345, 14 Temmuz 1295/26 July 1879.
66. For example, ED 4, 299, 16 Şubat 1294.
67. ED 4, 146, 22 Mart 1294/3 April 1878.
68. ED 4, 53, two documents, both dated 14 tl 1293/26 October 1877.
69. ED 4, 141, 15 Mart 1294/27 March 1878; on 250, 20 tl 1294/1 November 1878, stating that clothing had not been sent for one or two years.
70. ED 4, 144, 18 Mart 1294/30 March 1878; 174, 10 Haziran 1294/22 June 1878; 295, 5 Şubat 1294/17 February 1879; 346, 17 Temmuz 1295/29 July 1879. ED 4, 359, 28 Ağustos 1295/9 September 1879 and 360, 29 Ağustos 1295/10 September 1879.
71. ED 4, 22, 19 Ağustos 1294/31 August 1878; 29, 27 Ağustos 1293/8 September 1877.
72. ED 4, 344, 14 Temmuz 1295/26 July 1879; 357, 18 Ağustos 1295.
73. ED 4, 190, 5 Temmuz 1294/17 July 1878; also, 198, 17 Temmuz 1294/29 July 1878.
74. ED 4, 196–197, 16 Temmuz 1294/24 July 1878.
75. ED 4, 349, 24 Temmuz 1295/5 August 1879, for clear evidence of double dipping.
76. ED 4, 299, 16 Şubat 1294/28 February 1879.
77. ED 4, 331, 28 Mayıs 1295/9 June 1879.
78. Eldem (1994), 132, quoting the War Ministry.
79. See Zürcher (1996), 241–242.

80. Zürcher (1996), 256–257, and Zürcher (1999), 90. Eldem (1994), 132, quoting Yalman, offers similar figures.
81. Toprak (2003), and Toprak (1982).
82. Pamuk (2000), 223; Toprak (2003), 168.
83. İmer (1973), 52–53.
84. There is, however, only the circumstantial evidence presented here to support the assertion. The absence of statistics regarding imports or local agricultural production does not allow present resolution of this issue.
85. Toprak (2003), 164; Eldem (1994), 50–51.
86. Özeken (1944a), 26; Savaşkan (1993), 55–56; and Eldem (1994), 82, for a different 1916 figure. See table 2.2.
87. KU 143, 1–40, excluding office boys: 900 krs versus an average monthly wage of 326 krs for workers.
88. KU 143, 51–84. Among office boys, employment duration of about 9 months per person was three times that of administrative officials and just slightly longer than that of unskilled workers. Moreover, those working as office boys were called away from their jobs to military service at very high rates. Indeed, three of the five working at the Ereğli offices were drafted between June 1915 and November 1916. In total, around 30 percent of all office boys were drafted—a rate fifteen times greater than the professional staff's and four times more than that of unskilled workers; KU 143, 8, and 35.
89. Eldem (1994), 78 and 168.
90. İmer (1973), 52–53. Of course, he may have emphasized the positive to highlight the efficacy of his own actions. In his support, it should be noted that the wartime reports never blame bombardments for problems with mine operations.
91. In ED 16, 493, 10 April 1334/1918, Mustafa Fazil states that between October 1917 and 10 April 1918, he had been inspecting the mines in Zonguldak, Kozlu, and Kilimli and had filed the appropriate reports.
92. ED 16, 383–386, 30 ts 1333/30 November 1917.
93. ED 16, 360, 25 tl 1333/25 October 1917.
94. ED 16, 356–359, 25 tl 1333/25 October 1917.
95. ED 16, 363–364, 30 tl 1333/30 October 1917.
96. ED 16, 439–440, 31 kl 1333/31 December 1917.
97. ED 16, 474–475, 16 Mart 1334/16 March 1918.
98. ED 16, 482, 1 Nisan 1334/1 April 1918.
99. ED 16, 418–421, 21 kl 1333/21 December 1917.
100. ED 16, 439–440, 31 kl 1333/31 December 1917.
101. ED 16, 458–461.
102. ED 16, 383–386
103. ED 16, 468–471, 5 Mart 1334/5 March 1918.
104. ED 16, 380–282, 30 ts 1333/30 November 1917; 383–386, same date; 387–392, 5 kl 1333/5 December 1917; 418–421, 21 kl 1333/21 December 1917; 458–461, 12 Şubat 1334/12 February 1919; 468–471, 5 Mart 1334/5 March 1918. The amounts sometimes varied by mine and were specified variously in grams, dirhems, or *okka*s, usually either 200 dirhems or 0.5 *kiyye*, both equal to about 0.64 kgs. At one mine in 1919, bread was directly provided, but otherwise the ration came in the form of flour.
105. Zürcher (1996), 248–249. The reality, of course, was rather different, and in some theaters of war, the soldiers received only one-third of their official ration.

10

Conclusion

This book, I believe, makes a number of important contributions to our understanding of labor history, modern state formation, and the nature of capital. The encounters of the Zonguldak miners with state officials and private mine operators do not follow the expected patterns of labor-state-capital relations as predicted by the major explanatory paradigms of modernization or dependency. Indeed, few of the outcomes are as predicted. The fate of these workers thus has much to offer Ottoman and Middle East specialists and scholars of the developing world and, more generally, those interested in the connections between economic development and social and political change.

Part of the story is about a state's efforts to manipulate and direct the flow of labor. Governmental instruments of labor control included the brutally direct use of troops to literally drag young men from their home villages to the mines. On occasion, state officials even forced fleeing miners back into dangerous, gas-filled mines. More subtly, they implemented safety measures intended not only to save lives but also to serve as disciplinary tools for molding and controlling an unruly labor force. But despite these efforts throughout the many decades between the opening of the mines and the end of the empire, the Ottoman state did not create a reliable labor force to provide the coal essential to its core strategic concerns. Thus, the research reported here has complicated still-prevailing notions of the all-powerful Ottoman state. According to some basic assumptions concerning modernity, the modern state is said to evolve uni-directionally, along quite particular lines of development. The Ottoman state surely did come to reproduce many of the expected attributes of modernity, for example, the specialized bureaucracy knowledgeable in geology and mine engineering that embraced safety as a disciplinary tool. Or, for another example, recall Raghip Pasha, the chamberlain who ended the monopoly of local workers in underground mine labor with the help of a friendly provincial governor.

But within the state apparatus, other bureaucrats (whose names are not available in the sources consulted here) steadfastly pursued distinctly un-modern or

---

Notes for this chapter are located on page 234.

non-modern policy objectives. The War Ministry's insistence on draining the mines of their manpower—during both of the wars examined here—may be understandable from a narrow military standpoint. But it was strategically ill-advised since it reduced the flow of coal essential to the imperial war machine. The government's civilian wing should have but did not overcome the military's shortsighted demands, ones which derived from residues of the state's archaic character. Take, as another notable example, the government's stubborn retention of the compulsory rotational labor system. The negative effect on coal production was understood clearly among the engineering staff of the mine administration yet the system outlived the empire. Thus, the research presented here contributes to a literature that shows modern state formation to be an uneven process, fraught with considerable slippages, detours, and blind alleys.

There were vast visible changes in the coalfield over the decades of coal exploitation. The once-unbroken green of the hillsides was scarred with mining debris and by 1920 the beaches likely were already as black with coal waste as they are today. A town of thousands, Zonguldak, stood where a swamp once had been, fronted by a port with its great breakwater. Ancient centers like Ereğli and Devrek and smaller, newer, communities such as Kozlu and Kilimli held new populations and wealth. Ereğli itself had served as a mother city, providing many colonists for Zonguldak as well as the less important towns. Thanks to this migration and others from more distant places, the towns' populations had become more diverse than those of the villages of the hinterland. Whereas the countryside remained exclusively Turkish and Muslim, the towns contained majority Christian populations—many Ottoman and foreign Greeks had settled in them, alongside Bulgarians, Rumanians, Serbs, Croats, and other nationalities. Zonguldak even had a foreign quarter, whose intended permanence was marked by its own separate cemetery.

There had been considerable improvements in the mining infrastructure. Thanks to the French company, a mechanized port facility complete with scrubbers and cranes facilitated the rapid and efficient handling of coal. The Ereğli Company and other firms mechanized land transport in significant ways, using both railways and the less expensive, if also less efficient, aerial tramway system. Many mines possessed ventilators to move the air and mechanical pumps to drain water. Wagons on rails often transported coal to the surface. Such changes benefited the workers directly, since machinery meant fewer backbreaking tasks and safer work conditions. The construction of dormitories also aided many miners, as did the expansion of hospitals and medical care.

Yet work conditions overall continued to be poor. Accident rates remained horrific and likely worsened as the mines went farther and deeper into the earth. The increased attention to safety lamps partly derived from the new realities of Zonguldak mining where methane and other gases more frequently were being encountered. There were many lacunae in the infrastructure. Mechanization, despite the improvements, remained quite incomplete, and many mines remained lacking ventilators and the other equipment characteristic of safer modern mining. During the final years of the empire, animals, not steam engines, pulled wagons in many mines. While this perhaps is hardly surprising, the continuing reliance on human power for transport may be. Many workers continued to push coal cars within and outside mines, and basket carriers hauling coal within mines remained commonplace. The precise number of these workers in the Ottoman twentieth century is uncertain, but the unremarkable manner in which they are discussed in accident reports makes clear that they continued to form a routine and significant part of the work force.

Mine safety was not enforced merely with the self-evident intent to protect workers' lives and improve profits by reducing accident-related work stoppages. The emphasis on safety lamps, for example, derived also from state efforts to create a disciplined and responsible citizenry. Also, in common with contemporary nineteenth-century French companies that used safety to convince miners to accept work discipline, the safety campaigns in Zonguldak were part and parcel of the engineers' efforts, in tandem with the operators, to impose greater authority and control over the work force.[1] Yet if experiences elsewhere are any indication, the implementation of piecework wages by the Ereğli Company and perhaps other firms conflicted with the goal of better discipline through safety. In the United States and France, experience showed that piecework actually eroded safety. In the haste to meet quotas and maximize output, it was easy to neglect or reject time-consuming or questionable safety measures such as the placement of an additional support or the use of safety lamps offering poor illumination. Contrariwise, better safety regulations were more likely in the presence of fixed wages.[2] Also, recall the top-down approach to safety in the Zonguldak coalfield where, the state and operators assumed, workers could not be trusted to maintain safety standards on their own but required constant supervision. Such policies elsewhere had been counterproductive and increased the incidence of accidents. Take, for example, the Rocky Mountain West of the United States, where workers were more careful about safety in the absence of supervision. There, with increased supervision, workers became more careless about their own safety because they assumed that others were watching out.[3] Thus, in their zeal to impose discipline upon the workers, the Ottoman state and the Zonguldak operators actually may have created more, rather than less, dangerous working conditions.

The work force became increasingly complex, in several senses, over time. First, there was an increasing division of labor. Early on, there were scarcely any workers at all besides hewers, transporters, and mine support makers. But many other occupations soon joined the roster, thanks to the expansion of production and the ongoing mechanization of work, and tasks became increasingly differentiated. For example, toward the end of the era there were different technicians to care for locomotives' steam engines and the steam engines that pumped water or air. In addition, there now were many workers in coal scrubbers, foundries, carpentry shops, and repair facilities, as well as on the railroads and aerial tramways. Besides these, there were many workers at the port of Zonguldak.

Also, the work force became more differentiated in both the nature of the labor—unfree versus free—and its geographic origins. Over time, increasing inputs of free labor diluted the largely unfree character of the original work force—the rotational workers and the soldier-workers—as it had emerged after the 1867 regulations. Thus, workers from across the empire came to work in the aboveground tasks initially seen as too technical for the local work force. In addition, as of 1906, free-labor miners from Eastern Anatolia came to dig coal. To this mix were added a few foreign workers and foremen. Thus, unfree labor characterized the local work force in contrast to the free market labor from outside the coalfield.

Villager-miners in rotational labor formed the core of the work force and quite likely continued to outnumber the combined total of all other work groups present. The rotational supply of local villagers to the mines began to emerge in the 1860s and became marked by a dense web of trails and paths crisscrossing the region, connecting hundreds of villages to many scores of mines. Most villages, both large and small, provided one kind of labor, mainly basket carriers, to just one mine. But a large minority of villages sent several kinds of workers to two or more mines. The relationship between a particular village and mine remains generally invisible in the record, but operators' payments to village authorities and to labor bosses suggest the kinds of alliances formed to produce the desired labor supply.

The consequences of shared work experiences among workers of unfree and free status and different geographic origins remain uncertain. Rotational workers from one particular village routinely worked together. It also is clear that the assignments of rotational workers from different villages in the coalfield to the same mine also regularly occurred. Rotational workers at the mines remained powerfully influenced by village-centered patterns of authority and obedience—quite often foremen who had led the workers from the village directed their labor tasks. Every two weeks, the shift workers returned to the village and again faced the community authorities who were their recruiters, paymasters, and disciplinarians. But other factors also affected these village-based ties. First of all, rotational workers from one and more villages commonly labored with fellow Ottomans from outside the coalfield and with workers from outside the empire altogether. These rotational workers, whose primary experiences had been village-based and remained rooted in village life, often witnessed different behaviors among these full-time workers from outside. For full-time workers, who were cut off from home, work remained the central everyday experience of their lives. Mitigation of their worksite grievances was more pressing, since these went unrelieved by rotation away from work—and some of the outsiders brought with them experiences in strike organizing. In the many strikes that swept the mines after 1908, aboveground workers who were Ottoman subjects from outside the coalfield played the leading role. The impact of these actions on the evolving identity of the rotational workers presently is not visible in the records and merits further consideration. On the one hand, these kinds of experiences helped to mold the rotational workers' evolving notions of identity and labor goals (but the precise patterns have yet to be established). On the other hand, rotational workers' continuing ties to the village in turn shaped emerging forms of identity and mobilization.

The preponderance of the rotational work force did not go unchallenged. Private entrepreneurs, on a number of occasions, took measures that can be understood as efforts either to proletarianize the rotational workers or replace them with a proletarianized work force. In 1899, the Ereğli Company stepped up efforts to introduce piecework rates, a measure disliked by many of the rotational workers.[4] Similarly, lobbying by the court-connected operator Raghip Pasha broke the monopoly of rotational labor in 1906 and aimed to create a full-time wage-earning work force. There is no documentation that other elements in the state apparatus sought to block his effort. It seems significant that the state cooperated in a measure that, if it had succeeded, might have meant the end of the rotational labor force. The disappointment of the Ereğli Company in these new workers from outside is recorded and palpable. Raghip Pasha's reaction is unknown at this time, but he abandoned mine operations shortly thereafter. The disappointment derived not only from the alleged low productivity of the new workers, but also from the labor disturbances accompanying their arrival. Both the mounting frequency of piecework and the attempted introduction of a full-time outsider mine force potentially undermined the rotational labor system that dominated coalfield labor. But even though the central state followed the lead of mine operators in seeking to create a more proletarianized work force, it did not take the next logical step. That is, there is no evidence that the government directly attempted to end the compulsory rotational labor system and offer or compel full-time work to these villagers.

Two different explanations for this inaction come to mind. The first is a state-centered one in which the state remains primarily concerned with maintaining its stable agrarian population, social stability, and a steady flow of taxes. In this explanation, credit is given to the wisdom of the state in balancing multiple interests.[5] The second explanation, however, focuses on actions by villager-workers. Here, both the workers and village authorities struggled against the creation of the reliable, more productive, permanent work force that mine operators demanded. The villager-workers' resistance to the implementation of piecework is a key indicator of their efforts to escape being bound more closely to mine work and to a cash nexus. Village authorities supported these efforts to preserve the status quo, perhaps because they themselves were threatened by the prospect of a full-time labor force living at the mines and slipping away from their control.

Whatever the reason, rotational labor remained intact and productivity low. Although at least two and perhaps three generations of villagers had experienced mine labor, they continued to display, as the accumulated evidence in this volume has indicated, decidedly unsubservient and uncapitalist behavior. Their reluctance to accept piecework rates is noteworthy in this regard and is quite different from the behavior of miners in many areas of the world. Also, they insisted on week-long holidays in the Ramadan season despite state objections, and they continued to leave the mines to harvest the crops. Finally, many refused to show up at all. All this suggests the limited dependence of villager-workers on wage work.

Perhaps this should not occasion surprise. After all, data from the 1890s reveal that large numbers of workers never saw the cash they had earned. Instead, repeatedly, the money flowed to pay their taxes (or those of village authorities) or buy the bread they ate to work. These kinds of payments diluted but hardly eliminated the impact of cash on village life. Whether or not, for example, the populations of mine villages increased or decreased in patterns different from communities without mining ties, remains uncertain. Recruitment pressures may not have been sufficient to trigger population increases, and it is more likely that additional labor supplies were available from the existing pool of villages in the coalfield.[6]

Indeed, the recruitment of miners from outside the district perhaps can be understood better as a disciplinary matter than as a supply issue. Certainly, outside workers did fill gaps in the supply of workers. But for the state and the operators, targeting this new group of outside workers also was a means to the dual ends of accumulating a labor reserve and keeping the local work force more malleable and responsive to demands for increased numbers of workers. By recruiting outsiders, the employers served notice to local workers that their monopoly on mine work and the income it produced was no longer guaranteed. Such practices were employed in nineteenth-century Britain as mining became more capital-intensive and managers sought to reduce absenteeism.[7]

In their attempts to find alternatives to nearby village labor, the mine operators of Zonguldak are similar to those in diverse areas such as Chile, Peru, and Rhodesia around the end of the nineteenth century. There, mine operators became disenchanted with the performance of villagers they had recruited and new labor sources replaced the original work force. But the existing work force at Zonguldak, unlike the original sources of labor in these South American and African examples, remained pre-eminent in the mining labor supply. Zonguldak mine operators failed to introduce a viable alternative to the villager-workers who, outlived the empire and persist down to the present.

In the early 1920s, the new Turkish Republic formally abolished compulsion in the labor system but retained the rotational aspect. Over time during the post-Ottoman period, the duration of the rotation increased from semi-monthly to monthly, a change demonstrating that workers were not impervious to the demands of state and capital. The considerable pressures to convert the villager-miners into a full-time work force forced them to yield their labor and reluctantly, haltingly, move down the path toward full proletarianization. Indeed, by the late twentieth century, the Zonguldak miners had become the very paragon of labor in action, able to bring down the Turkish government itself.[8] Yet the persistence of rotational labor and the retention of village ties and identities connected to the village marks the ability of the labor force to protect itself from total encroachment by capital and the state. Thus, coal mining, which can be considered as the most capitalistic of capitalist enterprises, took place in the late Ottoman Empire and into the Turkish Republic thanks to a work force that is a particular hybrid of proletarian and anti-proletarian characteristics.

Having completed this study, I can try to imagine, since I generally cannot document, the gendering of community life over the decades of mine labor. There is nothing inherently masculine about mine work, although it has been thoroughly masculinized in most mining regions of the world, often with the aid of the state. For example, before an 1842 law excluded them from mine labor, women formed a full quarter of the labor force in Scottish mines, charged with carrying sacks of coal.[9] Women actively participated in the work life of the Zonguldak mines even though they often are not visibly present in the written records. At some of the smaller operations, women who lived with their owner husbands had unknown roles in mine operations. Some wives of mine operators worked in their husbands' mines while a few managed mines on their own accounts.

Women workers late in the Ottoman era are documented in the single miner's memoir that has come down to us. Ethem Çavuş devotes a separate section to "Women Workers in the Coal Pits" and names some of them, such as Adalı Sultan, Topçu Emine, and Gulsum Hatun.[10] But the language he uses to describe them is formulaic rather than personal, and he does not tell us how often they were present.[11] The memoir, however, does offer proof of women at work both outside and inside mines. In the official records, there are recorded instances of female labor during the Ottoman-Russian War of 1877–1878 and during World War I as well. Two sets of superintendency reports, separated by four decades, mention women in outside work, earlier as transporters and later as providers of mine supports. The 1878 era reports make clear that female labor was not common but was considered necessary nonetheless. In contrast, the World War I records note women's mine work as a routine event, unworthy of special comment. Comparing the memoir with the official sources allows for several tentative conclusions. Women worked inside mines less frequently than outside them. Within, they usually were members of small-scale, family-run operations. In outside work, they most commonly served as transporters, a task that likely brought them back to the village by nightfall.

Several generations of rotational labor must have created a more masculine culture at many worksites and in the housing and eating locations as well. For one-half of each month, workers had no female companionship, except for visits to prostitutes at mine sites or in towns. Even in the context of the highly gendered society of the late Ottoman era, the total maleness of the work and living environment at the mines seems stark—as does the pattern of two weeks away at work and two weeks at home. Whether this pattern caused female members of the households to assume tasks that once had been the duty of males at home remains beyond speculation in the absence of supporting materials, despite the importance of the topic. After all, how did the semi-monthly absence of the large numbers of males from villages affect life there and the assignment of tasks to various members of household and village communities? The consequent evolution of social and cultural patterns awaits another study. But there is an important clue to this puzzle in the workers' desertion of the mine in order to harvest crops. This behavior may indicate families' continued insistence that harvesting crops remain male work, more important than mining coal. That is, the return of the men to the village for harvesting suggests continuation of existing divisions of labor within mining households and villages.

The story of the mines in wartime illustrates that the state (and the mine operators) failed to achieve the goal of assured coal production in periods of crisis. Indeed, coal output levels during World War I barely equaled those attained during the Ottoman-Russian War era of the 1870s, despite the decades of control of workers and considerable financial investment in the mining infrastructure. Meanwhile, the state's ability to extract labor had improved measurably over the four decades. During the Ottoman-Russian War, civilian workers largely disappeared from the mines, and mobilized soldiers accounted for much of the work force. Thus, the mine administration utterly failed to protect the miners from conscription. In contrast, during World War I civilian workers formed the bulk of the work force present in the mines. From the state's perspective, this was an improvement over past performance in keeping civilians at work during wartime. But few persons of military age were present in the mines. Thus, the mine administration, as forty years before, could not keep draft-age civilians out of military service. Instead, it dipped more deeply into the remaining pools of civilian village labor, summoning the young boys and older men of the community. Despite the centrality of coal to the war effort, the labor system devised over the preceding decades failed the litmus test of wartime.

Notes

1. Reid (1981).
2. Dix (1977), 67ff., and Reid (1981).
3. Whiteside (1990).
4. Quataert (1983), 62–63.
5. This is the explanation offered in Quataert (1983), 68–69.
6. I hope to address these issues in a forthcoming study.
7. Church (1986), 234–246.
8. For example, see Kahveci (1997).
9. Church (1986), 191.
10. Quataert and Duman (2001), 172–173.
11. My thanks to Pamela Scully, Denison University, for her very helpful comments on the language used by Ethem Çavuş in discussing women workers.

Appendix on the Reporting of Accidents

Over the four decades following their first appearance in the late 1870s, accident reports become increasingly detailed. They offer progressively more information on the nature of the event as well as the matter of responsibility for its occurrence. They also present increasingly specific personal details about the victims and, later on, the witnesses of these accidents. In these ways, they reflect the increasing size and professionalization of the mining bureaucracy appointed to oversee mine safety.

Only a few specific reports relating to safety and accidents survived the chaos and confusion of the Ottoman-Russian War. The register book (ED 4) holds some 500 pages containing several thousands of documents within which are perhaps eleven accident reports. Most reports are very brief, noting the occurrence of an accident, the number of casualties, and sometimes, the cost of medical treatment when provided. One report is striking for its detailed and vivid account of an explosion. In its full and precise description of the accident, the 1877 report is comparable to reports issued thirty-five years later, in 1912–1913. But in most other respects, this report is dissimilar to the later ones. The 1877 presentation provides no personal information about the victims: the fact that there are wounded and dead is stated, as is the medical treatment they received. But only their occupations are mentioned—they are simply basket carriers or hewers, not individuals with names, ages, families, or villages of origin.[1] There is only one named exception: an injured worker who brought suit against the mine operator.[2]

In contrast to the scarcity of accident reports in the 1877–1879 register, the registers for 1893–1907 and 1912 and 1913 abundantly document accidents and contain rich details about the surrounding circumstances. Unlike the reports from the Ottoman-Russian War era, these later reports—at first in the registers of 1893–1907 and increasingly in the 1912 and 1913 reports—offer concrete personal information about the victims themselves. In the earliest

---

Notes for this section begin on page 240.

reports from the 1893–1907 register, the injuries are described quite precisely; trained medical personnel surely were present at the examination. For example, Hatipoğlu Mehmed bin Halil, "fully 35 years old," suffered "variously 1st, 2nd, 3rd, and 4th degree burns" on his "head, eyelids, ears, face, chest, arms, and hands."[3] It is likely that the medical doctors preparing these reports were stationed in the Zonguldak region to examine boys and men eligible for military conscription as well as soldiers who had become sick or injured or were seeking release from service. The doctors either submitted the accident reports personally or were directly involved in their preparation until around 1897, when the practice of noting physical features of victims and medical descriptions of the wounds fades from use.

In these 1890s reports, workers have become concrete individual persons with names and ages (and, in the first years, physical descriptions). Thus, a victim of a July 1894 accident is known by his district and village of origin, name, age, and his "yellow and white" complexion. Thereafter, in the reports issued between 1893 and 1907, we almost always learn a victim's name, occupation, place of origin and, sometimes, age (stated in years). A relationship to others present at the site, such as brother or uncle, occasionally is noted. Throughout, this information is presented in textual form, embedded in the narrative of the accident.

Beginning in June 1893, when an inspector notes that no one could be held accountable for an "unfortunate" gas fire that had burned two workers, the reports also begin to be concerned with issues of responsibility.[4] Thus, individual workers, foremen, and mine operators variously are held responsible, or not, for the particular accident. Quite often, the final assessment was neutral: procedures were being followed and the accident was unavoidable. In keeping with this concern for responsibility, around May 1902, the inspectors' reports begin adding phrases such as "as for the causes of the accident," reflecting a more formal presentation of the event.[5] Further details appear when a June 1905 report identifies not only the victims by name and village but, for the first time, also others present at but not harmed in an accident.[6] Shortly thereafter, witnesses formally appear and the reports begin to list their names, villages, occupations, and testimony.[7]

Diagrams depicting the accident site first appear in October 1905 and subsequently become routine practice.[8] In another innovation, reports of accidents occurring in August and December 1905 list the victims' and witnesses' names and occupations in tabular form at the head of the report and no longer in the text itself. This practice had become standard by 1912, but it appears on only these two occasions during the 1893–1907 period.[9]

The 1893–1907 reports anticipate those of 1912–1913 in yet another way. In the earlier reports, the engineer's detailed description typically reframes the various participants' words into their own narratives. For example, in a 1895 accident report, the engineer rephrases in his own words the accounts of seven different workers who had been involved in a gas explosion.¹⁰ Thus, he transformed the accounts of eyewitnesses into third-person statements. In three accident reports, however, the first in early 1895 and the last in 1900, we read the words of the witnesses themselves and not simply the engineer's assessment of their testimony. While the verbatim recording of such direct testimony remains unusual until 1912–1913, its appearance in the later 1890s is part of an ongoing, gradual transformation in the reports.¹¹

In sum, between 1893 and 1907 the reports begin to change in important ways. They become personally more informative, at first about the victims and then about all parties present at the site. Second, they are increasingly comprehensive in the information provided about the incident. Third, they become more formal in their presentation of the information. And finally, the reports increasingly are interested in assessing responsibility.

In an August 1909 report, an engineer on temporary assignment to Zonguldak from the Ministry of Forests, Mines, and Agriculture was touring the minefield when a methane explosion took the lives of six workers. The engineer, Behçet Bey, extensively reported it to his Istanbul superiors in an impressive accident report that anticipates some developments of the post-1912 era.¹² Notably, he offers no personal information about the victims, perhaps because the reports were being filed directly with the ministry. But his report forms a prolonged argument on the need for more scientific, safer mining procedures. In the many details that he provides regarding the accident and ways to avoid future misfortunes, he marks the ongoing evolution toward greater concern with mine safety that, already apparent in the 1893–1907 reports, culminates in those of the post-1912 era.

When engineers' reports again become available for 1912, 1913, and occasionally for 1914, the accident reports are found to have evolved in the direction anticipated in earlier years—toward the continuing personalization of the victims. We now also learn whether they were single or married. At first sporadically, but regularly after around December 1912, the reports also note the gender and age of the children dependent on the fatally injured. Just a few months later, in March 1913, this information is provided for the children of the wounded as well. Witnesses remain identified only by occupation and origin until March 1914. At that time, the recording format again changes slightly; tabular reports now specify the work that witnesses were performing at the accident site, their connection to the victims, and generally more commentary on all those recorded as present.¹³ By 1917, noting the age of the victims or witnesses has given way to recording their year of birth.¹⁴ Also, the testimony of the witnesses is recorded more schematically, with a separate paragraph for the statements of each person.¹⁵

Several other new practices appear to have become regularized by 1912. First, eyewitness testimony, by the wounded and by observers, surrounded by quotation marks in the original Ottoman and French texts, is commonplace. Quite extraordinarily, the first person voices of Ottoman workers now can be heard with some frequency. Take, for example, the testimony surrounding the March 1912 death of a 20-year-old worker, Devrekli Muradoğlu. The head engineer went into the Kozlu #33 mine and recorded the testimony of a number of eyewitnesses. Among them was a 30-year-old hewer from Tosunlar village who said:

> On the day of the accident, the foreman entered the mine together with us to show us the Haci Bey shaft which would be opened…. After giving us instructions, he went to another part of the mine. One or two hours later, as we were working and cutting the shaft a half meter, there was a sharp cracking noise and two big chunks of stone fell down. We tried to raise them up; it had fallen on our friend Muradoğlu who was in the pit. I have no information about the effort to get the stones off. I was working with coal sacks in the shaft at the scene of the accident.

Three other witnesses corroborated the account, and the head engineer concluded that since the workers and hewers were following the instructions of the foreman, there was no fault to be assigned.[16] Such verbatim testimony thereafter was standard procedure.

In a second reporting innovation, accident reports dating from March 1912 take on a more formal structure. Placed above the text, in a tabular format, are the names of the company operating the mine, its director, the accident date, and the names and biographical data of the victims and witnesses. Earlier reports contain this kind of information, but only within the narrative of the text.[17] The more formal method is practiced sporadically until the spring 1913, when it becomes standardized in the following format:

Concerning an accident which took place in Pavlaki mine:

Mine name:	Pavlaki
Administrator:	M. Jiru veledi
Name of dead workers:	Kurtoğlu Hüseyin, basket carrier, 45–50 years old, married with three children, from Kum Tarla
Witnesses:	Kahyaoğlu Hasan, hard rock miner, from Kum Tarla
	Yakuboğlu Hayri, hewer, from Kum Tarla
	Kahyaoğlu Şaban, hewer's assistant[18]

At this time, some parallel reports on the same accident begin to appear in both Ottoman and French. The first of the French-language reports is dated 26 March 1912 and overall these form a small minority, less than 5 percent, of all the accident reports available for this study.[19] Occasionally but not always, reports on the same accident appear sequentially in the two languages. There are almost always differences between the two versions, but the pattern of the differences is not readily apparent. Take, for example, a June 1913 accident in which three were killed and three wounded in a trainhopping incident. The French-language report directly criticizes the Ottoman government, in a remark not present in the Ottoman version.

Amidst the engineer's long description of the event, the following appears in only the French version:

> The prevention of accidents rests in the hands of the government and I am forced to state that it is necessary to procure a sufficient quantity of gendarmes and to send them to the station at Zonguldak.

Meanwhile, in the Ottoman but not the French version of this report, we find the following assessment:

> Some 100–150 workers force their way onto the coal wagons, either at the station or as it gets underway, using pistols or knives and two gendarmes can't do anything at all! The workers are traveling from Zonguldak-Uzülmez and Uzülmez-Zonguldak on trains from morning until night.

To which the French version adds: "Need to place three gendarmes at each station and 5–10 others circulating the length of the line."[20]

While these variations pertain to sensitive issues—critique of the state or discussion of disorder—at other times, the differences in the Ottoman and French-language reports on the same accident do not appear to have any particular significance. One exemplary case here concerns an attendant stationed at the doors installed to contain fires and explosions, who was struck by a wagon. Embedded in the long description of events are the following details, present in the French but absent from the Ottoman version. Some of the comments, here noted in CAPITAL LETTERS, in the French text reinforce the notion that responsibility could not be assigned since the injured could not be interviewed. But sometimes the added comments are simply more details about the nature of the wounds or of the accident, perhaps in anticipation of a court case.

> The doorkeeper was wounded in the head AND ARMS in a very dangerous manner. HE HAS INTERNAL BLEEDING, BLOOD IS FLOWING FROM HIS EARS, NOSE, AND MOUTH. HE CAN'T BE INTERROGATED ABOUT THE DETAILS OF THE ACCIDENT. The doorkeeper was in the space between doors one and two, that is, some 15–20 meters. The conveyer which brings out the coal of the day arrives at the second door. THERE WAS ALWAYS A LAMP ON THE FIRST WAGON. The entire gallery was ventilated for air.... etc.[21]

In the above cases, the French-language version usually was more specific, but sometimes it was the Ottoman version that was more detailed. I quote the following report at length to dispel the notion that the French-language reports necessarily were the more informative. The information in CAPITAL LETTERS is available only in the Ottoman version.

> From 7 June 1913 to 16 June 1913, I was at Ereğli. I inspected the mines at Çamlı, Kandilli, Alacaağzı, Armutcuk, Köşeağzı. At Çamlı, I checked up on the execution of tasks that were spelled out in my 1913 report, #22. I saw that all the workers were using safety lamps. But these lamps were being opened improperly by the workers.

I took precautions AND HAVE ORDERED SAFETY LAMPS WITH MAGNETIC LOCKS. THE WORKERS CAN USE THE OLD SAFETY LAMPS UNTIL THE NEW ONES ARRIVE IN A FEW DAYS.

According to the statement of the head official who administered the workings of the lamps which were closed as required, a few days would pass before this happened. Consequently, the Çamlı administration will take measures to be certain the lamps are closed in a way the workers can't open them and will check up on this.

Also, there is the issue of ventilators supplying enough air to prevent the methane from building up above a certain level.

Two recommendations:

1. When new safety lamps arrive, get rid of the old ones which are being used now.
2. At -4, have a wall at least two meters thick.

I inspected other mines and found things there were being done in a proper manner. I had reported on this in the 1329 #22 report. I HAVE ALREADY SPOKEN ABOUT THE CUTTING OF THE PILLARS IN MINE NO. 202 AT ARMUTÇUK, THAT OF MAHMUD BEY, WHICH IS BEING EXPLOITED BY SARICAZADE.

For mine 364, I gave a 1913 #30 report.

Here at Armutçuk, at the Mahmud Bey and mine #202 worked by Saricazade, I made a few remarks. ARE TWO STRATA.... ONE IS THREE METERS THICK AND THE OTHER IS VERY LARGE. THERE WAS A FIRE IN A STRATA AT KANDILLI WHERE A LOT OF COAL WAS LOST. SUCH LOSSES ARE NOT IN THE GOVERNMENT'S INTEREST, AND I HAVE PROPOSED TO THE ADMINISTRATION OF THIS MINE TO USE A CUTTING SYSTEM IN THIS LAYER THAT WOULD EASILY PREVENT A FIRE....[22]

Notes

1. ED 4, 78, telegram to Marine Ministry, 3 ts 1293/15 November 1877.
2. ED 4, 170, 171, 173, 31 Mayıs 1294–10 Haziran 1294/12–22 June 1878.
3. ED 3, 2, #12, 1 Haziran 1309/13 June 1893.
4. ED 3, 129–130, #2, 24 Mayıs 1309/5 June 1893.
5. ED 3.
6. ED 3, 218, #12, 29 Mayıs 1321/11 June 1905.
7. ED 3, 220 #19, 24 Temmuz 1321/6 August 1905.
8. ED 3, 225 #28, 17 October 1905.
9. Ed 3, 220, #19, 24 Temmuz 1321/6 August 1905 and 221, #20, 30 Temmuz 1321; 228, #37, 9 ks 1321/22 December 1905.
10. For example, ED 3, 145, 3 Eylül 1311/15 September 1895.
11. ED 3, 141 #43, 5 Mart 1311/17 March 1895; ED 3, 29 #135, 20 tl 1311/29 November 1895; ED 3, 159–160 #8, 5 Haziran 1316/18 June 1900.
12. BBA, DH.MUI.C.II (22f-2) Sira 552; Dosye 17-2, 18 Ramadan 1327. With this exception, no inspectors' reports could be located for the period between mid 1907 and spring 1912.

13. ED 16 Ottoman, 254–255, 18 Mart 1330/31 March 1914.
14. After a break of three years, accident reports again become available for the year 1917.
15. ED 16 Ottoman, 301, 12 Mart 1333/25 March 1917.
16. KU KD 2, 164; this is a translation of a report #80, 25 Şubat 1327/4 March 1912, first presented to the Ereğli mine engineer by the Ereğli mine head engineer and here certified on 26 Mart 1328.
17. KU KD 2, 189–192, in French, 29 Mart 1328.
18. ED 10, 427–428, 25 Haziran 1329, copied on 26 Haziran 1329.
19. Previously, there are several Ottoman-language reports stating that they are translations from the French.
20. ED 16, 65–66, French version; 67–70; Ottoman version in ED 10, 310–311, 3 Haziran/Juin 1329/16 June 1913 and 3 Haziran 1329.
21. ED 16, 86–88, is the complete French version of this document. ED 10, 350, 22 June 1913.
22. ED 16, 80-81, in French; ED 10, 347, 9 Haziran 1329/29 June 1913.

An Ottoman Miner's Glossary

aerial car	*uluk*
basket carrier	*amele* or *küfeci*
bathhouse	*hamam*
boat launcher	*felekeci* or *felenkeci*
boiler fireman	*ateşçi*
boiler waterman	*sucu*
brigade	*tabur*
carpenter	*dülger* or *marangoz*
coal chute	*oluk*
coalfield	*havza*
conveyer worker	*zincirci*
council of elders	*ihtiyar meclisi*
director	*müdür*
directorate	*müdürlük*
district	*kaza*
district official	*kaymakam*
foreman	*çavuş*
hamlet	*divan*
headman	*muhtar*
hewer	*kazmacı*
inclined plane	*varagel*
iron worker	*demirci*
labor boss	*sevk memuru*
lighterboatman	*kayıkçı*
locale	*mevki*
machinist	*makinacı*
mine support worker	*sütuncu* or *sütunkeş*
office boy	*odacı*
oiler	*yağcı*
post maker	*direkçi*
prayer leader	*imam*
preacher	*hatib*
quarry	*kesme*
Qur'an reciter	*hafız*
religious teacher	*hoca*
sub-district	*nahiye*
sub-province	*sancak*
superintendent	*nazır*
switchman	*makasçı*
town quarter	*mahalle*
transporter	*kiracı*
unskilled worker	*amele* or *küfeci*
village	*kariye*
worker	*amele*

ABBREVIATIONS

CAMS	Center for Asia Minor Studies, Athens, Greece
ED	Eğitim Dairesi, Zonguldak
Emmu	Ereğli madeni hümayunu müdürlüğü
KD	Kopya Defteri
kgs	kilograms
kl	Kanun-ı evvel
km	kilometer
krs	kuruş
ks	Kanun-ı sani
KU	Karaelmas Üniversitesi
OA	Osmanlı Arşivi
tl	Teşrin-i evvel
ts	Teşrin-i sani
TTBD	*Belgeler: Türk Tarih Belgeleri Dergisi*
vs	*Vilayet salnamesi*
Yurt Ansik	*Yurt Ansiklopedisi*

Notes on Calendar System

Several calendar systems were at work in the late Ottoman world that are relevant to the present volume. The lunar *hicrî* calendar begins counting from a crucial event in Islamic history—the day that the Prophet Muhammad left Mecca for Medina on 16 July 622 CE. These dates appear occasionally in this volume.

Most of the documents prepared by mining officials used the financial *malî* calendar that combined features from several dating systems. The financial calendar begins 622 CE, but it is based on a 12-month solar calendar of 365 to 366 days. It begins on 1 Mart (March), which corresponds to 13 March of the Gregorian calendar during the nineteenth century and 14 March in the twentieth century. In the notes, I often will present the original financial calendar date followed by its equivalent in the Gregorian calendar.

CAMS references are dated according to the system employed by that archive, in the Gregorian calendar by day/month/year.

Bibliography

Primary Sources

Nearly all of the primary sources utilized in this study are located in modern-day Zonguldak, Turkey. Most are stored at Karaelmas University and at the Education Department of the Turkish Coalmining Ministry. Unfortunately, a number of the registers in the latter location disappeared after my first visit in 1997. For a complete inventory of all the holdings in Zonguldak, see Quataert and Özbek (1999), cited in the bibliography.

I used a few documents from scattered classifications in the Ottoman Archives, Istanbul. I also had access to several documents from the archives of the Credit Lyonnais, Paris, that were not used in Quataert (1983). These were kindly provided by Marie Guillochon, History Department, Binghamton University, State University of New York. And finally, I utilized the resources of the Center for Asia Minor Studies, Athens, Greece—namely, recorded interviews of former Greek Orthodox subjects of the Ottoman Empire. I am very grateful to Margarita Poutouridou, History Department, Binghamton University, State University of New York, who selected and translated the interviews, conducted in Greek, of former residents of the coalfield.

The following Web site contains a host of photographs, illustrations, maps, and documents relevant to this volume. Please visit the following site: http://bingweb.binghamton.edu/~coal/index.htm.

Published Primary Sources

Bolu vilayet salnamesi 1334. 1334. Bolu.
Kastamonu vilayet salnameleri 1308–1317. 1308–1317. Kastamonu.
Quataert, Donald, and Yüksel Duman (2001). "A Coal Miner's Life during the Late Ottoman Empire." *International Labor and Working Class History* (Fall): 153–179.
Sabah. Various Issues, 1892–1908.
Tanin. Various Issues, 1908.
Turkey (1325). Orman ve Maden ve Ziraat Nezareti İstatistik İdaresi. *Maden Istatistiği Birinci Sene 1323 Senesi*. Dersaadet.
Turkey (1327). Maliye Nezareti. *İhsaiyati Maliye. Varidat ve Masrifat Umumiyeyi Muhtevidir. 1325*. Istanbul.

Turkey (1340). *Yeni Hukuk Kitaplar. Rehber. 1255 Tarihinden 1341 Tarihine kadar Vaz ve Neşredilen Bilumum Kavanin ve Nizamat ve Talimatla İradelerin Hurufi Hece Tertibiyle Fihristi.* İzmir.
Turkey (1947). *T. C. Ekonomi Bakanlığı. Bakanlığı İlgilendiren Mevzuat İI Müşterek Hükümler.* Ankara.

Secondary Sources

Abdulkadiroğlu, Abdulkerim et al. (1998). *Kastamonu Jurnal Defteri, 1252-1253/1836-1837.* Ankara.
Abou-El-Haj, Rifaat (1991). *Formation of the Modern State: The Ottoman Empire, Sixteenth to Eighteenth Centuries.* Albany.
Batatu, Hanna (1978). *The Old Social Classes and Revolutionary Movements of Iraq.* Princeton.
Beinin, Joel (2001). *Workers and Peasants in the Modern Middle East.* Cambridge.
Bildik, Cemaleddin (1950). *Kömür İşçileri.* Istanbul.
Brass, Tom, and Marcel van der Linden, eds. (1997). *Free and Unfree Labour: The Debate Continues.* Bern.
Brody, David (1990). "Labour Relations in American Coal Mining: An Industry Perspective." In Gerald D. Feldman and Klaus Tenfelde, eds., *Workers, Owners and Politics in Coal Mining: An International Comparison of Industrial Relations.* New York, 74-117.
Burke, Edmund III, ed. (1993). *Struggle and Survival in the Modern Middle East.* Berkeley.
Castles, Stephen (2003). *The Age of Migration: International Population Movements in the Modern World.* New York.
Cemal, Abdullah (1922). *Türkiye'nin Sihhi-i İçtimai Coğrafyası: Zonguldak Sancağı.* Ankara.
Cemal, Ahmed (1932). *Vilayetlerimiz: Kastamonu ve Zonguldak.* Istanbul.
Church, Roy (1986). *The History of the British Coal Industry.* Vol. 3, *1830-1913: Victorian Pre-eminence.* Oxford.
_____ (1990). "Employers, Trade Unions and the State, 1889-1987: The Origins and Decline of Tripartism in the British Coal Industry." In Gerald D. Feldman and Klaus Tenfelde, eds., *Workers,Owners and Politics in Coal Mining: An International Comparison of Industrial Relations.* New York, 12-73.
Cuinet, Vital (1895). *La Turquie d'Asie.* Vol. 4. Paris.
Çatma, Erol (1998). *Asker İşçiler.* Istanbul.
Çıladır, Sina (1970). *Zonguldak Havzasında Emperyalizm, 1848-1940.* Ankara.
Çıladır, Sina (1977). *Zonguldak Havzasında İşçi Harketlerinin Tarihi, 1848-1940.* Ankara.
Derickson, Alan (1998). *Black Lung: Anatomy of a Public Health Disaster.* Ithaca.
Deringil, Selim (1998). *The Well-Protected Domains: Ideology and the Legitimation of Power in the Ottoman Empire, 1876-1909.* London.
DeWind, Josh (1987). *Peasants Become Miners: The Evolution of Industrial Mining Systems in Peru, 1902-1974.* New York and London.
Dix, Keith (1977). *Work Relations in the Coal Industry: The Hand-Loading Era, 1880-1930.* Morgantown, W. Va.
Dominian, Leon (1913). *The Coal Resources of the Turkish Empire.* N.p.
Doumani, Beshara (1995). *Rediscovering Palestine: Merchants and Peasants in Jabal Nablus, 1700-1900.* Berkeley.
Du Velay, A. (1903). *Essai sur Histoire Financière de la Turquie depuis le Règne du Sultan Mahmoud II jusqu'à Nos Jours.* Paris.
Eldem, Vedat (1994). *Harp ve Mütareke Yıllarında Osmanlı İmparatorluğu'nun Ekonomisi.* Ankara.
Enver, Sadrettin (1941). *Zonguldak Kömür Havzamız.* Ankara.
Erkin, Engin (1999). *Dört Maden Kentinin Değişim Öyküsü 1973-1996.* Istanbul.
Etingü, Turgut (1976). *Kömür Havzasında İlk Grev.* Istanbul.

Faroqhi, Suraiya (1994). "Crisis and Change, 1590-1699." In Halil İnalcık with Donald Quataert, eds., *An Economic and Social History of the Ottoman Empire, 1300-1914*. Cambridge, 413-636.
Feldman, Gerald D., and Klaus Tenfelde, eds. (1990). *Workers, Owners and Politics in Coal Mining: An International Comparison of Industrial Relations*. New York.
Fisher, W. B. (1966). *The Middle East: A Physical, Social, and Regional Geography*. 4th ed. London.
Freese, Barbara (2003). *Coal: A Human History*. Cambridge, Mass.
Goldberg, Ellis, ed. (1996). *The Social History of Labor in the Middle East*. Seattle, Wash.
Graebner, William (1976). *Coal Mining Safety in the Progressive Period: The Political Economy of Reform*. Lexington, Ky.
Güran, Tevfik, ed. (1995). *Osmanlı Devletinin İlk İstatistik Yıllığı 1897*. Ankara.
Gürol, Mehmet Ali (1997). *Zonguldak Kömür Havzası Yapısı Sorunları ve bir Çözüm Önerisi*. Ankara.
İmer, Hüseyin Fehmi (1944). "Ereğli Maden Kömürleri Havzası." *İş* c. 10, defter 2, # 38 Nisan, 33-69.
_____ (1973). *Hayatı-Hatıraları (1871-1960)*. Istanbul.
Izmestieva, Tamara (2000). "Impact of Russian Protectionism upon the Donetz Coal Industry and Labour Force in the Late 19th-Early 20th Century." Paper presented to the European Social Science History Conference, Amsterdam, 12-15 April.
Jennings, Ronald (1975). "Women in Early 17th Century Ottoman Judicial Records—the Sharia Court of Anatolian Kayseri." *Journal of the Economic and Social History of the Orient* 17, no. 2: 53-114.
Kahveci, Erol (1996). "The Miners of Zonguldak." In Erol Kahveci, Nadir Suğur, and Theo Nichols, eds., *Work and Occupation in Modern Turkey*. London.
_____ (1997). "The Political Economy of the Zonguldak Coalbasin and Its Labour Force: 1848-1995." Ph.D. diss., University of Bristol.
Karpat, Kemal H. (1985). *Ottoman Population, 1830-1914*. Madison.
Kıray, Mübeccel (1964). *Ereğli: Ağır Sanayiden önce bir Sahil Kasabası*. Ankara.
Kırlı, Cengiz (2000). "The Struggle over Space: Coffeehouses of Ottoman Istanbul, 1780-1845." Ph.D. diss., Binghamton University, State University of New York.
Klubock, Thomas M. (1998). *Contested Communities: Class, Gender and Politics in Chile's El Tenninte Copper Mines, 1904-1951*. Durham, N.C.
Longuenesse, Elizabeth (1978). "La Classe Ouvrière au Proche Orient: La Syrie." *La Pensée* 197 (January-February): 120-132.
Mansur, Fatma (1954). "Zonguldak Ereğli Kömür İşletmesi Hakkında Rapor." Typescript. Ankara.
Mathis, Franz (1990). "Goodbye to Class War: The Development of Social Partnership in Austrian Coal Mining." In Gerald D. Feldman and Klaus Tenfelde, eds., *Workers, Owners and Politics in Coal Mining: An International Comparison of Industrial Relations*. New York, 315-360.
Murphey, Rhoads (2003). "Mineral Exploitation in the Ottoman Empire." *Encyclopaedia of Islam* (CD version), part of "Ma'din" entry, 963b-993a.
Murray's Handbook (1877-1878). *Turkey in Asia*. Constantinople.
Naim, Ahmet (1934). *Zonguldak Havzası (Uzun Mehmet'ten Bugüne kadar)*. Istanbul.
Nichols, Theo, and Erol Kahveci (1995). "The Condition of Mine Labour in Turkey: Injuries to Miners in Zonguldak, 1942-1990." *Middle Eastern Studies* (April): 197-228.
Oskay, Ülger (1983). *Geçiş Dönemi Tipi Olarak Zonguldak Kömür Havzası Maden İşçisi: İhsaniye ve Gelik Ocaklarında Çalışan Maden İşçileri üzerine bir Araştırma*. Izmir.
Ökçün, A. Gündüz (1960). "XX Yüzyıl Başlarında Osmanlı Maden Üretiminde Türk, Azınlık ve Yabancı Payları." In *Prof. Dr. Yavuz Abadan'a Armağan*. Ankara, 801-895.
Özbek, Nadir (2001). "The Politics of Welfare: Philanthrophy, Voluntarism and Legitimacy in the Ottoman Empire, 1876-1914." Ph.D. diss., Binghamton University, State University of New York.

Özeken, Ahmet Ali (1944a). "Ereğli Kömür Havzası Tarihi üzerinde bir Deneme 1840–1940." Umumi Tarihçe ve İdari Rejimler. Hukuki Mevzuat Tarihi—İktisadi Gelişim Merhaleleri. İstanbul Üniversitesi İşletme İktisadi Doçenti. Istanbul.
―――― (1944b). *Ereğli Kömür Havzası Tarihi üzerinde bir Deneme 1840–1940, Umumi Tarihçe ve İdari Rejimler. Hukuki Mevzuat Tarihi—İktisadi Gelişim Merhaleleri*. Istanbul.
―――― (1955). *Türkiye Kömür Ekonomisi Tarihi*. Istanbul.
Pamuk, Şevket (1995). *19. Yüzyılda Osmanlı Dış Ticareti*. Ankara.
―――― (2000). *A Monetary History of the Ottoman Empire*. Cambridge.
Peirce, Leslie (2003). *Morality Tales: Law and Gender in the Ottoman Court of Aintab*. Berkeley.
People's House (1933). Zonguldak Onuncu Cumhuriyet Bayramı Komitesi. *Cumhuriyetin On Yılında Zonguldak ve Maden Kömürü Havzası*. Zonguldak.
Quataert, Donald (1983). *Social Disintegration and Popular Resistance in the Ottoman Empire, 1881–1908*. New York.
―――― (1993). *Ottoman Manufacturing in the Age of the Industrial Revolution*. Cambridge.
―――― (2000). *The Ottoman Empire, 1700–1922*. Cambridge.
―――― (2001), ed. "Labor History in the Ottoman Middle East, 1700–1922." In *International Labor and Working Class History* (Fall): 93–179.
Quataert, Donald, and Nadir Özbek (1999). "The Ereğli-Zonguldak Coal Mines: A Catalog of Archival Documents." *Turkish Studies Association Bulletin* (Spring): 55–67. A Turkish translation of this can be found in: "Ereğli Kömür Madenleri." *Tarih ve Toplum* (Ocak): 11–18.
Ralli, G. (1895). "Le bassin houiller d'Héraclée." *Société Géologique de Belgique* 22: 151–267.
―――― (1933). *Le basin houiller d'Héraclée*. Paris.
Rebel, Hermann (1983). *Peasant Classes: The Bureaucratization of Property and Family Relations under Early Hapsburg Absolutism, 1511–1636*. Princeton.
Refik, Ahmet (1931). *Osmanlı Devrinde Türkiye Madenleri (967–1200)*. Istanbul.
Reid, Donald (1981). "The Role of Mine Safety in the Development of Working-Class Consciousness and Organization: The Case of the Aubin Coal Basin, 1867–1914." *French Historical Studies* 12 (Spring): 98–119.
Roy, Andrew (ca. 1905). *A History of the Coal Miners of the United States*. Columbus, Ohio. Reprinted Greenwood Press, 1970.
Roy, Delwin A. (1976). "Labour and Unionism in Turkey: The Ereğli Coalmines." *Middle Eastern Studies* 12, no. 3: 125–172.
Savaşkan, Bahri (1993). *Zonguldak Maden Kömürü Havzası Tarihçesi, 1829–1989*. Zonguldak.
Seltzer, Curtis (1985). *Fire in the Hole: Miners and Managers in the American Coal Industry*. Lexington, Ky.
Shaw, Stanford J., and Ezel Kural Shaw (1976). *History of the Ottoman Empire and Modern Turkey, II*. Cambridge.
Solakian, Archak (1923). *Les Richesses Naturelles et Economiques de l'Asie Mineure*. Constantinople.
Spratt, T. (1877). "On the Coal-Bearing Deposits near Erekli." *Quarterly Journal of the Geological Society of London* 31: 524–533.
Tenfelde, Klaus, ed. (1992). *Sozialgeschichte des Bergbaus im 19. und 20. Jahrhundert*. Munich.
Tesal, Necip D. (1957). *Zonguldak Vilayetinin İktisadi Ehemmiyeti*. Istanbul.
Thobie, Jacques (1977). *Intérêts et Impérialisme Français dans l'Empire Ottoman (1895–1914)*. Paris.
Toprak, Zafer (1982). *Türkiye'de 'Milli İktisat' (1908–1918)*. Istanbul.
―――― (2003). *İttihad-Terakki ve Cihan Harbi*. Istanbul.
Trischler, Helmuth (1988). *Steiger im deutschen Bergbau: Zur Sozialgechichte des technischen Angestellten, 1815–1945*. Munich.
van der Linden, Marcel (1999). "The End of Eurocentrism and the Future of Labour History: Or, Why We Should and How We Could Reconceptualise the Working Class." *Actas dos V Cursos Internacionais des Cascais (29 de Junho de 1998)*. Cascais, 159–192.
van Hentenryk, Ginette Kurgan, and Jean Puissant (1990). "Industrial Relations in the Belgian Coal Industry since the End of the Nineteenth Century." In Gerald D. Feldman and Klaus

Tenfelde, eds., *Workers, Owners and Politics in Coal Mining: An International Comparison of Industrial Relations.* New York, 203-270.
van Onselen, Charles (1976). *Chibaro: African Mine Labour in Southern Rhodesia, 1900-1933.* London.
Varlık, M. Bülent (1985). "Osmanlı Devleti'nde Madenlerde Çalışma Koşulları." *Tanzimat'tan Cumhuriyet'e Türkiye Ansiklopedisi*, 4. Istanbul, 917-922.
Weisbrod, Bernd (1990). "Entrepreneurial Politics and Industrial Relations in Mining in the Ruhr Region: From Managerial Absolutism to Co-Determination." In Gerald D. Feldman and Klaus Tenfelde, eds., *Workers, Owners and Politics in Coal Mining: An International Comparison of Industrial Relations.* New York, 118-202.
Whiteside, James (1990). *Regulating Danger: The Struggle for Mine Safety in the Rocky Mountain Coal Industry.* Lincoln, Nebr.
Winkler, Erhart (1961). *Die Wirtschaft von Zonguldak, Türkei: Eine geographische Untersuchung.* Vienna.
Yersel, Kadri (1989). *Madencilik bir Ömür: Anılar-Görüşler.* Istanbul.
Yıldırım, Nuran (1985). "Tanzimat'tan Cumhuriyet'e Koruyucu Sağlık Uygulamaları." *Tanzimat'tan Cumhuriyet'e Türkiye Ansiklopedisi* 5. Istanbul, 1320-1338.
Yurt Ansiklopedisi. 1982-1984. Ankara.
Zürcher, Erik Jan (1993). *Turkey: A Modern History.* London.
_____ (1996). "Between Death and Desertion: The Ottoman Army in World War I." *Turcica* 28: 235-258.
_____ (1999). "The Ottoman Conscription System in Theory and Practice, 1844-1918." In Zürcher, Erik Jan, ed., *Arming the State: Military Conscription in the Middle East and Central Asia, 1775-1925.* London, 79-94.

Index

Abdulhamid II, Sultan, 112, 114
Abdulmalik, 117
Abdulmecid, Sultan, 19n22, 39
aboveground workers
    estimated numbers, 60, 137–38
    housing and medical care, 80–81
    and military draft, 146, 218
    role in strikes, 53, 230
    types of, 61–62
    in wage ledgers, 66–71, 73–76
accidents, 3–4, 6, 8, 24, 45, 64, 69
    aboveground, 158–61
    belowground, 162–79
    death and injury rates, 150, 152–55, 187–88
    effects on miners' households, 151, 188–90
    frequency of, 152, 186
    international comparisons, 151, 153, 155–56
    statistics, 60, 153, 186–88
    testimonies on, 157–58, 163, 165, 171–74, 197, 237–38
    See also safety
accident reports, 4–5, 65, 109, 119, 155, 176, 193, 241n14
    changes in, 45, 109, 145, 235–38
    differences between French and Ottoman versions, 238–40
    as means to hear workers' voices, 157, 184, 235–38
    and soldier-workers, 134, 141
    structure of, 151, 153, 201, 235–40
accident victims, 4, 185

age distribution of, 145–46, 173, 187–88
families of, 151, 189–90
other characteristics, 119–20
Acılık, 33–34, 158
administration of coalfield, 31, 38–45, 50n126, 88, 98–99, 102–3, 158, 191, 209–10, 213–16, 228, 234
    campaign for safety, 4, 151, 161, 184, 194–202, 227, 229
    civilianization of, 16, 20
    military, 20, 41, 133
administrative districts, coalfield, 20, 34, 54–55, 59–60, 91
administrative personnel, 41–42, 81
    wages and job security, 75, 148n19, 218–19
aerial tramways, 69–70, 78, 218, 222, 228–29
agriculture, 20, 25, 33, 98. *See also* peasants
Akbaba, 117
Alacaağzı, 64, 84, 97, 102
    loading facilities, 31
    mines, 22, 104–5, 107, 113–14, 117, 122, 127n88, 135, 196, 198–99, 212, 239
Alaplı, 40, 47, 57, 103, 141, 212, 214–15
Amasra, 21–22, 44
    mines, 104, 142, 209
America. *See* United States
Ankara government, 60, 87, 194. *See also* Turkish Republic
apprentices, 73–75
Armenians, 34, 37, 125n52
army. *See* military
Artvin, 62

Balkan Wars, 133, 142, 145–46, 158–59
Barkley, John, Barkley brothers, 27, 54, 76n2, 84
Bartın, 79n74, 97, 99, 100, 102, 112, 118–19, 123, 137, 141–42, 144, 149n37, 166, 177, 187, 208–10, 213–14, 224
basket carriers, 31, 53, 55–57, 68, 82, 84, 86, 96–97, 104, 107, 117, 119–20, 122–23, 137, 208, 218, 229–30, 235
  as accident victims, 65, 154, 172, 185, 189
  selection of, 100, 221
  wages of, 64, 75, 105, 110, 116, 211
  See also workers
Behçet Bey, 44, 51n144, 78n67, 237
belowground workers, 7, 52, 81, 88, 132, 134, 138, 218. *See also* basket carriers; hewers
black-lung disease, 91–92, 152, 156
Black Sea, 1, 3, 16, 20–21, 24–25, 30, 35, 39, 59, 63, 65, 91, 96, 99, 117, 141, 187, 207–9, 216
boat launchers, 58, 79n73, 104, 135, 138, 149n37, 209
boatmen, 52, 60
  military draft in Ottoman-Russian War of 1877–78, 62
  role in transportation, 28, 31, 61, 101
  strike in January 1913, 62
Bolu, 19n22, 54, 98–99, 112–13, 118
Boyacıoğlu, Boyacıoğlu Company, 144, 167, 170, 220
bread money, 99, 106–7, 128n105. *See also* wages
brigands, 123
brothels, 35, 92, 233
bureaucracy
  mining, 20, 75–76, 109, 201–2, 218, 227. *See also* administration of coalfield
  professionalization of, 235
  state, 18, 44

cable cars, 30, 162. *See also* aerial tramways
capital, 5, 29, 42–43, 51n131, 129–30, 206, 227, 232–33
capitalism, 2, 8, 42, 109, 116
Cemal, Ahmed, 11–13, 204n39
chain migration, 63, 96
charitable contributions
  to accident victims, 114
  during Ramadan and Muharrem, 95–96, 113
  by mining companies, 112, 115–16

child labor, 85, 90–91, 132, 169
Cide, 27, 40, 141
coal loaders, 61–62
coal production, 5, 21, 26–27, 38–39, 42–44, 59–60, 67, 69, 81, 98, 115, 122, 154
  during wartime, 142, 145, 207, 211, 218–19, 223, 228, 234
  under French occupation, 65
  importance for Ottoman fleet, 1, 5, 41, 142, 206–7
company stores, 81, 88
compulsory workers, 41–42, 52, 54–58, 60–62, 69, 86–88, 98, 106, 129–30, 137, 184, 201, 207
  comparison to corvée labor, 52, 55
  during wartime, 132–34, 212, 214–15, 218–19
  lack of class-consciousness, 8, 53
  lack of medical care, 150, 184, 193
  recruitment of, 7, 20, 57–58, 80, 96–97, 99–104, 117–18, 122, 130. *See also* council of elders; village headmen
  resistance to proletarianization, 53
  tax privileges, 97
  wages of, 53, 63–64, 75, 136
  See also villagers; workers
council of elders, 4, 55, 80, 101
courts, judicial, 17, 95, 170, 179, 204n24, 239
Crimean War, 27, 31, 33, 37, 39, 54, 84–85, 92, 131, 215
Çamlı, 22, 31
  mines, 30, 87, 197–99, 205n64, 239–40
Çarşamba, 138
Çatalağzı, 22, 61, 76, 176
  mines, 29, 104, 122, 127n87
Çatma, Erol, 14, 17, 133–34
Çaycuma, 33, 142–43
Çay Damarı, 91, 160, 171, 176–77, 179, 199
Çaydere, 117
Çıladır, Sina, 14, 16, 57, 78n56

deforestation, 26
Devrek, 26, 32, 38, 47n35, 73, 97, 102, 122, 128n113, 136, 140–43, 148n27, 162, 167, 171, 212–13, 216, 228
  population of, 117–18, 121, 125n33, 126n55, 127n101
Dilaver Pasha, 17, 40
  regulations. *See* legislations, of 1867

diseases, 91–92, 192, 204n36
   respiratory, 152, 156
   venereal. *See* syphilis
   See also black lung; malaria
division of labor, 138, 229, 234
donations. *See* charitable contributions
drift mining. *See* methods of mining

Ebegümeci, 117, 121, 170
engineers, engineering staff, 14, 20, 44–45, 81, 109, 196–98, 201–3, 218, 220, 223, 229, 237
   foreign, 27, 59, 77n40, 78n63
England, 5, 15, 86, 88, 151–54, 195, 202, 216, 232
Ereğli, 9, 12, 14, 21–22, 27, 32–41, 44, 48n61, 58, 86, 97–99, 109, 113, 121–22, 137, 141–44, 208, 212, 215–17, 228
   mines, 149n37, 198, 239
   population of, 118, 125n33, 126n55
   port of, 25, 29, 61, 69, 123
Ereğli Company, *Société anonyme Ottomane d'Héraclée*, 62, 64, 81–82, 84, 90, 93n3, 122, 133, 143–44, 206, 220–21, 228
   accidents, 157–58, 160–68, 171, 174, 176, 178–79, 185
   coal production, 5, 66
   efforts to recruit workers, 60, 63, 81
   formation of, 29–31, 33, 48n42, 53
   government inspections, 91
   government vigilance, 5, 59, 185
   hospitals of, 157, 161, 167, 192
   housing for rotational workers, 86
   labor disputes, 65–66, 159, 194
   lower accident rates, 185–86
   negotiations with Ottoman state, 43, 51n131
   piecework system, 229, 231
   and safety procedures, 196, 199
Ereğli Imperial Mine Administration. *See* administration of coalfield
Ethem Çavuş
   on accidents, 155, 168, 177–78
   on commuting to work, 122
   on housing, 87
   on medical care, 193
   memoir of, 19n39, 56
   on piecework system, 65–66
   on selection of basket carriers, 100
   on taxes, 106
   on wage payments, 89, 108
   on women workers, 233
   on working hours, 87
ethnic division of labor
   as a myth, 69
explosions, 56, 84–85, 155–56, 176, 178, 185, 193, 196, 199, 202–3, 235, 239
   coal dust, 155, 197
   gas, 177, 179, 196, 237
   methane, 45, 65, 176, 178–79, 189, 199, 201–2, 237

female labor, 212–13, 233
Filyos, 24, 38
floods, flooding, 100, 169, 200. *See also* accidents; water accumulation
foremen, 7, 63, 65, 71, 75, 77, 81, 89, 107, 142–43, 154, 162, 219, 230, 236
France, 5, 22, 151–55, 177, 217, 229
   investments, 5, 29, 43, 93n20, 205n64. *See also* Ereğli Company
   mining concessions to, 43–44, 48n41, 48n43, 63, 185
free-labor, 7, 52–53, 58–63, 80, 91, 94n47, 129, 230

gas detection workers, 177
Gelik, 29, 162, 220–22
geology of coalfield, 11, 21–22, 24, 170, 227
   effects on mining, 82, 85, 156
Gerede, 121
Giurgiu Company, 22, 30, 155
   accidents, 171–72, 178, 184–85
   commercial fleet of, 206
   lower rate of charitable donations, 115
   methods of payments, 89, 106–7
   mines of, 65, 135, 162
   and soldier-workers, 144
Giurgiu Pano, 29–30
Grammar Hasan Pasha, 51n135, 106
Great Britain. *See* England
Greeks, 33, 34–37, 63, 69, 124n26, 125n52, 158, 228
Gregoviç, Petro, 30
Gümüşhane, 62, 164

Hacı İsmailoğluları, Hacı İsmail, 14–15, 19n28, 19n33, 209. *See also* Uzun Mehmed story

Hallaçyan Efendi, 110, 114, 119
Hallaçyan mine, 178, 196
health care. *See* medical care
hewers, 54–57, 59–60, 64–66, 75, 87, 97, 104, 117, 120, 142, 166, 174, 216, 220, 229
   ability to negotiate wages, 100, 107, 110
   as accident victims, 152, 154, 170–72, 176–77, 185–89, 197, 235, 238
   See also belowground workers; workers
history from below, 3, 17
holidays, 8, 53, 88, 103, 211–12, 232
hospitals, 38, 92, 134, 178, 184, 191–95, 228. *See also* Ereğli Company
hours of work, 66–67, 85, 87–88
households, 37, 119, 121, 189, 233–34
housing, 53, 80–81, 85–87, 92, 137, 192, 194, 228
Hühner, Wilhelm, 172
Hüseyin Fehmi, İmer, 9, 14, 31, 38, 45, 219

İkinci Makas, 65, 165, 199
İkse, 121, 221
immigrants/immigration, 34, 52, 59, 62, 70, 217, 228
   impact on coalfield, 7, 53, 58, 129, 230
imperialism, 16, 81
İnağzı, 22, 61
Industrial Revolution, 15
investors, 5, 11, 29
Ishak Ağa, 111, 116
Istiolyanos Istabolos, 44, 51

journeymen, 73–74, 149n56

Kandilli, 22, 31, 61, 176, 198, 204n36, 239–40
Karamahmudzadeler Company, Karamahmudzadeler, 14, 19n33, 30, 78n51, 117, 135, 142, 171, 197
Karamanyan Company, Karamanyan, 29–30, 107, 115, 135, 158, 162, 178
Kargarlar, 105, 111, 117, 120, 189
Kasap İsmail Ağa, 109–10
Kastamonu, 11, 19n22, 27, 31, 43, 92, 99, 113, 118, 210
Kayseri, 34, 36–37, 49n85, 140
Kemalism, 9, 13–14
Kestaneci, Kestanelik, 12, 14
Kılıç Mine, Kılıç Mining Company, 110–12, 117, 126n72

Kilimli, 22, 28, 31, 61, 64, 73, 104, 112, 134, 137, 142, 144, 173, 178, 191, 192, 196–98, 221–22, 228
Kirelik, 61
Konya, 36
Kozlu, 22, 24, 27–31, 33, 35, 37–38, 40, 61, 69, 71, 84, 86, 88–89, 111–14, 116–17, 134, 138, 144, 148n27, 191, 198, 215, 228
   mines, 44, 63–65, 86, 97, 104–5, 109–10, 119, 122, 127n87, 135, 140–42, 155, 162, 165, 167, 169, 171, 173, 178–79, 221, 226n90, 238
   port of, 27, 31, 48n41
Köşeağzı, 12, 239
Kurds, 34, 70, 79n74, 81

labor bosses, 53, 96, 102, 130, 230
labor force
   ethnic identity of, 34, 52–53, 88, 141, 150, 212–13
   foreign
      Croatian, 54, 58
      English, 58
      Greek, 22, 158
      Iranian, 59
      Italian, 59, 176
      Montenegrin, 54, 58–59, 64–65
   nature of, 1, 4–8, 20, 52, 54, 63, 67–71, 73–76, 91, 121, 130, 150–51, 153, 185–88, 230–34
   recruitment of, 31, 53, 56, 118–22, 132–33
   shortages of, 6, 31, 59, 62–63, 84, 88, 97, 125n36, 129, 133, 142, 144–45, 169, 208, 213–14, 220–23
   state's efforts to control, 4, 44, 55, 151, 194–95, 201–2, 206, 220–21, 227, 229
   turnover rates, 71, 73–75, 218–19
   See also aboveground workers; belowground workers; child labor; compulsory workers; female labor; soldier-workers
labor historians, 1, 6
labor history, comparative, 1–8, 227
labor market, 43, 59–60
labor unrest, 3, 53, 65, 70. *See also* strikes
laws, mine labor. *See* legislations
ledgers, 77n20, 104–9, 117, 191
   problems as historical source, 66–71, 74–75, 133–41

legislations
    of 1867, 17, 19n31, 40–41, 43, 50n107, 54–55, 57–59, 64, 86–88, 91, 96–97, 99–100, 106–7, 129, 193, 230
    of 1892, 101, 116, 127n93
    international comparisons, 90, 202
    of September 1921, 93n26, 194
Limancık, 12–13
local elites, notables, 4, 8, 13
    exploitation of workers, 106
long-wall system, 82

Mahmud II, Sultan, 10, 12
malaria, 33, 38, 91
mechanization of mines, 27–31, 61–62, 69, 170, 222, 228–29
medical care, doctors
    availability of, 53, 80, 85, 150, 191–94, 228, 236
    comparison to United States, 191
    See also hospitals
methods of mining, 31, 44, 82, 84
migrants. *See* immigrants/immigration
military
    administration of coalfield, 20, 41–45, 54, 133
    as disciplinary force in mines, 3, 55, 96, 159–61
    labor role in mines, 54–56, 212, 214. *See also* soldier-workers
    terms of service, 91, 130–31
    wartime conscription, 218–21, 228, 234
mine administration. *See* administration of coalfield
mine inspectors, 45, 51n144, 69, 81, 151, 164, 185–86, 201
    reports, 3, 18, 109, 153, 160, 174, 176, 178, 190, 196, 220, 236
mine operators
    bankruptcy, 8, 102
    charitable contributions, 95–96, 112–16
    and labor force, 5–7, 53–54, 57–66, 90, 98–102, 116, 142–43, 230–32
    negotiations with state, 42–44
    obligations, 41–42, 89, 133
    and safety procedures, 91, 156, 194–96, 198, 229, 236
    See also under proper names

mine superintendent, 9, 14, 17, 31, 38, 40, 45, 55, 57, 75, 89, 91, 99–103, 106, 123, 125n50, 169, 205n64, 219
    efforts to solve labor shortage, 97, 117, 133, 142–44, 208, 211–16
    implementation of safety procedures, 159–61, 177–79, 196, 198
    office of, 7, 44, 91, 100, 104, 111, 132, 134, 146, 157–61, 164, 201–3
    petitions to, 60–62
    provisioning problem, 208–10
mine support workers, 58, 96, 100, 104, 149n37, 211, 214, 229, 233
miners. *See* workers
Ministry of Commerce, Agriculture and Mines, 16, 38, 45, 76, 91, 144
Ministry of Marine, 16, 38, 40–42, 45, 142, 144, 149n39
Ministry of Public Works, 38, 45
Ministry of War, 41, 133, 142–44, 228
Muharrem, 114
    as a notable time for gift-giving, 112–13
Mustafa Fazıl, 219–22

Naim, Ahmet, 9–16, 50n127, 204n48
nationalism, 9–10, 13, 15
nation-state, 2–3, 9, 18
newspapers
    Sabah, 11–13, 15
    Zonguldak, 9
non-Muslims
    as mine owners, 16
    population in mining districts, 32, 35, 228
    as workers, 69

officials
    district/local, 38–40, 97, 99–103, 129, 133, 142–44, 177, 196, 209, 212–13
    mistreatment of workers, 103
    state, 3, 10, 18, 28, 43, 130, 155, 157, 194, 213, 227
    See also administration of coalfield; bureaucracy; mine superintendent
Ortaköy, 119
Ottoman Empire
    allowing free-market sale of coal, 16, 42–43, 59, 62
    coal imports of, 206
    comparison with Russia in coal-mining, 5

concessions, mining, 29, 40, 43–44, 63, 185
demand for coal, 1, 16, 29, 42, 206
ecumenical nature of, 115
efforts to discipline citizenry, 4, 151, 184, 195, 201, 229
failure to solve labor shortage, 7, 227
fiscal crisis, 210–11, 215, 217
impact of Ottoman-Russian War of 1877–78, 207–9, 212–16
impact of World War I, 145–47, 216–23
reforms, 2, 151
taxation, 27, 43, 97–98, 105–6, 110
Ottoman-Greek War (1897), 30
Ottoman historians, 2–3, 17–18
Ottoman history, 1–3, 17, 207
Ottoman-Russian War of 1877–78
impact on coalfield, 42, 62, 130, 142, 207–16, 218
Özeken, Ahmet Ali, 14, 16, 50n113, 77n33

Paris Mining School, 22
Pavlaki Company, 144, 169, 199
mines, 120, 135, 174, 238
payments and rates. *See* wages
peasants, 14–15, 17, 25, 35
policing, mines, 4, 101, 123, 159–61, 239. *See also* military
population statistics, 32–33, 35–38, 118, 121
Prime Ministry Archives, 3, 17
Privy Purse, 39–40
productivity, coalfield, 84, 134–35, 207, 231
during wartime, 218, 223

Raghip Pasha, 30–31, 62
as lobbyist for free labor, 43, 59–60, 227, 231
See also Sarıcazadeler
railroads, 22, 24–25, 27–31, 55–56, 58, 61–62, 69–70, 81, 157–60, 218, 222. *See also* cable cars
Ralli, 22
Ramadan, 71, 88, 211, 232
charitable activities in, 111, 113–16
regulations. *See* legislations
Republican People's Party, 9
revolutionary government. *See* Turkish Republic
Rize, 62

Rombaki, Rombaki Company, 144, 162, 192, 220
room-and-pillar system, 82, 85
rotational labor system. *See* compulsory workers
Russia, 5–6
bombardment of Zonguldak in 1914, 217, 219
See also Ottoman-Russian War of 1877–78; World War I

safety inspections, 45, 174, 197–98. *See also* mine inspectors
safety lamps, 85, 150, 177–79, 194–201, 228–29, 239–40
shortcomings of, 202
safety procedures
as disciplinary devices, 4, 151, 184, 195, 198, 201, 227, 229
efforts to establish, 44–45, 185–86, 194–95, 197–98, 229, 235–40
insufficiency of, 150, 199–200
international comparisons, 152–53, 229
Safranbolu, 27, 34–35, 225n44
Sarıcazadeler Company, Sarıcazadeler, 30–31, 62, 82, 86, 173, 176, 192, 196, 222, 240. *See also* Raghip Pasha
Savaşkan, Bahri, 14, 48n45, 48n53, 51n131, 205n64
Serbs, 33, 228
Setrak Efendi, 91, 161, 163, 219–22
shaft mining. *See* methods of mining
shifts, work, 35, 41, 56, 85–88, 100, 103, 116, 168, 211–12, 214
Sinop, 36
Sivas, 60
Sivriler, 105, 111, 119
skilled workers. *See* workers
slope mining. *See* methods of mining
soldier-workers, 54, 131–33, 139
comparison to civilian workers, 139
in peace time, 130, 134–37
wages, 129, 137–38, 140–41, 215
in wartime, 130, 142–47, 212, 215–16, 223
steamships, 16, 21, 36, 123
strikes, 53, 62, 65–66, 73, 159, 230
to receive medical care, 194
syphilis, 35, 91–92

Tabaklar, 105, 117, 189
taxation. *See* Ottoman Empire, taxation
technology, mines. *See* mechanization of mines
Tiran, 19n22, 27, 64, 117, 171
tithe. *See* Ottoman Empire, taxation
Trabzon, 60, 62–63, 65, 97, 99, 160, 162–63, 171–72, 179, 187, 208–9
trainhopping, 158–61, 167, 238–39
transportation
    mechanization of, 28–29, 81, 203n5, 207, 218, 228
    methods of, 27, 31, 56, 61, 69, 82, 158–61, 211, 229
    See also aerial tramways; cable cars; railroads; steamships
transporters, 24–25, 55–57, 59, 62–63, 80, 87, 96, 102–4, 110, 117, 119, 123, 210–12, 214, 229, 233
Tripolitanian War, 71, 133, 142, 158–59
Turkish Republic, 2–3, 9, 14–15, 87, 92, 94n44, 133, 180n24, 232–33
    Ministry of Health, 92
Turkish War of Independence, 53, 142

Uluköy, 117
United Kingdom. *See* England
United States
    coal mines, 5–6, 22, 64, 82, 90, 152, 229
    medical care for miners, 191
    mining accidents, 4, 150–53, 155–56, 177, 202–3
unskilled workers. *See* workers
Uzun Mehmed, story of, 3, 9–16
Üzülmez, 29, 33, 48n55, 81, 158, 239
    accidents at, 160–61, 178
    hospital at, 167, 192
    mines, 162, 171

villagers
    collective responsibility of, 101, 103
    and compulsory work, 8, 41, 95–97, 103, 201, 220, 230–32
    resistance to work in mines, 90, 96
    See also village headmen
village headmen, 4, 57, 97, 106, 211–12
    authority over villagers, 8, 53, 55, 96, 99–104, 116–17, 130, 132

wages
    of administrative personnel, 218–19
    in arrears, 53, 89, 95, 126n54
    in cash, 86, 90, 107
    daily and piecework, 57, 61, 63–66, 68, 70, 229
    deductions, 76, 106, 191, 204n48
    disparities in, 70–71
    in promissory notes, 8, 105, 107, 117, 210–11
    raises, 71, 73–76
    to soldier-workers, 129, 135–41, 147, 215
water accumulation, mines, 85, 168–70. *See also* accidents; floods
women
    employment in mines, 7, 213, 222, 233, 234n11
    and households, 233–34
    as mine operators, 222
    as mine support workers, 222, 233
    as transporters, 213, 233
    See also female labor
workers
    and absenteeism, 89, 102–3, 132
    commuting to work, 122–23, 158–59. *See also* trainhopping
    diets, 88, 222–23
    efforts to discipline, 4, 44, 55, 117, 151, 158–61, 164, 184, 195, 198, 200–202, 206–7, 229
    everyday life of, 56, 69, 109, 151, 220, 230
    identity formation, 8, 119, 230–31
    international comparisons 8, 153
    and masculine culture, 233
    provisioning of, 34–35, 98–99, 209–10, 222–23
    resistance to proletarianization, 8, 231–33
    resistance to safety procedures, 178–79, 200–202
    retention of village ties, 53, 232–33
    skilled, 52, 56–57, 62–63, 68–71, 88, 100, 130, 146, 218–19
    unskilled, 52–53, 55–56, 59–60, 68, 75, 87, 104, 142, 146–47, 185, 187, 214, 218–19
    See also aboveground workers; belowground workers; compulsory workers; labor force; soldier-workers

World War I
 impact on coalfield, 53, 130, 145–46, 169–70, 217–18, 233–34

Young Turk Revolution, 45, 142n51, 70

Zonguldak, 21, 25–26, 39, 118, 122, 141, 144, 156–61, 191–92, 196, 201–2, 206, 218, 220, 232, 236, 239
 geography, 24–27
 population, 35
 port of, 29, 31, 36, 61–62, 69, 134, 217–18, 229
 town of, 33–35, 45, 81, 86, 92, 158, 217, 228
Zonguldak People's House, 9–15